DEMOCRACY UNDER ATTACK

"Dean manages to convey the imperatives, intricacies and intractability of much real world policy-making in a sentence … policy-making is a complex process, a mix of new events, old promises, bureaucratic loyalties, party allegiances, manifesto pledges, pressure group campaigns, think tank or select committee reports, research findings and legislative cooking time among other factors."
Alex's Archives online

"Malcolm Dean's book provides a wealth of evidence on what has gone wrong, with many insights into why it has happened, and some pointers to a different way of doing both media and politics."
Counterfire

"A cogent, detailed and comprehensive description of UK drug policy shenanigans from 2000-2007, including contributions from Transform. "
Transform review

"A remarkably detailed book, an intricate and subtle study of the interplay between politicians, media pressure groups, civil servants, think tanks and social research funders"
Fifth Estate Online

"Malcolm Dean has had a ring-side seat as journalism morphed from observer into political player. The five years that Dean subsequently spent researching and collating this book shows in the breadth of subjects and some of the detail of the case studies. *Democracy under attack* is a book to dip into."
LSE IMpactblog book reviews

"The book is a fascinating interweaving of government policy decisions – especially in the Labour years – with the media's treatment of the same issues and how one shaped the other."
5★ review on Amazon

"An admirable companion reader for anyone following Lord Justice Leveson's inquiry into the *News of the World* phone hacking scandal and the culture, practice and ethics of the British media."
5★ review on Amazon

"A landmark publication. It surely must become a bible for anyone with an interest in the media, politics, the law or just old fashioned decency and integrity as an integral part of democracy."
5★ review on Amazon

DEMOCRACY UNDER ATTACK

How the media distort
policy and politics

Malcolm Dean

First published in Great Britain in 2013 by

The Policy Press
University of Bristol
Fourth Floor
Beacon House
Queen's Road
Bristol BS8 1QU
UK
t: +44 (0)117 331 4054
f: +44 (0)117 331 4093
tpp-info@bristol.ac.uk
www.policypress.co.uk

North American office:
The Policy Press
c/o The University of Chicago Press
1427 East 60th Street
Chicago, IL 60637, USA
t: +1 773 702 7700
f: +1 773-702-9756
e:sales@press.uchicago.edu
www.press.uchicago.edu

British Library Cataloguing in Publication Data
A catalogue record for this book is available from the British Library.

Library of Congress Cataloging-in-Publication Data
A catalog record for this book has been requested.

ISBN 978 184742 849 3 paperback

Cover design by The Policy Press
Front cover: photograph kindly supplied by Getty
Printed and bound in Great Britain by TJ International, Padstow

Contents

To: Clare, Sophie, Tim and Ben
for their support and subtle skill in ensuring
that for all the fantastic reviews the first edition
received – see two pages at front and cover – the
author's head did not get too big for
his shoulders

Foreword

Howard Glennerster, Emeritus Professor of Social Policy,
London School of Economics and Political Science

How are we to view the role of the press and the wider media in Britain today?

Does it hold politicians to account or merely scare them into submission? Does it raise issues of national concern or trivialise them? Does it trample on individuals' privacy or save them from bureaucratic indifference? Perhaps it does all of this but, if so, what does it do most?

There are plenty of views, individual complaints and an official inquiry under way. But this book is different – a retrospective and carefully documented account by one of the country's leading journalists of the part the media has played in shaping public and political attitudes to social affairs over the past 40 years. Malcolm Dean spent most of his journalistic life writing about social policy, observing politicians at work and immersing himself in the policy process. Here he distils that lifetime of experience. It is not just an account by an insider but by a hugely well-informed insider, one with a feel for history. Dean looks back at changes in social policy from the 1960s on and at changes that have overtaken journalism. But above all he looks in detail at the part the media have played in shaping policy on law and order and prison reform, on drugs policy, on child poverty, vocational education, housing, health and social care. He includes content from numerous interviews with people who others would likely not have reached and includes his own experiences. It is a unique blend. Having been involved in the policy debate myself, and the political process at times too, his accounts ring true.

Dean knows the specific academic literature that underpinned the debates, or should have done, and the day-to-day interaction between politics and the press room. What we learn is an arresting and sometimes shocking insight into the power of the press to shape the way politicians think and see the issues they are legislating about. It frames their world view.

Some academics have played down the role of the media, seeing it as a sounding board at best or a mere form of entertainment or perversion of reality at worst. This is a much more subtle and revealing account. Sometimes the press can be more even handed and well informed than politicians think and they would have done well to show courage: drug policy is one case. In other areas like housing the absence of specialist informed reporting helped take it off the agenda. Working with a well-informed press, policy can be developed that will win the public over, as in the case of child poverty or pension reform. But sometimes politicians are simply scared stiff by what they think the press will say and about how they judge the public will react. These detailed accounts give us all shades of grey and some glimpses of the sun too.

This will be an indispensable read for those wishing to understand the media and the policy process in the United Kingdom, whether they are interested in social policy or not.

Professor Howard Glennerster is one of the most respected academics of British social policy. The author of multiple books and papers, he has been at the heart of the LSE's social administration team, where he began teaching 44 years ago. He was elected Fellow of the British Academy in 2002.

Foreword

David R. Mayhew
Sterling Professor of Political Science
Yale University

Britain always offers an apt comparison for American readers worried about democracy and policymaking. Throw in the media, and the comparison becomes irresistible. This work by Malcolm Dean offers all that. Informed by long duty as social policy expert for *The Guardian*, Dean traces the nexus of media (especially the newspapers), politicians and policy-making in Britain during the last half-century.

It is not a pretty evolution. It has some bright points. British policy-making is vastly more transparent that it used to be. Dean notes his surprise, once back from a stint in America in the 1960s, in finding how closed the British government was back then. But there are adverse trends, many of which echo US experience. Newspapers and traditional television channels have been losing audiences. Specialist reporting in such policy areas as housing has fallen off. On the media side, Dean sees a growing bent for sensation, scandal-mongering, pack journalism and adversarial coverage. Souped-up crises have been crowding out real societal problems.

As with the US presidency, the Prime Minister's office has adapted to the 24-hour media cycle by centralising government power and deploying worldly-wise apparatchiks who are deft at 'spin' and 'shaping the narrative'. These moves, a signal success under Tony Blair especially, have constituted both offence and defence in a public policy space that can all too easily degenerate into media tropes. 'Keep Myra Hindley in prison' (in the wake of gruesome murders) led a vibrant media life in the 1980s and 1990s. 'Welfare scroungers' have enjoyed a starring role. 'One asylum claim every six minutes' became a caption for refugees entering Britain. The media hyped 'Herceptin the wonder drug', a bogus cancer cure, but delegitimised through scare stories the MMR vaccine for children, a real pharmaceutical protection.

Are the British media worse than the American? Well, the media scene in the United States has evolved into radio shock-jocks, nasty bloggers, and off-centre news coverage by the Fox and MSNBC cable channels. There are problems. But at least the United States does not have tabloid newspapers that reach a nationwide audience. That seems to be a great blessing. In Dean's account, British tabloids such as the *The Sun* and the *Mail* are truly awful. All by themselves they debase the public sphere. Lately, they have gotten themselves enmeshed in the phone-hacking scandal.

Democracy under attack can be read as a policy history. I was struck by the trans-Atlantic similarities. As in the United States, poverty blossomed as a British concern in the 1960s. Law and order and tax-cutting ensued in the 1970s and 1980s. Drugs hit the charts: The Americans created a drug 'czar', the British a drug 'tsar'. In sync with the Clinton era, Britain's politicians keyed on child poverty and welfare reform. Then the 'death tax' made an appearance. In the 2000s came concerns about terrorism, immigration, inequality and school testing. The British focus was often different. Asylum seekers and traditional A-level school testing drew attention in Britain, for example; illegal immigrants and new Bush-era testing in the United States. But a good deal has moved in tandem. For Americans, there is much to be learned by peering across the ocean. This book allows that.

Professor David Mayhew is one of the most eminent political scientists in the US. As Sterling Professor in Yale University's political science department, he has been awarded numerous visiting fellowships in the US and the UK. In 2004 he received the Samuel J. Eldersveld Award for lifetime achievement from the American Political Science Association.

Preface

How big a role do the media play in formulating social policy? Has this role changed over time? Are there some areas – asylum, crime, immigration, drugs, welfare, for example – where right-wing tabloids have more power because of their ability to fan public fears, prejudices and anxieties? To what extent do the media change public opinion? Perhaps more importantly, to what extent do ministers believe tabloids influence public opinion and adjust their decisions accordingly? And why was there a three-way breakdown of trust between the media, government and the public, as documented by the Phillis Report in 2004?

This book is an attempt to answer these questions. It begins by describing the rise and fall of mainstream media, which I watched through a *Guardian* window from 1969, and to a lesser extent the rise and fall of specialist journalists. Chapter Two describes the rise of the welfare state, how the media responded to its emergence, along with an insider's and outsider's look at policy-making. There then follow seven case study chapters examining the media's influence on policies across a wide spectrum: law and order, drugs, asylum, poverty, education, health and social care, and housing. These were all issues I tracked, first as *The Guardian*'s social affairs leader writer and later as its social policy editor. The media's influence is measurably greater in the first three areas, which is why they get more space. Collectively the seven illustrate the interplay between politicians, media, pressure groups, civil servants, think tanks and social research funders. I hope they give readers a taste of what goes on in newsrooms, departmental policy divisions and Parliament. Chapter Ten examines the seven sins – all legal, alas: distortion; 'dumbing down' content; being more interested in politics than policy; hunting in packs (group think); being too adversarial; being too readily duped; and worst of all, concentrating on the negative. Chapter 11 describes early origins of illegal media invasions of people's privacy, the *News of the World* hacking scandal, the Leveson inquiry into the media, and the resulting disagreements between and within proprietors, editors and political parties over the Leveson report's recommendations. The Afterword looks at what led to the decline in media ethics, the dangers raised by the delay in reaching agreement on Leveson's proposals, and the answer to the five questions raised in the first paragraph of this preface.

This is not intended to be an academic treatise. Rather, it is a look at the media's influence on social policy as observed by a journalist close to the scene for over 40 years. It draws on hundreds of different briefings I have been given by ministers, departmental policy-makers and social policy researchers over the last four decades, and is supplemented by interviews with 150 participants in the policy-making process since my association with Nuffield College, Oxford, which began in 2006: ministers, civil servants, pressure group campaigners, public service inspectors, think tank researchers, MPs, select committee members, along with fellow journalists, social policy academics, political scientists and media watchers. It has been improved by the extended reading I have been able to do on my fellowship at Nuffield, and with the support of the Joseph Rowntree Foundation (JRF). Sincere thanks to both institutions.

There is considerably more criticism than praise for journalism in this book, but before we get to the criticisms, I would like to pay tribute to the large number of serious journalists still 'out there', who, with much expertise and wide knowledge of the fields they cover, continue to provide an invaluable public service. The best are performing a crucial role in any democracy: making the government more open and accountable; keeping the public informed about the performance of public services; and identifying the unmet needs that society and government are still ignoring. I remain proud of the traditions of my trade, and feel privileged to have been able to spend 38 of my 50 years in journalism on *The Guardian* – I believe it is still producing some of the finest journalism in the country. They were a wonderful team – highly intelligent, collegiate, serious but not solemn, and good fun. Right up to the day of my retirement in 2006 I was still travelling to the office believing I should be paying them for the job.

There are too many people whom I interviewed to list here, but to all of them a deep thanks for their time, thoughts and encouragement. They made my entry into long-distance writing after more than 40 years of 24-hour deadlines much easier and yet challenging. Apart from my old colleagues at *The Guardian* – including the ever-helpful librarians – and new colleagues at Nuffield, who made me so welcome, there are some people I would like to thank in particular. Professor Richard Neustadt, a revered American political scientist and hero-figure of mine who sadly died in October 2003. His book on *Presidential Power*, which I read as a Harkness Fellow in the 1960s, received rave reviews. I got to know him well in later years when he came to live in England after marrying Shirley Williams. When I told him I was planning to write a book about media power, using case studies as he had done to tease out the amount of power, he could not have been more encouraging. There are large differences in the power of the President and the power of the media, but there are some similarities, as Neustadt readily agreed in our talks. What was novel about his book was the distinction he made between a President's formal and informal powers. The media have few formal powers, but considerable informal powers in terms of powers of persuasion. Power is only one of several goals of the media – alongside profits, sales, dominance, entertainment – but political influence remains important. Rupert Murdoch did his best in his appearance before the Commons Select Committee on the media and the Leveson hearings to downplay his influence, but 20 years earlier, he told his biographer, William Shawcross, 'That's the fun of it, isn't it? Having a little smidgen of power'. Some smidgen.[1]

Professor Peter Golding, who was an early practitioner of monitoring media coverage of social issues, could not have been more encouraging when I telephoned him about my project. He provided a helpful framework. A special thank you to Nicholas Timmins, an old media colleague, for writing such a superb book *The five giants: A biography of the welfare state*, to which I have made frequent reference to check essential facts. But above all, to Howard Glennerster, Emeritus Professor of Social Policy at the London School of Economics and Political Science (LSE), author of the other essential book on the welfare state, *British social policy: 1945 to the present*. He was not only extremely helpful in the early part of the project, and in advising on the structure of the book, but in the last stages took on the onerous task of reading through my first drafts. They were returned with rigorous and detailed comments, suggestions and insights. He even recalculated the pie charts from his own book – on the growth of the welfare state – bringing them forward to 2009/10, as set out in Chapter Two. Any current errors will not be his, but mine, for ignoring his advice. To Howard, and to Professor David Mayhew, the distinguished Yale political scientist, a sincere thank you for setting this book in context – the first for British readers and the second for an American audience, given the book's US publication – in their astute forewords above this preface. A huge thank you, too, to my wife, Clare Roskill, who supported my 'creative quarantine' in our second home hideaway in Bath, to write the book. She also proved a good proofreader.

I am sure readers will be as grateful as I am to Harry Venning, the *Guardian* cartoonist, for the delightful insights in his cartoons that I have selected for the book. He has uplifted *The Guardian*'s Society section – and generated smiles from its readers – for over a decade. David Austin, another brilliant cartoonist enlightening *Guardian* readers, died in 2005. His pocket cartoons – see pp 9 and 229 – used to appear daily. Finally, my sincere thanks to Ali Shaw and her great team at The Policy Press. They were my first choice of publisher. As an editor I was an admirer of the work they produced. As a client I am extremely grateful for their enthusiasm about the project, the support that has been extended from all branches of the firm – editorial, design, printing, proofreading and marketing – as well as the care and commitment that all have applied at all stages. I would particularly like to single out three people. Jo Morton, who for the first edition had the challenging task of accommodating daily developments that occurred with 'Murdoch's meltdown' in July 2011. The publisher readily re-opened the book and Jo calmly organised and took charge of mounting numbers of inserts that were filed in the right place. It has happened again with this paperback edition, which has needed to absorb multiple inserts on the many changes that have taken place in the intervening 18 months. Kathryn King, the head of marketing, who has been an enthusiastic supporter of the book from the beginning, has seized all manner of opportunities to publicise it through traditional as well as new media sources. Finally Caroline Wilding, who produced the superb index.

Malcolm Dean
January 2013

Note

[1] William Shawcross (1992) *Rupert Murdoch: Ringmaster of the information circus*, London: Chatto and Windus, p 550.

#democracyunderattack – please visit Twitter to see all the latest updates on the book and discuss with other readers

ONE

The rise and fall of mainstream journalism

Politicians who complain about the media are, as Enoch Powell MP once observed, like sailors who complain about the sea. But as the new millennium began, it was not just politicians who were complaining about the growing power of the media, but philosophers, the establishment and senior journalists too. It began with a Cambridge philosopher. Onora O'Neill, in her Reith lectures in 2002,[1] discussed the issue of trust in public institutions, noting that it was rather ironic that the main champions of ideas about transparency and accountability – the media – were themselves the least transparent and accountable of groups in our democracy. She spoke of the national press acquiring 'unaccountable power that others cannot match'. Then senior journalists took over.

Anthony Sampson, in his fourth edition of *Who runs this place? The anatomy of Britain in the 21st century*,[2] showed just how entrenched that perception was. Returning to interview the leaders of 24 other centres of power – Whitehall, Westminster, the City, industry, corporations, the Cabinet, political parties, banks, academia, the law, defence, trade unions, accountants, and so on – he noted that virtually every institution he had talked to complained of a weakening of their influence in the 40 years since his first edition, and the growth of media power in the same period. He found that the leaders he interviewed 'mention the media more often with fear or dislike rather than respect, and have a contempt for their short horizons, their superficiality and destructiveness'. The media were 'more pervasive, seeping everywhere into the vacuum left by the shrinking old powers'. And within the media, it was newspaper owners who were more feared and respected than the television tycoons, 'for they can express their own strong political views, humiliate politicians, and pursue vendettas through their newspapers without the regulations which restrict television channels'.[3]

John Lloyd, a senior writer on the *Financial Times*, followed up in *What the media are doing to our politics*[4] with an indictment of both broadsheet and broadcasting journalists for their sensationalism, distortions and exaggeration in the new 'adversarial journalism'. He noted: 'The media have claimed the right to judge and to condemn; more they have decided – without being clear about the decision – that politics is a dirty game played by devious people who tell an essentially false narrative about the world and thus deceive the British people.'

Concern about the media's influence was not just confined to these observers. Editors too became involved. Richard Lambert, of the *Financial Times*, delivered a long lecture in December 2004 – reprinted in *The Guardian*[5] – on the need for higher journalistic standards and more media accountability. He compared the storm of protests that broke out when Shell tried to dump an oil rig in the North Sea with the lack of protests over totally inaccurate media stories such as *The Sun*'s front-page splash about asylum-seekers capturing and cooking the Queen's swans (see Chapter Five on asylum). He noted that although there were a large number of national titles, because their ownership and location was too concentrated so was their power. As a result no politician from any of the main parties was ready to tackle the press barons head on. 'The result is a media that in some extreme cases is more of a threat to our democracy than its guarantor.'

Harry Evans, Editor of *The Sunday Times* who moved to New York in 1984 after disagreements with Rupert Murdoch, continues to monitor the British media. In an interview with the *Press Gazette* in July 2006, he hit out at the 'partisan reporting' and 'fratricidal nonsense that you read in the British press'. He condemned the way 'stories are twisted, particularly during election time – it's disgusting. Now I'm not saying that it should be stopped – it's a free country, so the more expressions the better. It is up to other papers to monitor the way news is reported, and they don't do that enough. *The Guardian* has done some good work in this area.' There were two consequences of bias and pollution in the news. 'First of all, it is demoralising to the journalist who has to do it – you have to take this angle and so on. Secondly, it destroys confidence in the press.'[6]

Alan Rusbridger, *Guardian* Editor, wrote to 50 people in high profile public service and private sector jobs asking them to evaluate the media coverage of their work. The responses ran to 26 pages, which were published in successive editions of *The Guardian*'s weekly Media section in January 2005.[7] The main concern of the respondents was the media's persistent negativity and destructiveness. David Bell, Chief Inspector of Schools at the time, declared: 'a lack of coverage of positive stories can create the impression that a system – in my case education – is in a perpetual state of crisis. This simply is not true.'[8] Trevor Phillips, former journalist and chair of the Commission for Racial Equality at the time, suggested 'journalists do now seem to believe that the person in charge is always wrong'.[9] Tony Wright, chair of the Commons Committee on Public Administration, in one of the most damning indictments, was unequivocal: 'Newspapers trumpet the collapse of trust in politics and politicians, as though they had not had a major role in bringing it about. They nourish a culture of contempt engulfing the whole of public life. The trend is clear. As circulations fall, the race is to the bottom.'[10]

A look back at media/government relations

Perhaps there could be no better acknowledgement of the increase in the media's influence than the declaration by former Prime Minister Tony Blair on his election as Labour leader in 1994, that 'the only thing that matters now in this campaign is the media, the media, the media'.[11] Compare that to Prime Minister Clement Attlee, who, on returning to Downing Street in 1951 after obtaining the Queen's consent to a general election, was asked by a reporter whether he wanted to expand on the campaign that he was about to lead and replied: 'No'.[12]

> Reporter: Tell us something of how you view the election prospects?

> Attlee: Oh, we shall go in with a good fight. Very good.
> Very good chance of winning if we go in competently.
> We always do.
>
> Reporter: On what will Labour take its stand?
>
> Attlee: Well, that is what we shall be announcing shortly.
>
> Reporter: What are your immediate plans Mr Attlee?
>
> Attlee: My immediate plans are to go down to a
> committee to decide on just that thing as soon as I
> can get away from here.
>
> Reporter: Is there anything else you'd like to say about
> the coming election?
>
> Attlee: No.[13]

Even in the 1970s, directors of information were still strictly rationing ministerial interviews. Norman Warner, Private Secretary to Barbara Castle, Secretary of State for Health and Social Security in the 1970s, remembers his boss being told by her director of communications that she had already done two broadcast interviews in one week and that was enough.[14] Compare that to Alastair Campbell's guidance to new recruits to Tony Blair's press office: 'If we do not feed them, they eat us.'[15]

There is nothing new about governments trying to manipulate the media. In the First World War Winston Churchill declared governments should either 'squash 'em or square 'em'. According to Lance Price in *Where power lies: Prime Minister v the media*, Lloyd George began the practice of 'employing a personal and somewhat thuggish spin doctor to help push his agenda' a century ago.[16] Price was a former BBC political journalist for seven years who then spent three years, first as a special media adviser in 1998 at Number 10 Downing Street, where he deputised for Alastair Campbell, and then as the Labour Party's director of communications. He now works as a freelance journalist and author. He suggests in his new, well-received book that Lloyd George was the first media-conscious prime minister. He reached that position in the words of his predecessor, Herbert Asquith, 'in a coup driven by newspapers'. Similarly, there is nothing new about public concern over the press taking over the role of the opposition in Parliament – during the First World War the creation of 'a coalition government had largely closed down debate about the war at Westminster, a vacuum the press was more than happy to fill'.[17]

In his ministerial period in the Second World War Lord Beaverbrook, a newspaper proprietor himself, declared his approach to the media was to 'kiss 'em one day and kick them the next'. Charles Wintour, former *Evening Standard* Editor, in his book *Pressures on the press* in 1972,[18] suggested: 'The attempt to squash 'em may have been dropped but the principle to square 'em is very much alive.' Ironically, for all Attlee's reluctance to seize media opportunities, it was under his government that media communications became more professional. This has all been set out by Martin Moore, in *The origins of modern spin*.[19] Perhaps it is worth remembering that even a government with postwar emergency economic powers that allowed it to ration the size of papers (4–6 pages), cap their circulations and even introduce distribution controls, was frustrated by a truculent press which, with a few exceptions, was not 'properly informing the electorate' in the eyes of ministers.

What was new in Labour's approach?

But for all this media history, what Labour introduced in 1997 was new. Blair's first appointment after becoming party leader was not a policy chief but a press chief. And he had to travel across France to persuade Alastair Campbell to become press director. Together with Peter Mandelson they created a formidable media machine complete with a computer-driven rebuttal unit, packed with stats and quotes that could provide instant responses to media or opposition criticisms. They covered the most important flanks with Campbell being a former political reporter with two tabloid papers, *The Daily Mirror* and *Today*, and Mandelson being a former television producer of current affairs programmes.

Thanks to the loss of confidence in the Conservative Major government and Labour's assiduous wooing of national newspaper editors and, more importantly in terms of *The Sun*, their proprietors, support for Labour was transformed. Where only 3 out of 10 national papers supported Labour in the 1992 general election, 6 out of 10 supported it in 1997, with one (*The Times*) staying neutral and three others (*Daily Mail*, *Daily Express* and *The Daily Telegraph*) offering only lukewarm support to the Tories. Indeed, in the run-up to the 1997 general election, Alastair Campbell was able to boast that for the first time Labour had both *The Sun* and the *Mail* on its side. But the support of the tabloids came at a price: first a swing to more right-wing policies as the case studies in the chapters that follow document. It was Lance Price, former BBC political correspondent, who became Alastair Campbell's deputy in 1998, who called Rupert Murdoch the 24th member of the Cabinet in a BBC Radio 4 documentary, 'Prime ministers and press barons', in March 2008. He suggested: 'His presence was almost tangible in the building and it was as if he was the 24th member of the Cabinet. In fact more than that. In some areas of policy, [he was] more influential on the Prime Minister and on the direction of the Government's policy than most of the other 23.'[20] Then there was also the dropping of three important media reforms that had been in the 1992 Labour Party manifesto but were not in the 1997 manifesto, to get Murdoch onside: restrictions on foreign ownership of British media; a stricter privacy law to curb tabloid invasions; and moves to outlaw predatory pricing which would have stopped *The Times*' price war that almost shut down *The Independent* and destabilised other broadsheets.[21] Remember that it was Rupert Murdoch who told his biographer William Shawcross of the attractions of political power: 'That's the fun of it, isn't it? Having a little smidgen of power.'[22] Some smidgen. Five years after Neil Kinnock was portrayed turning off the lights in 1992, it was Tony Blair's turn to be on *The Sun*'s front page on the day of the 1997 general election holding that day's paper which read: '*The Sun* backs Blair ... the people need a leader with vision, purpose and courage, who can inspire them and fire their imagination.'[23]

On victory, Labour's campaign media machine was taken into Downing Street. Once in power, New Labour had many more levers to ensure its belief in 'shaping the narrative' was achieved. It was regarded as the most essential element for success in politics: linking news stories to a single narrative, controlling their development and still being in charge of the debate. Senior media directors were replaced by more proactive ones – 25 heads or deputy heads changed in the first year. Presentation of policy became as important as its creation. Policies were never knowingly undersold. They were pre-announced, announced, post-announced and re-announced. Campbell's high command kept a grid of media announcements, parcelling out releases to fit the government's narrative. But as 24/7 news and later web news took off, a daily grid proved inadequate – news cycles shortened to hours. Journalists, particularly from *The Mirror*, joined the press machine. Ministerial special advisers asserted control over departmental press operations and attempted to deliver good headlines. Rebuttal was developed as never before in Whitehall. A coterie of sympathetic reporters was identified and favoured with leaks. The 'tyranny of momentum politics' – in the evocative words of Peter Hyman,[24] Blair's impressive speech writer and head of strategic communications – was an enormous challenge but also offered new opportunities for control. These were seized by Campbell's unit, which organised new convenient pre-packaged deals to television news teams that were eagerly snapped up even though they had little opportunity to check them out properly. The announcement of new policy initiatives in health, education and crime control miraculously found television reporters already on the site of successful pilot projects, hours before the better-informed newspaper specialists were told of the new programmes.

Blair was the first prime minister to allow his media director to attend all Cabinet meetings, the first to give his media director powers to instruct civil servants, the first to write regularly for the tabloids (150 articles in his first two years), and the first to have weekly sessions with his pollster. In its first four-year term, the Blair administration issued 32,000 press releases.[25]

As Martin Moore, Director of the Media Standards Trust, noted in an address to the Reuters Institute for the Study of Journalism in Oxford, when Prime Minister Baldwin first compared the press to a harlot ('power without responsibility') between the two world wars there were 44 people in the government involved in some form of communication. In 2008 there were over 3,000 press officers, 70 or so special advisers, huge departments of communication within each Whitehall ministry, some occupying whole floors, a Number 10 communication team, an advertising budget of over £230 million and 950 government websites. Surely that evens things up a bit?

Evaporation of goodwill

Initially there was immense goodwill for the new Labour government. In the early days senior civil servants conceded that Whitehall's communication system did need reform. It had to become more proactive in getting the details of new policies over and not leave it to just the publication day of Green and White Papers. But over time relations turned sour. It was a combination of spin, too much manipulation, too much favouritism to selected journalists, the needs of 24/7 news, a dubious favour to Bernie Ecclestone – whose £1 million donation to the Labour Party had been kept secret – of Formula One's exemption from the ban on tobacco advertising, along with, as time progressed, Iraq and 'dodgy' dossiers.

The emphasis on presentation pushed ministers into 'headline policy-making'. Lance Price admitted as much in *The Independent on Sunday*, where he suggested part of the problem was structure rather than mendacity. The huge increase in media outlets with more time and space to fill had left government with too few 'newsworthy' stories:

> We at No 10 had only a finite number of our own to offer to our hungry customers. For the rest we had to go to individual departments. I have no doubt that they felt under pressure constantly to come up with new announcements and new angles because I was among those putting pressures on them. And equally I have no doubt that, as a result, some 'news' that wasn't quite as new as it seemed was passed on to the papers. It may have been demand led but it was clearly counter-productive in the end.[26]

In his book Price is even more disparaging:

> Clever fingers are put to work to try to whip up the kind of stories Number 10 believes the voters want to read. No longer content to dole out the valuable news at its disposal to those journalists who can be trusted to

repackage it appropriately, Downing Street now creates valueless news in order to satisfy a perceived demand. Like candyfloss, stories are spun from very little to appear larger and more eye catching than they really are. Along the way the distinction between the public interest and what interests the public is quickly forgotten.[27]

From the beginning of the 1997 Labour government, as Andrew Marr, former BBC Political Editor, noted in a farewell to Tony Blair in May 2007 on the day the Prime Minister announced his retirement, 'there seemed to be a tendency to browbeat and cajole journalists,

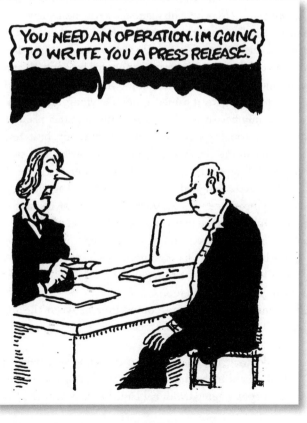

to fight for every comma and exclamation mark in every headline, contest every quote, challenge every piece of analysis'.[28]

Indeed when things were getting tough in 2000, they were made worse by two leaked memos. The first, in June, leaked to *The Sunday Times*, reported on the findings of focus groups that suggested 'TB is not believed to be real. He lacks convictions, he is all spin and presentation, he says things to please people, not because he believes in them.' [29] The second, written in April but published by *The Times* on 17 July 2000 was from Blair to his aides and followed his regular briefing from his pollster, where he learned his government was looking 'out of touch with gut British instincts'.[30] His memo was aimed at restoring some tough gut instinct: 'We should think now of an initiative, eg locking up street muggers. Something tough with immediate bite ...'. The leaks reinforced David Marquand's assessment in *Britain since 1918*, where he suggested a damaging new media-led circulatory policy-making process had been created: 'Media storms fed into focus groups; focus-group discussions fed into the Prime Minister's office; and ministerial reactions fed back into the media.'[31]

Conceding the accuracy of the observation, Lance Price also noted that the process gave the media, not Downing Street, the upper hand: 'the number of hours I spent with ministers planning new "crackdowns" on drugs, asylum-seekers and benefit cheats testifies to the accuracy of the assessment'.[32] Price acknowledges 'a significant proportion of the stories generated by Downing Street for the sake of headlines were designed to suggest that New Labour understood and even sympathised with the socially conservative instincts of most tabloids. Only rarely did they challenge the mindset of *The Sun* or the *Daily Mail*.'[33] But he went on to suggest that it was more complex than just bowing to media pressure: '... such ideas appealed to him [Blair] not just because he thought the *Daily Mail* and *Sun* would like them. He liked them too.'[34]

Price makes a fascinating comparison between the briefings Margaret Thatcher received with Blair's:

> Under Margaret Thatcher the media summary produced
> by Bernard Ingham had encouraged her to believe that
> the country agreed with her basic instincts. Under Tony

Blair the focus groups and other research carried out by his polling expert Philip Gould sent the opposite message. Gould would sit down with small groups of 'swing' or uncommitted voters and tease out their views. He told Hugo Young that 'every time I do a focus group I get the *Daily Mail* coming back at me. It's terrible'.[35]

Media relations get worse

Mistrust grew. Adversarial journalism expanded. A nadir in media manipulation was reached in September 2001 when Jo Moore, a Labour special adviser at the Transport Department, emailed officials to suggest the terrorist attacks on the US on 9/11 made it 'a good day' to publish and bury bad news. Senior advisers within the government became seriously worried by the state of government/media relations and the impact the government's bad press was having on public attitudes. Geoff Mulgan, former Head of the Prime Minister's Policy Unit and Director of the government's Strategy Unit, was later to confess: 'The Government's worse nightmare is not that its policies will fail, rather that they might succeed but no one would believe them because of the chronic distrust of statistics on hospitals, schools and the police.'[36]

As the report of the Phillis Committee, which was set up in February 2003 to look at the three-way breakdown of relations between the media, government and public, concluded, the decline in public trust was at its heart:

> Trust in government and politicians is at its lowest level, at least in modern times. Thirty years ago in 1974, 39 per cent of the population believed that government, of whatever political persuasion, would put the national good before party political gain. Today the figure is 16 per cent. Opinion polls repeatedly show that politicians and journalists are the least trusted professions ... the level of trust in politicians is lower than comparative figures from both Europe and the USA. It has become commonplace for commentators to say that the Government is no

longer believed and media coverage throughout the period of this review has referred consistently to this being the era of spin.[37]

It had not forgotten the media. It went on: 'The disturbing lack of trust in government and politicians is accompanied by a diminishing trust in the media and the press in particular. Recent research shows that only six per cent of respondents regard any newspaper as the most fair and unbiased source of news, compared with 14 per cent radio, and 70 per cent for television.'[38]

Alastair Campbell's *mea culpa*

Just a few months before the Phillis Committee was set up, Alastair Campbell gave a long, thoughtful speech at the inaugural meeting of the Media Correspondents Association in 2002.[39] He described the wooing of right-wing publishers and their editors as a basic step for a professional media operation of a major organisation.

> We did make a concerted effort to get a better dialogue with some parts of the media where before there had been pretty much none. This was of course about reaching their readers. It was also about preventing destruction by a hostile press. Competence with the media conveyed a general competence that was important to us in establishing ourselves as a competent Government. Without it, we could have been heavily undermined from the start. In the event, we had what was described as the longest honeymoon in history.... But therein lay the seeds of sin.

He continued:

> The consequences were greater than we anticipated. We appeared, and perhaps we were, over-controlling, manipulative. People stopped trusting what we had to say. I think what we underestimated was the extent to

which the changes we made in our relationship with the media, and in getting our media to act together, would itself become an issue and a story. That's in part because we carried on for too long in Government with some of the tactics of opposition. When you've got parts of the media that are, I'm afraid, more interested in process than they are in policy and outcomes, that gave them an excuse to focus on us. The centre of gravity moved from a position of basic support for the dynamic of New Labour to basic hostility, or at best, grudging recognition.

He then went on to speculate on a theme other media commentators had taken up, over the media turning into 'the opposition':

I think this was due in part to a large section of the media post-1997 feeling there was no opposition, that the Tories for whatever reasons had just become useless. There was a growing sense that it was their [the media's] job actually to stand up and try to do the job the Opposition was failing to do – conveniently overlooking the fact that you are supposed to get elected to do that. That has become a problem. Not only for us, but for all people with an interest in the democratic process.

(He overlooked the crushing defeat which the Conservatives had suffered – a mere 165 MPs compared to Labour's 418, which offered the Tories little chance of changing Labour's legislation when it had a majority of 197.)

He went on:

We can look at our own role and the mistakes we made in handling that change as it happened. I think we were too slow to see our part in the way the dialogue between politics and press was becoming devalued.... When we cooperated with Michael Cockerell on a documentary he made about our whole media operation – in part because we wanted to try to get out to the public a broader sense of perspective about what it is these terrible spin doctor people do – it sort of underlined the problem. Michael told me after the event that that programme generated more column inches than all the other programmes he ever made, combined.

That said, two things. One, media obsession. Secondly, our failings in adapting to this new discourse. There was a sense that politics and the media were involved in a dialogue from which the public was becoming excluded. It was as if something was going on that had absolutely nothing to do with them and with their lives. While I am willing to accept our share of the blame for this situation, it is not unreasonable to point out these other important factors responsible for this disconnection: a hostile and cynical media, a more demanding public living in a culture of immediacy, and less trust in established institutions. But whoever or whatever is responsible for getting us where we are, in the end we have to take lead responsibility for getting us out of here. For if the public comes to believe all communication is spin, no matter how much we may want to blame the media, it is ultimately our problem, a problem for our political culture.

There was more acceptance of his share of the blame in those passages than most of the media are ever ready to concede about their share. He made three other interesting points. The first concerned 24/7 news and the need for news organisations – and Downing Street – to find fresh angles and themes by the afternoon and evening for stories that had broken in the morning. He thought there was an inaccurate assumption within the media that readers and viewers had a basic knowledge of what stories were about even when they came in late. But unlike media people living in a bubble of 24/7 news on television screens in the office, surrounded by full sets of newspapers and with a flow of domestic and foreign news on their computers, the average person was only dipping in and out. A huge number of people no longer read newspapers and many of those that did were not interested in the news sections. 'So, again without overstating it, I'd say there is more media and there is a lot more noise, but there is less understanding by the public of what's actually happening within the political debate. And that inevitably, I think, leads to cynicism.'

Second was the major challenge of democracy, its processes being far slower than the demands of the people in an era of immediacy. 'Take an issue like asylum. People demand that something must be done, yet in the way stands the cost, the lords, an opportunistic opposition, and the courts.' He could have added inter-state cooperation, international law and global migrant smuggling rings but he went on:

> It's not easy. But viewers can take part in Sky News phone poll as to whether some new proposal is a good idea or a bad idea, and it gives a sense that it can be dealt with now, straightaway, easily. People sit at home, watch *Pop Idol* or *Big Brother*, hit these buttons on their phone and have an impact on the result. You can win the Champions League on PlayStation in a few hours. Yet, they say, in the real world the authorities can't even build a national stadium. But real solutions to real problems take time. And that can lead to a feeling of disempowerment, which adds to disillusion, exacerbated by the semblance, largely false, of some kind of quick fix of power elsewhere. This is the real paradox, and a real challenge for modern government: how do you deliver long-term, difficult change in this era of immediacy, and how do we keep the public interested, informed and engaged as we go?

Third, he turned to the addiction of journalism to negative stories (see 'sin seven' in Chapter Ten, this volume). He concluded:

> Journalists are an absolutely vital bridge between politicians and the public, and if journalists see their role as simply presenting the negative, that a story's only a decent story if it's a bad story, then that bridge exists only to be blown up. People begin to lose faith in politics. But

while it's true that respect for politics is lower, it is worth just bearing in mind that government and politicians remain more trusted to tell the truth than the press. The last Euro Monitor survey asked the public whether it trusts the press or doesn't. The UK distrust level is way, way, higher than anywhere else in the EU.

Alastair Campbell in retrospect

Few would dispute that Alastair Campbell became the most powerful Prime Minister's Press Secretary in the history of Number 10. This was partly due to his knowledge of the media along with his writing skills, partly his closeness to Tony Blair – they were true 'buddies', partly his forceful and implacable personality. The media dubbed him 'the real Deputy Prime Minister' quite early in his Number 10 position. Lance Price, Campbell's deputy, provides a vivid description of his operating skills and power:

> Campbell's self confidence was one reason.... The new dispensations he'd been given by the order in council were just the start. The real power he had was stripped, sometimes brutally, sometimes discreetly, from others. From departmental heads of information, from the Downing Street policy unit, from the Prime Minister's private office and even the Chief of Staff, Jonathan Powell, who preferred to work in a more low-key and conventional way. In a crisis, and in Downing Street the next crisis is never far off, it was Campbell's decisiveness and clarity of thought that Blair most valued. As a result the Prime Minister ceded some of his power to his press secretary, and not simply because Campbell had the authority to put words into Blair's mouth. Privately Campbell would joke to some of his team that the Prime Minister's 'indecision is final', and Blair often did prefer to keep his options open as long as he could. When the crunch came and a decision could be postponed

no longer, Campbell's judgment, informed by how he thought the media would react, often held sway.[40]

Long before he finally left Downing Street in the autumn of 2003, Campbell had wanted to depart. As early as the summer of 2000 he withdrew from the twice-daily lobby briefing of Westminster correspondents. Much of the media had turned sour, and some of it with justification for the brutal way Campbell had treated some reporters. Worse still, he had become 'a story' in his own right, which was fatal for a media director. For some time Blair, who had recognised the counter-productive use of spin and the time and energy Campbell was using fighting day-to-day battles with the media, persuaded him to stay on. His new remit was to concentrate on long-term strategy, but he got sucked back into the daily headline operations as well as speech writing for Blair. His vendetta against the BBC's coverage of the Iraq war, although exonerated by the Hutton Inquiry, made him even more enemies within the media that rightly regarded the report as a 'whitewash'. What was more damaging, as Anthony Seldon noted in his 2004 book *Blair's Britain 1997–2007*,[41] was the damaging disruptive diversion from long-term strategy that Campbell's campaign against the BBC had caused.

The Phillis Committee Reports

The Phillis Report, published in January 2004, found three major factors had contributed to the breakdown of trust: the communications strategy that Labour adopted in coming into power; the reaction of the media to this strategy; and the response of the civil service to the new communications demands that were placed on it.[42] Although in theory communication officers were part of the service – like lawyers, statisticians and economists – they were not seen as a core function of the mainstream. The report criticised 'the increased use of selective briefing of media outlets, in which government information was seen to be being used to political advantage' and acknowledged journalists' complaints about information 'being used as the currency in a system of favouritism, selective release and partisan spinning'.[43]

Chaired by Bob Phillis, then Chief Executive of the Guardian Media Group, the 12 other members were drawn from senior ranks of the media, government information officers, advertising and public relations (PR). The report quoted the evidence of Adam Boulton, Sky News Political Editor, who warned the Committee about the dangers of using both political special advisers and civil servant press directors to brief the media. He explained: 'the present elision of political and Civil Service information is benefiting no one. In the short term it gives the government more "wriggle room" because no one knows where they stand. But in the long run, it has damaged the credibility of government statements, including denials of allegations against it.'[44]

The Committee noted the usefulness of special advisers being able to be involved in political issues and party debate in a way that was debarred to civil servants. But it was also concerned about how many were concentrating their time on the lobby (the journalists based in Parliament) and a handful of specialist reporters. 'We have been told that this has created an "inner circle" of reporters who have good access, but a disenfranchised majority who do not. They can leave reporters dealing with a sometimes poorly informed and demoralised press operation.'[45]

The main thrust of its recommendations was to widen media access to government briefings, ensure much more was done on the record and live on television, with official transcripts on the web on the day. The report, which was fully endorsed by ministers, supported Labour's principle of making the presentation of policy as important as its development; it suggested that ministers should not be involved in selecting their communications directors; and called for the head of government communications to be a senior civil servant with Permanent Secretary status, rather than a political appointee like Alastair Campbell. The government had already accepted this last proposal before publication.

There was mixed reaction from the media. Many did not engage at all. But both *The Independent* and *The Guardian* welcomed the Committee's interim report. *The Independent*'s story reflected its headline 'A golden opportunity to start again'.[46] *The Guardian*, which observers might have concluded would support it without knowing there was an ambiguous relationship between the top editorial people and Phillis, did, in fact, back the report. It called its recommendations 'the chance of a fresh start, not just for government, but for our whole political culture ... they offer the biggest opportunity for mature modern political debate in many years and they deserve every support'.[47] The two papers were more restrained with the final report. *The Independent* declared: 'The Phillis Report is unlikely to deliver a fatal blow to off-the-record conversations between politicians and journalists. It might, however, help to end some of the worst excesses of the culture of spin.'[48] *The Guardian* noted that it was not just Downing Street that had to admit to the errors of its ways, but the media too. The blame had to be shared, as should the responsibility for rebuilding trust. It added: 'The report is right to say that until we in the press accept we are part of the problem too, it will be hard to begin to break out of the vicious circle.'[49]

Paul Routledge, in *The Daily Mirror*, was having none of this, suggesting the report was 'not about reviving trust between the newspapers and the Prime Minister. It is about conning the British people into believing that the government has kicked its spin habit – when it hasn't. It will take more than the resignation of Alastair Campbell, Blair's spinmeister in chief, to convince the voters.'[50] Peter Riddell, *The Times'* chief political commentator, was more measured. He welcomed the push for more openness, but rightly noted that the proposals made virtually no mention of ministers' accountability to MPs in the Commons. Parliament was in danger of becoming more marginal.[51]

Ivor Gaber, former journalist turned media academic, rightly questioned two of the procedural proposals. It was wrong to give presentation equal status with policy-making – it should be more than an afterthought, but should not have equal status. And it was also wrong to bar ministers from a role in recruiting their head of press. It was a crucial relationship in which senior press directors needed to know they had the full confidence of their ministers. But he had a much more sweeping criticism to make, suggesting the solution to restoring trust lay beyond the Phillis proposals:

> The problems are not just technocratic, they are systemic
> and ideological. They are systemic in that both our

political and media systems have become distorted and dysfunctional over the past two decades or more. The current state of the media – in terms of ownership, ethos and regulation – has clearly made a major contribution to the breakdown in relations with the government.... In political terms we have developed a culture, particularly on the back of the New Labour project, in which the 'appointed' appear to have grown vastly in power and influence, at the expense of the 'elected'. Can anyone doubt that the lowliest special adviser inside Downing Street now wields more influence than the most eminent Labour backbencher? Moreover, as for senior appointees, such as Alastair Campbell and Jonathan Powell, their influence and de facto power are far greater than virtually any member of the Cabinet. Only by re-invigorating the power of the democratic process – by expanding the power of elected politicians at the expense of appointed professionals – will the Labour Government be able merely to start to challenge the public's perceptions of deep distrust.[52]

The report did lead to on-the-record briefing, transcripts on the web, as well as monthly press conferences and appearances before Parliament's select committees. Campbell points to the response of Nick Robinson, BBC Political Editor, to the monthly press conferences to demonstrate the difficulties of change. In his 2008 Cudlipp speech[53] he reports Robinson as saying that Blair was so good at them, they became boring. What did not change after Phillis was the emphasis on presentation pushing ministers into 'headline policy-making'. There were leaks from a conference of senior government media directors in 2004, in which Sian Jarvis, head of communications at the Department of Health, was reported to have complained that Number 10 was still 'asking for announcements before we have policies'. Another, Julia Simpson, head of press at the Home Office, complained: 'Number 10 think they can rugby tackle you. They have made an announcement before you have thought through the policy.'[54]

And to demonstrate burying bad news on big news days was still in operation almost three years after Phillis, on 14 December 2006 the government aborted a corruption inquiry into an arms deal between Saudi Arabia and BAE, announced the closure of 2,500 post offices, confirmed two new airport runways, invited police into Downing Street to interview Blair about cash for peerages, and introduced plans to constrain the Freedom of Information Act – all on the same day that Lord Stevens, former Metropolitan Police Commissioner, released his report on the death of Princess Diana. No prizes for guessing which story got the most extensive coverage.

Two last lessons from a deputy chief press officer to the Prime Minister

Lance Price drew two other relevant lessons from his time in Downing Street. The first was the degree to which modern governments had become so alarmed about the public switching off from politics that prime ministers were ready to engage in any passing media fancy rather than risk appearing remote:

> What started almost tongue-in-cheek when Tony Blair called for the release from prison of a person who didn't actually exist, *Coronation Street*'s Deirdre Rachid, has become a matter of habit. Gordon Brown clearly thought somebody would be impressed that he had taken time out from dealing with the global economic crisis and the expenses scandal to call Simon Cowell and ask after the health of the talent-show contestant Susan Boyle. By indulging in the whims of popular journalism Downing Street has squandered its greatest asset – the authority of the office of Prime Minister. Where once the Prime Minister's words had scarcity value and were listened to with care, they are now devalued to such an extent that they jostle for attention alongside those of anybody else with access to the media. Worse. When they are heard they are now treated as toxic never to be taken at

face value, only to be handled as one, almost certainly unreliable version of the truth.[55]

In fact this runs wider than prime ministers. Specialist journalists on *The Guardian* were sometimes ready to pull out their hair in frustration when offered a genuine exclusive article by Cabinet ministers on a new policy initiative only to have the offer rejected by the comment page editors, suspicious that it would be only spin.

Price's other observation was the degree to which the influence of the media had become inflated:

> Why has this happened? Because most prime ministers, encouraged by the legions of press advisers and pollsters that surround them, have come to believe that journalists are far more powerful than they really are. That belief, in itself, has strengthened the media and weakened the office of the prime minister. And, in the process, far from winning the approval of the media, it has earned politicians in general and prime ministers in particular a mixture of ridicule and contempt. Having seen politicians demean themselves as they scrabble for their favour, the media have reported the sound bites and broadcast the pretty pictures but lost any respect they might once have had for those who supply them. It is hardly surprising that the public has followed suit.[56]

Price's conclusion of this century-long battle between prime ministers and the media is interesting: '... it is a consistent feature of the long battle for supremacy between Downing Street and the media that those prime ministers who fretted most about getting the support of the media not only failed to keep it, but also performed less well in office as a consequence of trying'. In this list he included John Major, Harold Wilson and Anthony Eden. He went on:

> Gordon Brown has demonstrated an excessive sensitivity to media criticism, sometimes publicly and much more often in private. And like the others he has been a less

successful prime minister as a consequence. Tony Blair's relationship with journalists was the most fascinating of all. He often said that complaining about the media was like complaining about the weather. It didn't make it any better. Blair used journalists to help him achieve much that he set out to do, but failed to pursue some of his most ambitious dreams in part, at least, because he thought the attempt would cost him too much support in the media.[57]

The 'feral beast' speech

It was just after his 10th anniversary in Downing Street on 10 May 2007 that Blair announced he would be standing down as prime minister on 27 June. In the following five weeks he gave some valedictory addresses, the most famous of which was on 12 June, on the media. His advisers were wary of the project and he himself admitted that he had made it 'after much hesitation'. He wrote it himself by hand. It was in this speech that he made his headline-grabbing phrase about the media ('hunts in packs ... like a feral beast'), which indeed has some truth but arrested attention away from a series of serious and valid other observations.[58]

He opened his speech by suggesting the relationship between politics, public life and the media was changing as a result of the changing context of communications. This was no one's fault but the effect of the change was seriously adverse to the conduct of public life, and it required a serious debate about how the future should be managed. He acknowledged that New Labour had paid 'inordinate attention in the early days ... to courting, assuaging and persuading the media', but given 'the ferocious hostility of parts of the media' in its 18 years of parliamentary opposition, 'it was hard to see any alternative'.

He did not ignore the history of fraught relations between previous prime ministers, but suggested this had become 'qualitatively and quantitively different'. The media had become fragmented, more diverse and transformed by technology. The main BBC and ITN news programmes used to have audiences of up to 8 or 10 million, but now average half that. In 1982 there were three television stations broadcasting in the UK, and in 2010 there were hundreds. In 1995 some 225 television shows had audiences of over 15 million. Now it was almost none. Newspapers were fighting for a share of a shrinking market. Many were now being read online, not the next day. Internet advertising had overtaken newspaper ads. There were roughly 70 million blogs in existence, with around 120,000 being created every day. Forms of communication were merging. Papers had podcasts, the BBC a website: 24/7 news had arrived.

In the 1960s the government would sometimes, on a serious issue, have a Cabinet meeting lasting two days. 'It would be laughable to think you can do that now without the heavens falling in before lunch on the first day ... things harden within minutes. I mean you can't let speculation stay out there for longer than an instant.'

Blair was leading with a glass chin on this issue. He was frequently criticised by commentators for centralising control and reducing the role of the Cabinet. It met less regularly, with much shorter meetings, far fewer official papers and far fewer official decisions taken there. His preference for informal discussion, often unminuted, became known as 'sofa government' or 'denocracy'. It was criticised by Lord Butler, Private Secretary to five prime ministers and Cabinet Secretary from 1988 to 1998, in his review of the quality of intelligence before the Iraq war, in a report in 2004 which spoke of 'a lack of reasoned deliberation' and 'too much central control'.[59] By 2005, when Blair was in a weaker position, he was making more use of Cabinet and its committees had grown from 27 to 59.[60]

Blair went on:

> I am going to say something that few people in public life will say, but most know is absolutely true: a vast aspect of our jobs today – outside the really major decisions, as big as anything else – is coping with the media, its sheer scale, weight and constant hyperactivity. At points it literally overwhelms. Talk to senior people in virtually any walk of life today – business, military, public services, sport, even charities and voluntary organisations and they will

tell you the same. People don't speak about it because,
in the main, they are afraid to.

The media were not the masters of this change but its victims. It had
produced a hugely more intense form of competition than anything
experienced before. The media were now driven to a dangerous
degree by 'impact'. Impact was what mattered. It was the way to
rise above the clamour and get noticed. But it was this 'necessary
devotion' that was unravelling standards, driving them down, making
the diversity of the media not the strength it should be but an
impulsion towards sensation above all else. The audience needed to
be arrested, held and their emotions engaged. Something that was
interesting was less powerful than something that made you angry
or shocked. Blair drew four consequences from this development:

- Scandal or controversy beats ordinary reporting hands down. News
  is rarely news unless it generates heat as much as or more than light.
- Attacking motive is far more potent than attacking judgement.
  It is not enough for someone to make an error. It has to be
  venal. Conspiratorial. What creates cynicism is not mistakes; it is
  allegations of misconduct. It is misconduct that has impact.
- The fear of missing out means today's media, more than ever before,
  hunt in a pack. In these modes it is like a feral beast, just tearing
  people and reputations to bits. But no one dares to miss out.
- Rather than just reporting news, even if sensational or controversial,
  the new technique is commenting on the news. It has become as
  important, if not more important, than the news itself. There will
  often be as much interpretation of what a politician is saying as
  there is coverage of them actually saying it.

He then picked out *The Independent* for criticism for merging the
two, commenting and news: 'avowedly a viewspaper not merely a
newspaper'.

The final consequence was that it was rare to find balance in today's
media. Things, people, issues, stories were all black and white. Life's
usual grey was almost entirely absent. Events were either a triumph

or disaster. A problem was 'a crisis'. A setback was a policy 'in tatters'. A criticism was 'a savage attack'.

He went on: 'Talk to any public service leader – especially in the NHS or the field of law and order – and they will tell you not that they mind the criticism, but they become totally demoralised by the completely unbalanced nature of it.'

He added: 'It used to be thought – and I include myself in this – that help was on the horizon. New forms of communication would provide new outlets to bypass the increasingly shrill tenor of the traditional media. In fact, the new form can be even more pernicious, less balanced, more intent on the latest conspiracy theory multiplied by five.'

His comment that caused most anxiety among the press was his suggestion that as technology blurred the distinction between broadcasters and newspapers, it was irrational to have different systems of regulation 'based on technology that no longer can be differentiated in the old way'. (Currently, broadcasters are required to provide balance; newspapers are not.) 'Change was inevitable and the regulatory framework at some point will need revision.'

His main reason for hope rested on a belief that the thirst for news remained. (In this respect he was contradicting his former media chief. Campbell rightly asserted in his speech to the Media Correspondents Association[61] that the thirst for news had diminished.) Blair acknowledged the media would fear that any retreat from impact would mean diminishing sales. But if tried, they would find the opposite was the case, with sales increasing.

The media's response

Although the media were divided in their response, they were agreed on one issue, that it was weak of Blair to attack *The Independent*, the newest, smallest and weakest paper. Adam Boulton, in *Memories of the Blair administration*, reported that out of office Blair conceded this mistake. 'His real target had been the *Daily Mail* but he feared what the paper would do to him and his family should he have targeted it.'[62] Alastair Campbell, in his 2008 Cudlipp lecture, declared: 'I certainly would not have singled out *The Independent* when the *Mail* is the most poisonous newspaper, and I know that is his view too'.[63]

Commentators clearly against the Blair analysis included Simon Jenkins in *The Sunday Times*, 'Blair was hounded too little by the feral beasts, not too much'; Stephen Glover, the media commentator, echoed the same feeling in the *Daily Mail*, 'for most of his 10 years as Prime Minister [he received] a more approving and more docile press than any British leader in living memory ... only one or two newspapers [of which the *Mail* was one] were regularly at odds with Mr Blair'; Matthew D'Ancona, Editor of *The Spectator* and *Sunday Telegraph* commentator, 'New Labour was very happy to tango with the media until it went wrong – most spectacularly over the Iraq dossiers and Hutton [Inquiry]'; Peter Hill, Editor of the *Daily Express*, 'It's just sour grapes. He's criticising journalists because they found him out. I'm afraid all that spin is Blair's undoing'; Trevor Kavanagh, Assistant Editor of *The Sun*, 'I thought it was an extraordinary ill-advised speech by a prime minister at the fag end of his tenure.... I think it has been sitting in the back of his mind for the last seven years, it's burst out and it's a big mistake'; Andrew Gilligan, BBC Radio 4 *Today* programme reporter, whose early morning broadcast on the preparation for the Iraq war sparked Campbell's war against the BBC, wrote in *The Observer*, 'To accuse journalists of "an impulsion towards sensation above all else", of making "accuracy ... secondary to impact", and then, literally seven paragraphs later, to describe the entire British media as a "feral beast, tearing people to bits", is surely, well, putting impact before accuracy. Might it even, perhaps, be sensational above all else?'.[64]

Senior journalists who supported Blair included Roger Alton, *Observer* Editor, who described the speech as 'spot on'; John Kampfner, *New Statesman* Editor, 'Tony Blair is right in much of his analysis but woefully wrong in the conclusions he draws'; BBC Political Editor, Nick Robinson, 'we must try harder to focus on policies not just personalities'; as well as Michael White and Simon Hoggart in *The Guardian*, although less wholeheartedly from Hoggart, who suggested it was difficult to disagree with what Blair said but added that New Labour were well aware of the faults in the modern media and used them for their own purposes – 'they knew all about demented competition, the need for exclusives, the terror of being left behind, the appetite for sensation, the relentless pressure to provide new material. Like drug dealers, they [New Labour] were happy to satisfy their [client journalists'] cravings.'[65]

The leader writer's response

Blair lost support in the editorial columns: 'spun out of control' (*The Daily Mirror*); 'those who live by the sword, die by the sword' (*The Sun*); 'Why Blair's legacy merits all of our "feral" criticism' (*Daily Express*); 'we do find his arguments deeply disturbing, founded on false premises and worthy of the strongest refutation' (*The Telegraph*); 'Blair's take on a decade of spin – some fair points but he still shoots the messenger' (*Financial Times*); and, in a front-page editorial by-lined by its Editor, Simon Kelner, in *The Independent*, 'What clearly rankles with Mr Blair is not that we campaign vociferously on certain issues, but that he doesn't agree with our stance.'

He got a fairer run in *The Guardian*'s Editorial: 'Right sermon, wrong preacher'; and *The Times*' leader: 'Journalists should be able to take as much criticism as they dish out'. It was this last point that Martin Kettle took up in a column on *The Guardian* website straight after the speech.[66] He compared the reaction of politicians to the decline in trust – 'in discussion after discussion and at conference after conference in recent years, I've heard politicians of every party be incredibly self-critical about themselves and the political process' – with the response from the media, which was quite the opposite. He went on, 'Most of the media are in denial about the fact that we are part of the problem too.... The reality is that the media don't think there is a problem. And as soon as a politician dares to suggest there might be, the media cries foul and accuses the government of trying to gag free speech.' The reaction of the media to Blair's speech only reinforced his argument.

BBC versus Fleet Street ethics

One week after the Blair media speech the BBC published a one-year long study it had commissioned on impartiality, providing its enemies – the Murdoch, *Mail* and *Telegraph* papers – a treasure trove of findings that they proceeded to selectively report.[67] *The Sunday Times* pre-emptively forecast that the study would conclude that the BBC was 'institutionally biased'.[68] It didn't. The *Daily Mail*, under the headline 'BBC comes under fire for institutional left-wing bias', declared 'senior figures at the corporation were forced to admit it was guilty of promoting left-wing views and an anti-Christian sentiment'.[69] That was not the conclusion. *The Daily Telegraph* headline declared 'BBC viewers angered by its "innate liberal bias"'.[70] They weren't. Unlike *The Sunday Times, Daily Mail* and *The Daily Telegraph,* the BBC had gone back to ask its viewers what they thought. They recognised impartiality and appreciated it. Like previous polls, it found that BBC television news had a much higher public trust rating than newspapers.

Richard Tait, former Editor in Chief of ITN News and a BBC trustee who chaired the review, was forced to correct the newspaper reports, declaring that the study 'doesn't say the BBC has a liberal bias – it says the BBC will have to work even harder to meet the trust of the audience in future'.[71] He was emphatic that the BBC had stayed within its impartiality guidelines. The report itself, as *The Times* reluctantly noted, judged coverage of mainstream politics as fair and impartial.

What it did pick up, as Richard Tait noted in a pre-release feature article in *The Observer*,[72] was that impartiality

> … can no longer be thought of as primarily about news. In some ways, news, where a tradition of tight editorial control has been ingrained in all broadcasters, is less of a problem than other genres. Nowadays the BBC Trust's editorial standards committee is more likely to deal with appeals about the impartiality of a film on the history of the Middle East or on a scientific controversy than on whether Newsnight was fair to a political party.

The idea that the Murdoch papers – *The Sun* and *News of the World* – along with the *Mail* would set up a standing committee to monitor their impartiality, let alone commission a year-long study on the issue involving audience research and extensive interviews with their staff, is unthinkable. The idea of their intimidated staff being allowed to question and assess the standards of their organisation is another fantasy world.

And yet that is what happened at the BBC, and some of its staff were not afraid to raise questions and make observations in an adult way. Many of these were included in the report,[73] but were not in the conclusions. Hence the selective reporting. At one of the open seminars, Andrew Marr, former BBC Political Editor, noted that the BBC was 'a publicly funded urban organisation with an abnormally large proportion of younger people, of people in ethnic minorities, and almost certainly of gay people, compared with the population at large'. All this helped create 'an innate liberal bias inside the BBC'.

There was an understandable backlash from some BBC staff members to the media coverage of the report. Peter Bennett-Jones, producer of *The Vicar of Dibley*, suggested in the *Guardian Media* pages that the study had 'given the BBC's enemies a stick with which to beat us'.[74] Too true. His programme had been criticised for including just a one minute-long clip in which the vicar, acted by Dawn French, watched a campaign video of Make Poverty History. The report stated: 'One view was that this was a laudable attempt to use the BBC's most popular comedy show to harness public interest for a worthwhile cause. Another (admittedly less widespread) view was that an unsuspecting comedy audience had been ambushed.'[75] Such were the stringent standards of the study. In response, Richard Curtis, the author of the comedy series, suggested Make Poverty History was more a movement than a campaign, which had won the support of all the country's main political parties and could not be regarded as controversial.

The report disagreed. It was equally critical about the length of broadcast of Bob Geldof's Live 8 concert in Hyde Park and a subsequent Africa season of programmes that also involved Geldof. It reminded producers of one of the new guidelines on impartiality that required 'particular vigilance when programmes purport to reflect a consensus for "the common good", or become involved with campaigns'. It warned about pressures on impartiality from the 'seductive mixture' of well-connected talent, high profile and well-meaning lobbyists, and the sympathetic involvement of production departments. It added: 'Increasingly manipulative and media-savvy pressure groups are hungry for free airtime.... Live 8 was not a one-off – it was the future writ large. Next time it will be a spectacular about conservation, cruelty to children or climate change.' So much for the complexity of modern broadcasting and the crudity of reporting in the press.

Gordon Brown takes over

When Gordon Brown took over from Tony Blair on 27 June 2007, he emphasised his 'moral compass' and signalled he was a man of substance rather than spin. In the words of his promoters: 'Not flash. Just Gordon.' But he had one of the shortest of honeymoons. He was given a good press for his handling of an early flood emergency and an outbreak of foot and mouth disease. But press goodwill began to evaporate not so much over his U-turn on calling an early general election, but more his absurd denial that he had ever contemplated calling one, which was blatantly untrue as subsequent memoirs documented.

For those of us who had thought Brown would make a better prime minister than Blair, we were in for a deep disappointment. As Chancellor he had been more serious about policy-making than Blair; more committed to the government's anti-poverty programme than Blair; more ready to recognise the shortcomings of choice, particularly in the field of health, when Blair was gung ho on markets. But there was concern over his choice of some close advisers. From the beginning of his time as Chancellor, specialist reporters were coming back to *The Guardian* office with astonishing stories of Charlie Whelan, Brown's spin doctor, reporting he was spending more time running down Labour ministers who were close to Blair than attacking the opposition. Once Brown was ensconced as prime minister, other faults emerged. There was his dithering over big decisions, his micro management of small ones (pay for prisoners), and his inability to set out a clear vision of where he wanted to take the country.

Worst of all was his last Budget before becoming prime minister, in which he abolished the 10p tax rate in order to reduce the basic rate from 22p to 20p in the spring Budget of 2007. It won him, as intended, plaudits from the right-wing press for recognising – like Tony Blair – the needs of Middle Britain. In the words of the *Daily Mail*: 'He can hold his head justifiably high.... His stewardship of the nation's finances has been remarkable.'[76] It wasn't until the following year, when the measure was due to come into operation in April 2008, that the effects of this change became apparent to the majority of Labour MPs. More than five million poor people were going to be worse off. Frank Field, Labour MP, had recognised this a year earlier and had unsuccessfully put down an amendment to the Budget demanding a compensation package for them. But only the Liberal Democrats, a handful of Labour MPs and one Conservative had voted for it. One year later Labour MPs began to hear from their less well-off constituents the problems they were going to face if the measure went through. For a month Brown continued to deny that people would be worse off, but Field, who, as the former Director of the Child Poverty Action Group was the expert in this area, had drawn up another amendment demanding compensation. A backbench Labour mutiny had not just begun, but achieved threatening momentum, fed by Brown's blatantly false denials about the numbers of losers. Belatedly Brown was forced to concede a compensation package. But by then his reputation as a friend of the disadvantaged had been seriously damaged. As Polly Toynbee, my colleague at *The Guardian* who had previously been an admirer of Brown, declared: 'The 10p tax fiasco is serious; in one iconic error Brown has blown away his most admirable reputation – a ten year record of directing money to the poorest. This does inestimable harm.'[77]

The two Gordon Browns

Andrew Rawnsley, *The Observer*'s chief political commentator, in his devastating account of the second half of New Labour's 13 years in government *The end of the party*, describes two different Gordon Browns of whom ministers spoke: the 'Good Gordon', a high-minded man from the Manse with an ambition to change the world, and the 'Bad Brown' who 'surrounded himself with thuggish acolytes, who used the press to carry out punishment beatings and character assassinations of colleagues who crossed or threatened their master'.[78] One year on from the 10p tax debacle both Browns were on centre stage. The first, in April 2009, was receiving the highest accolades of his premiership for the way in which he had organised, chaired and brought to a successful conclusion the G20 London conference that initiated collective international intervention in the world's financial crisis. One week later the mortifying 'smeargate' scandal broke that shone a wounding media light on the 'Bad Brown'. *The Sunday Times*[79] revealed a sordid Labour plan to set up a new Red Rag website to take on right-wing bloggers by running smear campaigns against leading Conservative politicians and their families. Damian McBride, Brown's spin doctor, was deeply involved in the plot. Emails which he sent to the website organiser, Derek Draper, setting out four early smears that could be run were passed to *The Sunday Times*. McBride, who said Brown had not been aware of the plan, resigned immediately, but this did not stop the media re-examining the spin doctors whom Brown had used. What made the scandal worse was that Brown had ignored repeated warnings from senior ministers and Gus O'Donnell, the Cabinet Secretary, to stop using McBride. In Rawnsley's words: 'McBride was not a lone wolf; he was one razor-toothed but sloppy dog in the Brown pack with a licence from the Prime Minister.'[80] In the aftermath of the scandal, a *Guardian* ICM poll found only 13 per cent of people thought Brown had succeeded in restoring trust in government; 82 per cent thought he had failed.

For media watchers there was another significant aspect to the scandal. The emails that convicted McBride had not been sent direct to *The Sunday Times* but to the internet blogger Paul Staines, known as 'Guido Fawkes', who runs a right-wing website. Staines decided this was such a major story that for maximum coverage it should be launched by a mainstream paper, rather than his own new media site, which other papers might have been wary of following up. The story dominated mainstream news for days. This is one of several good examples – see WikiLeaks below – of where the mainstream has been seen as a better way of achieving impact than the more suspect new media.

The MPs' expenses scandal

The MPs' expenses scandal proved another triumph for the mainstream media. It took the Labour government eight years from coming into office to implement its long-promised Freedom of Information Act. The Act was passed in 2000 but not implemented until 1 January 2005. Following on from that it took another four years to clarify how far Freedom of Information applied to the workings of Parliament. Protracted resistance from the Commons authorities, led by the Speaker of the House Michael Martin, required formal appeals to the Information Commissioner and the High Court before the issue was resolved in favour of the journalists pursuing the publication of MPs' expenses.

In March 2008 some indication of what was to come emerged with the revelation of the 'John Lewis list', setting down the maximum sums that could be claimed for second home household items. It was not just the generous allowances – for plasma television sets and desirable dining room furniture – but the fact that there could be substantial reimbursement for some items without even submitting receipts. In February 2009, media appetites were whetted when the *Mail on Sunday* revealed Jacqui Smith, the Home Secretary, had claimed £116,000 in expenses by designating her sister's house in south London as her 'main home' rather than the substantial house in the West Midlands she shared with her husband and children. Further humiliation followed when it was revealed her claims had included rented pornographic films watched by her husband. In March 2009, the same paper exposed Tony McNulty, Employment Secretary, for claiming £14,000 for the house in which his parents lived, which was just eight miles from his main home.

Then on 8 May – two months before the official publication – *The Telegraph* began a three-week long series of detailed expenses exposures, day after day, on the front page plus four, five, six full broadsheet pages inside, with most other papers and television and radio news programmes following up each day's disclosures. It was rightly regarded as 'a media frenzy' in which the old media led the new. It was known that a leaked disc containing the details of four years of MPs' claims – hundreds of thousands of items – was being touted round to editors. *The Daily Telegraph* forked out and did a brilliant job in exposing the scandal. It needed to do much more than just transcribe the CD-ROM. Over the next weeks it used up to 40 reporters checking multiple facts including with the Land Registry on the ownership of first and second homes and scrutinising the complicated 'flipping' arrangements in which some MPs indulged – making claims for mortgage interest and refurbishment on one home and then changing the designation of their 'second home' to start a new round of claims or avoid capital gains tax on a sale. Hazel Blears, who was required to pay back £13,332 in capital gains by the Prime Minister, claimed expenses on three different houses in one year.

For the first three days *The Daily Telegraph* concentrated on Labour government ministers, but this was to be a long series. It then switched to the Shadow Cabinet and then to Tory grandees. The latter provided a field day for political cartoonists and tabloids. The claims ranged from cleaning out the moat of his 13th-century manor house (Douglas Hogg), through the purchase of a £1,645 ornamental 'duck house' for his pond that the ducks didn't like (Sir Peter Viggers), to the purchase of a chandelier for his Worcestershire manor house (Sir Michael Spicer).

Andrew MacKay, MP, a senior adviser to the Conservative leader, and Julie Kirkbride, his wife, who was also an MP, claimed tens of thousands of pounds between them. He claimed his second home allowance on their London property that his wife claimed to be their main home. *The Telegraph* explained: 'This means they effectively had no main home, but two second homes – and were using public funds to pay for them.' MacKay was forced to agree to stand down as an MP at the next election in the face of angry opposition in his constituency. His wife announced she would stand down, changed her mind, then changed it again and stood down. They were jointly required to pay back £60,000.[81] Most of this would not have come out but for *The Telegraph* and its investigative team of reporters. The Commons fees office did not have the staff to carry out such investigations. When the official publication of the expenses was released, *The Guardian* put all 450,000 pages on its website to promote a 'crowd-sourcing' exercise, under which its readers were able to identify, log and discuss claims by their own MPs or others they were interested in. Within a month they had reviewed 209,000 pages.

James Murdoch's MacTaggart attack on the BBC

Undaunted by the worldwide respect for the BBC, James Murdoch, Rupert's son who is chair and chief executive of Murdoch's Asian and European businesses, broke into the headlines in August 2009, when he used an invitation to deliver the annual MacTaggart lecture to attack Britain's main broadcaster.[82] Rarely has there been such an arrogant, ill-judged and presumptuous presentation aimed crudely at a pending Conservative government. (Murdoch Senior was just weeks away from announcing – at the start of the Labour Party conference – that *The Sun* was swinging its support to the Conservatives.) The speech was a long sustained attack on public service broadcasting in general and the BBC in particular. It described the size and ambition of the BBC as 'chilling', and called for 'a far, far smaller BBC'. Murdoch Junior cited George Orwell's *1984* novel and the threat of an authoritarian state, while indulging in the gross form of 'Newspeak' that Orwell warned against. He described the BBC as a state-sponsored broadcaster, when in fact it is something quite different, not an arm of the state but a publicly funded body with fees direct from the public. He bitterly criticised the creation of the BBC website ('an expansion of state-sponsored journalism'), describing it as 'a threat to the plurality and the independence of news provision, which are so important to our democracy'. He made his own position clear: broadcasters such as his own BSkyB should be free from the long-standing requirement to produce impartial news, ludicrously describing the impartiality rule as 'an infringement on the freedom of speech'. What he wanted instead was the pathetic and ineffective self-regulation which newspapers in the UK enjoyed. Finally, he concluded with the most preposterous claim: 'the only reliable, durable and perpetual guarantor of independence is profit.'

Appropriately, the lecture was entitled 'The absence of trust', appropriate given the degree to which his own papers, *The Sun* and the *News of the World*, have eroded that most important value in serious journalism: public trust. Unsurprisingly, there was no mention of this. The speech won some isolated support, none more so than from Jeremy Hunt, then shadow minister for the media, who was quick to voice support for the tirade, picking out the size of the BBC website. While he said it was not on his agenda to make the BBC charge for its website, he did not rule it out.[83] One day later at a follow-up press conference, Murdoch Junior called on the Labour government to cut the licence fee funding so that the BBC would become 'much, much smaller'. As Amanda Andrews noted in *The Telegraph*: 'With the Murdoch view of the BBC now clearer than ever, the Tories will have to tread carefully to avoid rocking the boat with their most vital supporter.'[84]

Robert Peston, BBC Business Editor, quipped: 'Having just lived through the greatest failure in history to distribute financial resources in an efficient and equitable way, we certainly shouldn't assume that a commercial digital market in news will distribute information in a way that would support a healthy democracy.'[85] Others suggested that a fair market was the last thing that the Murdochs wanted. David Chance, former Deputy Managing Director of BSkyB and now chair of Top Up TV, told the *Financial Times*: 'Once Sky was a plucky new entrant – now it is the biggest of beasts – with a market share in excess of 80 per cent controlling virtually all pay-TV channels, and making hundreds of millions of pounds of profit each year, spending £900 million on marketing. Now it is using its influence to try to prevent new entrants such as BT Vision and Top Up TV from getting a foothold in the market.'[86]

Will Hutton spoke up for many journalists when he wrote in *The Observer* column: 'The biggest risk is not an Orwellian state. It is that our society is being taken over by a new class of super rich, unaccountable oligarchs – in finance and the media – with little interest in our culture, civilisation or vitality of the public realm.'[87]

Evidence-based media analysis

A four-nation report on the media, published in 2009, provided a devastating, evidence-based rebuttal of Murdoch's assertions.[88] It was designed to examine the implications of the movements towards entertainment-centred, market-driven media by comparing what was reported and what the public understood in four countries with different media systems. These were: public service television (Denmark, Finland), a dual model (UK) and the market model (US). It looked at the news provided across four dimensions: foreign and domestic, hard and soft. It then proceeded to test the citizens of the four nations to measure their understanding. The market model in the US – which includes Murdoch's right-wing Fox Television – came at the bottom in terms of public understanding. Almost two thirds of Americans did not know what the Kyoto Treaty was about while 70 per cent could not identify Nicolas Sarkozy as President of France even in a multiple-choice question with his name on the list. Among the benefits of public service broadcasting were that it:

- gives greater attention to public affairs and international news, which leads to greater understanding of these areas;
- makes television more accessible by using leading channels fostering a higher level of news consumption;
- narrows the knowledge gap between the advantaged and disadvantaged, contributing to a more egalitarian society.

The biter bit

The political ineptness of James Murdoch's speech became all too clear within a year, as the Murdoch Group began negotiating to obtain the 61 per cent of the BSkyB shares it did not own and then merge it with its UK press empire, which was already by far the biggest in the UK. When news of this broke, a ball of public opposition began rolling, collecting support from a wide spectrum of social and political organisations. All were agreed that it was not the BBC that was the 'Big Gorilla' causing the 'Big Chill', but the Murdoch Empire that should not be allowed to get any bigger. A merger would create a company owning 37 per cent of the national press and a broadcasting arm with almost £6 billion in revenues compared to the £3.5 billion the BBC receives from licence fees. Mark Thompson, Director General of the BBC, was invited to deliver the MacTaggart lecture in August 2010 in which he shredded James Murdoch's analysis of the previous year.[89] He noted that despite Sky

Television's huge budget, it was only spending £100 million a year – outside news and sport – on original UK content. This was less than Channel 5, 'despite the fact that Sky's turnover was 15 times that of Five'. He was able to point to a new opinion survey which showed the BBC had never been more popular with the public – rubbing salt in the wound by revealing that the readers of two of Murdoch's papers – *The Times* and *The Sunday Times* – which regularly attack the BBC, were in fact among the BBC's most enthusiastic supporters, with 83 per cent and 85 per cent respectively in support. He added, 'It's time Sky pulled its weight in using much more British talent and British content.'

In a House of Lords debate on 4 November 2010, inspired by David Puttnam, over 20 peers from the three main political parties spoke against the merger.[90] So did the Church of England in a memorandum to Ofcom, the television regulator, calling for Murdoch's bid to be blocked. Lord (Norman) Fowler, former Conservative chair of the House of Lords Select Committee on Communications, wrote a column in *The Guardian* calling on Vince Cable, the Business Secretary, to reel in Murdoch's bid for full control of Sky.[91] Claire Enders, media analyst, told Dan Sabbagh, former Media Editor of *The Times* who had moved to set up his media website, Beehive City: 'The level of concentration of [Murdoch Media] already seen in the UK is substantially greater than would be allowed in Italian law. We are already way past the Berlusconi moment in Britain.'[92] Other commentators, like Steve Hewlett, noted it would not be allowed in the US or Australia. And in an unprecedented move, newspapers and broadcasters came together for the first time – the Conservative-supporting *Mail* and *Telegraph* groups as well as *The Mirror*, *The Guardian*, BBC, Channel 4 and Channel 5 – to petition Vince Cable to stop the takeover.

On 4 November 2010, Cable referred the bid to Ofcom, asking it to carry out a public interest assessment of whether the move would damage media plurality. Six weeks later, on 21 December 2010, Cable was stripped of responsibility for media policy, after two undercover reporters purporting to be constituents recorded him telling them that he was 'declaring war on Murdoch'. Responsibility – along with

70 of his civil servants – was transferred to Jeremy Hunt, the Culture, Media and Sport Secretary of State.[94]

By the end of June 2011 Murdoch's bid to take over the whole of BSkyB was on the brink of being achieved. Hunt had signalled he would not be referring the bid to the Competition Commission in the light of a commitment from Murdoch to hive off Sky News into a separate and independent organisation to further plurality. (It would be independent of BSkyB but receive funding from it to ensure its survivability.) All Hunt was waiting for was the end of a consultation period, due in early July.

But then on 4 July 2011 two separate public battles in which Murdoch's media companies were engaged – the BSkyB bid and the investigations into serious allegations of widespread hacking of mobile phones owned by celebrities, MPs and ministers by the *News of the World* (NoW) – became conjoined. For the next 17 days the hacking saga kept Westminster – along with the media and the public – in its grip until Parliament went into recess for the summer.

The hacking scandal is looked at in Chapter Eleven, which is devoted to the issue. But in brief, it began in 2006 with the trial of two NoW employees who pleaded guilty to hacking the phones of Royal Family aides and were sent to prison. It was reopened by *The Guardian* in July 2009, when the paper reported that hacking was far more widespread than 'a single rogue reporter' and the tabloid's private investigator, as Murdoch executives had been strenuously suggesting. *The Guardian* suggested that as many as 3,000 people could have had their mobiles hacked. John Yates, the Assistant Metropolitan Police Commissioner, was asked to review the evidence in light of the *Guardian* story. He declared that the police inquiry had identified only hundreds, not thousands, of potential targets. He rejected the suggestion that the police investigation should be reopened – a decision which took him only a day and which he later admitted was wrong. Further revelations were made by Nick Davies, the leader of the *Guardian* investigation; new investigations opened in January 2011 by the Metropolitan Police suggested 4,000 phones could have been hacked; but it was not until 4 July 2011 that the story went viral.

The Milly Dowler story

It was sparked by a *Guardian* exclusive, initially on its website, that the mobile phone of murdered schoolgirl Milly Dowler had been hacked by NoW staff in 2002. The story was no longer a narrative restricted to Royal aides, MPs, celebrities, footballers and ministers, who some perceived could look after themselves, but ordinary families too. The story shot straight to the top of BBC bulletins and other national media websites, as well as the front pages of newspapers – *The Daily Telegraph, Daily Mail* and some other tabloid red-tops – which had been ignoring it until then. There was an eruption of public protests. Further allegations began flooding in, including claims that the phones of victims of the 7/7 London bombings and members of the armed forces killed in Iraq and Afghanistan had been targeted too. Protests mounted. A string of major advertisers, beginning with Ford and ending with 32 other large companies, announced a boycott of NoW. News International, the parent company, was facing the prospect of further damaging revelations, with seemingly no sign of them ending. Just three days after the *Guardian* splash, James Murdoch announced the paper was being shut down. In his published explanation, he acknowledged that his staff had acted illegally, covered up what had happened through a series of huge out-of-court settlements and misled Parliament. A 168-year-old paper, whose title Rupert Murdoch bought in 1969 at the start of his British acquisitions, would have only one further edition, which would carry no commercial advertising.

Yet not even that dramatic move failed to stem a tidal wave of new allegations involving the police, politicians and the Murdoch papers, along with new arrests of former NoW employees. A brave Editorial in *The Times* after publication of the last edition of NoW could not have pleased the chief proprietor or his son. It declared that those who thought closing the paper would resolve the issues facing Murdoch's News International were wrong. It went on: 'Mr Coulson, a former editor of the *News of the World*, has now been arrested over payments to the police allegedly made during his tenure. His arrest raises the prospect that, of all unanswered questions, the most serious of all may involve corrupt relations between journalists and the police.'

Noting an address that Rebekah Brooks – Chief Executive of News International and Editor of NoW when Milly Dowler's phone was hacked – had made about the NoW's closure to the tabloid's staff, *The Times* Editorial added: 'When the company says that worse is to come we can be assured that the full truth has not come out.'[94]

Several papers suggested that NoW had been sacrificed to protect the BSkyB bid, the highest commercial priority of Murdoch's global US-based company, News Corp.[95] But one week on from the Milly Dowler story, Murdoch was facing a more serious challenge. Ed Miliband announced on Monday, 11 July that Labour would be tabling a motion in the Commons calling for the decision on the BSkyB bid to be suspended until the police investigations had been completed. Nick Clegg signalled support from the Liberal Democrats. David Cameron, who had won the support of News International both before and after the 2010 election, initially resisted but by Wednesday, he too had signalled his support. Just a short time before the parliamentary debate was due to begin on 13 July, Murdoch formally withdrew his bid. The debate went ahead and won unanimous support. As *The Guardian* noted in an Editorial the next day: 'At the start of this month no senior politician dared to defy Rupert Murdoch. Yesterday all of them did.' [96] The national press headlines summed it up next day: 'Defiant MPs shift balance of power' (*Financial Times*); 'Rupert on the run' (*The Independent*); 'Murdoch takes stock after Sky Bid falls in' (*The Times*); and perhaps more worrying for the Murdochs, 'US campaign for probe gathers' (also in the *Financial Times*). That paper reported a growing number of US politicians calling for an investigation into whether News Corp had violated the US Foreign Corrupt Practices Act if the allegations of illegal payments to the police were upheld.

Unanswered questions

Questions still hung over Murdoch's BSkyB bid after Downing Street disclosed that Cameron had met senior News International executives 26 times since he had become prime minister 14 months earlier. In Parliament's final session before the summer recess on 20 July 2011, Cameron was repeatedly asked by Labour and Liberal

Democrat MPs whether the Murdoch BSkyB bid was raised during those meetings. Finally, after dodging several questions, for the first time he admitted the bid had been raised but insisted that the conversations were not inappropriate because he had not passed on the content to Jeremy Hunt, the minister who was in sole charge of handling the bid. *The Times* noted in its report:'This issue is awkward for the Prime Minister because it makes him vulnerable to the suggestions that his friendship with Ms Brooks and his closeness to News International gave Rupert Murdoch improper influence over a decision that is supposed to be non-political.'[97] *The Guardian* was blunter in its Editorial:'In a carefully parsed remark that echoed Bill Clinton's denial of sex with Monica Lewinsky, Mr Cameron said that he "never had any inappropriate conversations" with Mr Murdoch and his minions. But that is an awful lot of meetings with important friends and contacts in which to avoid subjects that were uppermost in News International minds.'[98]

The week before, Will Hutton, former Editor of *The Observer*, was even blunter. He noted that *The New York Times* was describing the July revolution as a 'British Spring' and went on to assert that 'the entire political class has freed itself of its fear of the tycoon – saying and doing things that would have been unthinkable just weeks ago. David Cameron, Jeremy Hunt and George Osborne saw their job – as Gordon Brown and Tony Blair would have done – to shepherd Murdoch's bid through while also serving the proprieties. The reward would have come in fulsome backing at the next election. All has changed.'[99]

There was one more humiliation facing Murdoch. Not only had he lost his bid to acquire 61 per cent of BSkyB, but he could lose his existing 39 per cent. As MPs headed for their holidays, Ofcom, the television regulator, announced it had begun an investigation into whether News International was a 'fit and proper' body to hold a broadcasting licence. The regulator said it did not have to wait for the end of the criminal investigations, nor was it necessary for any individual to be convicted for it to reach an adverse conclusion.[100] Two months later the broadcasting regulator concluded that BSkyB was a 'fit and proper' body to hold a licence, but declared that the actions of James Murdoch, who resigned as chairman in April 2011 but remained a non-executive director, 'repeatedly fell short of the conduct to be expected of him as chief executive officer and chairman'.[101]

A tumultuous three weeks in July ended with a report from the Bureau of Investigative Journalism disclosing that hospitality between Downing Street and News International had been a two-way process: Number 10's specialist advisers were hosted by senior employees of News International on 26 occasions in the first seven months of the government.[102]

All this – and much more – was closely scrutinised by the judicial inquiry, set up by Cameron in the middle of July 2011. The Chair, Lord Justice Leveson, Appeal Court Judge, Chair of the Sentencing Council and forensic former prosecutor, was given an advisory group of six independent figures with experience in media, regulation and policing. Its remit was to produce two reports, the first to look at the culture, practice, and ethics of journalism, including the relationships between politicians, the press and the police. In its hearings, which began in November 2011 and lasted until July 2012, some 330 witnesses gave evidence and a further 300 submitted evidence which was read into the record. Witnesses included over 200 media people (including former tabloid journalists), almost 50 police officers, 40 lawyers, 38 senior politicians or their aides, 36 academics, 21 regulators or watchdogs, and 14 charities or pressure groups. Transcripts of all nine months of the oral hearings, with an excellent index, are available on the inquiry's website (www.levesoninquiry.org.uk/). On 29 November 2012, a four-volume, 2,000-page report on the inquiry's findings was launched in London (also on the inquiry's website). It was the seventh time in 70 years that a report commissioned by a government concerned with the media had been produced, with the first six having had little implementation. Leveson was unequivocal about the need for a much stronger and more independent press regulator with statutory backing to ensure its independence and effective powers. The second inquiry would have looked at the 'extent of unlawful or improper conduct within News International and other organisations', as well as the 'extent to which the police received corrupt payments or were otherwise complicit in such misconduct', once the criminal investigations have been completed.

Doubts about the need for this second review were raised by Leveson during the hearing because of the scale and thoroughness of the police investigations. But Cameron declared when the report was published that he still wanted the second review. Even so, doubts must remain given the extent of the police operations. There were three separate teams of detectives comprising 170 officers examining three separate allegations: the hacking of mobile phones; computer tampering; and illegal payments to police and public servants. There was also the length of delay that would have occurred with the first trials not expected to begin until September 2013. In his first statement after his appointment, Leveson declared: 'the press provides an essential check on all aspects of public life. That is why any failure within the media affects all of us. At the heart of this inquiry, therefore, may be one simple question: who guards the guardians.'[103] At his first full press conference on 28 July, he warned that the inquiry might not be completed within the planned timetable of a year because its goals had been widened 'quite substantially'.[104] (See Chapter Eleven for a fuller account of the hacking story, the Leveson hearings, the inquiry's conclusions and the government's response.)

New curbs on the BBC

Meanwhile, what the new Conservative/Liberal Democrat Coalition government had ensured in its October 2010 comprehensive spending review was a deeply wounding reduction in the BBC's budget – through a six-year freeze in the licence fee, plus new obligations for which the government was previously responsible: rolling out a digital broadband, supporting a notionally commercial Welsh language service, plus the famous World Service. It amounted to a cumulative 16 per cent cut by 2016. The deal was criticised by the *Financial Times* for requiring the BBC to carry out activities previously funded by the government, as it 'dilutes the BBC's mission and weakens its independence'.[105] The 2010 cuts came on top of a succession of squeezes applied by Labour – a Freedom of Information request by *The Guardian* showed that the BBC had reduced its staff numbers by 2,200 to 21,360 over the four years up to 2007.[106] That same year, the BBC announced even more dramatic plans to fill a £2 billion shortfall in its budget – including a 500 job cut to its 2,000-strong news department and some 600 from programme makers. Even before the 2010 Coalition cuts, the BBC had been forced to cut back its investments in its website.

One of the worst aspects of the Coalition government's six-year deal was the degree to which the BBC World Service, run separately from its other services and funded by the Foreign and Commonwealth Office (FCO), is going to be cut back. Funding is meant to continue from the FCO until April 2014. In the meantime, the FCO requires the World Service – along with the British Council – to carry a hugely disproportionate amount of the cuts that the Department is being expected to make. By 2014 the World Service's £272 million budget, which funds its 2,000 staff, will be cut by well over £40 million. The chair of the Commons Select Committee on Foreign Affairs, the Conservative MP Richard Ottoway, estimated the World Service would be losing 16 per cent, while the rest of the FCO was being reduced by only 6 per cent.[107]

'The worst BBC crisis in 50 years?'

Then out of nowhere two separate 'scandals' hit the new Director General of the BBC, George Entwistle, who had taken over from Mark Thompson in September 2012. The first involved a six-week investigation by a *Newsnight* team into the late BBC presenter Jimmy Saville in relation to allegations of abuse of children, which was pulled by the programme's editor, Peter Rippon, late in 2011. This occurred at a time when, in a separate part of the BBC, plans were being made to run tributes to the presenter, who had only died on 29 October 2011, in the forthcoming Christmas schedules. The second 'scandal', which also involved *Newsnight*, occurred just five weeks after the first became public. This was a programme in which a victim of abuse that had taken place at a North Wales children's home three decades earlier, had claimed it had been perpetrated by a senior Tory peer of the Thatcher era. Although not named in the programme, it did not take the Twitter site long to name the wronged man, Lord McAlpine, a former Tory Treasurer.

Entwistle was facing a double whammy: a *Newsnight* documentary which should have been shown but was pulled; and a second *Newsnight* documentary which should have been pulled but was shown. A discordant symmetry, which the many enemies of the BBC in the newspaper world (the *Telegraph*, *Mail* and Murdoch's *Times* and *Sun*) lapped up and made more discordant. Had the first *Newsnight* programme been pulled because of the forthcoming tributes planned for the presenter? Had the BBC – and other institutions – covered up his crimes? One further complication for Entwistle, who was head of BBC television in 2011, was that he had been briefly told by the head of BBC News of the pending *Newsnight* programme but did not follow this up.

The news of the first wrong decision broke almost a year after it had been made, when an ITV documentary on the same theme was due to be shown on 3 October 2012. On the night before the ITV film was broadcast, Rippon wrote a blog explaining that a *Newsnight* programme on the same theme the year before had been pulled for editorial reasons. It had been unable to find anything wrong with the police or Crown Prosecution Service investigations into Saville. This later had to be corrected by the BBC when the team working on the programme said their focus had been on the victims of abuse.

Within a week of the ITV broadcast the Metropolitan Police had 120 leads. But it was no longer confined to Metropolitan London. Police out in the regions were alerted to allegations of abuse by Saville from people who had been in Stoke Mandeville hospital, Leeds General Infirmary, Broadmoor secure hospital and a children's home in Jersey, all institutions with which Saville was closely connected. As early as 25 October a Metropolitan Police commander described Saville as 'undoubtedly' one of the most prolific sex offenders, with the weight of evidence against him overwhelming.[108] Some of the allegations dated back more than four decades. Within a month some 450 people had been in touch with the police claiming to be victims. Entwistle announced two inquiries by independent outsiders within days of the first scandal breaking: one by Nick Pollard, former head of Sky News, into the reasons why the programme was pulled; the second, when the police were ready to give the go-ahead, by the formidable High Court judge Dame Janet Smith, on the BBC's culture during the period Saville worked there. Meanwhile, in an inspiring demonstration of independent journalism within the BBC, a separate documentary team from *Panorama* decided to carry out its own investigation into the first *Newsnight* blunder.

The film showed clips from *Newsnight* that had not been shown before of a woman who claimed to have been abused by Saville. It reported that the *Top of the Pops* programme over which Saville had presided for 20 years was a centre of abuse – and that Saville was not the only one involved. John Simpson, the BBC World Affairs Editor, in a much-quoted soundbite, said: 'This is the worst crisis that I can remember in my 50 years at the BBC ... I don't think the BBC has handled it very well.' What *Panorama* did assert was that it could not find any evidence that Rippon had been told to drop the programme. The day after the *Panorama* broadcast on 22 October, Entwistle had an uncomfortable time before the Commons Select Committee on the Media. But he was clear about one issue: the *Newsnight* programme should not have been pulled.

The second *Newsnight* blunder went out on Friday, 2 November. One week later the key witness in the programme said he had made a mistake. He had subsequently seen pictures of Lord McAlpine and McAlpine was not his abuser. The journalists had failed to show him a picture of McAlpine and had not checked their story with McAlpine. The following day Entwistle suffered a ferocious interrogation from John Humphrys on the BBC Radio 4 *Today* programme in which he confessed he had not seen the *Newsnight* programme, nor a story in the previous day's *Guardian* revealing that McAlpine had been wrongly identified. Later the same day, just 54 days after becoming Director General, he resigned. The Sunday front-page headlines summed up the story: 'BBC boss quits over "shoddy journalism" at Newsnight' (*Sunday Times*); 'Bloodbath at BBC as chief quits' (*Mail on Sunday*). But it was not quite over. A further row erupted when it was disclosed that Entwistle had been awarded a £450,000 pay-off, twice the minimum specified in his contract, by the BBC chair, Lord Patten. The Pollard review, released on 19 December 2012, concluded that no senior people had applied pressure on Rippon to pull the programme, but there was 'chaos and confusion' within the higher ranks and a lack of leadership once it had been shelved.

The national police investigation concluded on 11 January 2013 that Saville's predatory behaviour had involved 214 criminal offences over 54 years, involving 34 rapes and 120 indecent attacks. Some 24 of the offences were against children under 10, and 93 against those under 16.

Making Twitter more accountable

There was one important move that emerged from the saga. McAlpine's lawyers, who had negotiated £185,000 damages from the BBC, decided to take on Twitter too. The lawyers hired a team of experts to collate the offending Twitter messages, including those that had been deleted. Some 1,000 individuals had implicated McAlpine, and a further 9,000 retweeted those messages to a wider audience. Andrew Reid, McAlpine's solicitor, said: 'Let it be a lesson to everybody that trial by Twitter or trial by the internet is a very nasty way of hurting people unnecessarily and it will cost people a lot of money.'[109] Later, on 20 November, the lawyers announced that people with fewer than 500 followers could make amends with an apology and a donation to charity, the BBC's Children in Need. Tweeters with larger followings would face legal action. In an emotional interview on the BBC *World at One* radio programme, McAlpine said he had been 'shattered' when his name was 'spread all over the world'. He went on: 'Suddenly to find yourself a figure of public hatred – unjustifiably – is terrifying.'

The action was described as 'unprecedented' by Lord Woolf, the former Lord Chief Justice, who added there was no reason why Twitter users should be treated differently from newspapers that published defamatory comments. The government has drafted a bill on defamation with sections on the responsibility of website hosts. It seeks to hold the underlying author or primary publisher responsible where they can be identified. The effect, according to one lawyer interviewed by *The Economist*, could be to force web firms to keep more detailed records to identify users in order to protect themselves.[110]

A new Director General for the BBC

Twelve days after Entwistle's resignation, Tony Hall was announced his successor. The news was well received both inside and outside the BBC. He was both an insider, having risen over 28 years from BBC news trainee to head of news and current affairs, and an outsider, having spent the last 11 years as chief executive of the Royal Opera House. In both those institutions he proved to be an innovator. At the BBC he launched BBC News Online, BBC News 24, BBC Parliament and Radio 5 Live. The Royal Opera House, which was enmeshed in internal disputes and financial traumas – five directors in five years – when he got there, was transformed by his charm, calmness and innovations. It was made less stuffy by the introduction of big screen relays, low-price ticket schemes, innovative family performances and outreach work in Essex. Even the *Mail* had a good word for him, with Geoffrey Levy providing reassurance on his readiness to retain high journalistic standards. He quoted one senior BBC figure as saying that he would 'sort out any programme makers who want to replace serious investigative journalism with coffee-table magazine items'.[111] Lord Hall, who had become a crossbench peer in 2010, was due to take over in March 2013.

A fatally wounded stag

When I began thinking of this book in 2005, the mainstream media were still regarded as a big, bad, uncontrolled beast. By the time I delivered the biennial Scott Trust lecture at Nuffield College, Oxford, in 2008, they were widely regarded as 'a fatally wounded stag'. For over a decade the media were losing, at a frighteningly accelerating rate, readers, advertisers and viewers – all decamping to the internet. A fourth wound for media companies listed on the stock exchange was a catastrophic drop in share value. The circulation of national newspapers dropped by almost a third between 1987 and 2007, according to the Office of Fair Trading.[112] The economic recession that began in 2007 created a double whammy. Now the media were facing not just the internet threat but one of the deepest recessions, in which historically the media have always been one of the hardest hit industries. According to an Organisation for Economic Co-operation and Development (OECD) report[113] published in June 2010, UK national newspapers suffered the second most dramatic circulation decline – after the US – of any of the 30 member states between 2007 and 2009, losing 25 per cent of their circulation. This continued through 2010 where late in the year *The Guardian* was 12 per cent down on 2009, *The Times* 14 per cent and *The Telegraph* 18 per cent. Of *The Independent's* 182,000 circulation, only 96,000 copies were being purchased at the full price.

Thousands of journalists have been made redundant. The Trinity Mirror group slashed 1,700 jobs in 2009 alone and cut another 200 editorial jobs on *The Daily Mirror* in 2010. There were 200-plus redundancies at both *The Guardian* and *The Times* between 2008 and 2010. The Guardian Media Group lost £26 million in 2007–08, £37 million in 2008–09 and £33 million in 2009–10. *The Times* and *Sunday Times* lost £50 million in the year to June 2008, £88 million to June 2009, and in May 2010, according to an email to editorial staff from the Editor, were making a loss of £240,000 a day before introducing more cuts.[114] These helped reduced losses to £45 million in 2009–10. *The Independent* and *The Independent on Sunday* were also making losses, which reached £28 million in 2009. They were sold to Alexander Lebedev, the Russian billionaire and former KGB agent, for £1 by its Irish publisher, INM, on 25 March 2010, with a follow-on payment deal of £9.25 million.[115] By May 2011 only 73,997 people were buying *The Independent* at the full price.[116]

Regional newspapers, which play a crucial role in journalism training, have been hit even harder. Even before the internet began to make serious inroads and the 2007 economic recession began, regional editorial budgets were already being slashed to help bring down the debt that many groups had amassed buying up smaller competitors. The circulations of local and regional papers fell by 40 per cent between 1989 and 2009.[117] As they were more dependent on advertising (80 per cent) than nationals, this revenue stream halved in the decade up to 2009. Regional evening papers have tried all manner of variations, from free in the centre/paid for in the suburbs (*Manchester Evening News*) to the move from five nights a week to one (*Bath Chronicle*). For a decade weekly papers have been shrinking, merging or have been shut down. According to a survey conducted by Roy Greenslade, media commentator, with the help of the Newspaper Society, 53 local papers closed in the 13 months up to January 2009. Between January and August 2009, a further 101 local papers closed down.[118] The Guardian Media Group, which used to own the *Manchester Evening News* and 32 local papers, had shut most of the local offices to publish them from a central office but was still making a loss. It sold them all to Trinity Mirror in February 2010.

Claire Enders, media analyst, in evidence to the Commons Select Committee on Media Affairs in June 2009, forecast that half the 1,300 regional and local papers would be closed within five years.[119] Ben Bradshaw, former BBC journalist and Labour minister for the media at the time, declared his concern: 'Good quality news is vital for the health of our democracy – we face losing it completely unless something is done.' [120]

Television was in an equally bad state. The main BBC and ITN news programmes which used to have audiences of up to 10 million were averaging half that. Total revenue for ITV, Channel 4 and Channel 5 dropped by £458 million to £2,978 million between 2006 and 2009. Some 2,000 out of the 7,000 jobs provided by the three companies were cut in this same period. The fall in television advertising shrank by 17 per cent in 2008–09, prompting Lord Burns, Channel 4's chair, to suggest this was 'unprecedented'.

By the end of 2010, the picture was still grim, but there were some shafts of sunlight. By then the Telegraph Media Group reported a pre-tax profit of £53 million – up from a loss of £15 million in the previous year. The Mail Group's pre-tax profits rose by 23 per cent to £247 million – with profits at Associated News, which covers the national papers, up by 54 per cent to £95 million. In September 2010, the *Press Gazette* reported only six closures in the current year – and even in 2008 when 53 closed, it turned out that there were 11 new launches, which took the deficit down to 42. Claire Enders' five-year prediction looked as though it might be too pessimistic. The *Financial Times*, which generated a cumulative underlying operating loss of £84 million between 2002 and 2006, was making profits from 2007 thanks to a doubling of its cover price and an annual online fee for visits to its website, which rose from £65 to £170 in the three years to 2010 and a further £125 to £295 by 2012. It, too, was losing circulation in the UK – although not abroad – with its home circulation of 96,336 in January 2011 propped up by 32,686 free copies. But commentators were agreed that given the specialist nature of the paper and its affluent readership, pay walls were feasible. ITV, which cut its staff from 5,700 to 4,000 between 2007 and 2009, reported in June 2010 that it had made a small profit of £25 million in 2009. Archie Norman, chair of ITV, reminded city analysts that the television advertising market was still lower than in 1998. Despite the successes of shows such as *The X Factor* and *Britain's Got Talent* in drawing audiences and advertisements, he declared: 'In organisation, economics and culture, ITV is a legacy broadcaster in a highly regulated market that is static to declining.'[121] Newspapers remained thinner, much more under-staffed and with far fewer investigative and specialist reporters than they had had before. Tabloids dropped their education specialists; *The Guardian* thinned its team down. A move towards 'churnalism' – rewriting press releases, PR handouts and Press Association copy – damningly set out by Nick Davies in his *Flat earth news*[122] – continued. Desk-bound journalism increased; investigative journalism on many papers declined.

The battle between old and new media

2010 general election

One event, which some observers believed might have led to the new media gaining a larger role in the provision of news, remained firmly in the grip of the mainstream: the 2010 British general election. And that was essentially because for the first time in history, the leaders of the three main political parties agreed to have three separate 90-minute televised debates. The debates dominated the four-week campaign with endless curtain-raising features and trails before each debate, and even longer post-debate analysis and polling after each one. The debates themselves attracted large audiences: 9.4 million for the first on ITV; 4 million for the second a week later on Sky supplemented by the BBC 24-hour news channel; and 8.4 million for the third on BBC 1. Within a very short time after the first debate, five separate polls showed Nick Clegg to be the clear winner. This decisively shaped the media coverage of the next week and established a pattern for the reporting of the other two. With Labour relegated to third place in some of the polls that followed the first debate, and some polls showing Liberal Democrats almost equal with the Conservatives, the election had become a genuine three-party contest. Better still for the media, it suddenly became an election in which there was no foregone conclusion, thus making it more interesting to the public and more exciting.

Two of the Conservative-supporting papers, the *Daily Mail* and *The Daily Telegraph*, did their best to restore right-wing order. A cascade of critical coverage descended on Clegg. The *Mail* accused him of uttering a 'Nazi slur' on Britain. It had dredged up an eight-year-old quote from a *Guardian* article he had written in which he referred to the British victory in the Second World War having created a dangerous superior attitude to Germany.[123] *The Daily Telegraph* claimed an exclusive over a financial donation to Clegg, which he had already reported to the parliamentary register of members' interests.[124] The two stories rebounded more on the papers than the MP. Twitter users killed off the *Telegraph* story with a hashtag '#nickcleggsfault' being applied ironically to everything going wrong in people's lives in a satirical online flash campaign. The paper ended up spending more time trying to defend its story than Clegg spent in denying it.

But overall the election remained a mainstream event. The number of Twitter users, for example, engaged in real-time discussion during the first debate numbered just 36,000 compared to the 9.4 million watching ITV. The mass mobilisation of supporters that Barack Obama achieved through using new media in his 2008 presidential election campaign never emerged in the UK. It was the televised debates and their coverage in the national press that dominated.

Rupert Murdoch's pay walls

There was one front on which Rupert Murdoch did win sympathy and support within the media, and that was his decision to follow in the footsteps of the *Financial Times* and his *Wall Street Journal*, both specialist papers, and to erect a pay wall around his more generalist UK websites. Murdoch came late to the internet (1999 in the UK), and became increasingly angry with the way in which news aggregators, such as Google news, provided free access to his expensively acquired news columns. His wariness of the new media was not improved by the losses he was making on MySpace by 2010. In July 2005 he announced he had bought the MySpace social network for $580 million (£332 million) with the hope it would drive traffic to his Fox Television sites.[125] The purchase was just before it became the most popular social network site in the US, and in 2007, when a merger with Yahoo was being discussed, it was valued briefly at £12 billion. But it began a plummeting decline in 2008 and by July 2010 had fallen to 25th in the internet traffic league ranking. Murdoch's chief operating officer described its losses as 'neither acceptable nor sustainable'.[126] It was relaunched as a music and entertainment portal with the hope of making it easier to sell. Frustrated by the way in which advertising and circulation from his two serious British newspapers – *The Times* and *The Sunday Times* – were shifting to the internet, Murdoch announced in 2009 that he would be introducing a pay wall to protect them in 2010. In a speech in Washington DC organised by the National Press Club in April 2010 he condemned the internet's search engines, accusing them of stealing journalism from his outlets. He charged them with tapping into 'a river of gold' by aggregating content, but the days of free news had come to an end: 'We are going to stop people like Google or Microsoft or whoever from taking stories for nothing ... there is a law of copyright and they recognise it.'[127]

His gamble was based on his belief that although he might lose 90 per cent of the users of the websites, the other 10 per cent would pay to acquire the news and would still be an attractive audience for advertising and marketers. The charges, which began on 1 July 2010, at a modest £1 a day or £2 a week for access to both papers, removed them from the search engines. Four months on Murdoch officials announced they had secured 105,000 digital subscribers to either the papers' websites and/or their iPad and Kindle apps. James Harding, Editor of *The Times*, declared: 'This is the first time in 225 years that *The Times* is being sold on something other than paper.' Compare this to the 20 million unique users a month who were using *The Times'* website before the pay walls were erected. Harding emphasised that it was still early days. Ian Burrell at *The Independent* talked to media and advertising agencies, most of which gave the thumbs down. Rob Lynam at the media agency MEC, said: 'We are just not advertising there. If there's no traffic on there, there's no point advertising there.'[128] Almost two years later, in May 2012, numbers of digital subscribers for the two papers had only grown to 131,000.[129] *The Times* had doubled its subscription price to £4 a week in February 2012.[130]

Rupert Murdoch's second front

In November 2010, Murdoch announced a second front on which he hoped to raise money. He had been collaborating with Steve Jobs, Chief Executive of Apple, to launch the world's first 'newspaper' designed exclusively for new tablet-sized computers such as Apple's iPad, that would be called '*The Daily*', and would be launched in 2011. At an earlier press conference in April 2010, he had declared that Apple's iPad could be the saviour of newspaper journalism, albeit in electronic form, not print. He had picked up an iPad to demonstrate how to navigate his *Wall Street Journal*'s website, adding: 'If you have less [sic] newspapers and more of these ... it may well be the saving of the newspaper industry.' Seven months on, he had a lot more to say. There would be no 'print edition' or 'web edition'. Instead, the new publication would be dispatched automatically to an iPad or any of the growing number of similar devices. With no printing or distribution costs, the US-focused *Daily* would cost 99 cents (62p) a week. He was reported to be recruiting 100 journalists and ready to invest £20 million in the project. He described the move as 'a game-changer', providing a product that would have 'tabloid sensibilities and newspaper intelligence'.[131]

There were plenty of sceptics. Dan Sabbagh, former *Times* Media Editor, who moved to *The Guardian*, was one of them, who warned: 'the problem for anybody wanting to believe that the iPad is a newspaper or magazine replacement (as planned by Richard Branson) is that it is not. It's a digital device, which means people will get easily distracted and start playing Scrabble, or listening to music ...' Then, even more perceptively, he went on: 'a newspaper was once not just a source of information, but a statement of identity, most of whose buyers would not dream of picking up a competing title. Now, in an era where identities are altogether more protean, and when any app can disappear from view at a single touch of a key, it is not obvious that people will sit down and spend 20 minutes engaged in silent contemplation of a single title. It's not how the modernised mind works.'[132]

The Daily was launched in New York on 2 February 2011. Murdoch explained: 'Our target audience is the 15 million Americans expected to own iPads in the next year.' *The Daily* will be sold exclusively through Apple's iTunes store. It was reported that Apple would be receiving 30 per cent of the 99 cent subscription. The Poynter Institute estimated it would need to achieve 650,000 subscribers to break even. There were no current plans to bring it to the UK – its 100 journalists would be focusing on the US.[133] In September 2011 *The Daily* was averaging only 120,000 readers a week, less than a fifth of the number Poynter suggested would be needed to break even, and less than a quarter of the 500,000 that Murdoch said would be needed in February. News Corp did not release circulation figures but John Nitti, who worked with Verizon Wireless, a *Daily* sponsor, was given them.[134] In August 2012, News Corp announced it was cutting its staff by 50 in a bid to hold down costs. It was dropping its opinion sector and turning to Fox Sports for its sports reporting.[135] On 3 December 2012, Murdoch announced *The Daily* was losing $30 million a year and would shut on 15 December, which it did.

Alan Rusbridger, the embracer's response

If Rupert Murdoch has been at one end of the spectrum with respect to his approach to the internet – irritated, wary, suspicious and distrustful – Alan Rusbridger, *The Guardian* Editor, has been at the other: excited, enthusiastic, exhilarated and evangelical. The British media world has been watching a tussle between the resister and an embracer. In between them are a large group of editors and publishers waiting to see what happens to Murdoch's pay walls. Rusbridger objects to the very idea of an old versus new media divide, with *The*

Guardian having now spent over a decade integrating the two. 'We want to be linked in with the web – be "of the web", not simply on it.' He recognises the dire straits in which the media finds itself, describing the industry as collectively suffering from what deep sea divers refer to as the bends. 'We are travelling through a period of extreme change faster than our corporate bodies can cope with. It's painful – and if not treated quickly and correctly, can be fatal.'

He remains firmly opposed to universal pay walls because of the way they would cut off news organisations engaging with their vast new audiences as well as being financially ineffective. *The Guardian* examined six different ways of applying a universal pay wall. It concluded they would not raise as much as the current open access was generating online: £37 million in advertising, app fees, and digital services such as Soulmates in 2009/10 and an expected £47 million in 2010/11 with a target of £100 million by 2015. Rusbridger points to the predictions of Sir Martin Sorrell, head of WPP, the world's leading advertising agency, who expects one third of all advertisements to be digital by 2013. In June 2011 *The Guardian* announced that its digital service – not print – was its new priority. The number of unique browsers to its digital sites had reached 49 million. The paper would have less news and more analysis – a *Newsnight* rather than *News at Ten*.[136] In terms of the media industry, Rusbridger believes it is healthy that Murdoch is testing pay walls out. *The Guardian* was ready to charge for highly targeted, hard to replicate, specialist sites, but the main sites and platforms would retain open access: 'If you think about journalism, not business models, you can become rather excited by the future. If you only think about business models, you scare yourself into paralysis.'

Rusbridger set out his vision in three major speeches in 2010.[137] This is a merged summary of the three. He believes the media industry is undergoing the biggest revolution since Gutenberg's invention of printing 500 years ago. There have been transformative steps in communication over the 500 years since – the telegraph, radio and television – but essentially these were continuations of the idea of communications that involved one person speaking to many. That was still not a dead idea, but what was happening today – the mass ability to communicate with each other without having to go through an intermediary – was truly transformative.

In the old world communication was a one-way process:

> We had the information and the access; you didn't. You trusted us to filter news and information and to prioritise it – to pass it on accurately, fairly, readably and quickly. That state is now in tension with a world in which many (but not all) readers want to have the ability to make their own judgements; express their own priorities; create their own content; articulate their own views; learn from peers as much as from traditional sources of authority.

There was not one new kid on the block but two: the original World Wide Web (essentially another form of transition) and Web 2.0, the rapid maturing social or open media. On one level there was no great mystery about Web 2.0. 'It's about the fact that other people like doing what journalists do. We like creating things – words, pictures, films, graphics – and publishing them. So, it turns out, does everyone else.'

Rusbridger described how the internet had transformed the influence of *The Guardian*: some 37 million unique users on the website, roughly one third in the UK, one third in the US, one third in the rest of the world. Fifty years ago *The Guardian* sold more copies to Colwyn Bay (653) than to the rest of the world (650). More Americans were reading *The Guardian* now than the *Los Angeles Times*. 'This readership found us, rather than the other way round.' Total marketing spend over 10 years in the US was only £22,000.

> This is the opposite of newspapers decline-ism ... when I think of *The Guardian*'s journey and its path of growth and reach and influence, my instincts at the moment – at this stage of the revolution – are to celebrate this trend and seek to accelerate it rather than cut it off. The more we can spread *The Guardian*, embed it in the way the world talks to each other, the better. Many of *The Guardian*'s most interesting experiments at the moment, lie in this area of combining what we know, or believe,

or think, or have found out, with the experience, the range, opinions, expertise, passions of the people who read us, or visit us, or want to participate rather than passively receive.

Instead of trying to do everything ourselves we're increasingly a platform as well as a publisher. It started with Comment is Free in 2006. Soon our cultural coverage will be just as open and collaborative. We've done it with our network of environmental and science blogs: traffic on the former has risen by 800 per cent since the start of the year [2010]. We benefit from expert content and increased audiences.

It is not just in specialist areas that collaboration has helped. It has been crucial too for investigative reporters. There is a lengthening list of exclusives that have been achieved by old and new media working together.

Rusbridger described how he had required senior editorial people on the paper to join Facebook so that they could see for themselves how 'these new ways of creativity and connection work'. He himself was initially sceptical of Twitter, but had become such an enthusiast – 'forget the 140 characters restriction, a lot of the best have links' – he now lists 15 virtues of the website. Virtue three is its search capacity, as good as, if not better than Google, because it goes one stage further than the use of algorithms to 'harnessing the mass capabilities of human intelligence to the power of millions'. More than 450 *Guardian* and *Observer* journalists are now on Twitter, reaching a different audience from the core *Guardian* readership, seeking help, ideas and feedback.

It is not just in specialist areas that collaboration is working. It has played a vital role for investigative reporters:

- Paul Lewis, the first reporter to raise doubts over the death of Ian Tomlinson, the newspaper vendor who tried to get home through the G20 protestors in London. Lewis used Twitter to appeal for contact with observers of the events preceding Tomlinson's death. Among the many responses was a crucial one, a video, sent from New York but made by a fund manager while in London. It showed a police officer hitting Tomlinson with his baton and shoving him to the ground only a short time before the heart attack that killed him.

- New media were equally important in the paper's long series on tax avoidance by big corporations; among the many documents received was an explosive one on a major tax avoidance vehicle being used by a leading bank. The loophole was closed in the next Budget.

- And it was Twitter users who came to the rescue when a super-injunction imposed on the paper prevented it from even reporting that questions were due to be asked in Parliament on the gagging order. Twitter users ferreted away and discovered the origins of the ban: Carter-Ruck lawyers and its client Trafigura. The large but mostly anonymous trading company (which was facing a class action in the Ivory Coast from 30,000 Africans, who claimed its dumping of hundreds of tonnes of highly toxic oil waste had caused them serious injuries) wanted to end any further discussion of the case. Their secrecy strategy was blown open by Twitter. It became the most Tweeted issue of the day, until the company withdrew its order.

All this was not just one-way traffic, the new media helping the old. The new also sought the help of the old, as we saw with the exposure of Damian McBride by the Guido Fawkes website. Much bigger still were three successive releases by WikiLeaks in 2010 of massive collections of US files – on Iraq and Afghanistan war logs followed by 250,000 dispatches from and to 250 US embassies around the world – given exclusively in the UK to *The Guardian* several weeks in advance. This allowed a team of specialist reporters to work systematically through them and set them in context by deadline day for the online release. Similar exclusive advances were given to the *New York Times* in the US and *Der Spiegel* in Germany. Two more world-famous newspapers, *Le Monde* in France and *El País* in Madrid, joined in on the third round. The disclosures in the first two leaks included the killing of civilians in previously unreported shootings and the handover of prisoners to be tortured. The third release lifted the curtain on how the US deals with both its friends and enemies.

Let me close with Rusbridger's rallying cry at the end of his Cudlipp lecture on 25 January 2010, on the need for and extension of mutual journalism:

> We feel we are edging towards a new world in which we bring important things to the table – editing; reporting; areas of expertise; access; a title, or brand, that people trust; ethical professional standards and an extremely large community of readers. The members of that community could not hope to aspire to anything like that audience or reach on their own; they bring us a rich diversity, specialist expertise and on the ground reporting that we can't possibly hope to achieve without including them in what we do.
>
> Yes, there are lots of concerns about this world I'm describing, not least the ignorant, relentlessly negative, sometimes hate-filled tone of some of what you get back when you open the doors. That can sometimes feel not very much like a community at all, let alone a community of like-minded, progressive intelligent people coming together around some virtual idea of *The Guardian*. So there are a throng of issues around identity, moderation, ranking, recommendation and aggregation which we – along with everyone else – are grappling with. But let's grapple with them rather than dismiss them or turn our backs on them.
>
> Fleet Street is the birth place of the tradition of a free press that spread around the world. There is an irreversible trend in society today which rather wonderfully continues what we as an industry started – here, in newspapers, in the UK. It's not a 'digital trend' – that's just shorthand. It's a trend about how people are expressing themselves, about how societies will choose to organise themselves, about a new democracy of ideas and information, about changing notions of authority, about

the releasing of individual creativity, about an ability to hear previously unheard voices; about respecting, including and harnessing the views of others. About resisting the people who want to close down free speech.

If we turn our back on all this and at the same time conclude that there is nothing to learn from it because what 'they' do is different – we are journalists, they aren't; we do journalism, they don't – then, never mind business models, we will be sleep walking into oblivion.

The media scene in 2012

To sum up: the situation was still grim. The average rate of circulation decline among national dailies accelerated to 11 per cent in the first seven months of 2012. The serious papers were particularly badly hit with the following year-on-year falls: *Telegraph* 9 per cent, *Times* 11 per cent, *Financial Times* 16 per cent, *Guardian* 16 per cent, *Independent* 28 per cent – this last fall reflected the launch of a smaller, briefer and cheaper sister paper, *The i*, selling 220,000 at 20p.

Pay walls were not working for Murdoch, and although running losses had been reduced, other threats had emerged. In June 2012 Rupert Murdoch finally bowed to the demands of frustrated shareholders, and conceded that the businesses within his US-based News Corp, the worldwide media empire he had constructed, should be split in two, with newspapers in one group and the much more lucrative television and cable companies in another. He resigned from his remaining directorships of News International, the holding company of his remaining three British newspapers, *The Sun*, *The Times* and *The Sunday Times*. This led to much speculation that this could be a first step to a sell-off, which would make *The Times*, the biggest loss-maker of the three, more vulnerable. A news report on 27 January 2013 noted that, according to recent financial filings in the US, Murdoch's new publishing sector would have reported a £1.3 billion net loss in the year to June 2012 but for the financial protection provided by the profitable Fox Film and Television businesses. Losses on *The Times* and *The Sunday Times* were said to be running at £1 million a week.[138]

The open website was not working for *The Guardian*. Its website continued to mushroom – reaching 70 million in October – but the losses from the two papers (*The Guardian* and Sunday's *The Observer*) had increased from £31.1 million to £44.2 million in the financial year ending April 2012. Total digital earnings were still less than one quarter of the paper's revenue. Having already lost 200 journalists, the paper began a new round of redundancies to cut another 100 from the remaining 650 total. *The Guardian* is funded by the Scott Trust, a non-profit body that owns both papers and other enterprises. There was a £225 million cash balance and investment fund in April, but there was genuine concern over the slow growth of digital revenue.

Eugeny Lebedev, the proprietor of *The Independent* and the *London Evening Standard*, told the Leveson inquiry in April 2012 that he and his father, the billionaire and former KGB agent, Alexander Lebedev, had spent £75 million keeping the two papers afloat in the last three years. He estimated that *The Times*, *The Guardian* and *The Independent* were losing £100 million between them a year. He added that that there may come a day when there won't be "wealthy individuals and charitable trusts that will be willing to fund this journalism and that's the scary moment".

The tabloids could perhaps survive for longer. They've lost circulation, advertising and staff, as well as further deterioration of their reputation in the wake of the hacking scandal, but they still make a profit. The *Mail*'s Associated Newspapers made £76 million, Richard Desmond's *Express*, *Star* and other titles £36.6 million, and the Mirror Group £83 million. *The Sun* also was very profitable, but its profits are less easily identified in News International accounts.

It is not going to be comfortable future for the five serious papers, chasing a shrinking group of 1.4 million people in a hyper-competitive world. There is one other factor contributing to their problems: the decline of the independent newsagent. About 10 such newsagents are going out of business every week. True, there are supermarkets, petrol stations and the big chains such as W.H. Smith providing newspapers, but none of them deliver papers to individual purchasers' doors. It is part of the decline of the local high street – disappearing pubs, post offices and paper shops.

Notes

[1] Onora O'Neill, 'A question of trust', Reith Lectures 2002, Cambridge (www.bbc.co.uk/radio4/reith2002/).

[2] Anthony Sampson (2004) *Who runs this place? The anatomy of Britain in the 21st century*, London: John Murray Publishers.

[3] Ibid, p 223.

[4] John Lloyd (2004) *What the media are doing to our politics*, London: Constable & Robinson.

[5] Richard Lambert (2005) 'The path back to trust, truth and integrity', *Guardian Media* Supplement, 17 January (www.guardian.co.uk/media/2005/jan/17/mondaymediasection1).

[6] Harry Evans (2006) 'Just find the bloody facts', *Press Gazette*, 14 July.

[7] *Guardian Media* Supplement for two successive weeks: 10 January 2005 and 17 January 2005.

[8] Ibid.

[9] Ibid.

[10] Ibid.

[11] John Rentoul (2001) *Tony Blair, Prime Minister*, London: Sphere, p 230.

[12] Peter Hennessy (2001) *The Prime Minister: The office and its holders since 1945*, Harmondsworth: Penguin, p 183.

[13] Ibid.

[14] Private interview.

[15] Private interview with Number 10 senior press officer.

[16] Lance Price (2010) *Where power lies: Prime ministers v the media*, New York: Simon & Schuster, p 35.

[17] Ibid.

[18] Charles Wintour (1972) *Pressures on the press*, London: Andre Deutsch.

[19] Martin Moore (2006) *The origins of modern spin: Democratic government and the media in Britain 1945–51*, Basingstoke: Palgrave Macmillan.

[20] 'Rupert Murdoch "like a 24th member of the Cabinet", says aide', *The Scotsman*, 19 May 2006.

[21] Interview with Neil Kinnock, former Labour Party leader.

[22] William Shawcross (1993) *Rupert Murdoch: Ringmaster of the information circus*, London: Pan Books, p 550.

[23] *The Sun* front page, 1 May 1997.

[24] 'Tough on rhetoric', *The Guardian* Editorial, 8 February 2005.

[25] Andrew Marr (2004) *My trade: A short history of British journalism*, Basingstoke: Macmillan, p 180.

[26] Lance Price (2003) 'Feeding the hungry beast', *Independent on Sunday*, 31 August.

[27] Lance Price (2010) *Where power lies: Prime ministers v the media*, New York: Simon & Schuster, p 11.

[28] Andrew Marr (2007) 'How Blair put the media in a spin', BBC News Online, 10 May (http://news.bbc.co.uk/1/hi/uk_politics/6638231.stm).

[29] Andrew Grice (2000) 'The strange case of Benjamin Binman', *The Independent*, 28 July.

[30] Andrew Sparrow (2000) 'Blair shows worry on "out of touch" memo leak', *The Daily Telegraph*, 17 July.

[31] David Marquand (2008) *Britain since 1918: The strange career of British democracy*, London: Weidenfeld & Nicolson, p 364.

[32] Lance Price (2010) *Where power lies: Prime ministers v the media*, New York: Simon & Schuster, p 349.

[33] Ibid, p 349.

[34] Ibid, p 350.

[35] Ibid, p 349.

[36] Geoff Mulgan (2005) 'Foreword', in Ipsos MORI, *Who do you believe? Trust in government information*, London: Ipsos MORI.

[37] Cabinet Office (2004) *An independent review of government communications (Phillis Report)*, Presented to the Minister for the Cabinet Office, London: Cabinet Office, January, p 6.

[38] Ibid, p 6.

[39] Alastair Campbell (2002) 'It's time to bury spin', *British Journalism Review*, vol 13, no 4, pp 15-23.

[40] Lance Price (2010) *Where power lies: Prime ministers v the media*, New York: Simon & Schuster, p 338.

[41] Anthony Seldon (ed) (2007) *Blair's Britain, 1997–2007*, Cambridge: Cambridge University Press.

[42] Cabinet Office (2004) *An independent review of government communications (Phillis Report)*, Presented to the Minister for the Cabinet Office, London: Cabinet Office, January.

[43] Ibid, p 7.

[44] Ibid, p 10.

[45] Ibid.

[46] *The Independent* (2003) Editorial, 4 September.

[47] *The Guardian* (2003) Editorial, 4 September.

[48] *The Independent* (2004) Editorial, 24 January.

[49] *The Guardian* (2004) Editorial, 24 January.

[50] Paul Routledge (2004) *The Daily Mirror*, 24 January.

[51] Peter Riddell (2004) *The Times*, 24 January.

[52] Ivor Gaber (2004) 'Alastair Campbell, exit stage left: do the "Phillis" recommendations represent a new chapter in political communications or is it "business as usual"?', *Journal of Public Affairs*, vol 4, issue 4, November, pp 365-73.

[53] Alastair Campbell (2008) 'The Cudlipp lecture' (www.independent.co.uk/news/media/alastair-campbell-the-cudlipp-lecture-775278.html).

[54] Julia Simpson (2004) *The Sunday Times*, 26 September.

[55] Lance Price (2010) *Where power lies: Prime ministers v the media*, New York: Simon & Schuster, p 11.

[56] Ibid, p 14.

[57] Ibid, p 15.

[58] Tony Blair (2007) 'Blair on the media', 12 June (http://news.bbc.co.uk/1/hi/uk_politics/6744581.stm).

[59] Dennis Kavanagh (2007) 'The Blair premiership', in Anthony Seldon (ed) *Blair's Britain 1997–2007*, Cambridge: Cambridge University Press, p 11.

[60] Paul Fawcett and R.A.W. Rhodes (2007) 'Central government', in Anthony Seldon (ed) *Blair's Britain 1997–2007*, Cambridge: Cambridge University Press, p 99.

[61] Alastair Campbell (2002) 'It's time to bury spin', *British Journalism Review*, vol 13, no 4, pp 15–23.

[62] Adam Boulton (2008) *Memories of the Blair administration: Tony's ten years*, New York: Simon & Schuster, p 180.

[63] Alastair Campbell (2008) 'The Cudlipp lecture' (www.independent.co.uk/news/media/alastair-campbell-the-cudlipp-lecture-775278.html).

[64] All quotes from the national dailies are from 13 June 2007; those from the Sunday papers are from 17 June 2007.

[65] Ibid.

[66] Martin Kettle (2007) 'Blair's message for the media', *Guardian Media*, 12 June.

[67] BBC Trust (2007) *From seesaw to Wagon Wheel: Safeguarding impartiality in the 21st century* (www.bbc.co.uk/bbctrust/assets/files/pdf/review_report_research/impartiality_21century/report.pdf).

[68] Richard Brooks and Dipesh Gadber (2007) 'BBC report damns its "culture of bias"', *The Sunday Times*, 17 June.

[69] 'BBC comes under fire for institutional left-wing bias', *Daily Mail*, 18 June 2007.

[70] 'BBC viewers angered by its "innate liberal bias"', *The Daily Telegraph*, 18 June 2007.

[71] Torin Douglas (2007) 'Does the BBC have a bias problem?', BBC News Online, 18 June (http://news.bbc.co.uk/1/hi/6764779.stm).

[72] Richard Tait (2007) 'Impartiality is worth fighting for in the age of the internet', *The Observer*, 17 June (www.guardian.co.uk/media/2007/jun/17/broadcasting.politicsandthemedia).

[73] BBC Trust (2007) *From seesaw to Wagon Wheel: Safeguarding impartiality in the 21st century* (www.bbc.co.uk/bbctrust/assets/files/pdf/review_report_research/impartiality_21century/report.pdf).

[74] Leigh Holmwood (2007) 'Dibley producer hits back at impartiality report', *Guardian Media*, 19 June.

75 BBC Trust (2007) *From seesaw to Wagon Wheel: Safeguarding impartiality in the 21st century* (www.bbc.co.uk/bbctrust/assets/files/pdf/review_report_research/impartiality_21century/report.pdf).

76 *Daily Mail*, Editorial, 22 March 2007.

77 Polly Toynbee (2008) 'This buffeted Prime Minister must stop scrambling at every puff of wind', *The Guardian*, 11 April.

78 Andrew Rawnsley (2010) *The end of the party*, London: Viking Adult (Penguin), p 638.

79 *The Sunday Times*, 12 April 2009, front page splash.

80 Andrew Rawnsley, (2010) *The end of the party*, London: Viking Adult (Penguin), p 638.

81 BBC News Online, 18 November 2009.

82 James Murdoch (2009) 'James Murdoch hits out at BBC and regulators at Edinburgh TV festival', 28 August (www.guardian.co.uk/media/2009/aug/28/james-murdoch-bbc-mactaggart-edinburgh-tv-festival).

83 Amanda Andrews (2009) 'James Murdoch doesn't go far enough: slash the BBC's budget by a third', *The Telegraph*, 29 August (www.telegraph.co.uk/finance/newsbysector/mediatechnologyandtelecoms/6111007/James-Murdoch-doesnt-go-far-enough-slash-the-BBCs-budget-by-a-third.html).

84 Ibid.

85 BBC website, 28 August 2009.

86 David Chance (2009) 'How Murdoch's upstart became the status quo', *Financial Times*, 27 August.

87 Will Hutton (2009) 'The big issue: Murdoch v the media', *The Observer*, 30 August.

88 J. Curran et al (2009) 'Media system, public knowledge and democracy: a comparative study', *European Journal of Communications*, vol 24, no 1, pp 5-26.

89 Mark Thompson (2010) MacTaggart lecture, 27 August (www.guardian.co.uk/media/2010/aug/27/mark-thompson-mactaggart-full-text).

90 Jason Groves (2010) 'Lords condemn Rupert Murdoch's bid for control of Sky', *Daily Mail*, 5 November.

91 Lord (Norman) Fowler (2010) 'Why Vince Cable must reel in News Corp's bid for full control of Sky', *Guardian Media*, 11 October.

92 Claire Enders, Beehive City, 12 September 2010 and *Guardian Media* report, 20 September 2010.

93 Patrick Wintour (2010) 'Humiliated Vince Cable stripped of Sky role after "war with Murdoch" gaffe', *Guardian Media*, 21 December (www.guardian.co.uk/politics/2010/dec/21/vince-cable-war-murdoch-gaffe).

94 'All human life was there', *The Times*, Editorial, 11 July 2011.

95 James Kirkup (2011) 'Cameron prepares to delay the bid', *Daily Telegraph*, 11 July.

96 'The sky falls in', *The Guardian*, Editorial, 14 July 2011.

[97] Roland Watson (2011) 'BSkyB conversation "did not break the rules"', *The Times*, 21 July.

[98] The judgment thing', *The Guardian*, Editorial, 21 July 2011.

[99] Will Hutton (2011) 'British democracy can't live with Murdoch's BSkyB bid', *The Guardian*, 13 July.

[100] Ben Fenton (2011) 'Regulators begin their probe into BSkyB', *Financial Times*, 23 July.

[101] BBC website (2012) 'Ofcom says Sky fit and proper, but James Murdoch rapped', 20 September.

[102] Toby Helm (2011) 'How phone hacking took the shine off the PM', *The Observer*, 24 July.

[103] See 'Media Guardian's 2011 top 100 players, no 10: Lord Justice Leveson', *The Guardian*, 25 July.

[104] Patrick Wintour (2011) 'Inquiry may not conclude until 2015 election', *The Guardian*, 29 July.

[105] *Financial Times*, Editorial, 23 October 2010.

[106] *Guardian Media*, 8 May 2010.

[107] Richard Ottoway (2010) *Guardian Media*, 29 November.

[108] BBC website (2012) 'Jimmy Saville: number of victims reach 300, police say', 25 October.

[109] Steven Swinford (2012) 'It's time to end trial by Twitter', *The Daily Telegraph*, 16 November.

[110] *The Economist* (2012) 'Twitter and libel law – a little bird told me', 24 November.

[111] Geoffrey Levy (2012) 'Rise and rise of networker they call head boy', *Mail* online, 23 November.

[112] Natalie Fenton (2009) *New media, old news: Journalism and democracy in the digital age*, London: Sage Publications.

[113] OECD (Organisation for Economic Co-operation and Development) (2010) *The future of news and the internet*, Paris: OECD.

[114] *Guardian Media*, 13 May 2010.

[115] BBC and *Guardian* websites.

[116] May 2011 ABC circulation figures.

[117] Office of Fair Trading (2009) *Annual report*, London: The Stationery Office.

[118] Natalie Fenton, Goldsmiths Media Research Centre seminar, 2010.

[119] 'Half of local papers could fold, media experts warn', *The Daily Telegraph*, 16 June 2009.

[120] 'New Culture Secretary highlights "excellent" local newspapers', *NS: The Voice of Local Media*, 11 June 2009 (www.newspapersoc.org.uk/11/jun/09/new-culture-secretary-highlights-excellent-local-newspapers).

[121] *Guardian Media*, 28 June 2010.

[122] Nick Davies (2008) *Flat earth news*, London: Chatto & Windus.

[123] Tim Shipman (2010) 'Underfire Lib Dem leader tries to laugh off his Nazi slur on UK', *Daily Mail*, 22 April.

[124] Robert Winnett and Jon Swaine (2010) 'General Election 2010: Nick Clegg under pressure to explain private account donations', *The Daily Telegraph*, 22 April.

[125] 'Murdoch's $580 million honey pot dip', *The Observer*, 24 July 2005.

[126] Dan Sabbagh (2010) 'News Corp runs out of patience with MySpace', *The Guardian*, 4 November.

[127] Paul Harris (2010) 'Rupert Murdoch defiant: I'll stop Google taking our news', *The Guardian*, 7 April.

[128] Ian Burrell (2010) 'Has Rupert Murdoch's pay wall gamble paid off? Advertisers don't like it', *The Independent*, 2 September.

[129] Gordon Macmillan (2012) '*The Times* adds digital subscribers as numbers grow to 131,000', *The Wall: Social, marketing, media: blogged*, 15 May.

[130] John Plunkett (2012) '*Times* digital subscriptions to double in price', *The Guardian*, 23 February.

[131] Edward Holmore (2010) 'Rupert Murdoch creates "iNewspaper" – with the help of Steve Jobs', *The Observer*, 21 November.

[132] Dan Sabbagh (2009) 'The iPad may not be the great saviour of newspapers', *Guardian Media*, 29 November (www.guardian.co.uk/media/organgrinder/2010/nov/29/ipad-kindle-newspapers-games).

[133] Ed Pilkington (2011) 'Rupert Murdoch unveils next step in media empire – the iPod "newspaper"', *The Guardian*, 2 February.

[134] Dominic Rushe (2011) 'Rupert Murdoch's *Daily* averaging just 120,000 a week', *The Guardian*, 28 September.

[135] Matthew Flann (2012) 'Murdoch's iPad pub lays off a third of staff', *Crain'sNewYorkbusiness.com*, 1 August.

[136] Andrew Pugh (2011) 'Rusbridger: staking future on print is "truly reckless"', *Press Gazette*, 29 June.

[137] Alan Rusbridger's three 2010 lectures: the Cudlipp lecture on 25 January 2010; the Media Standards Trust seminar on 'Why journalism matters', 22 July 2010; and 'Splintering of the fourth estate' in Sydney, Australia, 19 November 2010.

[138] Mark Sweney (2013) 'News International's Mike Darcey strikes a deal for digital future', *The Guardian*, 27 January.

TWO

An inside and outside look at policy-making

This book has two themes: the power of the media was introduced in Chapter One, with the chapters that follow this one examining how that power has been applied across seven different branches of the welfare state. This chapter looks at the second theme: social policy and policy-making. The welfare state is at the heart of social policy – how did it start? What was the media's response? How did the relationship between social policy and the media develop?

The welfare state slowly emerged from the Second World War, which had helped generate a collective spirit through widespread bombing, severe austerity and serious loss of life. It was, however, a far from robust organisation at the start. Social and economic conditions in the UK were in a desperate state. Britain had been importing up to 70 per cent of its food needs before the Second World War. After the war, the rationing of almost all food, clothing and petrol that began in the war continued for some years afterwards. Millions of troops were returning home, a large proportion wanting to start families. Second only to the fear of unemployment was homelessness.

Over 400,000 homes had been destroyed or left unfit for habitation from bombing. Between one quarter and a third of all homes had received some damage. Building materials were in short supply and were being rationed. Britain had little or no foreign currency to pay for imports. Two thirds of the pre-war building workers were in the armed forces. And yet in a March 1945 White Paper by the war-time Coalition, a British government accepted for the first time the principle that there should be 'a separate dwelling for every family needing one'. The best accounts of the birth and growth of the welfare state are set out in *The five giants: A biography of the welfare state* by Nicholas Timmins, a widely respected *Financial Times* journalist[1]

, and *British social policy: 1945 to the present* by Howard Glennerster, Emeritus Professor of Social Policy, London School of Economics and Political Science, a pioneer in the field.[2]

The welfare state, a name first coined in the 1930s, had been a term of abuse against the Weimar Republic for allegedly burdening the state with too many social responsibilities and undermining the country's political and economic viability. It was the Beveridge Report in 1942, with its clarion call to take on the five giants (Want, Disease, Ignorance, Squalor and Idleness) that rebranded the term and gave it a glittering New Jerusalem ambition. For a war-weary nation, it proved a massive morale-booster. In William Beveridge's words, 'the purpose of victory is to live in a better world than the old world ... each individual citizen is more likely to concentrate upon his war efforts if he feels his government will be ready in time with plans for a better world'.[3]

The author was not just an academic and an administrator, but a journalist and broadcaster as well, which proved crucial in building public support for his proposals. Leaks and broadcasts before publication on 1 December 1942 built up anticipation of what was going to be produced. A Home Office intelligence report in the autumn before publication noted: 'Three years ago the term social security was almost unknown to the public. It now appears to be generally accepted as a post-war need. It is commonly defined as "a decent minimum standard of living for all".'[4] Publication of the Beveridge Report produced an ecstatic response from the press, the only critical voice being in *The Daily Telegraph*. The public, who had been queuing for copies, were equally enthusiastic. Some 100,000 copies were bought in the first month, with a shortened 40-page version including the introduction and summary pushing up final sales to 600,000. Copies of the report with its messianic message – 'a revolutionary moment in the world's history is a time for revolution not patching' – were sent to troops overseas. The BBC broadcast the message abroad in 22 languages.

Evolutionary rather than revolutionary change

In reality, implementation was more evolutionary than revolutionary given the economic and social conditions in the country. One measurement of the stark needs concerned bathrooms: half of all households lacked the use of one; two out of five did not have a bath; and nearly a quarter did not have their own exclusive lavatory. It took six years to build the first million of the three million new homes that the 1945 White Paper estimated would be needed as a minimum within 10 to 12 years. It took 12 years to achieve the three million target. The reform of education sprang from the 1944 Act that separated primary from secondary schools, abolished school fees, proposed day release for the education of young workers and introduced university scholarships. A guidance circular that followed set out a tripartite system for secondary schools: selective grammar schools, secondary moderns and technical schools for 13-year-olds intending to take up apprenticeships, the last of which hardly materialised (see Chapter Seven).

The National Health Service (NHS) replaced a mish-mash of municipal and financially impoverished voluntary hospitals along with general practitioners (GPs) who adjusted their charges to the incomes of their patients. Only roughly half the working population were part of the National Health Insurance scheme launched by Lloyd George in 1911 with access to panel doctors. Launched in 1948, the NHS provided comprehensive medical care, free to all in time of need, financed by taxation and a modest contribution from National Insurance. It became the most popular arm of the welfare state, even more popular than the Royal Family in their most popular period. A national social security system, with local offices run from the centre, providing flat-rate benefits for flat-rate contributions, replaced a myriad of local schemes. This was the one front on which Beveridge went into great detail. Alongside the social security programme was a separate means-tested benefit system, providing a safety net for people who had not made National Insurance contributions or whose contributory benefits had run out. The two were later brought under the same roof. So this, in brief, was how four of the five giants were dealt with: Want (social security), Disease (NHS), Ignorance (education reform) and Squalor (new housing). The fifth, Idleness, was met by a government commitment to pursue economic policies that would optimise the chances of full employment, plus a network of local offices providing guidance on jobs. In terms of spending, these changes were providing a cut-price safety net from the start.

Even by 1950/51 the defence budget still accounted for 24 per cent of all public expenditure – twice as much as social security (12 per cent) and more than the combined total of the NHS (8.4 per cent), education (6.8 per cent) and housing (6.9 per cent). Pivotal points in the first 20 years included Harold Macmillan imposing his strong Tory will on his Housing Department and the Treasury officials with his new target of 300,000 new homes a year – achieved in 1953 and 1954 although with less space and a lower standard than the first postwar homes built; and Anthony Crosland's famous circular in 1965 firmly 'requesting' local authorities to move to comprehensive schools, although more were confirmed under Margaret Thatcher's period in the Education Department between 1970 and 1974. For policy wonks the 1960s were an era of great commissions, particularly in education – with reports from Crowther, Newsom, Robbins and Plowden – that changed attitudes. The 1963 Robbins Report on higher education, for example, packed with facts and stacks of social statistics, sowed seeds which were still multiplying 25 years on (see below).

The welfare state post-1969

Even in early 1969, when I started at *The Guardian*, expenditure remained distorted – still reflecting the UK's presumed power status that no mainstream party was prepared to give up. Defence spending had been halved but was still bigger than education or health and twice as big as housing. There were still plenty of causes to fight for, with the 'rediscovery' of poverty in the mid-1960s (see Chapter Six). And all was not well in the NHS as an independent investigation into Ely long-stay mental hospital – documenting both cruelty and cover up – starkly set out in 1969. Richard Crossman, the forceful Secretary of State, overrode both departmental and NHS resistance and published the full report. Ely, alas, was followed by a chain of scandals in other long-stay wards in Farleigh, Whittingham, Napsbury, South Ockendon, St Augustine's and Normansfield. But Ely had led to the establishment of the independent Hospital Advisory Service – essentially a national inspectorate that dare not speak its name, with direct access to the Secretary of State – and put mental health on the agenda.

What was clear post-1969 was the acceleration in the expansion of the welfare state, even under Conservative administrations. I watched Sir Keith Joseph at the 1971 Conservative Party conference win resounding applause for new disability benefits he was implementing. They had been designed by the 1964–70 Labour government, but implemented by the 1970–74 Conservative government. Similarly, the sixth arm of the welfare state, personal social services, was set up in 1971. This sprang from the 1968 Seebohm Report and was the last act of the Labour government before it lost the 1970 general election. But once again the Conservatives implemented the legislation, widening the old children's departments so that they were joined by social workers and carers from mental health, residential care and community care for older and disabled people.

Perhaps the most dramatic change in social policy in my 40 years of observation was the huge spurt into higher education. In a speech shortly after his 1988 Education Act had passed, Kenneth Baker, Education Secretary, noted that in the 25 years since the Robbins Report participation rates of 18-year-olds entering university had doubled. He went on to speculate that in the following quarter of a century participation rates might double again. But it did not take 25 years; it took just five. Participation rates rose from 15 per cent in 1988 to 30 per cent in 1993. The Conservative government had temporarily removed the limits on places at university that they were prepared to fund although at much less per student. Much to the surprise of the Education Department and the alarm of the Treasury, the number of offers universities extended exploded. Whitehall hurriedly put the lid back on.

Some challenges have been constant through the 60-plus years of the welfare state. The growing number of older people has caused concern through all six decades of the NHS. Numbers had increased from seven million in 1951 to nine million in 1971. They are still causing concern in 2011 with even greater numbers and still no agreement on how to finance those needing community or long-term residential care (see Chapter Eight). Each decade health policy-makers have shed tears over the deletion or addition of management tiers. Sometimes there were three, sometimes four, and then only two under the initial Conservative/Liberal Democrat plan, later expanded to four. A *British Medical Journal* Editorial in July 2010, by a professor of health management, suggested there had been 15 identifiable major changes in the previous 30 years.[5]

The Thatcher/Major era

Where a slowdown in the rate of growth began was with Margaret Thatcher's election in 1979. The first line of her first White Paper on public expenditure read 'Public expenditure is at the heart of Britain's present economic difficulties'. This put the biggest social policy budget – social security – under a highly focused spotlight. Serious cuts followed by ending the earnings link of several benefits (basic pension, unemployment and sickness benefit) which, over time, achieved huge savings. If the index had been retained, the level of the basic pension, for example, by 2010 would have been two thirds higher: £158.60 rather than £95.25. The second state pension – SERPS, the 1978 State Earnings-Related Pension Scheme – received equally fierce cuts, particularly affecting women. And two thirds of the Social Fund's grants to meet exceptional needs were withdrawn (see Chapter Six).

The losses did not stop there. The huge sums raised by selling off council houses failed to be reinvested in much needed social programmes including social housing. In an undoubtedly astute political move – which Thatcher had opposed when first proposed by Edward Heath in the 1970–74 Conservative government – tenants of three years standing were given the right to buy their homes at extremely generous discounts, initially up to 50 per cent, but by 1989 the top discount had been raised to 70 per cent. It brought huge numbers of former Labour supporters into the Conservative fold. In its first 13 years this raised over £28 billion – more than the sale of gas, electricity and British Telecom put together. It was the biggest single privatisation of the Thatcher era. Between 1979 and 2000 the share of total housing stock owned by local councils fell from nearly a third to less than a fifth. And health and education were also being squeezed.

New Labour, new funds

After Labour's initial two years of following austere Conservative spending plans as they had promised – restrictions which, had the Conservatives won, they would certainly have slackened – resources began to flow. The NHS saw its longest and strongest period of growth since its founding, with spending doubling in real terms by 2008. By 2010 UK health and education were receiving 33 per cent of all government spending (20 per cent for health, 13 per cent for education) against 25 per cent when Labour came to power in 1997. Defence spending had fallen to 7 per cent.

Two pie charts in Howard Glennerster's *British social policy: 1945 to the present*[6] show just how dramatic the growth of the welfare state was by its 60th birthday. In 2004/05 absolute real spending on social policy was seven times its scale in 1950. By 2010 it was nine and a half times as large.

The size of the welfare state 1951/52 and 2009/10

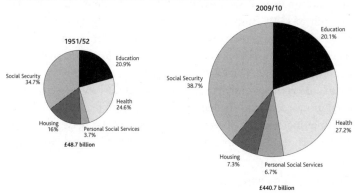

Note: The sums are in billions of pounds expressed in 2009/10 prices and on a UK basis.
Source: Glennerster (2007); HM Treasury (2010)

Irregular reports of the death of the welfare state

It was not just in the UK that the welfare state was expanding, yet this growth was accompanied by irregular forecasts of its demise. A US economist posted an early forecast. Writing in 1967 when New York's public services were near bankrupt, he suggested they were doomed because they could not match the productivity gains of the private sector.[7] In Britain commentators on the left were pessimistic about a country that wanted European levels of social provision but US levels of low taxation. And then on the right there was Charles Murray, another American brought over to the UK at irregular intervals by *The Sunday Times*, to wreak unsubstantiated gloom on the damage that the welfare system generated. Poverty in the UK is different than in US. For one thing, it is less persistent.

In an essay in the 2008 *Oxford handbook of comparative welfare states*,[8] Glennerster examined why the doomsters had got it wrong. He looked at 18 states between 1980 and 2003 with welfare state programmes. None collapsed nor went into decline. Indeed, in the 23-year period spending increased by billions on social security, social services, health and social housing. There were two big factors ignored by the critics. Politically the welfare state drew its robust resilience from the high proportion of people benefiting from the provision of health and social security. Republican presidents from Reagan through to G.W. Bush were thwarted from applying pension cuts because of the sharp-elbowed middle-class beneficiaries receiving state pensions worth 45 per cent (compared to 33 per cent in the UK) of average earnings. The major economic reason why there was not a switch to privately funded provision was that the private sector faced even more economic challenges. Private school fees in the UK, for example, increased by 40 per cent between 2001–06, twice the rate of the earnings rise of their managerial and professional customers.

The media's response

Glennerster carried out a content analysis of the media in the early years of the welfare state. He found it was dominated by coverage of imperial and international issues such as the forthcoming independence of India, the communist threat to Eastern Europe and the acute shortages of basic essentials at home, in the UK. But over time this was transformed by the political rise in importance of public services, although it did take time. When I joined *The Guardian* in 1969, the pecking order among its news journalists was clear. First came the political team (three), then two industrial relations reporters closely following the trade unions, which were at that time much more powerful, followed by the diplomatic/Commonwealth correspondent and the defence correspondent. Social policy specialists then filled the next rungs, but compared to later years, the numbers were thin: one education reporter, one health and social care, one housing and planning. When promoted in 1972, I was the first full-time social policy leader writer the paper had employed.

There was a similar hierarchy on the other broadsheets. There would have been bigger political staffs, particularly on *The Times* and *Telegraph* that devoted much more space then to what was said in Parliament. *The Times* was the only daily to have a home affairs correspondent, dealing with Home Office policy rather than crime. Most papers, particularly the tabloids, had crime reporters, but not *The Guardian* when I joined. Crime is not normally included within the remit of social policy, but it is included in this book because it is so related to the social conditions from which it springs (see Chapter Three).

As the welfare state became more important politically, so did the role of specialist reporters. They were also helped by the growth in the size of papers. In 1969 *The Guardian* was a single broadsheet daily paper of a mere 18 pages priced at 8p. Three decades on, there were never less than four separate sections each day (main, sports, G2 and a specialist section), with 10 sections on a Saturday. At its height in 2001, the daily editions averaged 250,000 words (a *War and Peace* every two days) and on Saturdays this rose to 400,000. There were similar expansions on other papers, but where *The Guardian* was a step ahead of its competitors was in capturing the public services audience. This was achieved through its *Education* section on Tuesdays launched in 1972, and *Society* section on Wednesdays (covering health, social services, welfare, housing, charities, environment and law and order), launched in 1979. By the first decade of the new century the social policy specialists on the paper had grown to 20 – including the staff on the two supplements – plus up to another 10 on *The Guardian*'s online site. The two specialist sections did not just boost the readership but also over time brought in huge amounts of classified advertising. At its peak at the end of the 1990s, *Society* grew to 160 tabloid pages, with 146 filled with classified advertisements. It was bringing in £50 million a year in advertising, almost one third of the paper's income at the time. Various papers – *The Times*, *The Sunday Times*, *The Independent* – tried to break into the market, but they had left it too late. *The Guardian* had captured 85 per cent of nationally advertised education jobs and 86 per cent of all other public service jobs in the national daily press.

What the pages did provide was ammunition for right-wing papers that combed through the advertisements for the more quixotic jobs to expound on public expenditure waste. These made regular appearances in the *Daily Mail* and *Telegraph*. They even led *The Telegraph*'s leader columns on one occasion. What also irked them was MI5 choosing the *Society* section for its first ever public recruitment advertisement for special agents. What was happening at *The Guardian* was being repeated across Fleet Street at a much slower rate. All papers devoted more space to health, education, welfare, asylum and immigration.

Whitehall versus Westminster

Whitehall – where key policies were formulated – was always a key focus for specialist correspondents, while Westminster was mostly left to the political staff. But there were other sources of information, particularly from the public service unions engaged in the negotiations over new policies: teachers, doctors, nurses, social workers, police, probation officers and prison governors. Within Whitehall there was a hierarchy of briefing ahead of important announcements on social policy. Leader writers would usually have access to the Secretary of State, sometimes in small groups, sometimes one to one, sometimes by telephone. The Home Office used to divide correspondents into two groups – broadsheet and tabloid – in the correct belief that tabloids were more interested in crime than criminal justice policy. Education would do this only on exceptional issues such as tuition fees. Tabloids and broadsheets alike were interested in falling standards, exam results, school league tables and annual reports from the inspectors, as long as they were negative.

Special advisers would be in constant touch with specialist reporters, which did make some of them, on occasions, too partial to the departments they were covering. Leaks would often have been made in the run-up to the announcement, usually to senior political correspondents rather than the specialists, for two reasons: to curry favour and in the knowledge they would be less likely to know the background to the new moves and the questions they raised.

As Chapter One has already documented – and the case studies in the chapters that follow demonstrate – Downing Street has become much more concerned with the tabloid press than the old broadsheet papers. With a circulation that has always been considerably smaller than *The Daily Telegraph*'s and which has played hopscotch with *The Times* (*The Guardian* was almost equal in the 1960s, ahead in the 1980s but behind since the price wars of the 1990s), it was not *The Guardian*'s circulation numbers that gave us access, but the key professionals whom we reached: teachers, NHS senior managers, doctors, probation officers, social workers and prison governors. With a Labour government in power, we had the added benefit of being read by an overwhelming majority of their MPs and a large proportion of their members. This was why, absurdly, some Labour ministers were particularly outraged by even small criticisms. Tony Blair pulled in *The Guardian*'s Editor in his early years in Downing Street but had to be told we were not a Labour mouthpiece. Ministers such as David Blunkett tried to rubbish such criticisms by describing them as 'the *Guardian* sneer', while sucking up to *The Sun* (which did not do him much good when his private life imploded).

The growth of specialist reporters has created a paradox – they are better informed than their predecessors. General reporters with no specialist background regularly attended policy department press conferences in the 1960s. Today, different groups of specialist reporters are an intimidating audience for most newly appointed ministers. They will know much more than the minister. Hence the pre-scripted statements and question and answers provided to ministers before press conferences. But overall, the end result is poorer for the reasons set out in Chapter Ten (the seven sins). The tabloids are much more serious serial sinners but the old broadsheets are not free from some of the seven deadly media sins: distortion, a general dumbing down of all papers, putting politics before policy, hunting in packs, too ready to be adversarial, too readily duped and putting the emphasis on the negative. As Anthony Sampson noted as early as 2004, the old broadsheet papers compete to attract a more popular readership and have become more like mid-market papers, such as the *Daily Mail*: 'The qualities can no longer survive commercially on a circulation of well-educated readers dedicated to serious news and analysis and high-minded editorials.'[9]

One reason for the relative decline in influence of editorials has been the rise of the columnist. When I joined *The Guardian* in 1969 there was only one, Peter Jenkins, but when I retired in 2006 there were 28 (including myself). There is no point in being nostalgic, but the beauty of a good editorial is that it has to engage in the arguments on both sides, frequently having to concede that there is some merit in both. Most editors like columnists who are fiercely polemical to engage – and even enrage – their readers, but how do you persuade people with the opposite view if you do not address their arguments? You can't.

Policy-making

Policy-making is a complex process, a mix of new events, old promises, bureaucratic loyalties, party allegiances, manifesto pledges, pressure group campaigns, corporate lobbyists, think tank or select committee reports, research findings, media pressure and legislative cooking time among other factors. Social reform frequently does not start in Parliament and sometimes does not even have to go through the parliamentary process. Pressure groups, think tanks and individual social entrepreneurs work up an idea and proceed to develop and implement it without parliamentary approval. As many as 5,000 charities can be created in a single year. Individuals or groups in public services develop new ways of delivering particular programmes, which then become adopted nationwide. What follows below is to provide readers with an insight into how a secretary of state's office functions. It takes a brief look at the different routes to social reform (charitable campaigns, research-driven or scandal-led change, individual initiatives, whistle-blowers), and then examines the degree to which British government has become more open in the last four decades. Finally it sets out 10 distinctive new approaches to policy-making that Geoff Mulgan, who was at the heart of government policy-making as Head of the Prime Minister's Policy Unit and Director of the government's Strategy Unit, identified during his time there.

Inside a secretary of state's office

One break which gave me an invaluable look at policy-making was an invitation in 1978 from David Ennals, Secretary of State for Health and Social Security, to replace Brian Abel-Smith, Professor of Administration at the London School of Economics and Political Science (LSE), as his special adviser in the last year of the 1974–79 Labour government on secondment from *The Guardian*. What was intriguing about the secondment was that for all the closeness you get to Whitehall as a leader writer, given one-to-one briefings by ministers and senior officials, constant contacts from special advisers, regular lunches with key people, you still do not get the full picture until you have worked inside. I remember how amazed my *Guardian* colleagues were on my return when I gave a seminar on the inside view: the systematic way in which ministerial telephone calls would be listened to on an extension phone by the principal private secretary, newly ironed handkerchief over the mouthpiece, so that the commitments made or not made were recorded. (This was before the age of modern phones, hence the handkerchief.) Then there was the detailed planning which preceded conferences called to debate the latest reports from advisory committees or special working parties. It even included listing the order in which delegates would be called to ensure those supporting the departmental side spoke last. And then there was the civil service's complex rankings and perplexing status symbols worthy of a medieval court: the nearness of your office to the secretary of state's, the width of the carpet – fully fitted or only partly fitted, all known to insiders but bewildering to outsiders. I was forever ringing up officials to ask if I could come over to discuss an issue, only to be told endearingly that they must come over to me.

Remember this was 1979 – over 30 years ago. It was a different era, particularly in terms of openness. Departments in those days kept the mass media at a distance. News was rationed. Many departmental directors of information regarded two media interviews in a week as more than enough. Compare that to the dozen or more one-to-one interviews ministers will give in a day on a White Paper in a 24/7 society with multiple numbers of radio, television and online outlets. There was no Freedom of Information Act then either. Any opportunity to withhold information was seized. One of my tasks as special adviser was to vet the replies that officials had drawn up in answer to written parliamentary questions from MPs. Time and again I would spot a reply suggesting we did not have the information, when we had some but not everything. For example, we would have the information from six of the regional health authorities but not the other eight. Officials had to be instructed to release what we did have.

There were some similarities with newspaper life in the secretary of state's office. The first job of the day was to review the papers before the early morning conference, but the schedules that followed were absurd. The pressure on the secretary of state was intense. The department was too huge, then dealing with health, every aspect of social security (all benefits as well as pensions), plus social care and social services. On some days there could be six separate policy meetings on the agenda, ranging through hospital complaints systems; benefits upratings (with detailed background papers showing their distributional effects); responses to any number of reviews of teaching hospitals, primary care, mental health nursing; new regulations concerning child protection, adoption or fostering; various departmental Bills proceeding through Parliament (plus briefings on other Bills from other departments which affected the department's brief); not to mention speeches that were being made inside and outside Parliament on a vast range of subjects along with newspaper articles that ministers wanted to write, or have written for them, and get placed.

There was not one culture within the department but several. Even within the social security side I was warned there were two – those working on National Insurance benefits and those dealing with welfare (supplementary benefits) where no contributions had been made. Morale within the social security side was much higher than health, but then they were operating a more predictable system. There were corridor-long stacks of information and statistics identifying the people most in need; they knew the decisions they took would be applied (that is, the benefit would go up, or down, or stay the same according to the decision taken); and they knew the distributional effects of all decisions. None of this applied over at the health side. The options were much wider, but the information base was much less precise. There were no simple and clear criteria – such as making society fairer – as there was with social security. Similarly, there was no guarantee that when the decision was taken it would be implemented. This was the age of 14 independent regional health authorities, which were known to have kept visiting secretaries of state waiting outside for ages while they completed their business agenda. All 14 were meant to have a secure centre for mentally disordered offenders, but a decade after this policy had been declared – and earmarked funds forwarded – only two authorities had built them. Finally the effects of decisions implemented were much harder to measure than in social security.

What the media don't see

Media assessments of ministerial competences need sceptical scrutiny. We see only about 10 per cent of their work: the performance in Parliament, outside speeches and media interviews. What we do not see is how good they are at mastering their briefs, how energetically they pursue the policies on which they were elected, how ready they are to hear both sides in a dispute and challenge existing departmental views, how diligently they pursue earlier decisions, which civil servants didn't like and were delaying implementing, the degree to which they encourage younger civil servants in policy meetings to speak up (they often know more about the particulars than the senior people), the respect with which they treat their staff and how firm a grasp they have on the management of their office. Not much of this is observable to outsiders. But that is why senior civil servants want ministers who are good parliamentary performers and media handlers. The mandarins believe they can handle the other 90 per cent, but not the public performances. And good performers help boost morale in the department.

David Ennals scored exceptionally high on the hidden policy-making virtues – as Richard Crossman noted in his *Diaries*[10] – but fell down politically having failed to keep in touch with his party's backbenchers through occasional visits to the Commons tearoom. He paid the price when disruptive industrial relations broke out in the health service in the 'Winter of Discontent' in 1979. When the predictable attacks by opposition parties of his handling of the dispute began in Parliament and he needed support from his own side, there was an ominous silence from his own backbenches, leaving him a lonely and vulnerable figure.

One reason I was invited in as a special adviser was the poor media coverage the department was receiving. The idea came from Patrick Nairn, Permanent Secretary, whom I got to know straight after his appointment. He was a refreshingly open-minded mandarin who was one of the earliest to recognise that government had to become more open. He had come from the Ministry of Defence with no previous experience of health or social security, and sensibly thought one of the best ways of immersing himself in the issues was to deliver a series of speeches. He didn't want to ask his officials for a reading list so he took me to lunch and subsequently got one from me. If I succeeded in this first mission, I totally failed in the later one of improving the department's media relations. A mischievous colleague on *The Guardian*, who in 2009 went to the release of the 1979 government papers under the 30-year rule, sought and received one of my 1978/79 vetting papers. It was from Downing Street's media director, Tom McCaffrey, who was clearly not keen for me to come inside. He wrote to Prime Minister Jim Callaghan, who had to approve the appointment, suggesting that I might be of more use to the government outside writing sympathetic leaders in *The Guardian* than inside providing policy advice. He might have been right.

The man in charge of media relations at the department at the time, Neville Taylor, had an impossible job handling media queries on what was happening in the health service during the 'Winter of Discontent'. The department itself did not know at the start. We were reading the daily newspapers to discover which hospitals had picket lines. But when all this was over Neville had a second problem. He had come from the Ministry for Defence, where it was much easier to keep control over information: the armed services are a disciplined force. There was no such discipline within the professional ranks under the Department of Health and Social Security (DHSS) – doctors, nurses, health managers and social security staff, all of whom had their separate channels of communication with the media and their own axes to grind. Leaks from policy meetings were a regular occurrence, which he found difficult to come to terms with.

The biggest benefit of the secondment for me was the large network of contacts I made within Whitehall, which was invaluable when I rejoined *The Guardian* after Margaret Thatcher took over as prime minister. I no longer needed the department's press office; I knew the direct lines to the relevant officials. Patrick Jenkin, the new secretary of state, complained bitterly about this loss of media control but could do little about it.

Politicians who felt 'we wuz robbed'

One last warning: be wary of politicians who leave office blaming their lack of progressive achievements on conservative civil servants. Michael Meacher, a junior minister in the Department of Trade in the 1974–79 Labour government, wrote just such a 'we wuz robbed' feature for *The Guardian* in 1979.[11] I watched the 1979 general election from inside the DHSS with a group of civil servants who had clearly been committed to improving the health service and raising benefits. They looked glum as the losses of Labour seats mounted up, and one of the few spontaneous cheers that night was for the election of a Labour-supporting man, who had caused them lots of trouble, Frank Field, Director of the Child Poverty Action Group (CPAG). Yet when Thatcher came in, these same people pushed through all the cuts she insisted on having. Ministers who know what they want will get their way. To be fair to Meacher, 18 years on, when he served in the Blair government as an effective environment minister from 1997 to 2003, he was by far the most ready to criticise his ministerial colleagues rather than the civil servants for the government's shortcomings on environmental policy.

What Meacher's 3,000-word article did generate in 1979 was a three-week debate in the letter columns of *The Guardian* on the art of government that is still relevant today, even though big changes have been made. Whitehall was a much more secretive place in the 1970s. There was no Freedom of Information Act, no special select committees, no Green Papers even. *The Sunday Times* tried to open up the system in 1965 by appointing Anthony Howard as Britain's first Whitehall correspondent. He had excellent contacts with the then Labour government, having served as the *New Statesman* political correspondent for the previous three years. His appointment was given a large splash in *The Sunday Times*, but the experiment failed. Harold Wilson, Prime Minister of the day, instructed ministers and civil servants not to talk to him.

Meacher was writing one year before the brilliant British political satire, *Yes Minister*, began on BBC television and taught the public just how devious the British civil service could be. We had had Richard Crossman's three-volume diaries of the 1964–70 Labour government and his battles with the civil service, including his formidable Permanent Secretary, Dame Evelyn Sharp, from which *Yes Minister* drew much material. But it was the 38 editions of *Yes Minister* and its successor, *Yes Prime Minister*, between 1980 and 1988 that brought the internal politics of Whitehall to millions of people in a vivid way. They were introduced to the guileful and eloquent Sir Humphrey Appleby, Permanent Secretary of the fictional Department for Administrative Affairs, subtly guiding the vulnerable and gullible Minister, the Rt Hon Jim Hacker, down paths on which he had no wish to tread. A master of obfuscation, manipulation and glorious circumlocutions, Sir Humphrey saw his prime role as defending the status quo. I was invited after the 1979 general election to a seminar organised by William Plowden at the Royal Institute of Public Administration, where one of the authors present was seeking real-life stories for their forthcoming first series. I left the meeting believing they could never make a comedy series out of the private office of a British Cabinet minister. It went on to win a succession of awards and be voted one of the best sitcom series ever broadcast.

Jim Hacker, Prime Minister in the BBC *Yes Prime Minister* series, demonstrating to his Permanent Secretary, Sir Humphrey Appleby, his understanding of the people who read the British national press:

Hacker: Don't try and tell me about the press. I know exactly who reads the papers: *The Daily Mirror* is read by people who think they run the country; *The Guardian* is read by people who think they ought to run the country; *The Times* is read by people who actually run the country; the *Daily Mail* is read by the wives of people who run the country; the *Financial Times* is read by people who own the country; the *Morning Star* is read by people who think the country ought to be run by another country; *The Daily Telegraph* is read by people who think it already is.

Sir Humphrey: What about *The Sun*?

Bernard (Private Secretary): *Sun* readers don't care who runs the country as long as she's got big tits.

Michael Meacher's 1979 *Guardian* article gave them some more material. It declared:

> There are three main ways in which the civil service subvert the effect of the democratic vote. One is the manipulation of individual Ministers, an exercise in man management which is skilfully orchestrated and on which a great deal of time and care is spent. Second is the isolation of Ministers and the resulting dependence on the Whitehall machine for which a heavy price in policy terms is paid. Third is the exploitation of the

> inter-departmental framework in order to circumvent Ministers who may be opposing the Whitehall consensus.[12]

He then added two others:

> In addition there is the close inter-lock with Establishment interests outside, which often means officials are acting in concert with the extra-parliamentary power structure against Ministers rather than in support of the political manifesto governing party. A further factor is the selective restriction on the dissemination of information, which keeps the power of decision-making limited in fewer hands and rebuts undesirable, undesired or public intrusion, especially into the most sensitive area of policy.

Many of Meacher's criticisms were answered by people who had worked in the same government as him. Charles Morris, former Minister of State at Education, pertinently asked in his letter: 'What action did the individual Minister take when he found that he had been manipulated, isolated, circumvented and browbeaten into submission?' Roger Darlington, a former political adviser at the Home Office, took a similar line. Yes there was manipulation, circumvention, purposeful isolation and selective information flows, but 'the Labour Party tends to blame civil servants for what are inadequacies of Labour ministers'.

It was clear that the Rolls-Royce service was not as smooth or as harmonious as it purported to be. *The Guardian* drew four conclusions from the debate.[13] First, that it was better to have a civil service with genuine creativity and imagination rather than a service of ciphers who would willingly obey the instructions of any regime, however arbitrary or authoritarian. Second, for all the attention that had been focused on civil servants, there had been little progress in leavening the service.

> What is needed is much more mid-career recruitment. But so far the number of senior men brought into the

service has been small. There are no new men at the top. They've all been there a long time. Not surprisingly, some of them are tired, weary and cynical. They've seen it all before. They know it will not work. New people could introduce new enthusiasm which could be contagious.

Third, providing select committees with adequate staff to monitor departments would make it more difficult for ministers to get away with half-answers and half-truths. And lastly was the need to reduce the intense hostility between politicians and civil servants. They lived in separate worlds. Meacher was right to contrast the undue deference extended publicly to ministers with the 'thinly veiled, condescending arrogance behind the scenes'. The barriers between the two worlds had become too high. It was not just inefficient; it had become quite counter-productive. It was time both sides stopped making each other into such stereotyped 'bogey men'.

Charity-driven reforms

Future social historians are likely to be shocked that it was only a decade ago that British society stopped prosecuting child prostitutes – rather than their pimps and adult clients – and finally recognised that they were victims, not criminals. This was primarily due to a joint campaign by two charities, The Children's Society and Barnardo's, which did eventually win widespread media support. But why did it take British society so long to take up such an obvious issue? And why had there been no parliamentary campaigns or media action until the two charities took up the cause? Part of the answer was the long process it took to identify the problem.

It started when The Children's Society began researching into what happens when children run away from home. No one until this research knew even the basic facts. Thanks to The Children Society's research we learned the size and scale of the problem: by the age of 16 one in nine children had run away for a night,[14] some 80,000 a year. Runaways were 'everybody's concern but nobody's responsibility'. They fell through the welfare net, often crossing social service boundaries. Most found a temporary home with relatives or friends, but 25 per cent slept rough, 13 per cent suffered physical injuries and 8 per cent sexual assault. About 1 in 14 ended up begging, stealing or drug dealing. And it was from this last group that most child prostitutes emerged, not just in big cities but in rural towns too. Worse still was the way they were sucked into the criminal justice system – as many as 4,000 in four years – through prosecutions or police cautions. Belatedly, new guidelines, backed by the police and social service chiefs, were issued in 2000 recognising child prostitutes as victims, not criminals. A new Sexual Offences Act in 2003 introduced much heavier sentences for their pimps and clients. But there is still a funding problem for refuges for runaways.

The late 1960s was one of the most fertile decades for the creation of campaigning groups. The two with the highest media profile were CPAG, under Frank Field, and Shelter, the campaign against homelessness launched by Des Wilson. Both were sharp media operators (meant as a compliment because it was an essential aspect of their job) and charismatic characters in different ways. Frank Field was more strategic, not worrying about being in the limelight as long as CPAG's policy proposals received wide coverage. Des Wilson loved the limelight but was also, as a former journalist, an astute judge of what would generate the maximum amount of publicity.

There were multiple other campaigning groups: the Brook Advisory Service providing better birth control; the Pregnancy Advisory Services helping women in need of an abortion; the Disability Income Group, which helped open up a new set of benefits for needs that Beveridge had not recognised; Gingerbread, which helped ensure the needs of lone parents were recognised by the benefits system; Release, which, under Caroline Coon, campaigned for a more rational approach to recreational drugs; and Tim Cook's Alcohol Recovery project addressing the problems of an older addiction problem. The same decade saw the emergence of the first law centres, the launch of Help the Aged and the birth of Alec Dickson's community service volunteers. In 1971 Erin Pizzey set up the first refuge in the world for battered women.

They all exuded energy, commitment, persistence and drive, with most having a proactive approach to the media. Some, indeed, had been given birth by newspapers. The Disability Income Group was launched following a well-crafted letter from two resolute disabled women, Megan du Boisson and Berit Moore, published on *The Guardian* women's page. That same page under Mary Stott, its Editor from 1957 to 1972, helped launch the Pre-school Playgroups Association, Invalids at Home, the National Association for the Welfare of Children in Hospital, the National Council for Carers and the National Housewives' Register.

But if the 1960s was an era for social entrepreneurs, one person stood out above the crowd. He had been creating institutions since the mid-1950s. Michael Young, Lord Young of Dartington, was described by Daniel Bell, one of Harvard's most famous social scientists, as 'probably the most successful "entrepreneur" of social enterprises in the world'.[15] He was a man of many parts: educator, author, academic, consumer advocate, policy-maker, political activist and rebel. Over and above these were two other roles: inventor and social entrepreneur, which made him a unique figure in British 20th-century social reform. As a social entrepreneur his innovations were designed to produce a public good, not a private fortune. The people he helped ran into millions.

Some of his projects – The Open University and the Consumer Association – are known round the world. The total number of his innovations comes to about 60. The majority were simple and practical, meeting an obvious need: Language Line, a telephone interpretation service which professional services – including health, the police and social services – can use when dealing with people who cannot speak English; brain trains on which commuters organise mutually beneficial tutorials for each other; Linkage, which brought together older people without grandchildren, and young people without grandparents; the College of Health, which produced hospital waiting-list guides as well as an advice line on ailments – a pre-cursor to NHS Direct; the Baby Naming Society, which provided advice to non-religious people wanting a ceremony to mark the birth of a child; and with others, the University of the Third Age for retired or near-retired people who want to pursue studies they were unable to follow while at work.

No one ever turned personal experience into more productive ends. In hospital with cancer, he devised the idea of the College of Health – or, as he was originally going to call it with his sense of fun, the Association of Trained Patients. Organising the funeral of his second wife, Sasha, he saw the need to improve the training of funeral directors: the National Funeral College was born. Those of us sucked into some of Michael Young's schemes could only admire the breadth of his personal network, the skill with which he handled the various prima donnas he brought together, and the boyish charm which made it impossible for even the busiest people to turn down his appeal for help.

Michael was very much aware of the importance of the media in providing momentum for his projects. When he launched the Consumer Association *Which?* magazine in 1957, the media, which had turned out in large numbers, failed to report a line for fear of libel. Undaunted, he persuaded Gerald Gardiner, a future Lord Chancellor but at that time the leading libel lawyer in the country, to add his name to the masthead. He then persuaded a *Times* leader writer to write a favourable review and lift-off was achieved. More than a dozen of his projects in his last 20 years were launched in *The Guardian's* weekly *Society* section, which I set up in 1979. One of the last was the School for Social Entrepreneurs, set up in London in 1997, and which subsequently sprouted off-shoots in Liverpool, Leeds, Cornwall and Sydney, Australia.

His two core institutions – the Institute of Community Studies and the Mutual Aid Centre, the first concentrating on research studies and the second ensuring practical projects blossomed – had run down after his death in 2002. But five years ago they were fused together as The Young Foundation and reinvigorated with the arrival of a new director, Geoff Mulgan. There was a certain neat symmetry to this appointment. Michael, who at the age of 29 drafted the famous 1945 Labour Party manifesto and went on to serve the 1945–51 Attlee government as Labour's head of research, left this centre of power to set up the Institute of Community Studies in Bethnal Green, one of London's poorest boroughs. Geoff Mulgan, left his dual position as Head of the Prime Minister's Policy Unit and Director of the government's Strategy Unit in 2005, to take up the challenge of merging the two core institutions and putting The Young Foundation back on the map. This too has been achieved with an elan that would have won Michael's admiration. By 2010 The Young Foundation was employing 60 people, involved in 40 new not-for-profit ventures in 35 local areas around the UK, with staff in New York and Paris as well as London. From an annual deficit of £300,000, the Foundation breaks even, with a turnover of £5 million. To declare an interest, I should add that I became a trustee of the Mutual Aid Centre after Michael's death, and was one of the founding trustees of The Young Foundation, where I still sit. Mulgan moved on to become Director of NESTA (the National Endowment for Science, Technology and the Arts) in June 2011.

The case studies in the chapters that follow document a wide range of other social issues raised by charities that have found a response from Parliament.

Research-driven change

Research-driven change has a long history, going back two centuries or more. The high points include Edwin Chadwick's epic report on the foul state of sanitation in London in 1842 that led to clean water pipes and public health inspection of housing conditions and sewage control; Joseph Rowntree's surveys of poverty in Britain in the 1860s; Charles Booth's 17 volumes on working-class life in London at the end of the 19th century; Beatrice Webb's minority report in the Royal Commission on the Poor Laws report of 1909; and Seebohm Rowntree's 1941 report on the living conditions of the poor in York, which greatly influenced William Beveridge's report in 1942.

Post-Second World War it was the research from Brian Abel-Smith and Peter Townsend in the 1960s that put poverty back on the agenda[16] – and the Joseph Rowntree Foundation's funding that kept it there for the next four decades, as documented later in Chapter Six. Victories for research in this field include the following:

- A doubling of support for younger children following a survey by social scientists in 1997 showed the inadequacy of their benefits compared to those for older children. Gordon Brown acknowledged the contribution which the report *Small fortunes: Spending on children, child poverty and parental sacrifice* had made.[17]
- The decision of the 1983–87 Conservative government to pay Family Credit, a benefit for those in work, to the caring parent rather than the wage earner was highly influenced by both research and a media campaign by CPAG.
- Jane Rowe and Lydia Lambert's 1973 report on *Children who wait*, which identified a large number of children trapped in care, led to the Children Act 1975 that freed up and improved adoption.[18]
- The EPPE (Effective Provision of Pre-school Education) research findings on the positive effects on children's development from pre-school provision between 1999 and 2004 helped drive forward Sure Start schemes and Early Years provision under New Labour.[19]

A fuller account of the role of research in social policy can be found in *Understanding research for social policy and practice* by Saul Becker and Alan Bryman.[20]

Although the Blair government arrived declaring it would be pursuing evidence-based policy-making and would concentrate on 'what works', we also know that in a succession of cases – drugs, crime prevention, sentencing policy and social services – inconvenient evidence was dumped, delayed or deleted from the press releases describing the work. In too many areas it was evidence-bent rather than evidence-based policy-making. (Chapter Three on law and order and Chapter Four on drugs provide a more detailed account of how it declined in the Home Office.) As Ken Young at the Economic and Social Research Council (ESRC) Centre for Evidence-based Policy and Practice noted, a wiser goal for ministers might have been 'evidence-based society' or even, as some cynics suggested had already happened, a concentration on 'policy-based evidence'.

The media's role, at its best, should be to give a platform to sound and critical research, to rescue the dumped or ignored research, to remind the public of it and to alert the public to the politically bent and selective use of research.

Scandal-driven change

Here is a front where the media has a high profile, with its reports of events that go wrong and its coverage of the subsequent court cases and public inquiries that follow. A 'scandal' does not normally become a scandal unless it is constructed as such by the media. Not all the 'scandals' labelled by journalists are genuine. The labels are too easily applied by a media thirsty to find someone to blame and over eager to point the finger at those in charge being always wrong, as Trevor Phillips noted (see Chapter One, p 3). Even so, that is not to deny that there are many genuine scandals, and they run across all areas of social policy: serious child abuse,[21] poor hospital care, inadequate teaching, unsafe or badly ventilated housing. But there is a particularly long history in the police where scandals, rather than research or managerial reviews, have driven change. A three-year study by David Smith, a highly respected researcher, into police–

community relations in London, provided a devastating picture that was published by the Policy Studies Institute in 1983.[22] Its evidence showed a clear readiness by the police to link black people to crime, that racial harassment and racial violence were not taken seriously at a senior command level, and that racism led to routinely aggressive and intimidatory policing. This was kicked into touch by the police just as promptly as the Sheehy Inquiry into police management in 1993 that documented the inadequacies of the current service.[23]

Scandals and their subsequent inquiries had far more success. Tighter controls over eyewitness evidence were introduced after the 1976 Devlin Report into two miscarriages of justice caused by identification parades.[24] Stricter regulation of police interrogation through audio and video recordings followed the Maxwell Confait miscarriage of justice case.[25] Much stricter rules controlling police evidence were prompted by the quashing of convictions in three successive Irish terrorist cases (the Guildford Four, Birmingham Six and Maguire Seven). All this occurred before the murder of Stephen Lawrence, a bright black sixth form student stabbed to death while waiting at a bus stop in 1993. Five white suspects were arrested but never convicted. The police investigation of the crime was condemned by the judicial inquiry into the case chaired by Sir William Macpherson.[26] The inquiry found that the police had made several fundamental errors: failing to give first aid on reaching the scene; failing to follow up obvious leads; and failing to implement key recommendations in the Scarman Inquiry into the 1981 Brixton and Toxteth riots. It concluded that the Metropolitan Police was 'institutionally racist'. This led to the biggest exercise in eliminating racism in public services ever conducted. A new law required 43,000 public bodies spending £400 billion on public services to publish their race equality schemes. These had to include action plans as well as monitoring procedures to ensure progress was tracked.

The media's involvement is equally intriguing. It was the right-wing *Daily Mail* that kept the case alive when the Conservative government was refusing to order an inquiry into the murder of Stephen Lawrence. The paper published photographs of the five suspects naming them 'killers' and inviting them to sue for libel. None did. Just why the paper did this remains uncertain. The paper's

Editor, Paul Dacre, was reported to have known Stephen's father, a decorator, who had carried out some work on Dacre's house. Yet by the time the Labour-appointed Lawrence Inquiry reported in 1999, the *Mail* had reverted to type. Along with *The Telegraph*, it distorted the Inquiry's findings by suggesting that its 'institutional racism' verdict meant everyone in the service was a racist. It meant nothing of the sort.

Service-driven change

One of the most important sources of innovation is professionals within public services who find new ways of doing things. Practitioners, independent of (or despite) government policy, find new ways of delivering services, which then mushroom from the local to the national level. This is happening right across the board. Within housing there are numerous examples. Neighbourhood wardens and stock transfers both emerged from local experiments, before going nationwide and being adopted by governments as 'theirs'. The same happened with council house sales (see pp 362–3). Multi-disciplinary teams working across health and social care dealing with long-term medical conditions began locally before becoming nationwide. The Expert Patient programme, which provides tools and techniques to help patients manage their long-term conditions is another example. Similarly there are numerous education programmes which have started in the same way, including various techniques adopted by The Open University which were later adapted by standard universities. But it is in health where local initiatives have become even bigger than national programmes and been adopted worldwide.

Contrary to the assertions of right-wing commentators on the lack of innovation in the NHS, numerous breakthroughs have been achieved. One early one was the work of Professor Ian Donald, Professor of Midwifery in Glasgow in the 1950s, who developed the use of ultrasound as a revolutionary method of medical diagnosis after seeing it being used in the Glasgow shipyards to look for flaws in metallurgy. With the help of Tom Brown, an engineer, and a fellow obstetrician he proved its feasibility as a key medical diagnostic facility. It is now used worldwide not just for diagnosis but for therapeutic procedures as well. A decade later Sir John Charnley, working in the Wrightington Hospital near Wigan, achieved a total hip replacement operation in 1962. By the 1970s his operation replaced almost all other hip procedures around the world and became the basis on which all modern hip implants have been based. It has brought relief to millions of patients suffering from arthritic conditions. In the US alone, there are 285,000 such operations a year. A third NHS breakthrough was achieved at Oldham General Hospital on 25 July 1978 when Louise Brown became the first person in the world to have been conceived by IVF. Her parents had been trying to conceive for nine years. The two doctors involved, Patrick Steptoe and Robert Edwards, were initially subjected to vitriolic criticism from religious leaders, journalists and politicians. Some 32 years later, Edwards was awarded the 2010 Nobel prize in medicine. Two years after that, the International Committee for Monitoring Assisted Reproductive Technologies (ICMART) calculated that the number of 'test tube babies' had passed the five million threshold.[27]

Whistle-blowers

There is a long history of reforms pushed by whistle-blowers. As long ago as 1854, Florence Nightingale, working as a voluntary matron in the British military hospital in Scutari during the Crimean War, used *The Times* correspondent to document the appalling conditions wounded soldiers were suffering to build up public support for change. For every soldier who died from war wounds, a further five died from typhus, cholera or dysentery, spread in the hospital by the unhygienic conditions. With the help of *The Times* and key contacts with ministers and Queen Victoria, she became the prime mover behind the establishment of two Royal Commissions – the 1857 Inquiry into the Health of the Army that led to the creation of the Army Medical School, and the 1859 Inquiry into the Health of the Army in India that led to the India Office setting up a sanitary department. Meanwhile, in 1860 she used the £45,000 that had been subscribed by the public to a Nightingale Fund to set up the

Nightingale School for Nurses at St Thomas's Hospital, London, the first of its kind in the world.

Some 130-plus years later Graham Pink, a night nurse on the acute geriatric ward of Stepping Hill Hospital, Stockport, wrote an avalanche of 90 letters to a pyramid of people above him about the appalling conditions in his ward. The recipients included health authority officers, district and unit managers, the nurses' regulatory authority, local MPs and the Prime Minister. A highly literate man, Pink graphically described the grimness of life at night for his geriatric patients: there was only one nurse and two auxiliaries for 26 highly dependent patients, all over 75, acutely ill, suffering from senile dementia, disorientation, some needing carrying to commodes, others having massive bowel movements before they could be got to one, important observations about blood transfusions being missed by the pressure of work, some patients frequently calling out for long periods, the lack of opportunity to sit quietly and talk to patients, even patients who had just been told they had cancer.

The letters were passed to *The Guardian* by an MP, not by Pink, but he was contacted and agreed to their publication because the local health authority was still refusing to increase staffing levels. They were published in 1990.[28] The health authority did not dispute Pink's account, but took issue with his assertion that patients were at risk and the wards needed more staff. The local manager insisted three people were enough, Pink wanted four, and a professional expert commissioned by the *Nursing Times* concluded there should be six.

Like many whistle-blowers, Pink was warned by his local managers not to persist with his campaign. This did not deter him. With no dependants or mortgage and near to retirement, he was immune from the usual threats that the NHS bureaucracy can apply. He was suspended when a local newspaper took up his cause, and was finally dismissed in May 1992, after refusing an alternative job. Unlike Nightingale, who also upset the officers and medics running the military hospitals, he did not have powerful contacts. Among Nightingale's close friends was the Secretary of State for War, Sidney Herbert, who had persuaded her to take 38 volunteers out to Crimea rather than the three she had originally planned.

But what Nurse Pink did generate was a national debate on the right of medical staff to speak out about unacceptable conditions. The Royal College of Nursing opened a confidential line for other whistle-blowers, to which 100 other nurses turned with concerns about the standards of care in their hospitals in just over a year. The College called on the Health Secretary, Virginia Bottomley, to ban 'gagging clauses' in health workers' contracts. It suggested the clauses were symptomatic of the 'macho' culture taking root in the NHS. The head of the College criticised NHS managers for 'imitating what they believe to be a business culture. In contrast, most successful businesses recognise that you cannot build a good corporate image on top of underlying problems over staffing and resources.' The College published a report on the helpline calls to coincide with a visit by Virginia Bottomley to address its annual congress.[29] Bottomley refused to ban the clauses, but just two weeks later, she leaked to *The Daily Telegraph* the exclusive news that she was intending to protect whistle-blowers.

The exclusive led the paper under a banner headline 'Bottomley to remove gag on NHS staff' with a sub-head 'Concern over hospital cover-ups brings "whistle-blowers" charter'.[30] The exclusive – along with widespread follow-ups by television and radio reports – coincided with Bottomley's visit to the annual conference of NHS managers in Bournemouth. Both managers and a contingent of health correspondents waited with eager anticipation. Gagging clauses were no longer just affecting medical staff; managers below the top executives were also complaining about gags and 'a climate of fear' in the NHS.[31] They complained about a new corporate structure that regarded any challenge as disloyal or destructive. With the restructured NHS divided into purchasers and providers still only in its second year, there was plenty to comment on. Their leader, Pamela Charlwood, had been given a rousing reception when she declared at the conference: 'It should not have to be a choice between discretion – that is silence – and valour.'[32] Bottomley left them totally confused – a confusion that became even more unclear at the press conference that followed, where many of her answers contradicted earlier assertions.

Optimists pointed to her assertion that 'there is no question of prohibiting staff from going to the press; they will continue to do that as a last resort'. But pessimists had lots of contradictory evidence concerning equally passionate assertions from the Health Secretary about the damage that was caused to staff morale when a colleague turned to the media to air complaints about unsatisfactory conditions. She emphasised that there should be 'a presumption of loyalty'. It was clear that the minister and her officials had clearly not thought through the issue since giving *The Telegraph* its exclusive. The experienced Health Department press officer present was in an invidious position after Bottomley had left, trying to achieve a consensus between the correspondents on what was meant. All that emerged was that staff would probably be given an avenue of appeal to the NHS Chief Executive – and that was dropped by the time the draft guidelines emerged four months later. The guidance, in effect, produced a nationwide gag. Under its proposals, any unauthorised disclosure to the media would represent 'a potentially serious breach of contract'. It sought to bring the NHS under the common law principle, which put employees under 'an implied duty of confidence and fidelity'. With this established, the guidance noted that staff may, as a last resort, 'contemplate' disclosing unsatisfactory conditions to the media, but before doing so they should 'contemplate' the consequences.

Whitehall's lumbering press operations

Although tiny compared to the huge media resources available to Whitehall, the best voluntary organisation press operations have always far outstripped the much larger government communications departments in the speed with which they can answer questions, the depth of knowledge and the recognition of the time and space restraints under which journalists work. All this was in marked contrast to lumbering departmental press procedures, where a three-stage process, riddled with possible misunderstandings and errors, required reporters to call a press officer with their questions; the press officer would then seek the officials who would know the answers; and then in turn relay those answers back to the journalist, but would often be unable to answer follow-up questions. Built on the principle of the children's party game Chinese whispers, where the sentence whispered into the ear of the first child in the ring becomes completely distorted by the end of the ring, Whitehall's media operation had similar distorting effects.

Some departmental media operations have improved – and there have always been some exceptionally good press officers – but overall Whitehall is still much slower, less nimble, and worst of all, often less truthful than the best charity press operations. The charities learned it was in their own interests to be honest. They would not be trusted otherwise.

Ivor Gaber, broadcaster, researcher and media academic, identified an institutional failing that undermines trust in government communications: the contradictory principles set out in the code of practice which Whitehall press officers are expected to follow. On the one hand, the code requires press officers to be 'objective and explanatory, not biased or polemical ... and not liable to be misrepresented as being party political'. But at the same time, they are also expected to 'present, describe and justify the thinking behind the policies of the minister, be ready to promote the policies of the department and the government as a whole and make as positive a case as the facts warrant'. As Gaber noted:

> Taking the two institutions together, civil servants (mindful of the demands of the code, the wishes of their ministers and their own careers) are being asked to make daily judgments of Solomon. For surely it is problematical, at the very least, to urge government press officers to 'justify the thinking behind government policy and ... help the public – by helping journalists – to understand the policies of the government of the day' without appearing to be anything other than cheerleaders for the government?[33]

He added one additional important problem: politicians want to maximise the positive and minimise the negative. In order to achieve this they have to 'play the media's game' by meeting the news media's own criteria as to what constitutes 'news'. This means presenting their information in ways that suggest:

- it is 'new' (when many government initiatives are not);
- it represents part of a coherent 'narrative' (when in the real world, many situations and processes are fragmented);
- it provides immediate and readily understandable solutions to recognisable problems (when in fact, life is usually more complex);
- it is 'dramatic' (when most processes of service delivery are not).

He went on: 'These journalistic imperatives create a situation in which the authors of government press releases clearly feel obliged to present an almost non-stop torrent of good news, exciting initiatives and departmental triumphs.' To prove his point he listed nine good news press releases from the Department of Health in the first three weeks of May 2008, and some 15 in April 2008. He suggested these unremitting good news press releases made it 'almost inevitable that press officers will find it difficult, if not impossible, to strike the right balance between delivering messages that "justify government policies ... and make a positive case" whilst at the same time being "objective, explanatory and unbiased"'.[34]

Access to information

Has there ever been a golden age for journalism? I would suggest there has never been a better opportunity than in the first six years of this century. We had never had access to more sources of information than in that period. Yet, because of the seven sins of the media set out in more detail in Chapter Ten of this book, we just didn't make sufficient use of them. I was shocked on returning from two years in the US to join *The Guardian* in 1969 at just how little information was available in the UK. There were few inspectors of services and none producing detailed reports of their inspections. There was little public audit; no Freedom of Information Act; no specialist select committees in Parliament; and a minimum of consultation documents from government departments before hard policy emerged.

The idea that newspapers can hold governments to account is a professional myth. In our scattergun way, we are able to pursue wrongs on many fronts, and indeed do so. These are important, but fall far short of what is actually necessary. Take education. The UK has 25,000 schools. Most newspapers had only one education reporter. *The Guardian* had six or seven if you added up the *Guardian Education* reporting staff. But how could even seven cover such a service, not just covering schools but all the many further education colleges, along with 150 universities? They could not. But Ofsted could, with its 2,000 inspectors, who not only provided detailed reports on each individual school (after a team of inspectors had spent days there), but also thematic reports. The same applied to the health service, housing, social services, the police, prisons, probation and the prosecution service. The inspectors of these services all wrote reports on the individual organisations within their field, and thematic reports addressing current problems and future challenges.

Add to this the Audit Commission, with another 2,000 staff, which was not even in existence in the 1960s, and a much beefed-up National Audit Office, which was. The Audit Commission, which the Conservative/Liberal Democrat Coalition now plans to close down, pioneered new ways of inspecting local authority services – its inspection teams included a chief executive and a political leader from one authority to help inspect another. In this way they learned from each other. Here was an inspection approach that was being applauded by the people it was inspecting, as I discovered at a conference organised to review its progress. Add in select committees with their specialist advisers scrutinising the field that Whitehall departments cover, the separate competency reviews of individual departments and a Freedom of Information Act, which was too constrained but did get more information disclosed, and there was real momentum in making British public administration more transparent. A further fillip was the much more consultative approach to policy-making – Green Papers before White Papers, consultative Bills before real Bills.

There was social change too. Permanent secretaries – not just ministers – being ready to meet over lunch; less coyness about civil servants briefing journalists in the absence of ministers; an increase in residential conferences where journalists rubbed shoulders with civil servants and got to know them socially; more direct contact by telephone with civil servants (despite control efforts by press officers). And change was also happening outside Whitehall. Professional associations – such as the British Medical Association (BMA), Association of Chief Police Officers (ACPO) and Chartered Institute of Housing (CIH) – which at one time had concentrated on their inside track to policy-makers, began using the media outside to gather support for their lobbying. Later, at the end of the 1990s, a burgeoning of think tanks, some with excellent inside contacts with government advisers, were eager to get media coverage of their pamphlets, reports and conferences. And over a longer period, the heavyweight research organisations continued to grow: the Joseph Rowntree Foundation (JRF) on poverty and housing; the Institute for Fiscal Studies on social security; The King's Fund on health; and the Pensions Policy Institute on pension policies. All were producing serious work along with the trio of penal reform groups – Nacro, the Penal Reform Trust and the Howard League for Penal Reform (mentioned later in Chapter Four).

Perhaps more important than the Freedom of Information Act was the spread of the photocopier. Prior to having photocopies, most policy leaks came from ministers over a lunch table or a weekend telephone talk with a minister or special adviser. The lunch had a choreography of its own: gossip first course; politics second; policy leak third, with dashes to the toilet to write it up before it all got forgotten. But the dear old photocopier changed all this. When I first joined *The Guardian*, the photocopier was in a locked room, for which you had to obtain the key from a very possessive Editor's secretary. But that was 1969. Government organisations even then were making much freer use of the machines. It was not just the disgruntled who were photocopying documents and forwarding them in brown paper parcels, however. It was easier for ministers to give you a photocopy to ensure you had the right statistics.

For self-confident secretaries of state, of whom there have been many, press briefings were a time to show off. Michael Heseltine at the Environment Department would have a string of civil servants down the side of the room and have no fear of demonstrating gaps in his knowledge, calling on the officials to deal with the specialist press, wanting technical details for house builders or developers. Barbara Castle, who delegated large amounts of her policy-making down to her ministers of state at the DHSS, would always insist on doing the one-to-one briefing of leader writers herself. This was often embarrassing as she clearly did not know the answers to many of the more detailed questions that needed clarification. Douglas Hurd, who took over the Home Office from Leon Brittan, was impressive in paying tribute at his first press briefing for home affairs specialists to his fallen predecessor's capacity for getting through paperwork – 'I will not be able to compete'. Hurd used to hold lunches for a quartet from *The Guardian* – the Editor, leader writer, political editor and home affairs correspondent – sitting round his huge desk, which was still able to accommodate large plates of sandwiches without disturbing his piles of personal papers. What he forgot was that one of us, from years of putting pages of type to bed, could read proofs upside down. On at least one occasion, we came away with an exclusive that we were not meant to have.

On the other hand, as leader writers used to say, the undoubted expansion of access to information did not remove all restraints. There is still restricted access to key background papers; much information is still only released after policy decisions have been made; a media spread across the political spectrum counter-balances to some extent each other's influence; public opinion is swung only by sustained campaigns, which the press is reluctant to engage in; and a limitation of space, made worse by modern design and smaller-sized papers, reduces impact.

There were many big stories we missed because of a deep-rooted British respect for discretion. Only in England could a Lord Chief Justice remain in office despite suffering from senile dementia, growing almost inaudible in court, and sometimes falling asleep on the bench. The tragic failings of Lord Widgery remained unpublicised until detailed by Hugo Young in his *Guardian* column in 1984, four years after Widgery's retirement.[35] At least his successor, Lord Lane, had his shortcomings scrutinised at length by a new corps of legal correspondents, who catalogued his irascibility, his seemingly unpredictable dislikes and his refusal to recognise the structural weakness of the criminal justice system.

New Labour's new approach to policy-making

In a fascinating chapter in *Social justice: Building a fairer Britain*, Geoff Mulgan, who between 1997 and 2004 worked at the heart of the Labour government's policy-making machine, sets out 10 new approaches adopted by New Labour.[36] He was quite open about the timidity of the government's initial approach and its ambiguous relations with the senior civil service:

> Labour was very timid in its thinking about policy tools and Whitehall machineries.... Labour in the past had tended to oscillate between a rather naive assumption that the civil service is a Rolls-Royce machine just waiting to be told where to go, and a paranoid assumption that its main objective was to frustrate Labour's radical intentions. Yet in power and particularly in social policy, Labour has been highly innovative, and has learned to use more finely tuned policy tools.[37]

The ten were:

• A move beyond the traditional linear approach to policy, which took ideas from manifestos, through Green and White Papers, to legislation. Instead it recognised that policy and delivery were much better understood as continuous processes of implementation, assessment and improvement in which every few years legislation symbolised change rather than being at the heart of it.

• Moving away from the old model dominated by a small cadre of specialist policy-makers, towards a much more open system in which large numbers of outsiders were employed within government. Half the staff in the Prime Minister's Strategy Unit and Social Exclusion Unit were drawn from universities, non-governmental organisations and business.

• Tighter performance management introduced across a wide area: literacy and numeracy in schools, treatment of cancer and heart disease, burglary and street crime. Mulgan conceded that targets could create perverse incentives and some had been ill designed, but 'the need to use some transparent metrics to judge success and hold agencies to account is now widely accepted'.[38]

- Policy that is more evidence-based, 'or to be more precise, more informed by evidence, with extensive use of pilots, pathfinders, trailblazers and systematic evidence reviews'.[39]

- More joined-up policies, among them Sure Start, New Deal for Communities, programmes for rough sleepers and youth justice.

- A host of new roles to supplement traditional professionals, including learning mentors and teaching assistants in schools, community support officers in the police and personal advisers in Jobcentre Plus.

- Tax credits, which after some serious teething troubles, relinked welfare to the workplace and transformed the living standards of millions of people. Mulgan conceded that the system still had some serious design problems to sort out.

- A stronger emphasis on contestability and diversity, breaking open public sector monopolies and allowing private and non-profit organisations to compete. Where this was once restricted to social care, it now applied in prisons, drug treatment programmes, employment services, welfare and health. Mulgan conceded that early private finance initiative (PFI) contracts had been flawed, cream-skimming had taken place, and the need to ensure there were sufficient numbers of providers was a challenge.

- More emphasis on prevention: preventing diseases and behaviours that cause health inequality, taking earlier action to prevent children falling into patterns of risk and raising spending on crime prevention, all disproving the cynical conventional wisdom that politicians will never spend in ways that will deliver results only in 10 or 20 years' time.

- More long-termism through five-year strategies and recognition that most things worth doing take time. This had been helped by relative economic and political stability – Mulgan was writing in 2005 – but it also reflected the seriousness of purpose of many ministers. As *The Times* had reported on the government's Strategic Audit in 2003: 'governments usually overestimate how much can be achieved in the short term, and underestimate how much can be achieved in the long term'.[40]

There will be many who will want to question some of these approaches. To be fair to Mulgan, in his own fuller version he did not duck the downsides. He acknowledged:

> Each of these innovative approaches is admirable and more likely to succeed than the traditional models of policy and delivery. But none of them is unproblematic. Ministerial understanding of, and interest in, the practicalities of delivery remain very uneven. The fact that so few Labour ministers had ever run anything before entering Parliament remains a problem and continues to encourage a spin culture which values announcements and the appearance of activity rather than real achievements and makes British government very different from counterparts in Europe that are largely populated with ministers who have run towns, cities and regions. This lack of practical delivery experience is also found amongst much of the senior civil service.[41]

The scale of change over the last 40 years between the different departments has been huge, but by no means uniform. Hence the need for the seven case study chapters that follow. They begin with issues where the media has had most influence – crime, drugs, asylum – but, as the later chapters show, they are not absent from other areas, particularly health and education. The last serious look at this issue was the well-received *Social policy, the media and misrepresentation*, edited by Bob Franklin, and published by Routledge. But this was 12 years ago in 1999. There have been huge changes since then.

Notes

[1] Nicholas Timmins (2001) *The five giants: a biography of the welfare state*, London: HarperCollins.

[2] Howard Glennerster (2000) *British social policy, 1945 to the present*, 2nd edn, Oxford: Blackwell.

[3] William Beveridge (1942) *Social insurance and allied services*, Cmnd 6404, London: HMSO.

[4] Paul Addison (1975) *The road to 1945: British politics and the Second World War*, London: Cape.

[5] Kieran Walshe (2010) 'Reorganisation of the NHS in England', *BMJ* 2010, 341: c3843.

[6] Howard Glennerster (2007) *British social policy: 1945 to the present*, London: Blackwell-Wiley.

[7] W. Baumol (1967) 'Macro economics of unbalanced growth, anatomy of urban crisis', *American Economic Review*, vol 57, pp 415–26.

[8] Howard Glennerster (2010) 'The sustainability of western welfare states', in *Oxford handbook of the welfare state*, Oxford: Oxford University Press, ch 47, pp 689-702.

[9] Anthony Sampson (2004) *Who runs this place? The anatomy of Britain in the 21st century*, London: John Murray Publishers.

[10] Richard Crossman (1977) *The diaries of a cabinet minister*, vol 3, London: Hamish Hamilton and Jonathan Cape, p 1306.

[11] Michael Meacher (1979) *The Guardian*, 14 June.

[12] Ibid.

[13] *The Guardian* (1979) Editorial, 5 July.

[14] Malcolm Dean (2001) 'Running battle to close the gap', *The Guardian*, 28 March.

[15] Daniel Bell (2005) 'The sociologist as man of action', in G. Dench, T. Flower and K. Gavron (eds) *Young at eighty: The prolific public life of Michael Young*, Manchester: Carcanet Press, p 125.

[16] Brian Abel-Smith and Peter Townsend (1965) *The poor and the poorest*, London: Bell.

[17] S. Middleton, K. Ashworth and J. Braithwaite (1997) *Small fortunes: Spending on children, child poverty and parental sacrifice*, York: Joseph Rowntree Foundation.

[18] Jane Rowe and Lydia Lambert (1973) *Children who wait: A study of children needing substitute families*, London: Association of British Adoption Agencies.

[19] DfES (Department for Education and Skills) (2006) *Final report on EPPE (Effective Provision of Pre-School Education)*, London: The Stationery Office.

[20] Saul Becker and Alan Bryman (eds) (2004) *Understanding research for social policy: Themes, methods and approaches*, Bristol: The Policy Press.

[21] Michael Little (1995) *Looking after children: Research into practice*, London: Dartington Social Research Unit for HMSO.

[22] David Smith (1983) *Police and people in London*, London: Policy Studies Institute.

[23] Home Office et al (1993) *Inquiry into police responsibilities and rewards (Sheehy Inquiry)*, London: HMSO.

[24] P.A. Devlin (1976) *Report to the Secretary of State for the Home Department of the Departmental Committee on evidence of identification in criminal cases (Devlin Report)*, HC 338, London: HMSO.

[25] (1976) Maxwell Confait (Inquiry into death): the case concerned_police interrogation of children and adults with learning difficulties without parent or guardian present.

[26] The judicial inquiry into the death of Stephen Lawrence, set up in 1997, was published by the Home Office in 1999 as *The Stephen Lawrence Inquiry: Report of an Inquiry by Sir William Macpherson of Cluny*, Cm 4262-I, London: The Stationery Office.

[27] James Gallagher (2012) 'Five millionth "test tube baby" ', BBC website, 2 July.

[28] 'Nurse Pink Letters', *Guardian Society*, 11 April 1990.

[29] *The Guardian*, 28 April 1992.

[30] 'Bottomley to remove gag on NHS staff', *The Daily Telegraph*, 12 June 1992.

[31] *The Guardian* (1992) Leader, 13 June.

[32] Ibid.

[33] Ivor Gaber (2009) 'Exploring the paradox of liberal democracy: more political communications equals less public trust', *The Political Quarterly*, vol 80, no 1, pp 84-91 (at p 84).

[34] Ibid.

[35] Hugo Young (1984) *The Guardian*, 2 July.

[36] Geoff Mulgan (2005) 'Going with and against the grain: social policy in practice since 1997', in N. Pearce and W. Paxton (eds) *Social justice: Building a fairer Britain*, London: Institute for Public Policy Research/Politico's, pp 88-106.

[37] Ibid, p 99.

[38] Ibid.

[39] Ibid.

[40] Ibid, p 102.

[41] Ibid.

THREE

Law and order

On 19 July 2004, the 10th anniversary of becoming the Labour Party's leader, Tony Blair delivered a speech preempting the official launch of a new five-year strategy for the criminal justice system the following day. At the heart of the new strategy was a welcome new system of community policing. Initially developed in Devon and Cornwall in the 1970s by Chief Constable John Alderson before spreading to other forces, community policing later became sidelined, but not before being exported to Chicago in the US from where it was now to be re-imported. It looked like a belated lesson had been re-learned: not even doubling the 140,000 officers at that time (instead of the 13,000 that had been added since Labour came into power in 1997) would be sufficient for policing a society of 60 million people. Policing required the help of the community. In return the Home Office was promising a new way of policing, with locally based neighbourhood teams meeting the priorities of the residents and answerable to them. There had already been successful public reassurance policing pilots on the Chicago model, much of the work concerned with low-level crime and public nuisance – noise, incivility and rowdy behaviour. Now this was to become more systematic.

A second welcome initiative in the package was a promise to press ahead belatedly with the alternatives to prison set out in the Halliday Report[1] just before the 2001 general election. The aim was a big expansion of community programmes – the number of youth inclusion programmes was to be doubled to 140; electronic tagging was to be doubled to 18,000; and by 2008 there was a promise of 200,000 drug treatment places. Add in the contribution to tackling the causes of crime from pre-school programmes such as 2,500 Sure Start children's centres, plus other family support projects, and this amounted to a major shift towards a more 'liberal' non-custodial direction.

There was a huge response to this speech, but very little concerned these new liberal policy developments. What put it on the front pages was the declaration in the Prime Minister's second paragraph. It began uncontroversially enough: 'Today's strategy is the culmination of a journey of change for progressive politics and for the country.'[2] But it then continued with the headline-grabbing line: 'It marks the end of the 1960s liberal, social consensus on law and order.' A surprisingly liberal crime programme from New Labour had to be packaged in hard-line wrapping. Once again most of the media was duped.

It was 'the end of the liberal consensus' that dominated the massive coverage of every television news channel, radio station and newspaper in the UK the following day. It was, of course, total nonsense, as *The Guardian* Editorial,[3] among a few others, noted. The liberal consensus had died over a decade previously, when a succession of hard-line laws introduced by Michael Howard were not only endorsed by Labour, but even implemented and extended after 1997. Professor Rod Morgan, Chair of the Youth Justice Board, noted later:

> With a single stroke the New Labour leadership achieved three things. The Prime Minister pre-emptively: set the stage for the Labour Party national policy forum due to take place at the end of July; fired the first Conservative-Party-out-manoeuvring shots in the general election then predicted to take place in May 2005; and further distanced New Labour from its old Labour roots.[4]

Polly Toynbee, in her *Guardian* column, had to give Blair some grudging praise:

> The man has a political genius. Public opinion flows in his veins before any report lands on his desk. Ten years as leader and he hasn't lost the knack of slapping a populist headline straight on to the front pages. So when he trumpets (and leaks in advance) that his new crime policy marks 'the end of the 1960s liberal consensus on law and order', this preposterous nonsense strikes

into every home. *The Guardian* was a prime target too. How they must have tee-heed with glee in Downing Street as he penned it (it was his own). This'll send those bastards apoplectic! Serves them right for their non-stop Iraq whingeing, give them something to get really incandescent about! And, indeed we are duly absolutely seething. But the angrier we are, the more certain he is that his one-line smart bomb went straight down the right chimney. Great shot, Tony![5]

But more seriously, she rightly went on to warn him about the longer-term consequences of his headline-chasing camouflage on crime:

So, 10 years on, Blair is back where he began. But how clever is that? Not very. All these years in power and a Labour government is still behaving like insurgents in a Tory Britain, as if no progress has been won since 1994. In all this time has Labour really made so little impact on public opinion that it still has to out-Tory the others on almost all fronts? Wrong-footing Tories may be good short-term politics, but if it's only done by occupying their ground then Conservatism keeps winning and not social democracy. The [Iraq] war is about the only issue on which Blair has sought to change public opinion. His social democratic deeds are mostly done sotto voce without explaining or persuading as he goes.

Who's to blame for penal populism?

As set out later in Chapter Four on drugs, disentangling the labyrinthine links between politicians and press in the field of law and order is a difficult challenge. They live in a symbiotic relationship. With drugs, the tabloids act as the host, the politicians as the parasite. With law and order it is the other way round. The main fault for the rise in penal populism in the last two decades can be laid more fairly at the feet of politicians rather than the press, although the tabloids have been eager accomplices. For the first 70 years of the 20th century, law and order was not a partisan issue. It was regarded as a difficult and complicated issue that was best left to the professionals in the field and the experts within the Home Office. Professors David Downes and Rod Morgan studied all the party manifestos post-Second World War and found there was no partisan mention of law and order until the 1970 general election. There were, of course, debates and votes on capital punishment, but the divisions on this issue were within parties, rather than between them, and the votes were free from whip pressure. In their chapter in the second edition of *The Oxford handbook of criminology*, these two leading criminologists note their surprise at their finding:

> This longstanding absence from party political discourse and contention is remarkable – law and order embraces highly emotive and fundamental issues. Few topics can routinely arouse such passionate debate. That law and order were relatively insulated from the realm of party politics for so long testified perhaps to the strength of belief that crime, like the weather, is beyond political influence; and that the operation of the law and criminal justice should be above it.[6]

Bipartisanship covered a wide field including the response to crime, the nature of policing and sentencing policy. 'Even at the fringes of political life, few challenges were made to so profound a consensus.' The series of Nuffield studies on British general election campaigns complemented the criminologists' findings.[7] These have noted that law and order topics did not figure in the elections of 1945, 1950, 1951, 1955 and 1959. Neither did the 'race riots' in Nottingham and Notting Hill in 1958 nor the Street Offences Act of 1959 impinge on the 1959 election campaign. Despite rising crime rates and heavy media coverage of youth cults of the day, there was no attempt by party leaders to exploit law and order. Even in the 1964 general election, after 13 years of continuous Conservative government, the Labour Party said nothing about law and order, or the government's record in the face of crime rates which had risen steeply since the mid-1950s. But in the 1966 election, after two years of governing with a narrow majority, the Labour Party's manifesto pledged to strengthen the police, reform juvenile justice and modernise the prison system. It was only implicitly critical of the Conservatives: 'For years Britain has been confronted by a rising crime rate, overcrowded prisons and many seriously undermanned police forces.' Yet even then, Downes and Morgan noted: 'There was no explicit suggestion that the level or form of crime was itself attributable to the politics of the opposition parties'.[8]

The first explicit sign of politicisation came in the 1970 general election, when it was raised in a modest way in the successful Conservative manifesto declaring 'the (1964–70) Labour governments cannot entirely shrug off responsibility for the present situation'. The 'situation' was the 'serious rise in crime and violence'. The Conservatives laid this situation at the door of the Labour government, pointing to their restricted 'police recruitment at a critical time'. More seriously, the Tories also drew a clear connection between crime, protest and disorders associated with industrial disputes, which until then had been quite separate issues. The Conservative manifesto declared that the current law 'needs modernising and clarifying and needs to be made less slow and cumbersome, particularly for dealing with offences – forced entry [squatters], obstruction [picketing], and violent offences connected with public order – peculiar to the age of demonstration and disruption' (brackets added).

Labour asserted it did recognise that it was the first duty of government to protect the citizen against violence, intimidation and crime, and undertook to prosecute vigorously 'the fight against vandals and law breakers'. But it also decried in wounded tones the breakdown of bipartisanship about crime: 'Nothing could be more cynical than the current attempts of our opponents to exploit for Party political ends the issue of crime and law enforcement.' It should be noted that by 1970 UK politicians would have seen the degree to which law and order was being used to achieve media coverage and political support in the US. It was not enough for Barry Goldwater to unseat the powerful Lyndon Johnson in his bid for the 1964 presidency, but it played an important role in helping Richard Nixon win in the 1968 election. (To be fair, divisions within the Democratic Party, the assassination of Bobby Kennedy and the violent police break-up of the anti-Vietnam War demonstrations outside the Democratic Convention in Chicago were in combination more important. I was there at the time, working for a Democratic congressman from New York, James Scheuer, and the Pennsylvania Democratic senator Jo Clark, on a Harkness Fellowship. Jim Scheuer was active in campaigning for safer streets in his Bronx congressional district.)

There were two UK general elections in 1974, the first in February, which with Liberal Party support allowed Labour to return to power, and the second in October, when Labour achieved a small majority on its own. In both elections Labour said little about law and order. By contrast the Conservatives devoted a substantial part of their manifesto to the issue. Downes and Morgan emphasised the Conservative Party's change of tack in the October 1974 election: 'It vigorously pursued the approach of attacking the Government's record, but with a significant difference. On this occasion it was the Government's integrity rather than its policies and priorities that was condemned.' The authors point to the veiled references in the manifesto of support for the National Union of Mineworkers in its successful deployment of mass picketing in 1973, by Labour MPs and key members of the Shadow Cabinet, such as Tony Benn. There was also the Clay Cross affair, in which the Labour government had refused to press for the prosecution of Labour councillors who would not increase rents in line with Conservative legalisation. After emphasising the importance of law and order in a civil society, the Conservative manifesto went on: 'recently the law has been under attack and these attacks have all too often been condoned and even endorsed by members and supporters of the present Government'.

This prompted Downes and Morgan to suggest that by 1974, the Conservatives had established that law and order could assume as much prominence in major party election manifestos as housing, transport and urban renewal. More worrying for Labour was the way the Conservative Party – now under the leadership of Margaret Thatcher – was fusing together criminal law-breaking with industrial relations disputes that at times involved aggressive strike-related actions. Given the strong links between the unions and Labour, the party's politicians felt inhibited from following the Conservative line on union actions. Nor was it ready to break with the more liberal traditions on penal reform that had been part of the party tradition best encapsulated in Roy Jenkins' tenure as Home Secretary.

Labour's 'Winter of Discontent'

Support for trade union action became even more difficult for Labour ministers in the 'Winter of Discontent' in 1978/79. Widespread strikes by public service workers under the Labour government's pay restrictions led to hospital picket lines, mountains of uncleared rubbish and seriously disrupted transport across the country. By this time I was a policy adviser within the DHSS on secondment from *The Guardian*, watching ministers facing a dilemma, when striking civil servants for a short period posted picket lines outside government departments. Most ministers used their offices within the parliamentary building to avoid the picket lines, but David Owen, Foreign Secretary, openly strode through the Foreign Office picket line, saying he was happy to do so. It had a good run on the television news. (Within the DHSS, where Owen had been a proactive health minister, the debate was over whether his public school education or his St Thomas's Hospital medical training prompted the move. A well-known aphorism 'You can tell a Tommy's doctor anywhere, but you cannot tell him anything' was widely quoted.)

By this time there were media stories on striking porters refusing to allow dead patients to be moved across hospital picket lines. There could only have been a handful of such cases, but the tabloids made the issue a defining one. The NHS was a centre of media attention because the government was under pressure to allow the nurses a more generous award. Just such a concession, which was eventually granted, was understandably seen by other Cabinet ministers as a breach that would break the dam. David Ennals, Secretary of State, was having a torrid time, not least because he had been diagnosed with a serious health problem. Feeling he had to be seen to be engaging with hospital staff, he went to a local hospital where disastrously he was pictured holding a new-born baby. The tabloids went for the jugular, accusing him of electioneering when the country was grinding to a halt. It all fell in to the main media narrative: was Britain ungovernable? All this was manna from heaven for Thatcher in the run-up to the 1979 election. She openly and persistently blamed Labour for rising crime and the disorder of the 'Winter of Discontent'. The tabloids were happy to relay the message. Her manifesto was studded with pay perks for the police, tougher custody sentences, extra spending on crime control, new 'short, sharp shock' regimes in detention centres for young offenders, along with revised laws on picketing to prevent 'violence, intimidation and obstruction'. Law and order had moved decisively into the realm of day-to-day party politics.

Margaret Thatcher comes to power

The Conservatives won a comfortable majority on 3 May 1979. In their book analysing the 1979 election, David Butler and Dennis Kavanagh suggested that Thatcher's use of tough law and order messages was one of the main drivers of her electoral success.[9] Opinion polls gave the same message: across a range of policy issues tested by MORI polls between August 1978 and April 1979, no policy placed the Conservatives so far ahead in terms of public confidence as law and order. They enjoyed a 30-point lead over Labour, compared to 11 points on unemployment, and equal scores on inflation and industrial relations. One third of Labour voters and almost half of the Liberal supporters expressing a clear preference on the issue thought the Tories had a better law and order policy than their own parties.

But for all the fire and brimstone in the 1979 Tory manifesto, for the first three of the four Conservative administrations that followed, law and order changes (as against the much tighter industrial relations legislation) were much more constrained than might have been expected. Unlike some of his successors, Willie Whitelaw (who served as Home Secretary from May 1979 to June 1983) did listen to the specialists in his department and accepted the need to divert from the prison system many of its non-violent offenders. A plan to do this through executive order was scuppered by the 1980 annual Conservative Party conference, which had always been seen by people on the left as a mere talked-to shop, but became a force to be taken seriously on law and order.

There was more success in dealing with the way juvenile offenders were treated. A new consortium of reform groups, New Approaches to Juvenile Crime, brought together Nacro (National Association for the Care and Resettlement of Offenders) with probation and social work professionals. They helped counter the 'short, sharp shock' rhetoric. Nacro, under Paul Cavadino in its press office, had developed a very successful media strategy. He spotted this was a world where a major report – of which there were many in the criminal justice world – would only get one bite by the media: just on the day of publication. Cavadino would monitor what was reported and then draw up other important facts and proposals that had not been relayed. These then, with a 'new nose', as introductory paragraphs are known in the trade, would be released through a series of Sunday-for-Monday press releases, a day on which fresh news stories are always in short supply. The 'old' news was frequently gratefully received in its dressed-up 'new' clothes. The new consortium eagerly followed the same tactic. Even better, through its chair, Lady Faithful, a former Social Services director and a Conservative peer, amendments were added to the Criminal Justice Act 1982 which led to a massive reduction in the number of juveniles receiving custody – it dropped dramatically from 7,000 in 1980 to 2,000 in 1987. Here in the 1980s, then, was a 'liberal', media-savvy pressure group not just changing headlines but also having a significant impact on legislation and, more importantly, the treatment of offenders. Nor was a Conservative government unreceptive to such pressure. This was a constructive period preceding one dominated by a rampant, sharp-toothed tabloid press.

A new charity, the Prison Reform Trust (PRT), emerged in 1981 which produced a succession of serious reports addressing the shortfalls in the criminal justice system. (It also helped launch Smart Justice, a separate crime reduction campaign between 2002 and 2008, which included wooing the popular press to take up serious criminal justice issues. It had some success, particularly with *The Daily Mirror*.) Together with Nacro and the Howard League for Penal Reform, which dates back to 1866, making it the oldest penal reform group in the world, this trio of charities neatly complemented each other. Nacro was running large numbers of prevention and resettlement programmes, helping tens of thousands of offenders or potential offenders; PRT was producing an impressive list of studies documenting how the criminal justice system could be improved; and the Howard League was membership-based, which later included separate student organisations as well as taking up individual cases – particular juveniles – to establish new rights through the courts. All three played a key part in creating a hidden consensus which all three main political parties supported by the mid-1980s. All three knew how to use the media well. It had three common strands:

- support for the police but recognition that the service needed to improve its effectiveness;
- ensuring crime prevention and victim support were priorities;
- accepting the need for extended custodial sentences where appropriate for the most serious offenders, but equally important

support for an enhanced range of non-custodial measures for less serious crimes.

Willie Whitelaw and Douglas Hurd, who each spent four years as Home Secretary (1979–83 and 1985–89 respectively), played crucial roles in steering the Conservative Party behind the consensus. Whitelaw, a former army officer, had been in favour of the 'short, sharp shock', but he accepted the new regime was not working so it did not last long. Even more to his credit was Whitelaw's readiness to support the launch of the first British Crime Survey (BCS) in 1982, a project over which even officials within the Home Office were divided at the beginning.[10] This was a period when only half of all crimes were being reported and only half those reported were being recorded. The case for a more accurate picture was pushed by Home Office researchers. The aim of the BCS was to conduct large surveys of individuals to record the criminal incidents in which they had been victims. This helped pick up the dark (unreported or unrecorded) side of crime and free the statistics from changes and variations in local recording practices.

Beyond capturing a truer picture of crime (although it missed shoplifting and most juvenile crime), the BCS also provided a much more detailed picture of fear of crime than any other survey had ever done. It eventually moved from an intermittent survey to a continuous exercise under New Labour. What was brave about Whitelaw's decision was that it was obviously going to record much higher crime numbers. I remember how nervous some of the key researchers were. But this was before penal populism broke out. The earlier surveys were treated seriously by the media and alarmist coverage was avoided. The four authors of its history[11] put this down partly to 'the professionalism of journalists in "reporting the facts"' in the 1980s. By the 1990s, when penal populism had broken out, all this was lost. Opposition politicians and the media began selecting whichever statistics – the BCS or recorded police crime – looked worse.

Most encouraging of all, the work of David Faulkner, Deputy Under Secretary at the Home Office who was in charge of policy for nine years, was bearing fruit under Home Secretary Douglas Hurd.

First came a White Paper (*Crime, justice and protecting the public*),[12] although, by publication day, David Waddington, a more right-wing minister, was in charge. But he too went ahead with its declaration that prisons were 'an expensive way of making bad people, worse'. This was partly put into effect through the Criminal Justice Act 1991, which included a clutch of alternatives to prison provisions – including restrictions on sentencing – reserving the use of prison for offences that were 'so serious that only a custodial sentence could be justified'. Partly in anticipation of the Act, and following its implementation, the prison population dropped from 50,000 in 1988 to 40,600 by 1992.[13] And all this under a Conservative government.

The 1991 report of the Woolf Inquiry[14] into the 25-day Strangeways prison riot and rooftop protest – the longest in British penal history – offered hope of more radical change. It described conditions in the Manchester prison that led up to the riot (which triggered a series of other riots in the system) as 'intolerable'. It criticised successive governments for failing to provide adequate resources for the service. Its recommendations – which included a national system of accredited standards and more emphasis on maintaining prisoners' contacts with their families – were enthusiastically endorsed by Kenneth Baker, who had become Home Secretary. Many commentators, including *The Guardian*, were describing it as the most important since the Gladstone Report a century earlier. However, the media had not served civil society well in covering the riot. A report from the Press Council – a much more proactive body than the current Press Complaints Commission – declared that 'many of the more gruesome events reported in the press had not occurred – nobody had been systematically mutilated, there had been no castrations, no bodies had been chopped up and flushed down the sewers'. There had been some violence in the first hours of the riot, but the torture suggested by many early reports had not taken place. Newspaper reporters had fallen into 'the ethical error of presenting speculation and unconfirmed reports as fact'.

Two events torpedoed Woolf's proposals. The escape of prisoners from two high security prisons, Whitemoor, and four months later Parkhurst, led to banner headlines and a tabloid demand that 'something must be done'. What happened was much tighter security, scuppering the Woolf plan for more community prisons. But before that, an even grimmer event occurred, the emergence of a penal populist war that began with Tony Blair becoming Shadow Home Secretary after Labour's 1992 election defeat. Blair specifically asked the new Labour leader, John Smith, for the post, with the intention of seizing the law and order crown from the Conservatives, without which he believed a Labour victory would be impossible.

The penal populism war begins

A huge increase in police-recorded crime (more than double) in the 13 Tory years between 1979 and 1992 and the grim death of Jamie Bulger, a Liverpool toddler killed by two young boys in 1993, provided Blair with powerful ammunition to attack the Thatcher/ Major record. His new mantra, 'tough on crime, tough on the causes of crime' – a rallying cry originally scripted by Gordon Brown – won him many headlines. All this was in place before Michael 'prison works' Howard became Home Secretary on 27 May 1993, and engaged in an epic battle with Blair over who could be the toughest. A former senior civil servant in Howard's office told me how amazed they were, as Howard ratcheted up his proposals in a series of Acts in the run-up to the 1997 election in an attempt to out-distance Blair, that were all accepted by Blair, by then the Labour leader. Even the draconian Sentencing Act 1997, with its 'two strikes and you're out' prison provision was passed by Howard, and was implemented by Blair.

Intriguingly, there is one front on which I cannot criticise Howard. In those days, parliamentary statements on new strategy documents, White Papers or Bills did not take place in the Commons until at least 3.30pm and frequently later if there were competing statements. In his four years as Home Secretary, despite the numerous editorials I wrote about how wrong his hard-line policies were, Howard was scrupulous in telephoning me for a 10- to 15-minute one-to-one briefing mid-morning on all the major statements that he was due to make later in the day.

The penal populism war did not stop once Blair had won office. He talked endlessly and inappropriately of the need to replace a

19th-century criminal justice system with a 21st-century model. He called for a victim justice system, ignoring the fact that a main driver behind setting up a justice system was to end blood feuds and lynch law. He held 13 criminal summits in his first five years, announced 33 'get tough' initiatives between June 2001 and May 2004[15] and passed 53 Acts dealing with crime, criminal justice and punishment in 10 years as though this was the key to crime control when in reality only three out of 100 offences ever get to court. But tougher Acts – and tougher rhetoric – led to longer sentences for a much wider range of offences in both magistrates' courts and Crown Courts. It took four decades between 1951 and 1991 for the prison population to rise by 11,000. Between 1992 and 2002, the first decade of Blair's penal populist assault, the prison population went up by another 22,000 – twice as fast in one quarter of the time; in other words, eight times as fast. Successive chief inspectors of prison along with successive directors of the prison service all complained about the number of inappropriate offenders imprisoned: young people, non-violent offenders, the mentally ill and drug addicts.

I watched, in amazement, at Labour's morning press briefings in the 1997 general election campaign. Labour was committed to following Conservative spending proposals – proposals the Tories would never have followed – so each day a series of austere and stringent improvements would be announced for mainstream services such as health, education, housing and social services. There was one notable exception: spending on the criminal justice system. A joint election press briefing by Gordon Brown and Jack Straw assured us of that. The 22,000 extra prisoners that arrived under Blair's 10-year reign cost £41,000 a year each in accommodation plus £100,000 in capital for each extra cell. We were spending a greater proportion of our gross domestic product (GDP) on the criminal justice system – 2.5 per cent – not just more than any other European Union (EU) state but the US as well.[16] Before Blair stepped down in 2007, a further 10,500 places were planned for 2014, including three Titan warehouses holding up to 3,000 each. Crime had been falling for 13 years – burglary, car crime and theft were all over 50 per cent down – but according to the Prime Minister's Strategy Unit, only 20 per cent of the fall was due to prison. So much for Blair and Howard's claims that 'prison works'.

If only politicians would read the reports from the specialists who are there to advise them. In 2000 Jack Straw commissioned the Director of Criminal Policy at the Home Office, John Halliday, to review both custodial and non-custodial sentences. Among the many interesting findings in his report in 2001, *Making punishment work*,[17] there is a rather important fact: it needs a 15 per cent increase in the prison population to achieve a 1 per cent fall in crime. This message was taken on board by David Halpern, chief analyst in Tony Blair's Strategy Unit between 2001 and 2007, who noted in his last book, *The hidden wealth of nations*,[18] the small contribution that prisons make in reducing crime. He estimated that of the 30 per cent fall in crime rates since the late 1980s, only 5 percentage points of the 30 were due to prison. The Prime Minister's Strategy Unit in 2007 made a similar point in its report, *Building on progress: Security, crime and justice.*[19]

Other factors leading to the decline in crime set out by the Strategy Unit and criminologists include greater economic stability, better security of cars and homes, falls in the value of electrical goods, a sharper police focus on persistent offenders and more investment in drug treatment schemes. Moreover, what Blair and Howard continued to ignore in their 'prison works' claims were places which were showing both falls in crime and falls in prison population: Canada, the Netherlands, New York and more recently, Chicago.

The irony of Blair's penal populism was that he was 'hoist by his own petard'. The main result of his tough rhetoric, hyperactivity and continuous criticisms of the criminal justice system was that a large proportion of the public came to believe the criminal justice system was not working. An analysis of the BCS by Professor Mike Hough, former Deputy Director of Research and Planning at the Home Office, showed that two thirds of people wrongly believed crime was still rising and blamed the government; one third rightly believed it was going down, but gave no credit to the government.[20] What politicians should pay more heed to was the second finding of the survey: people who were the best informed had the least anxiety about crime; those who were most ill informed were the most anxious. Hough noted there were various academic and political arguments about the cause of these findings, but he concluded that 'the simplest explanation for this trend is that people think crime is rising because they are told by the media that it is. It is striking that much lower proportions of people think that crime is rising in their area than nationally'.[21]

A separate important study on fear of crime, which needs more publicity, was produced by Jonathan Jackson of the LSE and Stephen Farrall of the University of Sheffield in May 2008.[22] They re-analysed the BCS data and identified three separate groups. The biggest (54 per cent) had never been victims of crime or only minor low-level nuisance and experienced low or no levels of anxiety about crime. They were 'unworried'. A second group (21 per cent) also had a low level or no experience of crime, but did have high levels of fear and anxiety. This group was analogous to the 'worried well' in health research. A third group (21 per cent) did suffer high levels of crime or local disorder and nuisance. Understandably they had high levels of fear and anxiety. This group tended to be the worst off in society according to other economic and social factors and should be the group that receive the most public attention and public resources. What politicians – and the media – should draw from these findings is that a majority of the people in the country manage to live their lives without fretting or worrying about crime.

How far were the media culpable in the penal populism war?

The tabloids regurgitated all the tough headline-grabbing soundbites that ministers – Tory and Labour – had emitted since the start of the penal populist war in 1992. Much of the media hysteria seen in the coverage of drugs in the next chapter also applies to the reporting of crime and punishment. And it does not just apply to tabloids. Serious papers are also at fault. Steve Hewlett's BBC Radio 4 programme, the 'Media Show', on 19 September 2008, elicited a striking insight into even a serious paper's outlook. *The Daily Telegraph's* Home Affairs Editor, Christopher Hope, was taken to task for downplaying the fall in violent crime figures and suggesting that knife crimes were spreading to rural areas. Yet there was only one set of recent statistics on this form of crime in such areas, from which you could not draw trends. In part of his defence he asserted: 'We try and get a picture which reflects what our readers are seeing every day ... some of us would say our readers see this lawless Britain is in some part of their life, they do not want to be told by the government that violent crime is falling.'

Neither are broadcasters exempt. Mike Hough has documented the BBC's online coverage of the Home Office publication of the quarterly BCS statistics. He looked at reports between July 2004 and January 2007. This was a period when the fall in violent crime recorded by the survey beginning in 1995 continued throughout the next 11 quarters he monitored. Yet the main headline on BBC Online contained some form of 'rising violent crime' message. He forwarded his evidence to the BBC and his complaint of seriously misrepresenting trends was upheld.[23] Yet it still continued after January 2007. In October 2007 the annual police statistics showed all recorded crime down by 7 per cent, more serious violent crime down by 14 per cent, lesser violent offences down 12 per cent and sex offences down 9 per cent. Firearms offences had fallen by 600 and serious injury from gun crime fell by 11 per cent. Yet *The Sun* headline declared '14% rise in crime'; *The Times* 'Violence is rising as confidence falls'; and *The Telegraph* 'Drug offences rise 14% after policy "shambles"'. Even *The Guardian* headline declared 'Crime down by 7% but drug offences show 14% increase'. It was cannabis that had caused this rise. The paper's Home Affairs Editor, Alan Travis, who does not write the headlines, explained why. It was not due to an increase in use but a change in police strategy: small-time users were no longer being taken to the police station, but instead given on-the-spot warnings that were quicker to record. The BCS was showing even more startling figures. The chance of being a victim was at its lowest since the surveys began in 1981. From the peak in 1995, burglary was down by 59 per cent, vehicle theft by 61 per cent and personal theft by 45 per cent. Did the BBC *Ten o'clock news* dwell on these startling figures? No, it gave them a glancing reference but concentrated on teen gun crime, of which there had been an abrupt spate (not set in context).[24]

In his *Law and order: An honest citizen's guide to crime and control*, an excellent guide for lay people, Professor Robert Reiner noted a significant rise in crime reporting. One study in which he was involved, looking at the proportion of crime stories in two British papers, found they had doubled after the 1960s, from 10 to 20 per cent of news space.[25] More seriously, he went on:

> Crime stories began to construct crime as a much more pervasive and threatening phenomenon than before. Stories about specific incidents were much more likely to represent a case as only part of a wider context of growing danger. Violent crimes, especially murder, have always been the main focus of news and fiction stories. But the concentration on stories of murder and sex crimes has become more marked. Stories about property crimes in which no violence occurred have almost disappeared from news and fiction, only appearing if they have a celebrity angle. Paradoxically, this means that although the media vastly exaggerates the risks of violent crime, characters in crime fiction are now in much less danger of victimization by property crime than the audience watching them.[26]

Reiner also shows how the modern media demonise offenders by the way they are drawn as one-dimensional evil villains inflicting frightening suffering on innocent and appealing victims. He contrasts this approach with how crime stories were handled six decades ago. A story on the front page of *The Daily Mirror* on 27 February 1945 involved a two-year-old girl who had been badly beaten by a 26-year-old living with her mother.[27] It listed the girl's injuries, which included black eyes, bruises and red weal marks that extended over her temple and across her cheeks. But two thirds of the story concentrated on the offender, who had been torpedoed three times during the war, and who was suffering from 'bad nerves'. What was noteworthy was the absence of demonisation of the perpetrator and concern to understand how he could have carried out such an act. Attempting to understand the offender was not seen as incompatible with the greatest concern for the victim. Condemnation of the act was taken for granted.

Myra Hindley: the ultimate evil offender

Nowhere was tabloid lust for demonising offenders and inflaming public opinion more overt than in their unrelenting campaign to keep Myra Hindley in prison for life. The gravity of the crimes in which she was involved was undeniable – the torture and murder of five young people – but even the prosecuting counsel at her trial, Elwyn Jones, accepted that she had been 'indoctrinated' by Ian Brady and was an accomplice, not a perpetrator. That is why in 1966 the trial judge, endorsed by the Lord Chief Justice, set her life sentence tariff at 25 years but Brady's at 40 years. In 1985, as she was approaching 20 years in prison, her local parole panel recommended release. Instead, the Home Secretary of the time, Leon Brittan, extended her tariff to 30 years. In 1990, yet another Home Secretary, David Waddington, increased her sentence to 'whole life'. She was the only person serving a 'whole life' tariff who was not an actual killer. Michael Howard reaffirmed this order, which was declared unlawful because he attempted to rule out any further reviews. In February 1996, the full Parole Board signalled its support for release in its recommendation that she should be transferred to an open prison – a preliminary step before parole. The Board ruled that there was no risk of her repeating her offence. It observed how the tongue-tied school leaver of 44 years earlier had become an Open University graduate of humanities and an advocate for her own cause. Instead, in 1998, Jack Straw, by then Home Secretary, reaffirmed her 'whole life' tariff.

On four occasions between 1991 and 2002, the courts used the European Convention on Human Rights to cut back the powers of home secretaries to decide how long lifers should spend in prison. In these successive cases, the courts rightly ruled that politicians had the right to establish sentencing frameworks, but not to determine the length of an individual's sentence. Under the terms of the European Convention – drafted by a Conservative British lawyer with another British lawyer chairing the legal committee that supervised the operation in 1952 – sentencing was reserved for judges. Ironically, the UK was the only country in the 47-member Council of Europe not following this rule. Hindley was the classic example of why it was necessary.

Sentencing requires calm and impartial judgments by people trained in applying cool criteria. Successive home secretaries were taking their decisions on Hindley against a background of widespread hysteria and hate, whipped up by the tabloid press, with the two main political parties trying to out-tough each other. The Parole Board, which does not have to worry about elections, had the independence to ignore the label tied round Hindley's neck by the popular press – 'the most evil woman in Britain'. The tabloids work on a different agenda. Natural causes of crime, complex though they are already, are not enough. Evil, the supernatural force, has to be invoked. It is not just irrational, with links back to medieval times, but dangerous. If killing is a product of evil, then secular society can be excused its failure. There is nothing that can be done. But there is a lot these days that can be done, both to prevent offences and to rehabilitate those who have offended. The damage which such tabloid campaigns wreak on civil society does not stop there. In their persistent returns for quotes from the parents of young murdered victims to boost media campaigns against the perpetrators, the tabloids unhealthily recharge these people's thirst for vengeance, an emotion which reduces their abilities to restore some equilibrium and internal peace in their lives. In 2002, as the Law Lords began hearing a case that would end the power of home secretaries to extend the tariff of life sentences set by the courts, David Blunkett had become Home Secretary. Recognising this would free Hindley, he threatened to introduce a new law to keep Hindley imprisoned. But this move, which undoubtedly would have been quashed by the courts, became unnecessary. Hindley died on 16 November 2002, 36 years after her conviction, still in custody. The tabloids had got their way. There was one final irony, however. Hindley, in prison, had fought for her freedom but failed; Brady, who had been transferred to a secure mental hospital after so many years in isolation, had rejected release but wanted to die. Prison policy allows inmates to starve themselves to death; secure hospitals do not. Hindley should have been given her freedom, Brady his right to die.

What criminologists say about the media's influence

This is one chapter in my book that has been crawled over by academics. In my residential year at Nuffield College I joined, among other things, a fascinating and enjoyable postgraduate course led by Oxford's intellectually invigorating Professor of Criminology, Ian Loader. The reading list for the course ran to 100 books. From one of the books I learned that Sonia Livingstone, an LSE researcher who had made a comprehensive survey of the literature, had concluded that 'since the 1920s thousands of studies of mass media effects have been conducted'.[28] In the 15 years since that report was published, no doubt a few more thousands have been added. The best summary I found within the reading list was a herculean effort by Robert Reiner in a 30-page essay in the fourth edition of *The Oxford handbook of criminology* entitled: 'Media-made criminality: the representation of crime in the mass media'.[29] This is not a summary but here are some key points I drew from it.

The many different academic critics are divided into two broad schools, 'polar opposites sharing in common only their demonization of the media'. (I should add that these studies were not confined to the media's news coverage and documentaries, but its entertainment, infotainment, fiction and soaps as well.) The first school believes that the media are a significant cause of offending and are fundamentally subversive. The second school believes that the media are not the cause of crime itself but of exaggerated public alarm about law and order generating support for repressive solutions. Some of us think we could join both of these schools. Content analysis – compared to criminogenic influence – is a less contested area and broadly familiar to many: the media's overwhelming concentration on violent crimes, an indirect consequence of which is an exaggeration of police effectiveness given they are more successful in clearing up such offences. A clear trend over the last three decades has been to make victims the pivotal focus of news stories. The demographic profile of offenders and victims is much more middle class and older in the media than in the criminal justice system. The old positive image of the success and integrity of the police and criminal justice system is now accompanied in both news and fiction with a critical trend questioning its effectiveness, justice and honesty.

Reiner suggests that the degree to which media and criminal justice systems are penetrating each other increasingly makes a distinction between 'factual' and 'fictional' programmes even more tenuous. He points to the O.J. Simpson car chase and trial in the US; live newscasts of particular police raids; amateur videos of Los Angeles police beating up Rodney King; and CCTV shots of Jamie Bulger being led away by his killers. As long ago as 1982, Roger Graef, producer of over 80 documentaries, showed how factual programmes could be as gripping as fictional, in his award-winning series on Thames Valley Police using a fly-on-the-wall technique that he himself pioneered. His programme on the insensitive handling of a rape victim – including a ruthless interrogation she was subjected to – helped change the way police handled such cases.

The role of the media in developing new (and eroding old) categories of crime – known in the criminological trade as 'labelling' – is probably acknowledged by both schools. Jock Young analysed how media representations amplified the deviance of drug takers (1971); Stan Cohen coined the influential concept of 'moral panic' in his study on how the media, along with the police, developed a spiral of respectable fear about 'mods' and 'rockers' (1972); and Stuart Hall analysed the 1973 moral panic about a supposedly new type of robbery, 'mugging', emphasising the crucial part played by the media. Geoffrey Pearson, in his 1983 book *Hooligan: A history of respectable fears*, far from inventing a new category of crime, documented how far back public distress over young people stretched. References to the research by Young, Cohen and Pearson make regular appearances in the serious media. To a lesser extent, so do the authors.[30]

The studies discussed above concentrate on the media's news coverage. The research on the wider media's influence through such issues as fictional violence has to include what Reiner describes as 'the apotheosis of agnosticism' in a 1961 US study by Wilbur Schramm: 'for some children, under some conditions, some television is harmful. For some children under the same conditions, or for the same children under other conditions, it may be beneficial. For most children under most conditions, most television is probably neither particularly harmful nor particularly beneficial.'[31]

Three and a half decades on, research on the media's influence had progressed. Reviews of the research literature by the US criminologist Ellen Wartella in 1995 concluded that there was 'a correlation between violence viewing and aggressive behaviour, a relationship that holds even when a variety of controls are imposed'. But as Reiner notes, the negative effects of media exposure seem to be small compared to other features in the social experience of offenders. Thus 'the question that remains is not whether media violence has an effect, but rather how important that effect has been, in comparison with other factors, in bringing about major social changes such as the post [second world] war rise in crime'. Reiner suggests that a sophisticated criticism of the research on media effects might be, in the words of a fellow criminologist, that 'repeated failures to find anything much out would ... suggest that the wrong question was being asked'.

How much were politicians the true drivers of penal populism?

This is one academic definition of penal populism that may provide a useful criterion:

> Penal populism: a combination of concern and lack of knowledge can present politicians with the temptation to promote policies, which encourage electoral advantage without doing much about crime. The more wilful that such politicians are in their disregard of the evidence about effectiveness and equity, the more we are inclined to regard them as penal populists.[32]

The points already made and those that follow suggest it was the politicians on this issue who were the main perpetrators of penal populism with the press being mere eager accomplices. Within months of New Labour being elected, *The Guardian* led its front page under the headline 'Crime "crisis" based on myth – ministers accused of playing to the gallery'.[33] It coincided with a Home Office publication, *Attitudes to punishment*,[34] drawn from the BCS by Professor Mike Hough and others. It noted that public ignorance about law and order was widespread and lay at the heart of a crisis of confidence in Britain's courts and judges. It observed that despite more than five years of 'prison works' and 'get tough' policies from the former Conservative Home Secretary, Michael Howard, there still existed a crisis of public confidence in the courts that needed tackling urgently. Drawing on its survey of 16,000 people, it found the public seriously underestimated just how severe the courts were. It suggested this ignorance of crime and sentencing was contributing to widespread public cynicism about law and order. The problem was compounded by the absence of easily accessible figures showing the 'going rate' for any particular crime. The public had a very jaundiced view of judges, with more than a third believing they did a poor job compared to much higher levels of confidence in the police, prison services and magistrates. It said the media had to carry some responsibility for such a large public misunderstanding of what was going on in the courts.

Two ways of rectifying the situation were set out – one new path for judges and the other for ministers. The Home Office publication scathingly concluded that judges may not be unique in continuing to use 18th-century trappings of pomp and ritual to sustain their authority, but that it was about time they started using a late 20th-century communications technique to let the public know about sentencing practice. It told politicians they had been wrong to 'play to the gallery' by basing their criminal justice policies during the 1990s on jailing more and more people to feed the public's mistaken appetite for tougher punishment. It added: 'These findings should warn politicians away from the populist responses to crime. They show that a populist sentencing policy will not actually change public perceptions.' Wise advice, which alas, the New Labour administration ignored.

Lance Price, former BBC political correspondent who became Alastair Campbell's deputy in Downing Street in 1998, is quoted in Chapter One of this book conceding how constantly the tabloids were pursued: 'a significant proportion of the stories generated by

Downing Street for the sake of headlines were designed to suggest that New Labour understood and even sympathised with the socially conservative instincts of most tabloids. Only rarely did they challenge the mindset of *The Sun* or the *Daily Mail*.'[35] Chapter One also quotes Julia Simpson, Head of Press at the Home Office, complaining about Number 10 searching for announcements before the department had fully developed policies, another sin Price pleads guilty to.[36] He admitted in *The Independent on Sunday* that the huge increase in media outlets with more time and space to fill had left government with too few 'newsworthy' stories: 'We at No 10 had only a finite number of our own to offer to our hungry customers. For the rest we had to go to individual departments. I have no doubt that they felt under pressure constantly to come up with new announcements and new angles because I was among those putting pressures on them.'[37]

He also acknowledged the damaging circulatory policy-making process which David Marquand identified in *Britain since 1918*[38]: 'Media storms fed into focus groups; focus-group discussion fed into the Prime Minister's office; and ministerial reactions fed back into the media'.[39] Price conceded the point: '... the number of hours I spent with ministers planning new "crackdowns" on drugs, asylum-seekers and benefit cheats testifies to the accuracy of the assessment'.[40] But he believed that this process gave the media, not Downing Street, the upper hand. This might have been the case by the time he got there, perhaps, but to ask the question raised after school playground fights, 'Who started it?', the evidence set out above indisputably points to the politicians.

No previous prime minister spent more time involving himself in criminal justice policy than Tony Blair. One of his aides who did not work in this area told my wife at a dinner that his biggest sin was not Iraq, but law and order. 'He believed in his policy in Iraq; he cannot believe in his law and order policy.' His 13 criminal policy summits were not just broad-brush events but went into fine-grain issues and micro-management. No prime minister has spoken as much about crime, or pushed through more penal populist measures. He had his own team of advisers. He brought in outsiders with no background in the field, such as John Birt, former Director General of the BBC, who was asked to carry out 'blue sky' thinking and draw up a '10-year crime plan'. Tim Newburn, an LSE criminologist, could find no evidence that it had much impact, but noted 'it is the fact of his appointment – with no experience in the field and working directly to the PM rather than the Home Secretary – that is significant'.[41] Worse still was the way in which the announcement of new crime initiatives was even used to divert attention from other political problems. In 1999, in the midst of the row over Peter Mandelson's home loan, the controversial 'two strikes and you're inside prison' provision for burglary, a section of Michael Howard's draconian Crime (Sentences) Act 1997 which had been put on hold by Jack Straw, was suddenly activated.[42] Later, as the story of the Home Office's mishandling of foreign nationals was unfolding (they were being released, rather than deported), the Prime Minister and his new Home Secretary, John Reid, began announcing a series of initiatives, including the possible introduction of a paedophile notification scheme along the lines of the US Megan's Law, floated but rightly rejected several years earlier.[43]

Blair's obsession with presentation, and an insight into how such ill-thought-out policies found their way into practice, can be seen from his handwritten memo to his staff in April 2000 (leaked to *The Sun* in July 2000):

> On crime, we need to highlight the *tough* measures: compulsory tests for drugs before bail ... the extra number of burglars jailed under 'three strikes and you're out'. Above all, we must deal *now* with street crime.... When the crime figures are published ... they will show a small – 4 per cent – rise in crime. But this will almost entirely be due to the rise in levels of street crime – mobile phones, bags being snatched. This will be in London. The Met Police are putting in place measures to deal with it; but as ever, we lack a tough *public* message along with the strategy. We should think now of an initiative, eg locking up street muggers. Something tough, with immediate bite that sends a message through the system.... But this should be done soon and I, personally, should be associated with it.[44]

Hugo Young's assessment

In July 2003, only weeks before he knew he was going to die from a rare form of cancer, Hugo Young, *The Guardian*'s political commentator, wrote an excoriating column on New Labour's record on human rights. Here is a much truncated excerpt:

Both Blair and Straw who might once have wanted to be seen at any rate lightly varnished with libertarian respectability, are now proud not to call themselves liberal. Straw is openly scornful, citing the message he gets from his Blackburn market square. His record as Home Secretary, except for his collaboration in the Human Rights Act, revealed a man true to his word. As for Blair his sabotage of freedom of information and his fervent defence of every measure the Home Office can dream up remind us that he is at heart – perhaps all prime ministers get that way – an unmitigated state-power man, guaranteed to come down on the wrong side whenever liberal principles vie with easy populist applause.

The need for certain fundamental laws to protect the people against arbitrary power has never been in more urgent need of discussion. It's extraordinary to see the Tory Party more interested in that than all the potent Labour progressives in our midst. But then the Tories do not have a Blunkett. At the apex of anti-liberalism, bragging his contempt, sits the most dangerous home secretary this country has ever had.... His attacks on judges who get in the way of his asylum orders or his penal ambitions betray constitutional illiteracy and mocking disrespect for the key upholders of law on a scale not even seen when Michael Howard had the job.

In all this Blunkett is Blair's lieutenant. They are a team of anti-liberals, goading each other on. Until now they did have one hurdle to surmount on the journey to that utopia where the judges had been put in their place. Lord Chancellor Irvine wasn't all that reliable a liberal himself. But he was the real begetter of the Human Rights Act, and above all a defender of the judges.... He could tell Blair what fundamental legal principle meant. Now I can't think of a single member of the cabinet who even cares.[45]

The authoritarian state

David Blunkett became Home Secretary immediately after the 2001 general election. Much to the annoyance of Jack Straw, his immediate predecessor, he had leaked the news long before it was announced or even possibly agreed by Blair. In the Whitehall pecking order, the office held higher status than Education, even given Blair's three famous priorities in the run-up to the 1997 election, 'education, education, education'. It was created in 1782 at the same time as the Foreign Office. At that time – before the era of social policy departments and large public services – it was responsible for all the government's domestic responsibilities, but law and order was at its heart from the beginning. Over time it lost a long list of responsibilities that included local government, public housing, local boards of health, highways, air traffic control, railway accidents, factory and mine inspections, reservoirs, infant and child care, adoption, mental health, not to mention Scotland, Northern Ireland, broadcasting and sport. Even so it still had a formidable range of services: asylum, immigration, border control, the three main law and order services (police, probation, prisons) plus legislative responsibility for all criminal justice and sentencing reform. Many progressives believed it was still too big and should be divided into two. And so it was, in March 2007, in one of Tony Blair's last initiatives. Criminal justice legislation and prisons were removed from the Home Office and incorporated into a Ministry of Justice, which also took over the old Lord Chancellor's Department's responsibilities.

I had run articles on David Blunkett in *The Guardian Society* section before he arrived in Westminster in 1987. He is a remarkable man. Born blind to a poor family in Sheffield, he was only 12 when his father died from a gruesome industrial accident – falling into a boiling vat of water. Educated in blind boarding schools from a young age, Blunkett won a place, against all the odds, at the University of Sheffield, where he gained a degree in political theory. He became Sheffield's youngest councillor in 1970 at the age of 22, and 10 years later leader in 1980, a position he held until 1987 when he arrived in Westminster. A decade later he was in Blair's first Cabinet as Education Secretary. I thought he performed well there, fully in charge of his responsibilities having had several years in the shadow post preparing himself for the job. He was known to be an adept media manipulator, boasting at his farewell dinner with the education correspondents to have placed, with the help of his well-regarded specialist adviser, Conor Ryan, 'exclusives' in the Sunday papers for 50 of the previous 52 weeks.

But his move to the Home Office in 2001 was a disaster in terms of progressive reform. He had no background in the area and quickly demonstrated that. An early forewarning of what was to come occurred at the Labour Party annual conference in 2001, where he made a crude attack on the judges and suggested Parliament was the seat of all reform, not the courts. This was to ignore what had been happening in Strasbourg where, in the previous three decades, the European Court of Human Rights had taken up the cause of a wide variety of vulnerable people whom successive British governments and Parliament had been ignoring. None of the new rights established there were trivial, and some were fundamental. It was Strasbourg, not Westminster, which forced the state to provide more protection to the weak (immigrants, prisoners and asylum-seekers) and applied necessary curbs on the powerful (police, prison officers and immigration officers). It was Strasbourg, not Westminster, that required the UK to lift unfair press curbs, to end illegal state telephone taps, and to stop unjust restrictions on prisoners' access to lawyers.

Unlike the other members of the Council of Europe, the UK was unique in not having a written constitution or a Bill of Rights. The advantage of an unwritten constitution is that nothing is illegal unless it is prohibited. The disadvantage is that the same principle applies to the state – hence in the UK the state's use of telephone tapping and its readiness to apply press curbs on reporting MI5 activities (*Spycatcher*), both of which were stopped in Strasbourg. Similarly, the curb on

The Sunday Times' investigations into the Thalidomide drug scandal was lifted there. I travelled to Strasbourg for *The Guardian* between 1972 and 1992 to watch some of the key decisions. By then it had made some 50 rulings against the UK. Equally interesting was the way in which the Court forced Whitehall to start anticipating the European Convention and improve the safeguards protecting civil rights in new social policy.

But all this changed after the 9/11 terrorist attack in the US in 2001. A better-informed Home Secretary would have been more aware of the dangers that terrorist laws can pose in terms of polluting the criminal justice system. Look no further than the Prevention of Terrorism Act (PTA) 1974 passed in the wake of two IRA terrorist bombs in Birmingham. Rushed through Parliament within 48 hours by the 1974–79 Labour government, the PTA was originally supposed to have lasted for six months. Sixteen years later it was still in place and was only abolished by the equally draconian Terrorism Act 2000. A Home Secretary with a criminal justice background would also have been aware of how prosecutions of suspected terrorists in the 1970s led to police perjury, bent police evidence and breach of court rules that were used in the trials of three groups of Irish suspects – the Guildford Four, Birmingham Six and Maguire Seven. It was not until the late 1980s and early 1990s, after lengthy appeal processes, that these abuses were exposed, belatedly quashing all the convictions and freeing the three groups.

There are few better examples of the poison which anti-terrorism laws were capable of leaking into the criminal justice system in the first decade of the 21st century than the ruling on torture given by a three-member Court of Appeal in 2004. The issue before the court was whether it was permissible in Britain to use evidence against terrorist suspects that may have been obtained by torture in other states. To the alarm of human rights lawyers, the court concluded – by two votes to one – that although there was no evidence in the case before it that torture had been used, even if there had been evidence of torture, the material gained would still have been admissible as long as Britain had not 'procured or connived' at torture. Belatedly but definitely, seven Law Lords 16 months later unanimously quashed the decision. Lord Bingham, the senior Law Lord, in a celebrated lead judgment, spoke of the abhorrence which 'torture and its fruits' had been held in English law for over 500 years. He went on: 'I am startled, even a little dismayed, at the suggestion (and the acceptance by the Court of Appeal) that this deeply-rooted tradition and an international obligation solemnly and explicitly undertaken can be over-ridden by a statute and a procedural rule which makes no mention of torture at all.' There was an understandable and almost audible sigh of relief from domestic and international human rights groups at this reversal. And with good reason. Under international law there is an absolute prohibition on the use of torture. The Court of Appeal had ignored obligations under a succession of international treaties and human rights conventions.[46]

The seven Law Lords also ruled that the 10 foreign suspects involved in the appeal should not be required to prove the prosecuting evidence was based on torture. As Lord Bingham acerbically noted, the suspects held without charge or trial for two years did not know under what evidence or witness statements they were being detained. He went on: 'It is inconsistent with the most rudimentary notions of fairness to blindfold a man and then impose a standard which only the sighted could hope to meet.'[47]

Ironically, this restoration of fundamental human rights on 8 December 2005 by the Law Lords almost coincided with another parliamentary battle over a new attack on civil liberties – the 300-year-old habeas corpus principle that every arrested citizen has the right to be either charged or set free. London had suffered two suicide bomber attacks in July 2005. In the first, on 7 July, over 50 people died and 700 were injured in a coordinated attack by four bombers – three on different tube trains and one on a double-decker bus. In the second, two weeks later, there were another four bombers but only the detonators went off, not the bombs. Only one person was injured. But Britain had suffered its first attacks by suicide bombers and worse still they were home grown. Understandably ministers felt they had to respond. Britain already had 200 pieces of anti-terrorism legislation before the bombings. No country in the EU had sterner laws. But given the scale of the injuries and the fear of looking complacent, Blair insisted a fourth anti-terrorism Bill in five years be drawn up. Charles Clarke had become Home Secretary after Blunkett had been forced to resign on 15 December 2004. (He had survived the startling revelation of his affair with Kimberly Fortier, the US publisher of the Tory-supporting *Spectator* magazine and wife of the managing director of *Vogue*. But he was doomed when an independent inquiry he had set up showed his private office had helped fast-track a visa for the Filipina nanny of his illegitimate son with Ms Fortier.)

David Blunkett resigns, Charles Clarke takes over

Charles Clarke was a much more impressive Home Secretary than Blunkett. Unlike Blunkett he was ready to engage in his critics' arguments rather than crudely deny and dismiss them. Appearing before a Commons Select Committee on Home Affairs on the day before the new post-London bombing Bill against terrorism was published, Clarke rightly identified intelligence as the key to combating further terrorism. But behind him there was a gung-ho Downing Street with a 12-point plan, drawn up post the July bombs, intent on pushing the Home Office beyond its hastily drawn line in shrinking civil rights sands. In December 2004, the government had suffered a severe setback when the Law Lords, in an eight-to-one judgment, declared the detention without charge or trial of 12 foreign suspects of terrorist activity under the 2001 anti-terrorism legislation was unlawful. It was described by one legal scholar as 'the beginnings of a much-belated judicial awakening to the fact that even in the context of national security, the courts have a responsibility to ensure that the rule of law is respected'.[48] Sir Louis Blom-Cooper, a veteran observer of the courts, was more effusive, describing it as 'a judicial tour de force, the likes of which have not been witnessed since the 17th century, when judges sided with Parliament, not the Crown'.[49]

In response to the Law Lords ruling, the government passed new anti-terrorism legislation in March 2005 that allowed the Home Secretary to impose 'control orders' on terrorist suspects. It could, in effect, be 'house custody', with a range of restrictions controlling the use of IT, phones, who could be seen, curfews and electronic tags. But that was March, before the July 2005 bombs exploded. Blair wanted more after the bombs. He was intent on trying again to get the police the powers to detain terrorist suspects for 90 days without charge or trial and he had the support of most tabloids but not the *Mail, Telegraph, Independent* or *Guardian*. Even the police were divided. The most senior Metropolitan Police officers wanted it, but a Scotland Yard assistant commissioner conceded: 'I do appreciate that there may be concern in some quarters regarding whether this is too long a period.'[50] Clarke originally thought so too, before being over-ruled by Downing Street. The Attorney General, Lord Goldsmith, was reported to oppose the move. Lord Carlile, the independent reviewer of terrorist legislation, was also opposed – the issue involved suspects, not terrorists. Of the 895 people arrested under terrorist laws in the previous five years, 500 were released without charge. The Prevention of Terrorism Act 1972 had set seven days as the limit, a length that continued through the height of the IRA campaign in the 1970s and 1980s. This was extended to 14 days under the Criminal Justice Act 2003, which was traumatic enough. But 90 days risked innocent people losing their jobs, homes, families and friends. A Foreign Office survey of other states could find none seeking similar powers. Nothing was more likely to unite communities in opposition to anti-terrorist activities, cutting off the police from the vital intelligence they needed.

There was widespread media debate. *The Sun* launched a campaign urging its readers to 'Tell Tony he's right'. It also compiled a 'list of shame' that named the MPs from all parties who were opposing the Bill. There were intense pressures on Labour MPs, who were all aware of the serious threat posed by suicide bombers. They had been briefed by an assertive prime minister, a reconstructed tough-talking home secretary, and the Scotland Yard's most senior anti-terrorism commissioner. There had been a succession of opinion polls signalling widespread public support for the plan. But on 9 November 2005, the Commons rejected the detention clauses, Blair's first Commons defeat since his election in 1997. Some 49 Labour MPs joined Conservative and Liberal Democrat members to achieve the defeat. Instead, a rebel Labour amendment, increasing the right of the police to detain terrorist suspects from 14 to 28 days, was passed. Intriguingly in his autobiography, Blair all but suggests that he refused to compromise as much for image as principle: 'contrary to conventional wisdom when it came to the vote I decided not to compromise on the essentials, but to lose without having yielded. Of course, when we lost there were all sorts of articles about the Prime Minister's vanishing authority etc; but I could sense that the very recklessness of it, on something I believed was right, got me more traction with the public.... I felt instinctively more comfortable losing than winning through compromise.'[51]

June 2006: Tony Blair re-examines UK civil rights

On 7 June 2006, in a preliminary exercise to delivering a lecture in Bristol on civil rights, Tony Blair hosted a seminar at Downing Street to which he invited policy-makers, leading criminologists, lawyers, criminal justice managers and senior researchers. The first two of five questions to which they were invited to respond to were:

- Do we agree that the UK criminal justice system is no longer protecting liberty in the way it was designed to do?
- Is it true that the balance between the rights of the criminal and the rights of the victim has shifted too much in the direction of the former?

It is clear from what has been said already – and the way in which the questions were phrased – where the Prime Minister stood. The best response came from Ian Loader, Professor of Criminology at the University of Oxford, in an addendum. Noting the mass of legislation that the previous two decades had produced, Loader suggested:

> None of these administrations has been particularly supportive of what the invitation letter revealingly called 'the rights of the criminal'. Yet you are now asking us to believe that during this period the criminal justice system has become 'unbalanced', such that it today unduly privileges the rights of criminals (we should of course say suspects) over those of the victim in ways that have led society to be poorly defended against crime. I simply think you need to offer more serious evidence than any

I have seen that this is in fact the case, rather than simply assert that it is so, or that 'the public' believes it to be so. One needs also to exercise some care here with the metaphor of 'balance'. The idea of balance almost always functions in these discussions as a piece of rhetorical trickery (who, after all, is in favour of 'imbalance'?). It offers no criteria whatsoever for determining what the right 'balance' looks like, sets up a whole debate as an entirely zero-sum game between 'criminals' and 'victims', and offers no resources from protecting the criminal justice from utilitarian calculation.

Picking up on assertions by the Prime Minister in the seminar, that the government had to respond to public concern with a criminal justice system being perilously close to crisis point, Loader accepted there were angry people but that they were in a minority, albeit one that made lots of noise. He went on:

It is not clear to me that governments can or should respond to their demands in the terms in which they are expressed. Listening to you speak about these matters, however, you seem to take the view that the role of government is to act as an uncritical cipher for public anger and demands viz crime and disorder. It is as if – on this issue at least – you have lost confidence in the capacity of government to engage in a dialogue with the people, to point out some facts (about resource limitations, or the capacity and effects of prisons, or the constraints on what can be done to tackle crime in a liberal democracy), to put another view, to be a voice of reason and restraint rather than a conduit or cheer-leader for longer sentences and more punishment. But this, it seems to me, is precisely the sort of public conversation that our society urgently needs to have about questions of crime, justice and security.

There is, further, plenty of evidence to suggest that many members of our society do not feel as concerned or angry or let down by the system as you seem to think that they are. This is the lesson that emerges from the research conducted by Mike Hough and others which suggests both that people know very little about how the system operates (why should they?) and that they are often less severe than judges when asked how they would sentence in actual cases. And it is also the lesson of initiatives such as restorative justice, mediation and now community courts.

Loader had three concerns about more legislation:

> First, I think the government is in danger of over-investing in criminal justice and forgetting the lesson that we tell every novice criminology student – namely, that policing, criminal justice and punishment have an important but ultimately small and peripheral part to play in the production of orderly societies; second, it often sounds as if you think the criminal justice system is a delivery arm of the government. But it isn't. I know this must seem frustrating from where you sit, but courts are meant to function as checks and constraints, both on government over-zealousness and on police forces who may too easily presume to know that they have 'got the right person'. Third, you run the risk, once again, of raising public expectations in what the criminal justice system can deliver in ways that risk the government being hoist by its own petard, and which do nothing to break the vicious circle of scandal, media frenzy and 'firm' government response that has come to surround this area of public policy making in the last decade.

Instead, he urged the Prime Minister 'to think instead about how to dismount the tiger that politicians have in recent years collectively convinced themselves they have no alternative but to ride'.[52]

Looking for alternatives to prison

Mike Hough's research, which Ian Loader referred to, involved both his work in the Home Office with the annual BCS and his work with the Esmée Fairbairn Foundation's £3 million programme on Rethinking Crime and Punishment that concluded in 2004. One of the important issues it explored was the public's view of sentencing. It did this through presenting to the people it was interviewing an outline of a crime and then asking what they thought the offender *would* have got from the court and then what they *should* have got. The case involved a 22-year-old burglar with two previous convictions who entered an old man's house in daylight and stole some electrical goods. About a third of the people over a 10-year survey period said he *would* go to prison and two thirds thought he *should* do so. This was more lenient than the current system that was operating at the time, under which with two previous offences (as long as they were post-1999) the offender faced a three-year mandatory sentence. This experiment has been tried by others with the same result. Ask people an abstract or general question on crime – 'Are courts too soft?'; 'Are judges too lenient?' – the public will, frequently with some anger, agree. Give them more information and they are more reflective.

Rethinking Crime and Punishment aimed at raising the level of debate about the use of prison and alternative forms of punishment. It involved some 60 different projects, research exercises and public surveys. Its in-depth study on the media's influence[53] was undertaken by a team at The Open University that carried out nine separate focus groups.

Among its findings were:

- tabloid newspapers were more influential than television in shaping punitive attitudes;
- participants learned a lot about crime and policing from television but little about sentencing and punishment;
- as much information was gained from dramas and soaps as from factual programmes;
- regular viewers of soaps, especially *EastEnders* with its ongoing crime stories, showed a higher awareness of crime and punishment

and a more precise knowledge of criminal justice than regular viewers of some other fictional formats;

- *Crimewatch*'s regular fan base was informed about how crimes were committed, which crimes were prevalent, and what to watch out for, but was also blamed for heightening fear of crime;
- most viewers had little understanding about alternatives to prison;
- punitive attitudes were often articulated through the language and phrases of tabloid and mid-market newspapers;
- over half of the respondents commonly expressed punitive attitudes. In order to tackle extreme forms of punitiveness, viewers' emotions as well as their reason need to be engaged;
- entrenched punitive attitudes were resistant to change as they were founded on beliefs about the value of punishment formed in childhood and deeply held political values. Group discussions enable participants to work through some of the contradictions in their views and opinions and to shift position. But more meaningful knowledge of alternatives to prison is essential if community sentencing is to gain legitimacy.

It has been a long haul. Community Service Orders (CSOs) were enacted in 1968. Even through the 1980s Conservative ministers sought to sell alternatives to prison to both the courts and their supporters. I watched people like David Mellor and John Patten arriving at the Home Office in junior posts, becoming converted to the cause, toughening their labels (Community Service 'Punishment' instead of 'Orders') and going out to sell them. Yet 35 years on from enactment, their legitimacy was still being questioned.

A separate study on non-custodial sentences involving 12 focus groups in Scotland had a more positive message. Community service, curfews and tagging once explained had positive associations. But 'statistical arguments about the effectiveness of non-custodial sentences had much less impact than arguments about the values and principles underlying them: paying back, making good, and learning "how good people live"'.[54]

A third study led by Mike Hough for the PRT clearly showed what was pushing up the prison population: not more offenders but a more punitive approach by the courts. Offenders were being imprisoned who would previously have received community penalties, and those who would previously have been sent to prison were being given longer sentences.[55] Between 1991 and 2001 the custody rate for magistrates' courts increased over threefold, from 5 to 16 per cent. Use of custody by the Crown Court rose from 46 to 64 per cent. This was partly prompted by legislation and sentencing guidelines but also by a more punitive political and media debate that influenced sentencing practice. The five senior judiciary members that sat on an advisory board of this project were unanimous in saying political and media pressure on judges and magistrates was leading to more severe sentences. The same message came from a survey of 133 judges and magistrates. One of their key explanations for the rise was 'the climate of political and media debate about crime and sentencing becoming more punitive'. At the launch of the report Mike Hough declared: 'Ten years ago people thought that the courts were far too soft on crime. Judges and magistrates have responded by getting progressively tougher. But the public simply haven't realised this, because they haven't been told clearly enough. It is perverse for sentencing policy to be driven by misrepresentation and misunderstanding in this way'.[56] Responding to the report at its launch, the Lord Chief Justice, Lord Woolf, said: 'This important report shows that there is an answer to the continually increasing prison population. The answer is a change in rhetoric from all those with a leading role in the criminal justice system.'[57]

Evidence-based policy-making

It certainly looked like 'a new dawn' for the 150 people in the Home Office's Research Unit when New Labour came into office in May 1997. The clashes between the Home Secretary and the Unit under Michael Howard had been numerous and serious. Most did not surface publicly, but Alan Travis exposed one row in 1994 in *The Guardian* when ministers were suppressing research findings that contradicted the effectiveness of Howard's hard-line approach.[58] The conflicts became so bad that at one point Howard threatened to disband the Unit, a threat which led to an unprecedented exodus of staff.[59] But New Labour swept into power, declaring it was intent on evidence-based policy-making. No Whitehall department was better based to adopt such an approach, with a unit of 85 researchers, 40 statisticians and support staff. As Hough and Morgan, both of whom have worked inside government, noted: 'In the early years the political commitment to evidence-led policy and to partnership between policy and research were very evident – and to our minds sincere.'[60] Governments that have been out of office for almost two decades tend to be hungry for new ideas and usually want support in implementing them. After the initial two years following Conservative restricted spending patterns, new flowers bloomed – new youth justice provisions, new drug prevention programmes in and outside prison, with evaluation budgets attached. The BCS was greatly extended – to a sample of 40,000 – and converted into a continuous rolling survey. The annual research budget rose from £11 million at its lowest point under Howard to £40 million. But the pièce de résistance was the 1999 £250 million 10-year Crime Reduction Programme with a £25 million evaluation budget to cover the first three years. It was intended that it be phased in over the decade with each new phase incorporating the lessons of its predecessor – an upward spiral of effectiveness. Alas it all turned sour. As Morgan and Hough explain, the challenges were immense: a multiplicity of disparate initiatives implemented in parallel in the same areas; tight timetables; political pressure for 'quick wins'; an underestimation by the agencies of the demands for data by the evaluators; and a recognition by poor performers that it would be in their interests to drag their heels. Evaluators fed back their findings of endemic failure to their policy paymasters, who found themselves in an impossible position. Operating in an increasingly demanding 'can-do' work ethos, they were reluctant to admit failure to ministers. It limped on for three years before there was a silent retreat. And as for the research, some went unpublished, some long delayed, some unpromoted but published elsewhere.

As the authors note, the potential visibility of Home Office research means there will always be close political scrutiny of the programme. Ultimately the research programme is managed for political ends – to enhance the reputation of the political party in government. At best it aims at the fine-tuning of policy, not challenging it, and certainly not discrediting either it or the agencies delivering it.'The ministerial thumb on the research pipeline occurs when an administration has accumulated an extensive policy record to defend, or when it feels under threat from the Opposition',[61] they suggest.

But under New Labour's 'can-do' administration there was a clear shift from officials to ministers long before there was any threat from the opposition. External contracts – and a large chunk of the budget has always been spent on them – became more specific in context, of shorter duration, subject to closer supervision, covered by stricter rules of confidentiality and subject to firmer control over the use of data and publication. And it did not stop there. The authors give various examples of where unpopular findings were delayed, not published, reworked or even turned from failure into success – the latter a re-analysis of Tim Hope's work, which found various projects to cut burglary had initially failed, but could be seen to have succeeded when 'anticipatory benefits' were included. A favourite trick was to pick out the ripe cherries for the department's press release and delay the bad fruit for a much later and fuller version, which was less likely to be read by the media.

Certainly the anger of criminologists in the field, even those who did not bid for research grants, grew. The Centre for Crime and Justice Studies, based at King's College, London, devoted a large part of its quarterly journal, *Criminal Justice Matters*, in February 2006, to the state of research in the criminal justice system, and produced a monograph series that began in 2008. The opening work by Reece Walters, Professor of Criminology at The Open University, pointed to the pause on research publication imposed in May 2006 by John Reid, brought in to replace Charles Clarke, who declared the department as 'unfit for purpose'. The Home Office announced 'the pause' on research to allow the new Home Secretary to 'take a look at what is on the stocks and in the pipeline'. Walters declared:

> For those of us in academic criminology who for years declared the biased controlling and manipulative practices of the Home Office criminological research, this was nothing more than home secretarial endorsement for what we have known for years – that the RDS [the

renamed Research Unit – Research Development and Statistics Directorate] is 'not fit for purpose'. Home Office suppression of criminological research that contradicts ministerial policy and opinion is a feature of this arm of government.[62]

On a front where news stories are few and far between, *The Sunday Telegraph* suggested Reid was trying to bury bad news by blocking research findings.[63] A gun crime research study by Chris Lewis at the University of Portsmouth was poised to reveal the ease with which criminals could access firearms. Without the pause, that leak may not have been given.

Can the penal populist toothpaste be pushed back into the tube?

The Commons Select Committee on Justice held some well-structured hearings on *Cutting crime* – alternatives to prisons – part of which looked at the rise in penal populism and the media's influence on law and order in 2008/09. (I presented a very brief summary of this chapter at one of the hearings.) The Committee noted that even the Lord Chief Justice, Lord Phillips, had conceded that the rise in custody and increases in the length of sentences 'may well be attributable in part to media pressure'. In a lecture 'Who decides the sentence?' in 2008, he had noted that 'part of a sentencer's job is to reflect, at least to a degree, the public's view as to the proper response to crime'. He also thought the negative media coverage of some bail and parole decisions had led to both the courts and the Parole Board becoming more risk-averse.[64] But the Committee also heard from politicians that they should not escape censure. David Howarth, Liberal Democrat Shadow Solicitor General, said: 'There is a lot of debate about the influence of the media on policy; you have just had a whole session about that ... the toxic bit was the politicisation of crime which we did as politicians and it is up to us to draw that poison out. Until we do that, it is not possible to move ahead but I think it is possible for us to do it.'[65]

Several witnesses including Lord Dubs, former Labour MP, and the New Economics Foundation referred to an apparent absence of political leadership in challenging media perspectives on crime with equally powerful voices. The same concern over an apparent lack of political will was reflected in the Committee's e-consultation process. One respondent declared: 'First you have to stop national politicians grovelling to the *Daily Mail* ...'[66] The Committee noted the extent to which the government still acquiesced in 'tough' criminal justice messages. A Ministry of Justice press release on a new ICM survey, which had found relatively strong support for community sentences, had been sent out under the heading: 'Victims of crime want punishment'. In response, Gillian Guy, Chief Executive of Victim Support, asserted: 'If the criminal justice system is to truly serve victims, we need to prioritise effective rehabilitation rather than using victims to justify harsh punishment.'[67]

The Committee was in no doubt about the counter-productive penal policies of the previous 17 years:

> We do not contest that crime and responses to it are important political issues but we believe that the extreme politicisation of criminal justice policy is counter-productive, undermines rational policy-making, and conceals the consensus that does exist around the future direction of the criminal justice system. The Government has found itself in a problematic position on two counts. The need to be seen to be tougher than the opposition has contributed to the massive expansion of the system which has in turn caused the current lack of prison and probation capacity. At the same time it has undermined the pursuit of the Government's aspiration to be tough on the causes of crime and provide offenders with the real opportunities to reform.[68]

But most interesting of all, the Committee noted that there were some signs of the political landscape changing. The two shadow ministers who had appeared before the Committee, the Conservative Nick Herbert and the Liberal Democrat David Howarth, thought all parties could begin moving to a political consensus 'if the direction of policy centred on reducing re-offending and preventing re-victimisation'. The then Justice Minister, Labour's David Hanson, echoed similar views giving his evidence: 'I can say genuinely that on some issue of rehabilitation I share very similar views to some of the Members of the Opposition'.[69]

Cometh the hour, cometh the man

The emergence of the Conservative–Liberal Democrat government following the May 2010 general election – the first coalition in the UK since the Second World War – saw Kenneth Clarke, the most experienced minister in the alliance, return to the Cabinet wearing a Justice Minister/Lord Chancellor hat. Here was the ideal candidate to take on the daunting challenge of tackling penal populism, a minister who was popular with the public, liked and respected by the media, seen to be fearless in pushing controversial policies (Thatcher's internal health market), robust in defending his position and resolute in refusing to bend to media campaigns. I followed – and wrote about – his climb through the most senior Cabinet posts between 1988 and 1997: Health, Education, Home Office and Chancellor of the Exchequer. The British Medical Association spent £1 million in a personalised advertising campaign to undermine his health changes ('What do you call a man who does not listen to his doctors? Kenneth Clarke') without disturbing his affability. You could write the most excoriating editorial about aspects of his policy only to be met the next day with a genial greeting, 'Thought you were rather gentle this morning, Malcolm'.

As speculation rose towards his first public speech in his new post in June 2010, *The Times* reported 'a certain nervousness in Number 10' on the morning of the speech.[70] At the Conservative Party annual conference in October 1993 David Cameron had been special adviser to Michael Howard when Howard delivered his infamous 'prison works' speech – throwing red meat to right-wing Tory lions and the tabloid carnivores. But, true to the speculation, Clarke ruthlessly attacked the failings of penal policy in the previous 17 years. Noting the prison population had doubled to 85,000 since he was last in charge of prisons in 1993, he declared: 'This is quite an astonishing number, which I would (once) have dismissed as an impossible and ridiculous prediction.'

Despite more and more offenders being warehoused in outdated facilities, the public did not feel any safer. He went on: 'Too often prison has proved a costly and ineffectual approach that fails to turn criminals into law-abiding citizens ... in our worst prisons, it produces tougher criminals.' In a scathing passage about the failure of prison to prevent re-offending, he said: 'Just banging up more and more people for longer without actively seeking to change them is what you would expect of Victorian England.' He highlighted that it cost more to keep one criminal in jail for a year (£38,000) than to send a boy to Eton, yet re-offending rates were stubbornly high. Half of all crime was being committed by people who had already been through the prison system. 'We must now take action to shut off the revolving door of crime and re-offending.' There needed to be more effective penalties. The speech, which had been well trailed in the morning papers, was defended by David Cameron at Prime Minister's Questions in the Commons.

The *Mail* Editorial thought 'one of Kenneth Clarke's attractive qualities is that he's always been something of a maverick. But the new Justice Minister's astonishing attack on his own party's policy over prisons takes independence too far.... Mr Clarke needs a short, sharp, shock.'[71] *The Guardian* Editorial thought Clarke's hand had been strengthened by the government's partner, the Liberal Democrats: 'Their manifesto proposed a presumption against all short term jail terms [as prison governors had been urging], and although the Justice Secretary did not go that far, his failure to mention the Conservatives' own pre-election plan to double the sentencing powers of magistrates suggests the coalition brokering has borne progressive fruit.'[72] Jack Straw, in a column in the *Mail*, headlined 'Mr Clarke and the Lib Dems are wrong. Prison DOES work – and I helped prove it'. And in a box below the headline, the *Mail* added: 'No, you're not going mad. Here, a former LABOUR Home Secretary accuses the Tories of going soft on crime.'[73]

By the time of the release of the new government's Comprehensive Spending Review on 20 October 2010, the picture was much clearer.

The Justice Department suffered a 23 per cent cut, reducing its budget to £7.3 billion with strict limitations on its capital spending. Labour's plan to increase accommodation in prisons to 96,000 by 2014 was abandoned. Clarke was promising a 3,000 fall in prison numbers, to 82,000, by 2014. The Treasury endorsed Clarke's claims that his sentencing reforms and 'rehabilitation revolution' would 'stem the unsustainable rise in the UK prison population'.[74]

Kenneth Clarke's Green Paper

Just over six weeks later, on 7 December 2010, Clarke published his sentencing and rehabilitation Green Paper, *Breaking the cycle*, to the acclaim of *The Independent* and *The Guardian* and the despair of *The Sun*, *Express* and *Mail*. The consultation document promised a full working week for prison inmates to prepare them for working life outside, more 'demanding' community programmes, tougher curfews, and diverting more offenders with drug or alcohol problems to community treatment schemes. It became clear that three of the ways in which the prison population would be reduced was by increasing the discount in prison for early guilty pleas, from 33 per cent to 50 per cent; reducing the number of suspects held on remand by not using it for offences which rarely lead to prison on conviction; and speeding up the removal of foreign prisoners. The document confirmed the probation service would lose its monopoly over alternative-to-prison schemes. It promised a 'revolutionary shift' in the way rehabilitation was financed and delivered through performance-related contracts with voluntary organisations and private firms which would be paid according to their 'rehabilitation results'.

Perhaps most important of all for penal reformers was Clarke's promise to restore some judicial discretion and deal with the critical overcrowding crisis being generated by a new indeterminate sentence introduced by David Blunkett. He said he would sweep away the statutory sentencing framework, erected by Blunkett in his Criminal Justice Act 2003. This laid down statutory minimum 'starting points' of 15 years, 30 years and 'life must mean life' for specified types of murder. Clarke described them as 'fair old nonsense', 'ill thought out' and 'overtly prescriptive'. He explained: 'We do not need to tell judges that murder is a serious offence. They are perfectly capable of setting a minimum term. We need a more sensible approach that is not too prescriptive in cases such as mercy killings, fights between partners, or husband and wife killings.'

He promised further curbs on the indeterminate sentence of imprisonment for public protection (IPP). This was one more of Blunkett's 'declamatory sentences' in his 2003 Act – a sentence which was hastily passed with hardly any parliamentary debate and even less media scrutiny despite the evidence from overseas of the dangers of such sentences. It was designed to sit next to Britain's only indeterminate prison sanction, the life sentence. Like life, it had a mandatory minimum term (the tariff, as it is known) to be served in custody, and then an indeterminate period determined by the Parole Board according to the risks related to release. It was designed for a lower order of 'dangerous' offenders than those served with life. However, the number of cases for which the IPP sentence was mandatory turned out to be much higher than the Home Office had originally envisaged.

From its implementation in April 2005, large numbers were imprisoned for relatively minor offences, receiving modest tariffs – just months or even weeks – but who could not be released because they could not get onto offending behaviour courses to prove their readiness for release. They numbered 2,000 in the first 20 months. Urgent amendments applied in the Criminal Justice Act 2008 provided some relief, but they did not apply retrospectively to people caught in the first three years nor end the disproportionate numbers still being imprisoned. By 2010, some 6,000 had received the sentence, with 2,500 still being held beyond their tariff. On 13 July 2010, in a valedictory lecture as Chief Inspector of Prisons, Anne Owers urged ministers to look at the IPP and learn 'how not to do it'.[76] In a special report commissioned by the PRT, the authors, Mike Hough and Jessica Jacobson, described the sentence as 'the least carefully planned and implemented piece of legislation in the history of British sentencing'.[77] One of the problems highlighted in the report was the way in which public concern was exacerbated by 'media coverage of grave crimes, which does little to set risks in context'.[78]

On 18 September 2012 the European Court of Human Rights declared the IPP sentence 'unlawful'. The Court ruled that the sentence had become 'arbitrary' in its operation through the lack of access to rehabilitative programmes. This was in breach of the European Convention on Human Rights. The Ministry of Justice responded by saying it would be replaced with a new regime of determinate sentences.[79]

One week after the Green Paper, the divisions within the Coalition were on public view – and highlighted by the media – when Home Secretary Theresa May echoed the 'prison works' mantra used by Howard, Straw and Blunkett when she appeared before the Commons Select Committee on Home Affairs. Paying tribute to the Green Paper's push for more alternatives to prison, she went on: 'I think we must all recognise that in looking at the wider issue of sentencing, prison works, but it must be made to work better.'[80] They proved sweet words for the tabloids. *The Sun* declared in its Editorial: 'Potty Ken Clarke is fighting a losing battle in his attempts to empty the jails.... Home Secretary Theresa May was "echoing the views of millions of *Sun* readers".'[81] Michael Howard waded in with a column in *The Times* declaring Clarke's proposals were 'fatally flawed'.[82]

Penal populism returns

Alas, five months after the Green Paper, the heart of the plan was abandoned. It was triggered by a BBC Radio 5 live phone-in on 18 May 2011 by a woman caller, Gabrielle Browne, who had suffered a sexual assault. She described Clarke's plan to increase discounts on sentences from one third to one half for early guilty pleas as 'devastating' because they would apply to rapists. This was all the tabloids needed to reignite their campaign against the plan. Ironically, the woman later changed her mind when she met Clarke and learned more women would be spared from the trauma of going through a trial process. She told *The Times* that the government should not jump to a hasty conclusion based on emotion but 'give this idea more thorough consideration before ruling it out'.[83]

But she didn't change Cameron's opinion. Until the broadcast and the reopened tabloid tirade, Cameron had warily supported Clarke, but after the broadcast he took over the plan and did not just eliminate the 50 per cent discount for rapists but for all offences; vetoed the new release test for IPP inmates which would have reduced their number; and introduced a new mandatory sentence of six months for carrying a knife. These changes, announced on 21 June 2011, received ecstatic responses from the tabloids. The headline to *The Daily Mail*'s Editorial 'Finally Mr Cameron acts like a Tory PM' and *The Sun*'s front page headline 'Can we claim victory over Justice Secretary? – YES WE KEN' succinctly summed it up.

We were back in penal populist wars. In the wake of the BBC May 2011 phone-in, Ed Miliband, the Labour leader, called for Clarke's resignation for suggesting that there was more than one form of rape. When Cameron announced his new hardline measures in June 2011, Miliband restricted his criticisms to the fact that he was making another U-turn – ignoring the fact that if he was not supporting them, he was too.

Abolition of Anti-social Behaviour Orders?

Theresa May had, however, earned some liberal cheers when she announced in July 2010 that she would be abolishing Anti-social Behaviour Orders (ASBOs).[84] The controversial ASBO was conceived by Labour as a flagship crime policy in 1996 and launched in April 1999. The original aim was to combine banning orders – imposing curfews or applying banning orders on visiting specific estates or shopping centres – together with parenting programmes to tackle the roots of 'yobbish' behaviour. Initially, the orders were unpopular with both the police and councils. In the first 21 months only 240 were issued and just 350 in 2001. But in Labour's second term, when placed at the heart of Blair's 'Respect' programme, numbers multiplied, reaching a peak of 4,100 in 2005. Critics condemned them for criminalising children. They were imposed for non-criminal but anti-social behaviour, but many of those on them ended up committing a criminal offence by breaching the conditions order. They were popular with the public, but only 39 per cent believed they were effective in curbing anti-social behaviour. The response from the media was mixed. The tabloids were generally in favour, but they too reported the contradictions – more than one offender found they were unable to visit their probation officer because the office was in a banned zone, and one order was even imposed on a 48-year-old woman forbidding her from making excessive noise during sex anywhere in England.

More than half the 17,000 orders imposed between 1999 and December 2008 – the latest year for which statistics are available – were breached. By 2007 the breach rate reached 61 per cent. The National Audit Office, in a report in 2007, found that a third of ASBOs had been breached five or more times. Almost 5,000 of these offenders were given immediate custodial sentences. Given these statistics, the number of orders had dropped to 2,000 in 2008. Jacqui Smith, in her term as Labour Home Secretary between June 2007 and June 2009, had sought to reduce them by urging more early intervention programmes. Theresa May, in declaring it was time to 'move beyond the ASBO', echoed the critics, in stating the orders 'too often criminalised young people unnecessarily acting as a conveyor belt to serious crime and prison'.[85] She promised more streamlined police powers to deal with anti-social behaviour.

What was evident was that anti-social behaviour was a genuine issue, which has been made dramatically clear by the case of Fiona Pilkington, a timid and depressed single parent with learning difficulties, who killed herself and her severely disabled daughter in October 2007 by setting her car on fire after years of continuous harassment by local youths. Over the years she had made 33 calls to the police that had failed to lead to any arrests or proper protection. A report from HM Inspectors of Police in September 2010 estimated 14 million anti-social incidents a year are reported to the police, who respond to fewer than 50 per cent.[86] Sir Denis O'Connor, Chief Inspector, criticised the police force for not recognising anti-social incidents as 'real police work'. He added: 'This kind of behaviour matters a lot to people but it doesn't count in the criminal justice system. It is a festering subject that is lingering in the background and we want to bring it forward.'[87] As *The Times* noted: 'Fears have been raised that with forces facing budget cuts of up to 25 per cent, the issue will fall down the agenda.'[88]

Anti-terrorism laws revisited

Behind the scenes a second law and order battle took place within the Coalition government over the reform of anti-terrorism legislation. The final compromise emerged – after a succession of contradictory media leaks – on 26 January 2011. The package included reducing the time that terrorist suspects could be detained pre-charge, from 28 to 14 days (although still retaining a procedure to temporarily revert to 28 days in exceptional circumstances); new restrictions on stop-and-search counter-terrorism procedures; and a watering down of 'control order' sanctions. The latter included tighter exclusion zones replacing forcible relocation; an 'overnight residence requirement' of 8–10 hours replacing the 16-hour house-based nocturnal curfew; and the lifting of some restrictions on day-time movements but with increased surveillance.[89]

Lord Macdonald, former Director of Public Prosecutions, who was commissioned by the government to report on current national security provisions, praised the first two moves but criticised the third for being too restrictive. This position was echoed by *The Independent*, *The Times* and *The Guardian*, but received a more mixed response from the tabloids. The *Mail* declared 'the fudged security measures unveiled yesterday, after months of haggling, show exactly what we feared ... the feeble compromise over control orders and curfews ... would be risible if they weren't serious'. *The Sun* welcomed 'the Government decision not to scrap the orders. They will be varied but the key elements remain.' Under the headline 'New look control orders to spare Clegg's blushes', the *Daily Express* believed control orders were not a threat to fundamental rights but the Liberal Democrat leader, Nick Clegg, had promised to abolish them in the last election. It added: 'Given all the promises he has been content to break it says much about Mr Clegg that obtaining a cushier deal for suspected terrorist masterminds was the one he fought hardest to keep.' But *The Mirror* insisted that the Coalition should have done more than just 'fudging the issue instead of abolishing restrictions which are ineffective and fundamentally illiberal'. *The Telegraph* was the most satisfied paper under a first leader headline that asserted: 'A sensible balance of liberty and security'.[90]

The 2011 summer riots

The riots began in Tottenham two days after 29-year-old Mark Duggan was shot and killed by London Metropolitan Police (the Met). Family and friends of the dead man marched peacefully to Tottenham police station on Sunday, 7 August but failed to be given a sufficiently senior officer to get satisfactory answers to their questions. The riots began shortly after a three-hour wait at the station proved fruitless. From Tottenham rioting spread to 10 other areas of London, five major cities (Birmingham, Manchester, Liverpool, Nottingham and Leicester) and a score of other local authorities. By 10 August when it stopped, five people were dead, 180 police officers and 10 firemen injured, 100 houses destroyed by rioters, and 48,000 local businesses – shops, restaurants, pubs and clubs – suffered serious financial losses from the looting and arson. It was the biggest outbreak of civil unrest in the country since the 1981 riots in London (Brixton), Liverpool (Toxteth), and Manchester (Moss Side). The Association of British Insurers faced payouts of an estimated £200 million and the uninsured losses of a further £200 million. The Riots Communities and Victims Panel, set up by the government, reported on 29 November 2011 that scores of firms had still been unable to get compensation despite pledges from the Prime Minister.

The Met were slow to anticipate the extent of the looting and delayed putting up adequate numbers of officers on the streets until outrage from Westminster, City Hall and the media helped tripled the number to 16,000. In the aftermath, over 4,000 arrests concerning 5,100 individual riot-related crimes were made across 10 police authority areas. Some 68 per cent (3,401) of the arrests were by the Met. Just over 50 per cent of the crimes involved commercial property, particularly electrical and clothing shops. Some riots broke out in unsuspected affluent areas like Sloane Square or in comfortably off outer London towns, such as Croydon, which lost an historic furniture store. The 150-year-old shop had survived two world wars, but went up in flames when a looter, who was filmed, stepped through a shattered window and set fire to a sofa. The fire, which was so fierce it spread to residential buildings forcing some inhabitants to jump to safety, became an iconic picture of the riots. The looter received an 11-year prison sentence.

A Ministry of Justice report, published in February 2012, provided demographic statistics of the people charged: 41 per cent were white, 39 per cent black, 12 per cent mixed race and 6 per cent Asian. These proportions varied according to the areas concerned. In Salford 94 per cent of those arrested were white, only 2 per cent black. Rioters brought to court were disproportionately male (90 per cent), disproportionately young, with 26 per cent aged 10 to 17 and 27 per cent aged 18 to 20, only 5 per cent over 40. Some 76 per cent had previous convictions, of whom 26 per cent had more than 10 previous convictions.[91]

Prosecutions and sentencing were swift. The average sentence was 16.8 months, making the penalties much longer than the average prison terms for similar offences in 2010. But of the 1,291 people given prison sentences by the end of June 2012, some 242 had been released under home detention curfews before serving half their sentence. These included 162 burglars and 44 thieves.[92] Britain's most senior prosecutor, Keir Starmer, Director of Public Prosecutions, in an interview in *The Guardian* questioned the heavy sentencing by the courts and said he believed the speed with which rioters and looters were brought before the courts was a far more powerful deterrent to reoffending than the severity of the sentences. He explained: 'I don't think people gamble on the length of the sentence particularly. They gamble on "Am I going to get caught?"'[93]

Most immediate analysis proved wrong. Many wanted to blame gang culture but only 13 per cent were group members. Others spoke of 'tourist rioters', but the average rioter lived only 2.2 miles from the scene of the crime. There was general agreement among researchers that contributing factors included: opportunism, perceived social injustice, deprivation, and frustration at the way their communities were policed, particularly the latter. Social media played a part – particularly BBM (BlackBerry Messenger), with a 37 per cent share of the teen market – in inflammatory incitement but the messages and photos were later invaluable to the police in bringing suspects to prosecution. Some academics pointed to the poor information flow to the Met, suggesting an inadequate implementation of neighbourhood policing and a failure to monitor social media. Others wondered why there had not been more rioting given the one million unemployed young people in the country.

There were some uplifting moments during the riots. One heroine, Pauline Pearce in Hackney, was filmed chastising looters for their criminal and selfish behaviour, the video subsequently going viral on the web. Tarik Jahan, the father of one of three men killed in a deliberate hit-and-run incident in Birmingham, was rightly hailed as a hero. His son, with two friends, had been trying to protect Asian shops from looters. A grieving father, Jahan helped quell rising community anger by publicly calling for calm, social unity and an end to violence just hours after holding his dead son in his arms.[94] And in the immediate post-riot period, large numbers of volunteers turned out to help the owners of wrecked shops or houses clear up.

In the wake of the government's refusal to set up a public inquiry, like the Scarman tribunal which documented the causes of the 1981 riots, *The Guardian* joined forces with the London School of Economics to create a 'Reading the Riots' project. The *Guardian* website contains an index with the same name, *Reading the Riots*, which contains hundreds of different reports, interviews, analysis, data, photos and videos grouped under 20 headings. One of the biggest exercises involved recruiting 30 researchers to carry out in-depth interviews with 270 rioters, only 30 of whom had been arrested. The authorities even allowed the researchers access to some who were in prison. A second study, undertaken by Manchester University, analysed 2.5 million Twitter messages made during the riots to conclude that they played a larger role in mobilising volunteers to clear up the wreckage rather than encouraging the rioters. In phase two of the exercise large numbers of police, prosecutors, court officials and judges were interviewed. The site includes all the conclusions of the various exercises.

Future prospects for the criminal justice system

There were several concerns for progressives following Clarke's bold Green Paper. The first was the chronic shortage of resources to fund the expansion of alternatives to prison. Community programmes are considerably cheaper than prison, but they are not cost free – good schemes cost money. Yet it was not just the prison budget that suffered in the department's 23 per cent cut but probation and community programmes too. Worse still, savings being made by the reductions in inmate numbers were due to go back to the Treasury, not to investment in expanded community programmes. This breached the principle of 'Justice reinvestment', which had received such an encouraging endorsement by the Commons Select Committee on Justice. Thus an obvious danger ahead is that community programmes, which have a better rehabilitation record than prison, will suffer from this financial squeeze, which could end up badly damaging their reputation. It would have been difficult enough if the Green Paper had been implemented. But with the new hardline measures announced by Cameron on 21 June 2011, instead of there being 3,000 fewer prisoners by 2014, there may be considerably more than at present. This will put an extra squeeze on community programmes and the legal aid budget, already suffering a £50 million cut to housing, debt, employment and welfare benefit cases.

Second, to his credit Ken Clarke negotiated an extra £50 million to fund the health programmes to which offenders with mental ill health can be diverted. But mental health services, like the rest of the NHS, are facing a serious squeeze. The NHS is notorious for gobbling up funds from even earmarked specialist services, such as the budget for secure units for mentally disordered offenders in the 1970s, into general service provision. Third, the large increase in youth unemployment – and cuts to youth services and some employment training programmes – may drive up crime rates, putting the system under more pressure.

The final blow was the removal of Clarke from the Justice Ministry in Cameron's first major ministerial reshuffle in early September 2012, seen by several media commentators as 'a transfusion of Toryism'. Clarke lost the Department but remained in the Cabinet as a minister without portfolio – a government 'wisehead', which he accepted, after some resistance, with commendable insouciance. Tory right-wingers had been arguing for such a move for some time. They didn't just achieve an ejection, but were given a right-wing successor, Chris Grayling, who openly boasted of wanting to be 'a tough justice secretary'. Some of this could have been camouflage – or persiflage – to keep the party's raw meat-eaters' wing happy. For instance his first move to change the law to allow householders whose homes have been broken into to use 'disproportionate' physical force in retaliation, won rapturous approval from the tabloids and delegates. 'Batter a burglar' was *The Sun*'s splash headline. In reality there had been only seven such cases in the previous 14 years, where householders who had retaliated had been arrested. It clearly was not such a big issue, but the rhetoric demeaned his position.

One reason why the UK had avoided having a Secretary of State for Justice for so many years was, in the wise words of a former Director of Public Prosecutions, Ken Macdonald, because 'we retained a lingering post-totalitarian belief, forged in European war, that Ministries of Justice were alien ... they were bad for freedom and above all they would turn our innocent courts into something cruel and partisan. So instead we preferred someone in government who wouldn't look to his party, still less to the worst instincts on its wider fringes, but instead act as though he didn't have one, and who would take care of the law, staring out above the political fray, someone more or less immune from crouching leader-writers and bullying radio phone-ins.'[95] Judged by this criteria, Clarke had been magnificent. Grayling's early speeches, particularly his address to the 2012 annual Conservative conference, miserably failed the test, with his tailor-made titbits for the wider fringe, but with less excuse, because unlike earlier years, the hall was only half full.

Cameron ratchets up the rhetoric

Cameron officially delivered his 'first' law and order speech on 22 October 2012, which – with 14 bullet points of 'new tough policies' – was straight out of the Tony Blair handbook on how to survive 'a bad week in politics'. The recipe was straightforward: make it an emotive headline-grabbing speech, pretend it's a first on the issue and the proposals are all new, leak it to a tabloid and throw titbits to the others. The speech followed one of his worst weeks in Number 10 in which he had botched the announcement of a new energy-pricing policy; suffered a vexatious Prime Minister's question time in which he refused to give more details about a cache of emails and texts that he had sent to Rebekah Brooks but, according to *The Independent*, had not forwarded to the Leveson inquiry;[96] saw his Chancellor become embroiled in a dispute over sitting in a first-class rail carriage with a standard ticket; and been humiliated by the belated resignation of Andrew Mitchell, his Chief Whip. Leaving Downing Street four weeks before on his bicycle, Mitchell had been stopped by the police at the main gate and asked to wheel it through the smaller pedestrian gate for security reasons. According to the police he had sworn and called them 'plebs'. Mitchell belatedly agreed he had sworn, denied saying 'pleb', but refused to say what word he had used. The police account was later challenged first when a person purporting to be a member of the public informed his MP that he had heard the alleged words, only to turn out to be a police officer who was not present at the gate. Doubts were reinforced when Channel 4 TV news relayed CCTV footage of the gate at the time of the event, which showed there was no one standing there to hear the words, contrary to police evidence. What made the last two incidents for the Tories so toxic was they both played into the tabloid narrative that this was a government of 'toffs'. What made the resignation worse, was that Cameron had spent the previous four weeks trying to keep his Chief Whip, much against the wishes of many of his MPs.

Thus it was on Sunday, 21 October 2012 that newspaper purchasers were faced with some dramatic front pages: in *The Sunday Times*, 'Tory alarm over No 10 "meltdown"'; in *The Observer*: 'Tory grandee in assault on "this dog of a government – Tebbit hits out at coalition incompetence"'; in *The Mail on Sunday*: 'Cameron: "It's time to mug a hoodie". PM promises to seek "retribution" against law breakers in new anti-crime crackdown following catastrophic week'. *The Mail on Sunday* went on: 'He will refuse to apologise for taking a more authoritarian approach on the issue, declaring "retribution is not a dirty word". Measures include fines for failing prison bosses, life for gun runners, community sentences to be "punishment" ... and a possible withdrawal of the £46 given inmates on leaving prison.'

But on the next day, still before the speech had been delivered, there was a headline in *The Guardian*: 'Cameron's attempt to move on runs into trouble', under which it reported: 'Aides admitted there would be no additional money to pay for either more prisoners – who each cost the state £40,000 – or for extending rehabilitation to more offenders.' And on examination, many of the bullet points were old proposals dressed up as new.

Penal populism was back at the top of the political agenda. As *The Mail on Sunday* noted: 'Mr Cameron's initiative will be seen by many as proof that he has finally abandoned the so-called "hug a hoodie" policy associated with him when he became Tory leader in 2005.' Liberal Democrats, to their credit, were converted to a more rational approach to the complex challenge of criminal justice policy-making years ago. A succession of Lib Dem Shadow Home Secretaries, Simon Hughes, Mark Oaten and Chris Huhne, refused to indulge in penal populism. Sir Alan Beith, chair of the Commons Select Committee on Justice, which looked at the damage of penal populism, was a Lib Dem MP.

Ed Miliband signalled in an early *Guardian* interview after his election as Labour leader support for the new Coalition government's drive to reduce the prison population.[97] But his opposition to the Green Paper's proposals in May and his lack of opposition to Cameron's new hardline amendments in June 2011 retreated back to the Blair/Straw/Blunkett fold. As noted at the beginning of this chapter, Labour in government behaved like insurgents in a Tory Britain, refusing even to try changing public attitudes. Then came some hope with Miliband, now dissipated. Changing public attitudes in opposition is more difficult than in government. Miliband was right to try. Unfortunately it was not much of a try. The Liberal Democrats should not give up. It is time evidence-based rational policy-making trumped media-driven gut instincts – not least since the gut was never designed for thought.

Notes

[1] Home Office (2001) *Making punishments work: A review of the sentencing framework for England and Wales*, London: TSO.

[2] Tony Blair, 'A New Consensus on Law and Order', Speech, 19 July 2004.

[3] *The Guardian* (2004) Editorial, 20 July.

[4] D. Downes and R. Morgan (2007) 'No turning back: the politics of law and order into the millennium', in Mike Maguire, Rod Morgan and Robert

Reiner (eds) *The Oxford handbook of criminology* (4th edn), Oxford: Oxford University Press, p 20.

[5] Polly Toynbee (2004) *The Guardian*, 21 July.

[6] D. Downes and R. Morgan (1997) 'Dumping the "hostages to fortune"? The politics of law and order in post-war Britain', in Mike Maguire, Rod Morgan and Robert Reiner (eds) *The Oxford handbook of criminology* (2nd edn), Oxford: Oxford University Press, p 87.

[7] Ibid, p 96.

[8] Ibid, p 90.

[9] D. Butler and D. Kavanagh (2008) *The British general election of 1979*, Basingstoke: Macmillan.

[10] M. Hough et al (2007) 'The BCS over 25 years: progress, problems and prospects', *Crime Prevention Studies*, vol 22, pp 7-31.

[11] Ibid.

[12] Home Office (1990) *Crime, justice and protecting the public*, London: HMSO.

[13] Ibid.

[14] D. Downes and R. Morgan (1997) 'Dumping the "hostages to fortune"? The politics of law and order in post-war Britain', in Mike Maguire, Rod Morgan and Robert Reiner (eds) *The Oxford handbook of criminology* (2nd edn), Oxford: Oxford University Press, p 101.

[15] M. Tonry (2004) *Punishment and politics: Evidence and emulation in the making of English crime control policy*, Cullompton: Willan, p 41.

[16] E. Solomon et al (2007) *Ten years of criminal justice under Labour*, London: Centre for Crime and Justice Studies.

[17] Ibid.

[18] David Halpern (2009) *The hidden wealth of nations*, Cambridge: Polity Press.

[19] HM Government (2007) *Building on progress: Security, crime and justice*, London: Prime Minister's Strategy Unit.

[20] M. Hough (2005) 'Public attitudes to crime and punishment', *VISTA Probation Journal*, vol 11, no 2.

[21] Ibid.

[22] J. Jackson and S. Farrall, ESRC research project *Experience and Expression in the Fear of Crime* (see www.esrc.ac.uk and www.lse.ac.uk).

[23] M. Hough (2005) 'Public attitudes to crime and punishment', *VISTA Probation Journal*, vol 11, no 2.

[24] National newspapers, 22 October 2007.

[25] R. Reiner (2007) *Law and order: An honest citizen's guide to crime and control*, Cambridge: Polity Press, p 142.

[26] Ibid.

[27] Ibid.

[28] Sonia Livingstone (1996) 'On the continuing problem of media effects', in J. Curran and M. Gurevitch (eds) *Mass media and society*, London: Arnold, pp 305-24.

[29] Robert Reiner (2007) 'Media-made criminality: the representation of crime in the mass media', in Mike Maguire, Rod Morgan and Robert Reiner (eds) *The Oxford handbook of criminology* (4th edn), Oxford: Oxford University Press, ch 11, p 302.

[30] Ibid, p 316.

[31] W. Schramm et al (1961) *Television in the lives of our children*, Stanford, CA: Stanford University Press.

[32] J. Roberts et al (2002) *Penal populism and public opinion*, Oxford: Oxford University Press.

[33] Alan Travis (1998) *The Guardian*, 6 January, p 1.

[34] M. Hough and J. Roberts (1998) *Attitudes to punishment: Findings from the British Crime Survey*, Home Office Report No 179, London: Home Office.

[35] Lance Price (2010) *Where power lies: Prime ministers v the media*, New York: Simon & Schuster, p 310.

[36] 'Blair's own spin gurus savage No 10', *The Sunday Times*, 26 September 2004.

[37] Lance Price (2003) 'Feeding the hungry beast', *Independent on Sunday*, 31 August.

[38] David Marquand (2008) *Britain since 1918: The strange career of British democracy*, London: Weidenfield & Nicolson.

[39] Lance Price (2010) *Where power lies: Prime ministers v the media*, New York: Simon & Schuster, p 349.

[40] Ibid.

[41] Tim Newburn et al (2007) 'Crime and penal policy', in Anthony Seldon (ed) *Blair's Britain 1997–2007*, Cambridge: Cambridge University Press, ch 15, p 333.

[42] Ibid, p 334.

[43] Ibid.

[44] *The Sun*, 17 July 2000.

[45] Hugo Young (2003) *The Guardian*, 15 July.

[46] *The Guardian* (2005) Editorial and reports, 9 December.

[47] Ibid.

[48] Adam Tomkins (2005) 'Readings of *A v Secretary of State for Home Department*', *Public Law*, Summer issue, pp 259-66, at p 259.

[49] L. Blom-Cooper (2005) 'Government and the judiciary', in A. Seldon and D. Kavanagh (eds) *The Blair effect 2001–5*, Cambridge: Cambridge University Press.

[50] *The Guardian* (2005) Editorial, 13 October.

[51] Tony Blair (2010) *Tony Blair: A journey*, London: Hutchinson, p 584.

[52] Although this was quoted on the Number 10 website, it has now been removed, but see Ian Loader's blog (http://conservativehome.blogs.com/platform/ian-loader/).

[53] M. Gillespie and E. McLaughlin (2003) *Media and the shaping of public attitudes towards crime and punishment*, June, London: Esmée Fairbairn Foundation.

[54] M. Stead et al (2002) *What do the public really feel about non custodial penalties?*, November, Strathclyde: Centre for Social Marketing, University of Strathclyde for the Esmée Fairbairn Foundation.

[55] M. Hough et al (2003) *The decision to imprison*, June, London: Prison Reform Trust.

[56] PRT press release, 1 July 2003.

[57] Ibid.

[58] Alan Travis (1994) *The Guardian*, 4 July.

[59] R. Morgan and M. Hough (2007) 'The politics of criminological research', in R. King and E. Wincup (eds) *Doing research on crime and justice*, Oxford: Oxford University Press.

[60] Ibid.

[61] Ibid.

[62] See the Centre for Crime and Justice Studies website at www.crimeandjustice.org.uk.

[63] *The Sunday Telegraph* (2006) 'Reid accused of burying bad news by blocking research', 2 July.

[64] Commons Select Committee on Justice (2009) *Cutting crime: The case for justice reinvestment*, London: TSO, para 190.

[65] Minutes of the Oral Hearing on Justice Reinvestment by the Commons Select Committee on Justice, 25 November 2008, in response to Q500.

[66] Commons Select Committee on Justice (2009) *Cutting crime: The case for justice reinvestment*, London: TSO, para 213.

[67] Ibid, para 214.

[68] Ibid, para 200.

[69] Ibid, paras 220-1.

[70] *The Times*, 30 June 2010, p 1.

[71] *Daily Mail* (2010) Editorial, 1 July.

[72] *The Guardian* (2010) Editorial, 1 July.

[73] Jack Straw (2010) 'Mr Clarke and the Liberal Democrats are wrong. Prison DOES work – and I helped prove it', *Daily Mail*, 30 June.

[74] *The Guardian*, 21 October 2010, p 8.

[75] Ministry of Justice (2010) *Breaking the cycle: Effective punishment, rehabilitation and sentencing of offenders*, London: TSO.

[76] See PRT website (www.prisonreformtrust.org.uk) for copy of speech.

[77] M. Hough and J. Jacobson (2010) *Unjust deserts: Imprisonment for public protection*, London: Prison Reform Trust.

[78] All national newpapers, 15 December 2010.

[79] Alan Travis (2012) 'Strasbourg judges rule indeterminate sentences unlawful', *The Guardian*, 18 September.

[80] Alan Travis (2010) 'Prison works, says Theresa May', *The Guardian*, 14 December.

[81] *The Sun*, 15 December 2010.

[82] *The Times*, 14 December 2010, p 20.

[83] Richard Ford (2011) 'Give Clarke's jail plan a chance, says his radio nemesis', *The Times*, 11 June.

[84] National press websites, 29 July 2010.

[85] *The Times*, 29 July 2010, pp 14–15.

[86] *The Times*, 23 September 2010, p 3.

[87] Ibid, p 3.

[88] Ibid.

[89] See the BBC and national press websites, 26 January 2010.

[90] Ibid, or see national newpapers for 27 January 2010.

[91] Ministry of Justice (2012) 'Statistical bulletin on the public disorder of 6th to 9th August 2011 – February 2012 update', www.justice.gov.uk/downloads/statistics/criminal-justice-stats/august-public-disorder-stats-bulletin-230212.pdf

[92] *The Guardian* (2012) 'One in five jailed rioters let out of prison early', 18 August.

[93] Paul Lewis (2012) 'Rapid riot prosecutions more important than long sentences', *The Guardian*, 3 July.

[94] Daniel Hannan (2011) 'Amid all the bad news, Tariq Jahan made me feel proud to be British', *The Daily Telegraph*, 11 August.

[95] Ken Macdonald (2012) 'Chris Grayling will need a soul, not a law degree', *The Times*, 10 September.

[96] Nigel Morris (2012) 'PM pressed to come clean over secret Brooks emails', *The Independent*, 18 October.

[97] *The Guardian*, 22 November 2010, pp 12–13.

FOUR

Drugs: tabloid puppets and pawns

DRUGS: how government ministers act like Murdoch editors: they don't need to be told what to do. They already know.

The title of the report published on Monday, 28 March 2000 far understated its importance. It was simply and plainly entitled *Drugs and the law: Report of the Independent Inquiry into the Misuse of Drugs Act 1971*. It was far more significant than that, as the media were aware. Both broadsheets and tabloids cleared large spaces on their front and inside pages to set out its proposals and to allow commentators to respond. Over 60 reporters were present at the report's launch. As *The Economist* noted at the end of the week, it was the most comprehensive review of drugs legislation for a quarter of a century. Yet rarely has a government so completely misjudged the way the media were going to respond to such a serious report.

There are several reasons why what happened to the Runciman Report – as it became known – is an important event in studying the influence of the media on policy-making. Perhaps the most intriguing is the insights it gives on how ministers adopt postures in anticipation of how the media will respond to an issue. There is a parallel to be drawn here between the influence that the tabloid press applies to ministers and the influence Rupert Murdoch applies to his editors. He does not need to issue daily edicts because his editors know what he wants. Ditto with the tabloids and ministers. Ministers know what the tabloids want and too frequently on major social issues – drugs, asylum, law and order – policy is adjusted accordingly. The Runciman Report is a more rare event in that for once, ministers misread the expected response and had to backtrack.

It was not unreasonable for ministers to believe that the tabloids would give the Runciman Report a hard time – there was a long tradition of drugs being used by the media to stereotype, vilify and sensationalise drug abuse. As Roy Greenslade, media commentator and former *Daily Mirror* Editor, noted in *Druglink*, a serious bi-monthly journal that tracks drug treatment, policy and legal developments, run by the charity DrugScope:

> There are many complex dilemmas that are, to a popular newspaper editor, so straightforward that the solutions do not require a second thought. Among the most glaringly obvious is the matter of drugs. It is just common sense, isn't it? All drugs are evil. They lead to criminality. They screw up the people who use them. They threaten the orderliness of our society. The people who supply them are scum....
>
> From the middle of the 1960s onwards it has been a roller coaster ride, with the media 'discovering' new forms of evil at regular intervals, starting with cannabis and progressing through heroin, LSD, speed, cocaine, ecstasy and all manner of combinations and spin-offs. None of this occurred in isolation. From the beginning the police and successive governments played their parts in the panics too. Indeed it is impossible to analyse why media coverage of drugs has been so wayward unless we understand the inter-relationship between press, police and politicians. Each of these institutions, working in a loose partnership, tend to cloud the issue, creating myths rather than informing the public about reality.[1]

As the Royal Society of Arts (RSA) Commission on Illegal Drugs, Communities and Public Policy noted seven years after Runciman in 2007: 'Much of the current debate about illegal drugs, especially in Parliament and the press, strikes us as positively medieval, with drug users demonised as though at the beginning of the 21st century we were still in the business of casting out demons and burning witches. As one of this commission's members put it, "it's time to get real".'[2]

Just one year after Runciman, the Chief Executive of the National Treatment Agency responsible for improving treatment programmes for drug users complained in evidence to the House of Commons

Select Committee on Home Affairs in 2001 about the media's refusal to recognise the different levels of harm posed by different drugs: 'Cannabis may as well be heroin, a weekend amphetamine user a crazed addict, a young woman who gives a friend an ecstasy tablet a drugs baron.'[3]

And just five years before Runciman reported, the apocalyptic tone of some politicians is well illustrated by the Secretary of State for Scotland introducing the 'Scotland Against Drugs' campaign in 1995: 'The drugs epidemic is a scourge as terrible as any medieval plague. Let us, as a nation, make a New Year resolution that 1996 is the year in which we will turn back the tide of drug abuse which is engulfing our young people and threatening our civilisation.'[4]

The toughest laws – but the most drug users

Another reason why the Runciman Report was important was that it coincided with a period when attitudes were changing, both at home and abroad. There was an opportunity for reform. The 30-month study by the Runciman Committee provided a solid base on which a progressive government proudly declaring its belief in evidence-based policy-making could have fruitfully built. The current war on drugs policy, as the Committee documented in detail, was not working. A survey by the European Monitoring Centre for Drugs and Drug Addiction (EMCDDA) in 1998 concluded that, despite the UK having some of the toughest enforcement laws in the EU, Britain had by far the highest proportion of drug users – 35 per cent of teenagers taking cannabis compared to 25 per cent in France, the next highest country. It was a similar picture with ecstasy, with 9 per cent of British youth having tried the drug compared to 3 per cent in Germany and France and 1 per cent in Sweden.[5] 'Drug-taking Britain worst in Europe' was becoming a familiar headline.

There had been a succession of calls for a more liberal approach towards soft drugs. In evidence to Runciman the British Medical Association (BMA) noted that the toxicity of cannabinoids (constituent parts of cannabis) were 'extremely low; they are safe drugs and no deaths have been directly attributed to their recreational or therapeutic use'. The BMA Scottish Committee called for cannabis to be legalised for recreational use in June 1999. The following month, a senior Scottish judge called for a Royal Commission to look at the case for decriminalising cannabis and examining the sentencing of drug offenders.[6] The EMCDDA survey showed that Europe was shifting towards decriminalising the possession of drugs for personal use. Its report revealed that the hard-line UK policy of continuing to criminalise all those arrested for cannabis possession – even cautions were placed on criminal records – was beginning to look like an old-fashioned stance. Public opinion polls were suggesting the same – a MORI poll found 80 per cent wanted a more relaxed approach to cannabis.

Finally, just before the Runciman Report was published, the Cleveland Police Service, which includes Teesside, was the first force to warn the government that its war on drugs was not being won. It declared that it was time to consider 'the only serious alternative – the legalisation and regulation of some or all drugs'. Previous chief constables had called for a more liberal approach but only on retirement, not when they were in office. The Cleveland Report, written by the force's Assistant Chief Constable and endorsed by its Chief Constable Barry Shaw, was the first call for decriminalisation from a senior serving officer. The force's police authority also endorsed the report.[7]

Calls for a Royal Commission into drug misuse had begun within months of Labour winning the 1997 general election. A Labour backbencher, Brian Iddon, had called for one in August 1997, when a five-year-old boy in his Bolton constituency was shot dead in an underworld drug shooting and his three-week-old brother was in hospital with a heroin addiction contracted from his addict mother. Two years later Charles Kennedy, as the newly elected Liberal Democrat leader, backed a similar call from his party. But Tony Blair had been adamant that there would not be such a commission set up; it was the voluntary sector that stepped in and ensured that there would.

Charities step in where the PM fears to tread

The man who broke the log jam was Dr Barrie Irving, the founding director of the Police Foundation, an independent research group set up in 1980 with the aim of making the police more effective. He was aware of the huge increase in drug-taking in the UK and the large number of young people at risk of getting criminal records for possession of cannabis as police sought to boost their arrest numbers. Irving, an exceptionally clever social psychologist, was educated at Cambridge and at the University of California in Berkeley, Los Angeles. He had worked at Cambridge and at the Tavistock Institute of Human Relations, but had come to the attention of the police from two inquiries. The first was the Maxwell Confait Inquiry into how a young man with severe learning difficulties had been wrongly prosecuted for murder – this led to stronger protection procedures for those with severe learning difficulties.

The second was his research for the 1977–79 Royal Commission on Criminal Justice where, among other things, he demonstrated that the concept of voluntary confessions in conditions of custodial interrogation was an oxymoron. It confirmed research in the US, which led to a famous US Supreme Court warning in the Miranda case that confessions in custody, where the police are in control of when a person eats, drinks and gets information, are suspect. What Irving's Royal Commission study also demonstrated – based as it was on many months' work in Brighton police cells – was that he was able to 'get on' with police officers of all ranks, even while he was documenting their shortcomings. His reputation as a constructive critic quickly spread among senior police ranks. For journalists interested in policing issues, he is a dream contact – his conversation fizzes with ideas, research findings, witty anecdotes, memorable quotes and interesting paradoxes.

Irving was able to persuade his somewhat reluctant Police Foundation trustees – the issue was clearly controversial and liable to be politically contentious – that it was time for a thorough examination of the present system of drug controls. He was helped by a strategy paper, drawn up by the Association of Chief Police Officers (ACPO) in 1996, which had reached the same conclusion. He was told he could 'give it a try' as long as he was able to raise the necessary funding. By 1996 Irving was one of the most experienced researchers at raising funds. He had been doing it for over 20 years at Tavistock and the Police Foundation. In drawing up his grant applications, he was able to quote the ACPO strategy paper and the fact that three senior ACPO members – the Metropolitan Commissioner, the ACPO President and the President of ACPO Scotland – were trustees of the Police Foundation.

It worked. He eventually persuaded nine charitable funds to back his idea. The first funder to which Irving turned was the Prince's Trust because Prince Charles was head of both institutions. Eight other trusts later joined in, bringing the total funding to about £500,000. Although the Police Foundation conceived the idea, raised the resources and provided the secretariat, once appointed, the committee was completely independent.

An impressive team of 13 commissioners was selected. They were as distinguished in their separate fields as any Royal Commission could have wanted. They were drawn from all the relevant specialties: drug treatment work, pharmacology, policing (two chief officers), law (the author of a definitive book on drug offences, plus a senior solicitor), mental health, as well as an inner-city college principal, Cambridge philosopher, economist, sociologist and a former *Times* Editor.

Viscountess Runciman sets to work

Viscountess Runciman, the first to be appointed to the commission, helped select the other 12 commissioners. She was an ideal chair, familiar with the policy areas the committee had to cover and with an enviable network of contacts in the fields of criminal justice, mental health, drug treatment, drug laws, HIV and community risk. Brought up and educated in South Africa, she had come to Britain to obtain a second history degree at Cambridge. Married to Lord (Garry) Runciman, a Cambridge scholar and chair of the 1991–93 Royal Commission on Criminal Justice, Lady Runciman had worked in the voluntary sector for 30 years. She had a long association with the Citizens' Advice Bureaux, was one of the founders of the Prison Reform Trust (PRT), served as chair of the Mental Health

Act Commission and then began a 20-year-plus association with the government's Advisory Council on the Misuse of Drugs (ACMD). As chair of two of ACMD's sub-committees she produced six reports on drugs. The first three helped change government strategy at the end of the 1980s, with its blunt conclusion that AIDS was a greater threat to individual and public health than drug misuse. The Thatcher government had initially found such conclusions hard to accept, but gradually adopted the policy of harm reduction – including needle exchanges – with, in Lady Runciman's words, 'immense and commendable rigour'. Would the Runciman Report of 2000 achieve the same delayed response?

Despite her daunting CV, Lady Runciman in person is warm, compassionate and self-deprecating about her abilities. But beneath the friendly, benign exterior runs an implacable determination to make the world a better place. By the launch of the inquiry in 1997 she was an expert chair of working parties, cleverly using her charm rather than her chair to ensure awkward maverick members – such as Simon Jenkins, former *Times* Editor, who is known to want more than the reclassification of drugs – stuck with the team. She was also well schooled in the politics of national commissions – they had to understand the art of the possible and not push for the politically impossible because they would not get a hearing.

This is what the Runciman Committee duly did following a normal Royal Commission procedure, holding 28 meetings over 30 months, cross-examining 34 expert witnesses and receiving written evidence from over 100 other individuals and organisations. Thanks to the funds generated by the trusts, the committee was able to recruit two key staff members. Joy Mott, who was due to retire from the Home Office where she had been steeped in drug research and criminal statistics in the role of liaison officer with the ACMD, proved an invaluable guide through the mountains of research and statistical papers. James Addison, a second mandarin and former secretary of the 1991–93 Royal Commission on Criminal Justice, was recruited to minute the meetings (some of which lasted for seven hours) and draft much of the report in clear and elegant English. The Permanent Secretary of the Home Office agreed to the cooperation of various parts of his department – research, statistics, drug unit – providing information and help including the release of previously unpublished data. Bill Saulsbury, Deputy Director of the Police Foundation, supervised the complex coordination and management of the exercise.

There were meetings with three groups of young people, two separate surveys of attitudes of school children and adults by MORI, specially commissioned papers on how young people make decisions to take drugs, the law on confiscation of assets, and the regulatory alternatives to criminal law in dealing with drugs. The Institute for the Study of Drug Dependence (ISDD) conducted a special analysis of the legal approaches of six other EU states. Two senior Netherlands officials from the health and justice departments flew over to brief the Committee on the Dutch system. Close contact was established with a separate working party on drugs by two Royal medical colleges – physicians and psychiatrists – which published one day after the Runciman Report and rejected the idea that cannabis was 'a gateway' to harder drugs.

The conclusions of the Committee followed the evidence, concluding that:

- eradication of drug use was not achievable and was not therefore either a realistic or sensible goal of public policy;
- far too much police time was targeted on users caught in possession of a drug, predominantly cannabis, rather than the dealers providing drugs;
- there was no evidence suggesting severe custodial penalties were deterring traffickers, and similarly no evidence that enforcement was having a significant effect on supplies;
- Britain had among the toughest drug laws of all major Western states, yet it also had the highest consumption of drugs and some of the worst addiction rates;
- despite record seizures of illicit drugs (£700 million in 1998, the last recorded year at the time) the quantity, quality and price of drugs on the street had remained unaffected. Indeed some prices had fallen;
- the current system which was supposed to be switching to treatment (which can work) from enforcement (which does not)

was still disproportionately spending 62 per cent on enforcement and a mere 13 per cent on treatment (a Rand study in the US estimated that every $1 spent on treatment saved $7);

- by any harm test – mortality, morbidity, toxicity, addictiveness or cause of crime – cannabis was less harmful than alcohol or tobacco. But the current annual criminal statistics showed cannabis possession accounted for at least 70 per cent of all 113,000 drug offences;

- a public opinion poll commissioned by the Committee found only 0.5 per cent of the public thought action against cannabis should be a police priority, a mere 8 out of 1,600 surveyed;

- the liberal approach of the Dutch – regarding drug use as a health problem rather than a criminal problem – was not without contradictions, but had contributed to a lower level of cannabis use, a heroin group which was ageing, unlike the UK where many young people were still joining, and the lowest overall rate of drug-related deaths in Europe.

The report concluded that the 30-year-old drugs law, passed to categorise drugs by harmfulness, no longer reflected modern scientific, medical or sociological evidence. It rejected the legalisation of drugs, but called for radical changes to current classifications, along with the introduction of a much less punitive approach to possession offences and a more effective punitive approach to supply.

Redrawing the criteria

The Committee drew up the first set of criteria against which objective assessments of relative harm of different drugs could be made. This was crucial if classifications were to have any rational backing. The criteria were: addiction potential; toxicity; risk of overdose; longer-term risk to life and health; potential for injecting; association with crime; association with problems for communities; and public health costs.

Using these criteria they drew up a more accurate 'hierarchy of harm', and recommended that:

- heroin, cocaine and crack cocaine should remain in class A, as they were the most addictive drugs and cause the most deaths;
- LSD (which is not addictive and has low toxicity) and ecstasy (closely related to amphetamines) should be reclassified from class A to the less harmful class B, putting them on a par with amphetamines – a change recommended to the inquiry by ACPO;
- cannabis should be downgraded to class C, the least harmful class – the report noted 'the law on cannabis causes more harm than it prevents';
- prison should no longer be available as a penalty for possession of either class C or class B drugs. At the time of the report possession of a class C drug was liable to two years' imprisonment and for a class B drug up to five years. The maximum for class A (then seven years) should be reduced to a year and/or an unlimited fine, and only imposed where community sentences had failed or been rejected.

The existing maximum sentences were among the toughest in Europe, but the report was not as radical as it might seem. Only 4,852 people of the 113,000 arrested for drugs in 1997 – the last year of completed statistics at the time of the report – were imprisoned. Most were dealers, many of them minor dealers. But in the five years up to the Runciman Report, between 500 and 1,000 young people a year were being imprisoned for possession. The number of drug offenders cautioned rose from 3 per cent of the total in 1974 to 50 per cent by 1997. More than 20 per cent were fined. Hence the system was already moving with the help of police discretion in the direction Runciman had mapped out. Even more reason, as *The Economist* argued, for ministers to accept the report.

At the launch Lady Runciman made three important points:

- the most dangerous message of all, that all drugs were equally dangerous, was untrue, lacked credibility and risked young people discounting the warnings about genuinely harmful drugs;
- the harm that drugs undoubtedly caused would not be reduced by disproportionate penalties on young people, whose occasional

drug use could be tackled more effectively by earlier more credible education;

• what was needed was a less punitive approach to possession offences combined with a more punitive approach to dealers.

Downing Street rebuttal

But even as Lady Runciman sat down, Downing Street and the Home Office were signalling to reporters that there would be no reclassification of the drugs identified in the report, nor would there be any lightening of penalties. Worse still was the response of the government's drugs tsar, Keith Hellawell, who had initially been a liberal chief constable with respect to drugs but within Whitehall's embrace had become a defender of the government's hard-line position. He said the report was sending out all the wrong messages. As *The Telegraph* later noted: 'Mr Hellawell, theoretically an independent player, seems to have been caught up in a government spin machine that does not admit the plain truths.'

Lady Runciman's public response to the rejection of the report by Tony Blair and Jack Straw proved prescient: 'Our report has a longer shelf life than them.' Within days Mr Straw was having to alter the line of his attack. Lady Runciman and Dr Irving had gone to the Home Office three days before publication to present the report to Jack Straw, Home Secretary, and Mo Mowlam, Drugs Minister. They were met by a bleak rejection by Mr Straw. He spoke of the political imperatives he faced and the importance of maintaining a strong anti-drugs message. He was opposed to reclassification and believed a reduction in prison penalties was politically impossible. Mo Mowlam, who had spoken of the need for a more progressive approach and continued pushing privately after being called into line publicly by Downing Street, suggested to the Home Secretary, 'Don't you think it would be better if we read the report first?'.

But the Home Office did not wait to read the report; they got their retaliation in first. Ministers received the report on the Friday, three days before the Monday publication date, and immediately went to work on the Sunday papers and television broadcasters. Sunday dawned, with the *Sunday Express* declaring 'Pleas for softer drug laws will be thrown out'; the *Mail*, 'Drugs hard line stays – Home Office rejects call to relax law on ecstasy'; *The Independent on Sunday*, 'Government to reject drug law relaxation'; and *The Observer* forecasting 'Police drug advice will fall on deaf ears'.[8] Charles Clarke, Home Office Police Minister, went on BBC 1's Sunday morning political show, *On the Record*, to reinforce the war on drugs message. There would be no weakening of the penalties for possession because that would send a signal that 'taking drugs is OK'.

Jay Rayner, in a column in *The Observer* on the following Sunday, noted: 'Tony Blair said his party would "campaign in poetry but govern in prose". The reality is less romantic. New Labour campaigns in thick black headlines....'[9] Polly Toynbee suggested in her *Guardian* column that the pre-briefing from Downing Street on the report could not have been more 'acidly laconic'. Downing Street spin doctors had concluded: 'to say the chance of reform happening is minimal would be an exaggeration'.[10]

Mike Trace, the deputy drugs tsar and a former drug treatment adviser in prisons, later described to *The Guardian* what had taken place on the Friday the report was delivered to the Home Office. Straw had taken over control of the government's response. 'As history will tell, we rebutted its key recommendations within 24 hours. Mo was too much of a loyalist really to make a stink about that, but basically she did not have a say in it, although she was nominally in charge of drugs policy.'[11] Both the tsar and deputy went to 10 Downing Street for the first time to discuss with ministers and the Prime Minister the response to the report. Tony Blair told Mo Mowlam that he knew she had strong views, which might even turn out to be right, but he was concerned about how a liberal line might play with the press and public. Blair indicated that his personal sympathies lay closer to Straw's position. 'End of chat, and that was it for the next two years,' Trace added.[12]

Fleet Street's unpredicted response

Not quite. The media did not respond as anticipated. Even on the eve of publication, there was a hint of what was to come: the *Mail on Sunday* ran a skewed three-page splash on the report under the quite erroneous suggestion that 'Prince Charles will this week place himself at the centre of a national debate over whether jail sentences for users of drugs such as Ecstasy should be scrapped'.[13] (The phoney tie was the fact that the Prince held honorary positions with the Police Foundation and the Prince's Trust, but had no direct control of either.) But it was not the skewed story, which was par for the course in the *Mail on Sunday*, but its Editorial that should have alerted ministers to changing tabloid attitudes. Under the headline 'We should all join the drugs debate', it declared 'this paper bows to no one in its vehement condemnation of the misuse of drugs', but then noted that British teenagers headed the European table for experimenting with drugs; that more than 4 out of 10 under-16s in Britain had used cannabis; that the Netherlands, where cannabis was partially legal, had fewer such users of cannabis; and went on to say, 'the depressing conclusion must be that the current regime of anti drug laws and enforcement is failing'.[14]

The next day, on publication day, in another paper in the *Mail* stable, London's *Evening Standard*, there was more support for the report. In an Editorial headlined 'Now let's have a proper debate', it declared: 'Lady Runciman must be right in arguing that education and treatment are more effective in curbing drug abuse than punishment', and condemned the government's pre-emptive criticisms. It went on: 'The Police Foundation, whose president is the Prince of Wales, is a well-respected organisation with far greater experience of the practical problems of curbing drug abuse than anyone on the Labour front bench. It is deplorable, therefore, that the Government should have dismissed the inquiry's findings before they were even published, in a casual statement by a Home Office minister on Sunday.'[15]

There was no surprise that *The Guardian* and *The Independent* both endorsed the report – they had campaigned for a more enlightened approach. Opposition from *The Times'* leader column was not a surprise, nor was the fulsome support for the report from its columnist, Simon Jenkins, a member of the Runciman Committee. His main reservation was that it had not gone further and adopted the Dutch approach, but he believed that the government's opposition would 'cheer every trafficker and pusher' in the country.

But it was the reasoned tone of the tabloids that surprised media commentators, who noted that they made Jack Straw appear more reactionary than the *Express*, *Mirror* and *Mail*.[16] The *Express* noted, ministerial 'knee jerk reactions won't help the police battle'; *The Mirror* insisted it should be 'discussed intelligently and with an open mind'; while the *Mail*, which placed an extract of its editorial in the middle of its front page, declared: 'despite this paper's instinctive reservations over a more relaxed approach to drugs, we believe that the issue deserves mature and rational debate'.[17] Inside it gave a full page to John Casey, a Cambridge don, to defend the decriminalisation of class B and C drugs – opposite an argument by Janet Betts, the stepmother of Leah Betts, who died taking one ecstasy tablet, on why ecstasy should remain a class A drug.

Most dramatic of all was the response of *The Daily Telegraph*. In an extraordinary editorial, given its previously hard-line approach, it declared: 'We are moving reluctantly to the view that Lady Runciman is asking the right questions. The "war against drugs" of which politicians and police officers like to speak, resembles those permanent wars between super powers that are a feature of George Orwell's *1984*: it is never won, though its victories are constantly trumpeted.' It looked at both sides of the argument and acknowledged that: 'Anyone of a conservative cast of mind is bound to take the objections to reform seriously.... And yet, and yet. We increasingly incline to the view that the banning of all drugs causes more harm than good. People like substances that alter their mind, and only strict puritans believe they should never use any of them.' It went on: 'Given that we live in an age in which the drugs of the world have found their way to our shores, surely the true conservative answer to the problem is to find ways of acclimatising drugs to bourgeois society rather than yelling vainly into the wind.' *The Telegraph* acknowledged this could be a tricky process for politicians and could be electorally vulnerable. But it continued: 'The first thing to do is to have a proper public debate. This is why Lady Runciman should not be getting the brush-off from the government.' But then, most radically, it declared: 'The second thing to do, we tentatively suggest, is to experiment with legalisation. As with the abolition of capital punishment, the thing should be tried out for a period, so that Parliament can easily vote to restore penalties if the experiment failed. But on that basis, we would argue that the government should draw up plans to legalise cannabis.'[18] *The Telegraph* followed up its editorial with a week of articles and commentaries maintaining the report's high profile.

The *Sunday Express* helped keep the story alive into a second week with a report suggesting that the Metropolitan Police Commissioner, Sir John Stevens, would not oppose decriminalising cannabis.[19] But before then ministers were already back-pedalling in the face of this unexpected outburst of media liberalism. *The Observer* reported that Jack Straw had indicated to them that there was 'a borderline case' for softening the law on ecstasy generating a three-line headline: 'Straw retreats from his hard line on ecstasy'.[20] But in a column in the hard-line *News of the World*, Straw adopted a different tone, insisting the government would not accept the reclassification proposed for cannabis. The headline summed it up: 'Why we won't be going soft on cannabis'.[21] He was, however, considerably more conciliatory about the need for a debate and expressed his 'genuine respect for the report's authors'. Indeed, for the first time he conceded there was 'a coherent argument' for legalising cannabis – which Runciman had not proposed but *The Telegraph* had – but went on to reject the proposal. As *The Telegraph* noted the next day, he had belatedly recognised he had misjudged the public's mood.[22] It could have added 'the media's mood' too. Ian Hargreaves, former Editor of *The Independent*, in a media column in the *New Statesman*, noted how the liberal leak had gone to a liberal paper (*The Observer*) and the hard-line position to a hard-line paper (*News of the World*). He went on: 'Surely one day, New Labour will realise the counter-productive effect of this duplicity.'[23]

The back-pedalling continued into the second week. *The Guardian* reported on the Monday that Home Office sources were insisting that the report was well regarded and had not been 'dismissed'.[24] The Metropolitan Police Commissioner, who was in New York, also clarified his position: 'If cannabis was legalised we'd be fine with it, because that's a policeman's job. I'd work with it.... I'm not saying legalise it. If policemen start querying laws, we're in trouble.' Scotland Yard emphasised that he was not in favour of decriminalisation, but he could work with it.

There was even support from the *Police Review*, an independent weekly journal on policing issues: 'The sizeable community who use soft drugs recreationally want a change in the laws, which reflects what is already happening at social gatherings, small and large, every night of the week. It is dismal that this reality, reflected in the Police Foundation report, carries no weight with the government and its disappointing drugs tsar, who appears to be performing a huge U-turn on the more enlightened approach he adopted as a senior police officer.'

But what caused newspapers, with a long record of resisting drug reform, to take the report seriously? After all, just seven weeks earlier the *Mail* was still being true to its tradition of traducing drug reformers with a front-page splash reporting 'a storm as anti drug chiefs go soft on cannabis', with an editorial that denounced the primrose path of easier drug laws. There was the MORI poll for the Runciman Committee, which showed clear public support for a more liberal approach to soft drugs. It was not the first to do so. But opinion polls documenting changing attitudes to drugs would not have been enough for the *Mail*. It had been resisting large shifts in public attitudes for three decades on a host of social and moral issues: divorce, cohabitation, pre-marital sex, homosexuality, discrimination laws against race, gender, disability, ageism and sexual orientation. Personal contact played a big part in the *Mail*'s shift. By luck, Lady Runciman was a member of the Press Complaints Commission on which the Editor in Chief of the *Mail* papers, Paul Dacre, also sat. He had many opportunities to see how well informed and intelligent she was, and is known to be influenced by the people he meets – he had begun the campaign to find the killers of Stephen Lawrence, the young black student murdered by white racists in the London suburb of Eltham, as Stephen's father had been a decorator at his own house.

The measured tone of the *Express* was not a surprise. Rosie Boycott, who in her days as Editor of *The Independent on Sunday* had campaigned for the decriminalisation of cannabis, had become Editor of the *Express*. The reaction of conservative papers became a story in itself. *The Guardian* interviewed the Editor of *The Telegraph*, Charles Moore, asking him, why now and what's changed? Moore replied: '... a lot of people have come to realise that we are making criminals of hundreds of thousands of people even though they are not particularly wicked. They know drugs can cause harm, but they don't want to think that they or their children could have a criminal record because they got caught smoking a joint.' Ian Hargreaves, in his *New Statesman* media column, pointed to other factors. He thought 'a touch of it, I suspect, is the pleasure all newspaper editors get from tickling the feet of a humourless and politically unassailable government'. He thought newspaper editors, having been children of the 1960s and 1970s, were more familiar with drug issues than they were with refugees and poverty. And then there were the editors' teenage children: 'Some half of those under 25 have used illegal drugs, the harsh hand of the law is raised not merely against frightening black youths in faraway inner cities, but against golden progeny of Fleet Street too.'[25]

Political change

What was going on politically was also important. There were multiple splits, divisions and U-turns in both main political parties. In a post-mortem on Labour's response to Runciman, Mary Ann Sieghart, a *Times* columnist, like several others, sought to find out 'why are ministers so scared of the drug debate'. She wrote in her column on 31 March 2000: 'I am told that when ministers met to decide how they should respond to the Police Foundation report, there was much discussion about what the press would make of it, but no expectation that the right wing papers would be as liberal as they were.'[26] She compared the media's serious response to the Runciman Report with the turnaround of public attitudes to global warming following Margaret Thatcher's Royal Society lecture on 27 September 1988. She went on: 'Yesterday was another such day, this time for advocates of new thinking on drugs.' She forecast that the reform of the drugs law would no longer be regarded as 'a crank's issue ... but a matter of mainstream political concern'. Alas the forecast proved wrong. At a Cabinet meeting the week before the report was published – which by then had been well leaked – it was agreed, according to *The Economist*, that with just over a year to a possible election Labour 'must not allow itself to be outflanked by its Conservative law-and-order critics'.[27]

Drugs was one of the more specific pledges that Labour had made in the run-up to the 1997 election. In an address to fifth formers at Dyce Academy in Aberdeen in April 1997, Tony Blair spoke of the need for a figurehead to lead the drugs battle. He went on: 'Today I am announcing that Labour will appoint an anti-drugs supremo, what they call in America a drugs tsar, to co-ordinate our approach.'[28]

The drugs tsar starts work

Keith Hellawell was appointed in October 1997 as drugs coordinator across 16 government departments on a salary higher than the Prime Minister's at the time: £106,000. As Chief Constable of West Yorkshire he had shown a liberal streak, advocating the reform of the 'absurd' laws on prostitution, and said in an interview on *Panorama* that he foresaw the day when cannabis would be legal. After being appointed to his Whitehall post, he disowned the comment. This was not the last comment that he wanted retracted – he was not keen to see an earlier comment to *The Guardian* in May 1994 being regurgitated: 'The current policies are not working. We seize more drugs, we arrest more people, but when you look at the availability of drugs, the use of drugs, the crimes committed because of and through people who use drugs, the violence associated with drugs, it's on the increase. It can't be working.'[29]

He had been given an impossible new post, with no budget of his own, few staff and far less power than the US prototype. He had few contacts in Whitehall and had neither the experience nor the intellectual clout to form a bridge between the departments, particularly the big two, the Home Office dealing with punishment and the Health Department responsible for treatment. These were huge departments, each with powerful staff, policy-making teams, well plugged into the Whitehall network, and perhaps even more important, large press offices with which the tsar could not compete.

I was invited with *The Guardian* Editor in early 2000 to a sandwich lunch in the tsar's large and dark Whitehall room in the Cabinet Office. It was a sad and embarrassing occasion. He looked absolutely lost and was in a desperate search for allies in an increasingly hostile media world that was questioning his pay, effectiveness and various U-turns.

His gaffes were numerous, from suggesting in an early interview that doctors could not prescribe heroin (they can, with a licence) to the launch of a 10-year strategy in May 1999, when, on top of unrealistic targets (a 50 per cent reduction in addiction) it was discovered that the government had not compiled the necessary base statistics against which the promised cuts in addiction could be measured.[30] He did not help his relations with teachers in the run-up to the new strategy by telling them to stop talking to children about soft drugs. He insisted on Labour's mantra that a drug was a drug and that they must all be treated with equal severity.[31]

As tsar he was also initially a harsh proponent of cannabis being 'a gateway drug' – a gateway to heroin. Roger Howard, former Chief Executive of DrugScope, punctured that assertion: 'It is like saying as the M1 goes from London to Leeds, everyone who gets on it is going to Leeds.' A Home Office research report[32] in 2002 rejected the theory. By early 2000, the tsar had changed tack and was urging the police to lay off cannabis users and concentrate on heroin and cocaine. But both this message and *The Observer* front-page headline, 'Drugs tsar defies spin machine',[33] produced menacing frowns in Downing Street. Number 10 was still dismissing suggestions that the ban on cannabis for medicinal purposes might be eased. Both the BMA and the Lords Select Committee on Science backed the change, but ministers were insisting that there would be no change until the outcome of medical trials was completed. What hardened Downing Street attitudes even further was an extraordinary speech on 8 February 2000, by William Hague, the Tory leader.[34] It was seen by Downing Street as a response to the more liberal lines of the drugs tsar and Mo Mowlam.

The war cries get louder

A beleaguered William Hague, still trailing badly in opinion polls, had ended the liberal line on social issues with which he began his leadership in 1997 and had gone back to wooing hardcore

Conservative support. Just seven weeks before Runciman reported, he signalled a much tougher line on drugs. He accused the government of 'turning a blind eye to soft drugs', and said: 'A Conservative government would move clearly in the opposite direction – not more tolerance of drugs but less; not softer policing, but tougher enforcement; not making excuses, but locking up offenders.' There would be automatic prison sentences for those in possession of drugs within 400 metres of a school. Given the density of schools in big cities, this would apply to almost all cannabis users. As the London *Evening Standard* front page noted, it was the hardest policy yet from a mainstream party.

Labour's response to Hague's new moves was immediate. Number 10 called in the father and stepmother of Leah Betts, who had died on her 18th birthday after taking one ecstasy tablet. Paul Betts, a former police inspector who had worked with the drugs squad, and Janet Betts, a nurse, who had managed to resuscitate Leah initially after her collapse but not save her, had become prominent anti-drug campaigners in the five years since her death. They had set up a helpline and were frequent commentators on the need for a firm line on drugs in interviews with the tabloids and broadcasters. What rankled in progressive circles was the way in which Janet purported to be Leah's mother. In fact Leah, who was three when her father had left her mother, had continued to live with her mother until she died from a sudden heart attack when Leah was 15. Even then she continued to live with her mother's partner for a further two years before going to live with a school friend's family. She was only a weekend visitor to Paul and Janet.

The drugs minister and drugs tsar were ordered to attend Downing Street to meet the Betts and recant their liberal words 'loudly and humbly'. Keith Hellawell used that lowest of ploys, 'I was misquoted'. Mo Mowlam came out of Downing Street and said tersely, but without recantation, 'our policy has not changed, but we believe it should be a combination of tough on drugs but also treatment and education'. The last thing Downing Street wanted was to be outflanked by the Conservatives.

Who's afraid of evidence?

Nine months on it got even worse. The Joseph Rowntree Foundation (JRF), which had astutely handled the Runciman Report's launch as well as being one of the nine trusts that had provided grants, sponsored an all-day conference on the report in London. The aim was to move the drugs debate forward. It was held at the Royal College of Physicians, who, with the Royal College of Psychiatrists, had brought out their own critical report on current drugs policy one day after Runciman. The opening session of the conference was entitled 'Who's afraid of evidence?'. Whoever else was intimidated, it was not the police or drug specialists who turned up in droves. But there were two missing parties at this biggest gathering of drug experts for years: the drugs tsar and the drugs minister. The drugs tsar, who had received an early invitation, was not too busy to turn up for both morning and evening BBC interviews – on the Radio 4 *Today* programme and BBC *Newsnight* – to declare the government had a good case to make against the Runciman Report, but was unable to make it to the conference. Home Office ministers, who had initially said they would attend, dropped out but unavoidably found they did have to publish a major robbery report that lured several home affairs reporters away from the JRF conference.[35]

Ironically, even before the JRF conference opened, the Conservatives had been forced to change their policy towards drugs following a Shadow Cabinet revolt over its hardening line. It was prompted by an even more draconian speech than William Hague's February speech, delivered by Ann Widdecombe to the annual Conservative conference in October 2000. To adoring cheers from her blue-rinse audience, she asked: 'Surrender to the drugs menace? We couldn't do that. We shouldn't do that. We won't do that. From the possession of the most minimal amount of soft drugs to the large importer there will be no hiding place. What does that mean? It means zero tolerance of possession. No more getting away with just a caution, no more hoping a blind eye will be turned.'[36] She declared an automatic minimum fine of £100 for possession and for people found a second time with even a tiny amount of cannabis 'penalties comparable to dealing', that is, prison. For the second time in a year, politicians pursuing a 'get tough' approach to drugs that had played so well in previous years were heavily panned by the media. This time it was the Tories who received a trashing.

Doris the Dope

The Mirror filled its front page with a picture of 'Doris the Dope' (a reference to Doris Karloff, the evil character with spiked shoes in a Bond thriller, to whom Ann Widdecombe was likened by some tabloid critics). The broadsheet papers reported the plan was in disarray after the police declared it unworkable. Their crucial criticism was followed by censure from some senior figures in Widdecombe's own party. Even William Hague was forced to admit on *Channel 4 News* that the police had not been asked whether it was a workable policy.[37] All this was reported in the Thursday papers. Worse was to come. A *Mail on Sunday* reporter began a survey, following a tip-off by a senior party aide, asking each Shadow Cabinet minister whether they had ever used cannabis. Those who became known as 'the magnificent seven' said they had in their youth, 11 said they had not, two would not say and two could not be contacted.[38] It dominated the news for three days – front pages, inside pages, analysis and comment pages – overloaded with damning headlines: 'How Tory drug policy went up in smoke' (*The Guardian*), 'Dump the Dope' (*The Daily Mirror*) and 'Widdecombe is left fuming over "cannabis plot"' (*The Times*).[39] Several papers reported that the source of the revolt could have been allies of Michael Portillo intent on damaging any bid by Widdecombe for the Tory leadership.

The inevitable U-turn within a week of the new policy being announced was also reported at length. As the *Express* noted: 'Mr Hague ran up the white flag after no fewer than seven shadow cabinet ministers admitted to experimenting with soft drugs in their youth. He claimed he was not altogether abandoning Miss Widdecombe's ideas, but was instead putting them up "for further debate and consultation" – political code for scrapping them.'[40] *The Times* Editorial moved the paper closer to Runciman than on publication day, with its declaration: 'Mr Hague was wise to signal a retreat rather than defend a proposal that lacked any credibility ...

a crackdown on the possession of cannabis for personal use would be an inexcusable distraction from the struggle against addiction to cocaine and heroin.'[41]

The disarray within the Tory Party prompted Charles Kennedy, the Liberal Democrat leader, to become the first leader of a mainstream party to call for cannabis to be decriminalised. Peter Riddell, in his political column in *The Times*, made some pertinent points:

> What a difference a year makes. When Charles Kennedy, in almost his first remarks as Liberal Democrat leader in August 1999, suggested taking a fresh look at the decriminalisation of cannabis, via a royal commission on drug laws, he was attacked by the Tory and Labour leaderships. The implication has been that serious, grown up politicians do not talk about drugs, but only maverick figures such as Clare Short and Mo Mowlam. Mr Kennedy was, and is, right to urge a review of the law. Blowing away conventional cant is what the Lib Dems partly exist to do. The taboo on discussion has been absurd and hypocritical. What a rich irony that debate has been opened up by the clumsy intervention of someone who wants even tougher action rather than liberation. There are parallels with the debates in the 1950s and 1960s which led to the abolition of capital punishment and homosexual law reform. What Mr Kennedy has openly urged, and now Mr Hague has been forced to concede, Tony Blair can hardly resist. It is time for the taboo on debate about drugs policy, and particularly decriminalisation of cannabis, to be dropped.[42]

Fran Abrams in *The Independent* noted another significant social event: 'Tony Blair bluntly told his biographer, *The Independent*'s John Rentoul: "I don't do drugs". But later his assertion was tempered by his press spokesman Alastair Campbell, who perhaps fearing his boss's street-cred was about to plummet, told journalists "If he had come across drugs, you can be sure he would have inhaled".'[43] By the following weekend, 14/15 October, the media even detected a change of tone by Tony Blair. Interviewed by John Humphrys on the BBC Radio 4's *Today* programme before an informal European summit in Biarritz, he was asked whether he would prefer his children to 'get drunk' or have 'the odd spliff'. He said he would prefer his children to not have anything to do with drugs, but that might be wrong and other parents might feel differently.[44] *The Sunday Times* suggested, 'in other words he believes in an individual's decision and, implicitly, it has very little to do with the law'.[45] Asked by Humphrys if ministers were free to smoke pot if they wanted to, Mr Blair ducked the issue. *The Sunday Times* interpreted this response to mean '"it is up to people to do what they want to do" – [it] could not have been more libertarian'.[46] Labour peer Helena Kennedy, who supported decriminalisation, told *The Mirror* that there were a lot of people in the Cabinet who took her view, but it would be difficult to turn it round when Blair, Blunkett and Straw were so opposed.

A new Home Secretary

Labour won the 2001 election with another landslide. An even more populist Home Secretary than Jack Straw took over: David Blunkett. Although he was a disaster in terms of law and order (see Chapter Three, this volume), on drugs he did signal his support for the downgrading of cannabis from B to C, and the use of cannabis for medical conditions, where it was shown to be effective. He formally announced his cannabis decision in October 2001 and it came into effect in January 2004. By then the *Mail* was back in a more traditional role with a hard-hitting piece about 'Cannabis, conspiracy, and how the liberal elite made a dope of Blunkett'.[47] In the year after reclassification, arrests for possession fell by one third, from 68,000 to 44,000. Researchers estimated that the police had saved 199,000 hours of time, drug use remained stable, and the police had more time to concentrate on dealers of harmful drugs.

The downgrading – done with the support of a report from the ACMD, an expert group of advisers whom governments are required to consult before making changes to categories – did not end the debate. Michael Howard, who succeeded Hague as the Conservative leader, vowed on the day of the downgrading that the next Conservative government would upgrade it. Fourteen months on, two new reports – one from New Zealand and the other by Dutch researchers – gave Mr Howard the ammunition he needed to suggest the government was 'soft on drugs' in the run-up to the 2005 election. The New Zealand study suggested 'regular cannabis use increased the risk of developing psychotic symptoms later in life'.

The conclusion of the Dutch study, published in the *British Medical Journal*, repeated findings of earlier research that cannabis could increase the risks of psychotic symptoms in young people, particularly in those with a predisposition for psychosis. The two reports prompted loud drum beats from the tabloid press without too much attention to the caveats the researchers made. The lead New Zealand researcher emphasised: 'There are not huge increases in risks.' Professor Jim van Os, one of the authors of the Dutch study, was even more robust. He told *The Guardian* that the fact that cannabis could trigger psychosis in a small minority of people was a good reason to legalise it, not ban it. This would allow governments to promote and advise on its use and control more dangerous forms like skunk. Packets could carry how much THC the drug contained (the most dangerous compound) along with how much CBD it contained (the compound believed to provide beneficial effects). But instead of setting out robust reasons why the downgrading had been right, ministers hid behind sending the new reports to the ACMD to see whether it would change its mind. It did not.

The ACMD was aware of the risks that cannabis posed to a tiny proportion of the population, but this loss was outweighed by the damage that extra policing of cannabis would generate. It noted that about 1 per cent of the population suffered from some form of schizophrenia and estimated that the prevalence of this mental condition would be reduced by 10 per cent if the use of cannabis could be totally eliminated. In other words, cannabis was threatening a tenth of 1 per cent of the population. Moreover, even if the drug was restored to class B, that would not in itself reduce consumption. (Indeed, consumption dropped while the drug remained in category C.) The leading schizophrenia charity, Rethink, supported the ACMD's conclusions.[48] But by the time the ACMD had reported, the Home Office had backtracked. It retained cannabis in category C but in an amendment to the Serious Organised Crime and Police Act 2005 made possession of cannabis an arrestable offence.

Harry Shapiro, Editor of *Druglink*, noted in a special issue of the journal on media coverage in 2006 that the government had recently published a lengthy study on how media reporting of people with mental health problems promoted discrimination. He went on:

> It is about time a similar spotlight was turned on those with drug problems. Phrases like 'drug fiend' and 'junkie', first coined in the 19th century, still litter the popular press ... so does it matter? Well yes it does. The underlying subtext is that in all cases such people are mad and evil and not deserving of sympathy. Nobody is suggesting that when drug users commit crimes, this should not be reported. And there are plenty of nasty heroin users, just as there are vicious accountants and horrible lawyers. But how is this unrelenting prejudice supposed to encourage those thinking of coming forward for treatment? Or persuade desperate families to seek advice and counselling?[49]

In the same issue a survey of key people in treatment agencies found some who had seen some improvement in media coverage. Rosie Brocklehurst of Addaction said 'the word "treatment" will appear where once punitive language of "lock 'em up and throw away the key" was all you got from right leaning red tops and the middle market press. There is a consensus across the media that help is what drug users need, even if they are uncertain about what "help" really means.'[50] Mike Linnell of Lifeline thought 'generally speaking, I think the media has improved greatly the way they report stories'.[51] But Vic Hogg, head of the Home Office Drug Strategy Unit, explained: 'our frustration with the national media is not what is said about the government, but over the lack of credit for what is happening on the ground. So we are looking to deal more directly with regional media ... from the first meeting it was very positive.'[52] Jeremy Dear, General Secretary of the National Union of Journalists, conceded 'all too often the nature of the reporting on drug-related issues is superficial, relies on stereotypes and scare stories of the latest epidemic'.[53] Martin Blakebrough, who believed addicts suffered from 'everyday attack' from the media, asked some of his clients at Kaleidoscope what they felt the wider community thought of them: 'of 12 people asked 8 used the word "scum". Interestingly, when sitting with them outside Kaleidoscope, car drivers would wind down their window and shout this word at them.'[54] Wily Victor Adebowale of Turning Point noted what was missing from media reports: 'In a perfect world, the media would reserve the "shock horror" headlines for government travesties: poor investment in alcohol services, a failure of services to meet complex needs, and a lack of housing and after care for those in recovery.' [55]

What the voluntary agencies might also have condemned is the tabloid thirst to expose celebrity drug-taking. Yet, as Roy Greenslade, ex-*Mirror* Editor, noted in his article in the same special edition of *Druglink*: 'What the media tend to achieve, however, is surely the opposite of their proclaimed intention. Rather than turn young people away from drugs it entices them. Both the act of drug-taking and the fact that it is done illicitly is glamourised. Instead of turning people away from drugs and from crime, it reinforces their desire to mimic the famous.' [56]

Government Strategy Unit 'endorses' Runciman

But it was not just cannabis that was causing the government problems. Its own Strategy Unit documented in devastating detail the failures of current drug policy. It was set out in two reports commissioned by the Prime Minister and produced in 2003 but which did not appear until 2005. The first report in May, *Understanding the issues*,[57] analysed what was happening and reinforced the Runciman message that enforcement was not working and probably could not work. It called for a much bigger treatment programme. The second, in December 2003, produced recommendations. The reports were not published until released in edited form under a Freedom of Information (FOI) application on 1 July 2005. They were slipped out on the Downing Street website at 5.45pm with no accompanying press release. Half the final report was missing, with the government claiming it was exempted from the FOI order. Downing Street spin doctors had clearly hoped that the released material would be swamped by media coverage of the massive Live Aid concert at the G8 meeting on 2 July. But the plan backfired with a leak of some of the withheld parts to *The Observer*[58] followed by further leaks to *The Mirror* and *The Guardian*.[59] The media had a field day, not just reporting on the failure of the government's drugs policy but also long pieces on 'The bad news on drugs that No 10 tried to bury', to use the headline of *The Mirror* on 6 July 2005.

The first report won high marks from drug reform groups. Transform, a drugs think tank that campaigns for a regulated and legalised market, described the report as 'a thorough and clinical analysis – by some of the best policy minds in the UK – of the counter-productive effects of national and global drug enforcement'.[60] The report estimated there were 280,000 high harm users (heroin and cocaine/or crack). The rising use of these seriously harmful drugs in the previous 20 years had had 'an increasingly adverse impact on users, their families and the rest of society'. In the previous decade (1990–2000) heroin and cocaine consumption had doubled while the purity-adjusted price halved. While there were no recorded deaths from cannabis with three million users and just 25 from ecstasy with 650,000 users, there were 670 deaths among 400,000 heroin and/or crack users in the last statistical year. Seizures of heroin and crack accounted at the most for 20 per cent of the total when to disrupt the market required 60–80 per cent.

The report went on to say that even if supply seizures 'were more effective it is not clear that the impact on the harm caused by serious drug users would be reduced'. Even if prices went up, consumption might not go down – it might lead to an increase in crime to fund the increasing cost of drug use. Drug-motivated crime accounted for 33 per cent of the cost of all crime, but 48 per cent of the volume – some 36 million out of 75 million crimes. Drug-motivated crime was skewed towards property but also involved robbery. It accounted for 85 per cent of shoplifting, 80 per cent of domestic burglary, 55 per cent of motor crime and 50 per cent of robbery. Drug-motivated crime had risen fivefold between 1995 and 2000 and then decreased threefold and subsequently remained steady. The Strategy Unit estimated that crime cost £16 billion a year, with health and social functioning harms costing a further £8 billion. At any one time only 20 per cent of the high harm-causing users were receiving treatment. Those engaging with treatment tended not to stay long; many caught by the criminal justice system were not identified as users; and a third were not engaged with either treatment or the criminal justice system. A detailed presentation of these findings was made to ministers so that none had any excuse for believing that current policies were working.

The second report, drafted by John Birt, the former BBC Controller recruited to be a 'blue-sky' thinker for the Prime Minister, led to the clauses in the Drugs Act 2005 that made the existing Drug Testing and Treatment Orders more coercive and called for an expansion of heroin prescribing, which used to be much more widespread in England in the 1960s. The free prescriptions for heroin addicts did not emerge until after the election in a leak to *The Observer* in July 2005.[61] The purpose behind legal heroin prescribing was to undercut the £4 billion-a-year illegal market and to stop the 280,000 heroin users in Britain having to commit crimes to pay for their supplies. Birt believed the most effective way to reduce the £24 billion-a-year harm caused by heroin and crack was 'identifying and gripping' its users and placing them in treatment. The main role of the police should be to 'identify, arrest and drive' drug users into treatment and keep them there, rather than trying to curb the inflow of drugs into the UK.

2005 general election

The run-up to the passing of the Drugs Act 2005 coincided with the run-up to the 2005 election in May, putting extra pressure on the government to 'look tough' on drugs – one reason why compulsory testing on arrest and mandatory treatment was made more coercive than drug reformers liked. Indeed most informed observers believed it was rushed through Parliament to protect ministers from Tory charges of being 'soft on drugs'.

Michael Howard, the Conservative leader, ran the most right-wing campaign – on asylum, crime and drugs – in my 40 years watching parliamentary elections. He set out the tough Tory position on drugs at a Conservative conference in November 2004. His rhetoric was as populist as Ann Widdecombe's in 2000, but he prudently avoided her prescriptions. His description of life in Britain, however, was as bleak and distorted as lurid tabloid tales: pensioners living in fear 'of the junkies on their streets', teenagers struggling to avoid 'drug dealers eager to prey on them'. He went on: 'It is time we stopped blurring the distinction between right and wrong ... we need to send a clear message: drugs are wrong. No quibbling. No hedging.' [62]

There was one liberal element to the Tory package: a tenfold increase in the existing 2,500 residential treatment places for drug users, who faced long waiting lists. David Davis, the Tory home affairs spokesman, was even more abrasive than Mr Howard. He declared: 'Labour's only significant policy on drugs to date has been to reclassify cannabis. We have opposed this lunacy and we will reverse it.' Another favourite Davis election soundbite was: 'Some people say we've lost the war on drugs. But Labour have not even begun to fight it. They have capitulated. Our country deserves better.' [63] He claimed that drug use and drug crime had gone up since the decision to reclassify cannabis in 2001, whereas Home Office surveys showed they had remained stable. The Tory view was also not reflected in a pre-election survey of treatment agencies and specialists in 2005 by *Druglink*. Mike Hough, former Deputy Director of Research and Planning at the Home Office, London, praised Labour for its expansion of treatment services but warned it was tilting too far towards coercion of such services. He went on: 'Labour's record on cannabis legislation is lamentable. They resisted classification when the Runciman report was published; they went for it when the popular mood seemed to change; and they back-pedalled furiously when the public – or, more accurately, the press – changed their minds again. Most people are now totally confused about the legal status of cannabis.' [64]

The Liberal Democrats, who had supported the Runciman proposals, provided an alternative definition of 'tough': not saying what you think people want to hear, but facing up to the reality of what is going on. Mark Oaten, the party's home affairs spokesman, who coined the term 'tough liberalism', defended the party's use of 'tough' to describe its drugs policy because it had taken 'a tough policy decision to get a tough message across'. Asked whether the fact that all three parties were talking 'tough' was a sign of the bankruptcy of the debate, Mr Oaten had replied with disarming candour: 'I think it is a sign that we are all fairly scared of the *Mail* and *Express*. With an election approaching, it's hard in this climate to be able to talk as openly as you might like about what you believe are solutions.' [65]

Marcus Roberts, head of policy at DrugScope, reflecting on the politics of drug reform, noted another example of 'pre-election stress disorder' that caused both major parties to switch lines in 2005: 'In an interview with the *News of the World* in February 2004 the Prime Minister offered a cautious endorsement of drug testing in schools. With the whiff of election in the air, New Labour has thrown caution to the wind and its endorsements are now ringing, not tip-toeing. Eager to sound equally as zero-tolerant, the Tories are now calling for an "acceleration" of random drug testing in schools – despite describing Blair's *News of the World* interview at the time as "another headline grabbing plan launched without proper consultation with either teachers or drug experts".' [66]

The election of a new Conservative leader, David Cameron, following the party's defeat in the 2005 general election, prompted some optimistic flutters among drug reformers. Prior to his election, Mr Cameron had signalled a more progressive approach to drug reform. He was a member of the Commons Home Affairs Committee Inquiry into drug misuse in 2002 and voted in favour of downgrading cannabis from B to C as well as recommendation 24: 'We recommend that the government initiates a discussion within the UN Commission for Narcotic Drugs of alternative ways – including the possibility of legalisation and regulation – to tackle the drugs dilemma.' In the run-up to his election as party leader in 2005, Mr Cameron refused to comment on whether he had used drugs before he became involved in politics. But in a debate on television on 3 November 2005, during his leadership bid, he bravely said that downgrading ecstasy from A to B would help make policy more 'credible' to young people. [67]

Fifteen months on, in February 2007, *The Independent on Sunday* began serialising a new biography of the Tory leader, which suggested he had smoked cannabis while a teenager at Eton. [68] It reported that he had been disciplined by the headmaster, but not expelled, unlike seven other unlucky pupils. Mr Cameron did not deny the allegations to the crowd of reporters camped outside his constituency home in Oxfordshire on Sunday, 11 February 2007, but he did say: 'Like many people I did things when I was young that I shouldn't have done and that I regret'.[69] To his credit, the current Home Secretary, John Reid, described the allegation as a 'so-what moment', going on to tell the *Politics Show* and BBC 1 on the same day that politicians should not be expected to be plastic models produced off some 'colourless and characterless conveyor belt'.[70] Neither Downing Street nor the Liberal Democrat Party sought to make an issue of the revelation.

Several newspapers reported that the restrained response from the public in the Tory leader's constituency, Witney, and across Conservative websites underscored a shift in public attitudes to drugs, reflected in a 2005 survey by the Economic and Social Research Council (ESRC) showing 41 per cent of the public supported the legalisation of cannabis. What did not change was the Conservative commitment to reclassify cannabis from C to B and opposition to reducing ecstasy and LSD from A to B. Yet there is no evidence to suggest that where a drug sits in the system acts as a deterrent to use or supply. Indeed, the drugs with the highest growth rates in the past 25 years have all been class A drugs – heroin, cocaine and ecstasy.

A new commission – same recipe, with a media twist

Seven years on from Runciman a second independent commission reported on the state of drug laws in March 2007. Set up by the RSA, it had, like Runciman, collected a cross-section of distinguished people under the chair of Anthony King, Professor of Politics at the University of Essex. The 330-page report said the 35-year-old strategy aimed at eradicating drug abuse was driven by 'moral panic'. It suggested the main aim of public policy should be to reduce the amount of harm that drugs cause, not send people to prison. It concluded that a majority of drug users were able to use drugs without harming themselves. Where there was serious addiction, it should be seen as a health matter rather than a criminal offence. It also supported the prescribing of heroin by state clinics to keep it out of the hands of criminal dealers – a proposal that David Blunkett signed up to, but by then he was on the backbenches. Like Runciman, the main thrust of the RSA report – reclassification – was rejected by the government on the day of publication.[71]

What it did highlight, which previous reports had not, was the way the demonisation of drug users by the media had serious detrimental effects on the quality of policy and debate. It explained:

> Cool deliberation and informed dialogues become difficult or even impossible, and public debate becomes overheated and polarised. Politicians often seem afraid to raise the subject in general terms lest they be quizzed in a hostile way about their own experiences. An exaggerated interest in individual drugs and their properties distracts attention from the social factors – poverty, homelessness, and unemployment – that often underlie drug use. In addition, policy itself may be skewed by the fear and distaste surrounding the whole subject.[72]

It noted that policy may be stalled altogether if drug users were treated as a class or caste apart and provided a damning example. It pointed to the growing alarm of drug treatment workers at the rise of hepatitis C among injecting drug users 'and the apparent lack of official interest in tackling it' even though the disease constituted a serious public health risk. If left untreated, hepatitis C can lead to cirrhosis, cancer and liver failure. It went on: 'The demonization of drug use appears to have led to the situation where drug users infected with hepatitis C are not considered worth the money it would cost to treat them.' It added:

> The effect of the demonization of drugs on public opinion in general is very hard to gauge. The media wield the most influence where a phenomenon is new and people have not had an opportunity to judge it for themselves. The information about drugs that they pass on to the public is inevitably mediated by the public's own experience of drugs, and it may well be that people

dismiss much of what they see on television or read in the tabloids as inaccurate and sensational. But the effect of the demonization of drugs on the practical politics of the issue is impossible to ignore.[73]

The Commission proposed that Britain's 'crude and ineffective' drug laws should be replaced and the Home Office stripped of its control over policy. All this was also ignored by Downing Street.

Tabloid entrapment

Even worse is the way tabloids entrap people and the extent to which they go to 'capture their prey'. The *News of the World* plot to catch Lawrence Dallaglio, the England rugby captain, stretched out over weeks. It began with a reporter purporting to be a creative director of 'a major American multi-national client' having two meetings with Dallaglio's agent. There then followed a lobster and champagne dinner between Dallaglio and his agent and two reporters – one a comely woman – purporting to be Gillette executives at a Mayfair restaurant. This was followed by a further two hours and reported five bottles of champagne back at the Gillette executives' suite at the Park Lane Hotel, hammering out the details of an endorsement contract that would give £500,000 to inner-city rugby clubs. There then followed a photo shoot at the Conrad Hotel in Chelsea, 'which finally led to the front page splash with Dallaglio allegedly confessing to taking ecstasy and cocaine that lost him the England captaincy'.[74] In the US, journalists are not allowed to impersonate people. As one lawyer noted, 'Once you start lying, where does the lying stop?'. In the UK, the Press Complaints Commission Code of Conduct expressly forbids misrepresentation and subterfuge except in the public interest – but the Commission is hopeless at enforcing its own rules.

On 18 March 2007, the media itself created a story. *The Independent on Sunday* splashed across its front page an apology for its campaign to decriminalise cannabis that it had launched in 1997. It declared: 'if only we had known then what we can reveal today'.[75] Inside there were seven other pages. What it reported was that the number of teenagers treated for cannabis addiction in 2006 was 10,000 – said to be 10 times the figure for 1997. What the report failed to note, although the Editorial did, was the huge increase in treatment places in the decade. What neither the reports nor the Editorial noted was that the statistics were not comparable. According to the National Treatment Agency, comprehensive data on young people being treated only got incorporated into national figures in 2004/05. Until that point there was no systematic collection because not all youth services were supplying data. The National Treatment Agency said that the proportion of people using cannabis requiring treatment in the 1990s fluctuated between 6 and 10 per cent. In 2004/05, when young people were included, it rose to 11 per cent, and in 2005/06 to 12 per cent. The rate for adults only in 2004/05 was under 9 per cent.

But several leading scientists supported this change of heart by the Sunday paper. Professor Colin Blakemore, Chief of the Medical Research Council, who had backed the paper's 1997 campaign, was one. He was reported by the paper as saying 'the link between cannabis and psychosis is quite clear now; it wasn't 10 years ago'.[76] Robin Murray, Professor of Psychiatry at London's Institute of Psychiatry, pointed to the increased strength of the drug. There was no dispute about that. Skunk, for example, a high-octane version of the more benign weed, is cultivated here in Britain hydroponically (without soil) indoors, under lamps, where it is specially bred to increase the content of the main psychoactive ingredient, THC (tetrahydrocannabidinol). A cannabis joint may contain 10 to 20 times more THC than the equivalent joint in the 1970s. About 60 per cent of cannabis used in the UK is now produced here. But the ACMD was aware of this when it approved for the second time in three years the downgrading of the drug.

The scientific defenders of cannabis made three persuasive points. First, there had been no increase in schizophrenia in this country despite a massive increase in cannabis smoking. Second, there was no evidence that cannabis-growing populations such as Jamaica had a higher incidence of psychosis. Third, you can show an association between the drug and the illness but you cannot show a cause. Scientific defenders believe a more likely explanation is that people who are in the early stages of mental illness may turn to the drug as a form of self-medication. They note that cannabis is widely used by patients on mental health wards to the despair of psychiatrists who say that it worsens their condition. Even *The Independent on Sunday* was backtracking the following week with an Editorial that stated: '... it may be, though, that last week's headline did not do full justice to our special report ... our "apology" was not a complete reversal of everything this papers stands for ... we still believe that adults should be free to live their lives as long as they cause others no harm'.[77]

Gordon Brown searches for tabloid brownie points

By the summer of 2007 the ACMD was being asked yet again, this time by the new Prime Minister, Gordon Brown, in his first month in office, to take a third look at cannabis in five years. Several media commentators interpreted this move as a policy offering to woo the support of the *Daily Mail*. Once more the ACMD, after a comprehensive review, rejected an upgrading, but this time it was ignored. The Home Secretary was instructed by the Prime Minister to upgrade the drug. Even worse, when it came into operation on 26 January 2009, the Home Office press release announcing implementation blatantly implied at three different points that this was in line with the ACMD when it was certainly not. A shocking distortion of the truth. Pure spin of the very worst variety.[78]

The flag carriers

Among the many voluntary groups in the drug policy field, two stand out. DrugScope, a merger in 2000 of two previous charities, one giving guidance on treatment and the other providing information, research and policy briefs, is the UK's leading independent centre of expertise on drugs. It has an impressive library, extensive files and a savvy press team. Martin Barnes, former head of CPAG, became DrugScope's chief executive in the week that cannabis was downgraded in January 2004. It was a baptism of fire. The tabloids had turned nasty again. His charity was damned by the *Mail*, shot at on BBC Radio 4's *Moral Maze*, and became a victim of a hoax 'confidential memo' purporting to come from a meeting of pharmaceutical companies eager to move into a legalised drug market claiming DrugScope to be 'a good ally'. The accusation from the *Mail* was that the group was a closet legaliser. It was not, as Mr Barnes made clear in his first week. It pushes for evolutionary reforms, based on hard evidence. That was why it backed the Runciman reforms and why it supported earlier tried and tested schemes such as needle exchanges and safe injecting rooms to reduce harm. Although he had worked in the charity world for 20 years, he had never worked in an institution under a tabloid blitz. 'I was used to welfare claimants being bashed and labelled "scroungers" by the tabloids at CPAG, but they always treated the organisation with respect. This was a shock. It was a torrid beginning. Even the Home Office had not been prepared for the extent of the media backlash.'[79] Fortunately for DrugScope, Barnes is robust, intelligent and a survivor. In more recent times he has acted as the voice of the ACMD as one of its most experienced members in dealing with the media.

Danny Kushlick, the other high-profile policy reformer, could not be more open about his support for a legalised and regulated drugs market. A former drug user turned drugs counsellor, he gave up his counselling job 15 years ago to begin campaigning for legalising drugs. Initially it was just himself, from his front room in Bristol, financed only by the dole, but gradually he began to win grants from respected funders, and the Transform Drug Policy Foundation emerged. It now has patrons from all three major political parties as well as retired senior police officers. Its funders have included the EU. In August 2007, Transform was granted special consultative status at the United Nations (UN). Transform's 40-page report, *After the war on drugs: Options for control*,[80] details how legal regulation of drug markets could operate, and was the basis of a seminar series at the LSE. Kushlick has submitted evidence and been an expert witness to a succession of drug reform inquiries: Runciman, Commons Select Committees (Home Affairs and Science and Technology) and the RSA. He is a regular speaker at conferences, seminars and workshops.

But the key to Kushlick's influence is his emails and internet site. Every ministerial move on drugs is documented with an immediate response by email to his long list of media contacts, including high-profile commentators. He is regularly invited by right-wing as well as liberal papers for comment pieces, blogs or a response to a new 'shock horror story'. His research files on who said what and when are exhaustive. He is convinced that 'the media play a crucial role. Politicians are just too slow and reluctant to move. Despite swings in the polls to a more liberal position, they still fear alienating the voters'.[81] The best compliment to Danny Kushlick – and a mark of how far his cause has come – is the space given to legalisation in the 2007 RSA report.[82] The arguments in favour of legalisation run over six pages, the arguments against over five. In the end it called for a new legal framework, not legalisation, but noted: 'powerful arguments can be advanced on both sides of this long-running debate. No one in this field has a monopoly of truth.' [83]

The UK back in the 1960s

To introduce a personal note: I spent most of the 1960s outside the UK. In 1968 I worked as a speech writer and aide to a New York congressman in Washington, and made many trips to New York. Walking the streets in those days you automatically carried a $10 or $20 bill – a lot more money then – in your back trouser pocket to pay out immediately if confronted by the many thousands of desperate heroin addicts in the city searching for funds to finance their habit. When I got back to London in 1969, the scene could not have been more different. There were about 350 registered addicts in the country. They did not need to rob for their drugs: they could obtain them from their GPs. But this scene was to change dramatically. To meet complaints that some doctors were over-subscribing – and their patients selling on the unneeded part of their dose to those who were not registered – a new system of licensed doctors and specialist clinics was set up. Initially offering injectable heroin on a maintenance basis, they moved on to oral methadone on a reducing base. The number of heroin-prescribing GPs rapidly dwindled, and the number of addicts dramatically rose as the emphasis in a succession of Drugs Acts (1964, 1967 and 1971) switched the lead role for dealing with the problem from medics to the criminal justice system. Now there are almost 350,000 heroin/crack addicts. Where once we led the world in dealing with serious drug abuse, we now lag behind even conservative nations such as Portugal, Switzerland, Spain and Luxembourg.

Heroin prescribing has been supported in the last decade by ACPO,[84] the Commons Select Committee on Home Affairs,[85] and the RSA Commission as a means of relieving the most chaotic and dependent users from relying on criminal sources, which require them to commit crimes to buy it and where there is no control over the drug's purity. Yet there is still no widespread programme at the time of writing. Drug consumption rooms in which dependent users are allowed to bring their illegally obtained supplies in supervised hygiene conditions are now operating in eight countries. In 2002 the Select Committee on Home Affairs proposed that they should be introduced here to reduce drug-related deaths, prevent needle sharing and reduce injecting in public places. The government rejected the idea on numerous grounds: legal concerns, public hostility, attracting dealers. A JRF working party chaired by Lady Runciman sat for 20 months examining the overseas schemes, and found none of the ministerial fears were realised. It proposed pilot schemes here.[86] This, too, was rejected.

It is the same story with soft drugs. Cannabis is the world's oldest euphoric drug. According to a chronology produced by the Campaign to Legalise Cannabis International Association (CLCIA), the earliest reference dates back to 2737BC when it was described as a superior herb in the world's first pharmacopoeia, Shen Young's Pen Ts'ao in China. It was praised by Roman Emperor Nero's surgeon, and its cultivation encouraged by Elizabeth I and George Washington. It was reputedly taken by Queen Victoria to relieve her period pains. I was not in England when the famous full-page advertisement in *The Times* signed by leading figures from the arts, politics, medicine, media and pop world (all four Beatles taking care to add their MBEs) called for the private use of cannabis to be treated at worse as a misdemeanour. It began an era of pro-cannabis agitation. Some 3,000 people staged a 'smoke-in' in Hyde Park; Mick Jagger and his Rolling Stone partner Keith Richards were jailed on drug charges, although they were quickly freed and their convictions quashed.

The 1968 Wootton Committee report that followed came near to persuading Harold Wilson's Labour government in 1970 to relax cannabis penalties. The state papers for 1970 – released in January 2004 – showed that James Callaghan, the Home Secretary of the day, wanted to create two categories: 'hard' and 'soft', with cannabis listed as a hard drug along with heroin. Cabinet ministers, particularly those who had been to university, revolted and asked for three categories with cannabis in the middle restricted to a maximum penalty for possession of a £200 fine. Callaghan conceded, but when this was leaked to *The Guardian*, both the Home Secretary and the Prime Minister, with the 1970 general election pending, decided to 'kowtow to public opinion'. Cannabis stayed in the middle category, but backed by a maximum penalty of five years' imprisonment and an unlimited fine for possession.[87]

Ignoring public attitudes

Successive governments have refused to respond to changing public attitudes monitored by the polls. They have been too intimidated by the tabloids, too worried about what opposition parties would do, too ready to talk tough when in reality they were weakly bowing to what they wrongly believed was a populist agenda, ignoring the serious arguments for downgrading cannabis. Michael Howard was at his worst in the week before cannabis was downgraded in January 2004. I have only quoted one *Guardian* Editorial in this chapter, but here is the start of one responding to Howard's intemperate attack on the move in January 2004:

> Michael Howard signalled his wish this week to divert a wide swathe of police officers from serious offences to trivial; to wage war on almost 50% of young people; and to ensure that tens of thousands of them should be given a criminal record and some a prison sentence for an activity that more than three million of them will engage in quite safely during the year. He did not quite put it this way. Indeed with his usual eager eye for an opportunistic response to a serious policy change, he clearly thought he was on to another populist winner.[88]

Five weeks after the RSA report, a new independent UK Drug Policy Commission was launched with a remit to reduce the emotion and heat and raise the national level of debate on drugs over the three years of 2007–09. Funded by the Esmée Fairbairn Foundation for three years and chaired by Lady Runciman, it was timed to coincide with the government's review of its 10-year drug strategy. Instead of bringing out one massive report, the Commission began publishing a series of briefing papers reviewing what was working, what was not and where there were gaps in the research that needed to be filled. At its Westminster launch Lady Runciman observed that there had never been a sustained scrutiny of the effectiveness of current drug policy. She explained that some policy was working well, some was not, and we needed to know about both and the causes behind the successes and failures. The goal was to involve the media, politicians and the public in a more rational debate about current policy. She went on: 'Politicians, policy-makers and the media are the real players. Politicians obviously call the shots and make the decisions but they need more headroom to be able to do this. We need to get better media coverage to enable this to happen. There has been too much media coverage of the polarities and too little of the national middle ground.'

In October 2012 – 12 years after her first report – Lady Runciman's second group of experts delivered their 175-page final report. They proposed that the possession of small amounts of drugs for personal use should be a civil offence, not a criminal offence. They concluded that the move would not lead to a significant increase in use. Instead the criminal sanctions imposed on 42,000 people sentenced each year for possession of drugs – and a further 160,000 given cannabis warnings – should be replaced by a fine, or an order to attend a drug awareness session, or a referral to a drug treatment programme. The report also suggested that withholding or imposing only minimal sanctions on people growing cannabis for their personal use could go some way to undermining burgeoning illicit cannabis factories controlled by organised crime. It ruled out any more radical move towards legalising drugs, saying that allowing the legal sale of drugs such as heroin or cocaine could cause more damage than existing drug laws.[89]

Two weeks before the Commission reported, the Home Office's annual report on illicit drug use for 2010/11 was released, confirming a downward trend in drug use. It estimated three million people, or 9 per cent of the population aged between 16 and 59, had taken an illicit drug, the lowest level since the annual crime survey for England and Wales began in 1996. Cannabis remained by far the most popular, with 2.3 million people having used it, but its use too was dropping, particularly among young people aged between 16 and 24. Proportions in this age group having used it had dropped from 26 per cent to 16 per cent. [90] Harry Shapiro, Editor of *Druglink*, said the fall – which was reflecting international trends – showed for the first time since illicit drugs became a political issue in the 1960s that their use was now on a firm downward curve. 'Drugs don't appear to be "cool" these days as they once were,' he said. He acknowledged there was still a significant issue, with over 300,000 serious drug users, but 'to suggest, as some do, that we are currently going to a drug hell in a handcart is just a wilful refusal to acknowledge the facts'. [91]

Two days after Runciman had reported, Simon Jenkins, a member of Lady Runciman's earlier Commission, suggested in his *Guardian* column that drug policy did not need any further research, but drug politics did. He explained: 'Each year governments re-legislate their "war on terror" despite the minimal threat, but reject any need to revise the 1971 Misuse of Drugs Act. They refuse to see it is not working and do nothing but waste public money.... Britain on drugs is where China is on hanging, Saudi Arabia on beating, Russia on censorship, and the Taliban on girls' education.... It has petrified home secretaries of left and right alike.' [92] True to this diagnosis, Theresa May, the Coalition Home Secretary, had ruled out any move towards decriminalisation one month before the Commission reported. She told MPs she regarded cannabis as a gateway drug, ignoring the research her own department had published in 2002 dismissing the theory. An opinion poll carried out by the Commission among MPs reinforced the columnist's call. It found that 77 per cent of MPs believed the UK's policies were ineffective in tackling the problems caused by drugs. Two thirds wanted a change in the policing process and three quarters believed more use should be made of evidence and research. But there was little consensus on what was needed to be done and most MPs would resist a change in the drug laws.[93]

Some of the ground which any review would have to carry out has already been cleared by the report of the 2007 RSA Commission, chaired by Anthony King, Professor of Government at the University of Essex. It was too sweeping in its legislative proposals, but it did have an excellent section on the media and politicians. It stated:

> There is no escaping the fact that the formulation and implementation of drugs policy takes place in a peculiar atmosphere, one that differentiates drugs policy from most other fields. The field of drugs policy is not 'ordinary', 'matter of fact', or 'routine'. It is highly charged, sometimes even hysterical, with people, including the media and politicians, emotionally involved in quite an unusual way. The emotional climate in some policy fields is relatively cool. The emotional climate of drugs policy is almost always exceedingly hot.[94]

It suggested, over and beyond concerns about health and crime, that the emotional climate is generated by drugs being seen as 'a peculiarly moral issue': a conviction in the US and Protestant Europe that seeking to alter consciousness through drug use – whether for enlightenment, pain relief or simply fun – is terribly dangerous and morally wrong. 'This conviction may be rooted in fundamental values, it may be unreasoned and emotional, and it may be, and often is, both at the same time. We do not presume in this report to lay down what we believe people's moral stance on this over-arching issue should be. That is not out business.'

What it did urge the media and politicians to change was the demonisation of drugs and drug users. Echoing Roy Greenslade, quoted earlier in this chapter, it went on: 'Demons are diabolical, evil spirits and are therefore to be slain. In our view, using such language and thinking in such terms is childish, if not mediaeval. It stifles rational and realistic debate and makes it harder, not easier, to deal with the very serious matters at hand.' Or, as Greenslade concluded: 'The single lesson to draw from all this? Whether drugs are bad for you or not, reading about them in papers and viewing programmes about them on television certainly is.'[95]

They are both right. The most serious charge against the media on this issue is denying the public a rational debate. Democracies are strengthened by serious well-informed debate and subverted by being denied one.

Notes

[1] DrugScope (2006) *Druglink*, London: DrugScope, March/April edition.

[2] RSA (Royal Society of the Arts) Commission on Illegal Drugs, Communities and Public Policy (2007) *Drugs – Facing facts*, London: RSA Commission, March, p 25.

[3] Ibid, p 35.

[4] *Herald Scotland*, 29 December 1995.

[5] EMCDDA (European Monitoring Centre for Drugs and Drug Addiction) (1998) *Country overviews, 1998 survey*, Portugal: EMCDDA.

[6] *The Independent*, 13 July 1999.

[7] 'Police force urges legislation', *The Guardian*, 17 February 2000.

[8] All four pages published on 27 March 2000.

[9] *The Observer*, 3 March 2000.

[10] *The Guardian*, 2 March 2000.

[11] *Guardian Society*, 12 December 2001.

[12] Ibid.

[13] *Mail on Sunday*, 27 March 2000.

[14] Ibid.

[15] *Evening Standard*, 28 March 2000.

[16] Media correspondent, *The Independent*, 30 March 2000.

[17] *Daily Mail*, 29 March 2000.

[18] *The Daily Telegraph*, 29 March 2000.

[19] *Sunday Express*, 2 April 2000.

[20] 'Straw retreats from his hardline on ecstasy', *The Observer*, 2 April 2000.

[21] Jack Straw (2000) 'Why we won't be going soft on cannabis', *News of the World*, 2 April.

[22] *The Daily Telegraph*, 4 April 2000.

[23] Ian Hargreaves (2000) *New Statesman*, 7 April.

[24] *The Guardian*, 10 April 2000.

[25] Ian Hargreaves (2000) *New Statesman*, 7 April, p 54.

[26] Mary Ann Sieghart (2000) *The Times*, 31 March.

[27] *The Economist*, 1 April 2000.

[28] 'Blair at odds with Church', *Herald Scotland*, 26 March 1997.

[29] *The Guardian*, 23 May 1994.

[30] 'Ministers pledge to halve UK drug abuse', *The Independent*, 26 May 1999.

[31] 'Stop talking to children about "soft" drugs, teachers to be told', *The Times*, 2 January 1999.

[32] *Cannabis*, House of Commons Research Paper 00/74, 3 August 2000, London: House of Commons.

[33] 'Drugs tsar defies spin machine', *The Observer*, 2 February 2000.

[34] 'Hague wants exclusion zone round schools', *The Independent*, 9 February 2000, and see national newspaper websites.

[35] Malcolm Dean (2001) 'High times for a joint change', *The Guardian*, 17 January.

[36] Full text of the speech is available on *The Guardian* website (see www.guardian.co.uk/politics/2000/oct/04/conservatives2000.conservatives1).

[37] *Channel 4 News*, 5 October 2000.

[38] *Mail on Sunday*, 8 October 2000.

[39] All national newspapers, 9 October 2000.

[40] *Daily Express*, 10 October 2000.

[41] *The Times*, 10 October 2000.

[42] Peter Riddell (2000) *The Times*, 10 October.

[43] Fran Abrams (2000) *The Independent*, 9 October.

[44] John Humphrys, BBC Radio 4 *Today* programme, 14 October 2000.

[45] *The Sunday Times*, 15 October 2000.

[46] Ibid.

[47] *Daily Mail*, 27 January 2004.

[48] *The Guardian* (2006) Editorial, 12 January.

[49] DrugScope (2006) *Druglink*, March/April.

[50] Ibid.

[51] Ibid.

[52] Ibid.

[53] Ibid.

[54] Ibid.

[55] Ibid.

[56] Ibid.

[57] Prime Minister's Strategy Unit (2003) *Strategy Unit Drugs Report: Phase one – understanding the issues*, 12 May.

[58] *The Observer*, 3 July 2005.

[59] 'The bad news on drugs that No 10 tried to bury', *The Daily Mirror*, 6 July 2005, and Tania Branigan (2005) 'Ministers "used Live 8 to bury" critical report', *The Guardian*, 4 July.

[60] See Transform website (www.tdpf.org.uk/), July 2005.

[61] *The Guardian* (2005) News story and editorial, 5 July.

[62] See the BBC and national press websites, 7 October 2004.

[63] 'Drugs war tops Tory crime plan', BBC News, 6 October 2004 (http://news.bbc.co.uk/1/hi/uk_politics/3718904.stm).

[64] DrugScope (2005) *Druglink*, March/April.

[65] Ibid.

[66] Ibid.

[67] See BBC website (www.bbc.co.uk/), 4 November 2005.

[68] J. Hanning and S. Elliott (2007) *The rise of the new Conservative*, serialised in *Independent on Sunday*, 11 February, p 30.

[69] BBC/*The Guardian* websites, 11 February 2007.

[70] BBC *Politics Show*, 11 February 2007.

[71] RSA Commission on Illegal Drugs, Communities and Public Policy (2007) *Drugs – facing facts*, London: RSA Commission.

[72] Ibid, p 38.

[73] Ibid, p 39.

[74] For a full account, see *The Observer*, 30 May 1999.

[75] 'Cannabis: an apology', *Independent on Sunday*, 18 March 2007.

[76] Ibid.

[77] *Independent on Sunday*, 25 March 2007.

[78] Home Office (2009) Press release on new move on cannabis, 25 January.

[79] Personal interview, 12 February 2007.

[80] Transform Drug Policy Foundation (2006) *After the war on drugs: Options for control*, updated edition (see www.tdpf.org.uk).

[81] Personal interview, 30 March 2007.

[82] RSA Commission on Illegal Drugs, Communities and Public Policy (2007) *Drugs – facing facts*, London: RSA Commission.

[83] Ibid, p 310.

[84] 'Police want to supply free heroin', *The Daily Telegraph*, 9 December 2001.

[85] Commons Select Committee on Home Affairs (2002) *The government's drugs policy: Is it working? Third report*, 22 May, para 164.

[86] Independent Working Group on Drug Consumption Rooms, Joseph Rowntree Foundation, 23 May 2006.

[87] Alan Travis (2004) *The Guardian*, 29 January.

[88] *The Guardian* (2004) Leader, 24 January.

[89] UKDPC (UK Drug Policy Commission) (2012) *A fresh approach to drugs: The final report of the UK Drug Policy Commission*, free to download at www.ukdpc.org.uk

[90] Home Office (2012) *Drugs misuse declared: Findings from the 2011/12 Crime Survey for England and Wales*, September, London: HMSO.

[91] Alan Travis (2012) 'Downward trend in substance use as drugs fall out of fashion', *The Guardian*, 28 September.

[92] Simon Jenkins (2012) 'It's drugs politics, not drugs policy, that needs an inquiry', *The Guardian*, 17 October.

[93] Jamie Dowd (2012) 'Britain's drug policies don't work, say 77% of MPs', *The Observer*, 9 September.

[94] RSA Commission on Illegal Drugs, Communities and Public Policy (2007) *Drugs – facing facts*, London: RSA Commission, March, p 32.

[95] DrugScope (2006) *Druglink*, London: DrugScope, March/April.

FIVE

Asylum: an oppressive media campaign prompts a cowardly political response

It was not the most auspicious of new policy launches, but it was certainly audacious: the halving of asylum numbers within seven months. Like some of Tony Blair's other big pledges – such as the commitment to increase health spending to the European average – it was made on television, not in Parliament. This time the exclusive was given to Jeremy Paxman on BBC *Newsnight*, not David Frost. It was delivered on Friday, 7 February 2003 and could not have been more specific: 'I would like to see us reduce it [asylum numbers] by 30 per cent to 40 per cent in the next few months and I think by September of this year we should have halved it.' He did not stop there either, adding 'I think we can get below that in years to come'.[1] Here was a major Western political leader openly admitting he was intending to breach the founding principles of the 1951 UN Convention on Refugees by making it extremely difficult for people fleeing from persecution to reach the shores of the UK.

It was a declaration that not even David Blunkett, Home Secretary, had been told about. Keith Best, Chief Executive of the Immigration Advisory Service, called it 'pie in the sky', unachievable. David Blunkett was reported by *The Sunday Telegraph* to have told colleagues it was 'undeliverable'.[2] A senior minister told the paper: 'David said he is treating it as a direction, rather than a target.' By Sunday, the Home Office was watering it down even further, describing the pledge as 'a longer term objective for years to come'.[3] By Monday Downing Street was describing it as 'an aspiration'. And by then, Home Office spin doctors were explaining to Home Affairs correspondents by what criterion the reduction would be measured: the October 2002 figures would be taken as a baseline.

Much fun was being had by the opposition parties. Simon Hughes, Liberal Democrat Shadow Home Secretary, declared: 'When the Home Secretary turns a prime ministerial target into a Home Office direction, everyone can see the muddle the government is in.'[4] But challenged at his weekly Prime Minister's Question Time in the Commons on the Wednesday, Blair remained unequivocal about his pledge: he expected to see applications from asylum-seekers halved by September 2003 compared to the previous year.[5]

To put this in perspective, Labour had been in power for over five and a half years. It had arrived in Downing Street in 1997 at a time when asylum was way down the list of public concerns. Only 3 per cent of people polled put it into their top three concerns. And in the next three years it was never higher than 10 per cent.[6] But, as the number of asylum applications began to rise – due to turmoil in Iraq, Zimbabwe, Somalia and Afghanistan – so did tabloid interest. This in turn fed more public concern. Numbers of asylum applicants grew from 32,500 in 1997 to 92,000 (including dependants) by 2001, and were still climbing. By then they were higher than in Germany, the country that had once been the most popular destination for refugees. They continued to rise through 2002, reaching a peak in October when the monthly total rose to 8,770 asylum applications. In early 2003 *The Sun* launched its 'Stop Asylum Madness' campaign, which by 1 March 2003 had collected one million names, the day the official statistics showed that for the first time the total annual numbers had breached 100,000. For the year ending in October 2002, total asylum numbers (applicants plus dependants) had reached 110,700.[7]

Media pressure mounts

A selection of press headlines in the run-up to Blair's announcement give a taste of the hostility Labour was facing: 'Now there's one asylum claim every six minutes' (*Daily Mail*, 9 December 2002); 'Britain "has more than EU share of refugees"' (*The Daily Telegraph*, 28 December 2002); 'How "soft touch" Britain tops the asylum league' (*Daily Mail*, 31 December 2002); 'Asylum flood – immigration up fivefold in 10 years' (*Daily Express*, 31 January 2003); '110,000 asylum seekers slipped in unnoticed' (*The Daily Telegraph*, 6 January 2003); 'The school where the pupils speak 33 languages' (*Daily Mail*, 28 January 2003); and '200 asylum seekers vanish every day – 329,000 now live here illegally' (*The Sun*, 10 February 2003).

A survey of content in seven national dailies over a 12-week period at the end of 2002 revealed that the *Mail* and *Express* were the most obsessive.[8] A second survey the following year found that the *Express* had become even more obsessive, running 22 front-page splashes in one 31-day period about asylum-seekers.[9] They had discovered that it sold papers. Many stories rested on statistics from unofficial sources that were no more than guesstimates. When journalists on the *Express* complained to the Press Complaints Commission (PCC) about their paper's campaign, they were told that the issue could not be examined because journalists were not the victims, it was the asylum-seekers who were.[10] And the effects of this on the public? One opinion survey in 2003 showed the British public believed that the UK was receiving 23 per cent of the world's refugees.[11] The true proportion was just under 2 per cent.

Tony Blair's autobiography does not mention his February 2003 policy 'bounce' on Blunkett in his *Newsnight* interview. And Blunkett restricts himself to just 11 lines in his 872-page *The Blunkett tapes: My life in the bear pit*. He simply records: 'Tony and I had a very strange time during the early part of the week because of his remarks on the target of a 50 per cent drop in asylum. It is not clear that it is understood that it's a drop in people coming in and claiming. That's the crunch.' That was certainly understood by the media. He went on:

> The upshot was that the Monday papers were very bad. When I'd spoken to Tony late on Monday night I didn't know that No 10 had been briefing, and we'd had a very pleasant and sensible conversation. When he rang me, it seemed to me that it was a deliberate move to try to heal the breach – and I thought we had. Then I opened the papers on Tuesday morning, particularly the *Daily Express* and we had Andrew Adonis [director of No 10 policy unit] writ large. He was in No 10 later in the day and I just told him to lay off, that I wasn't prepared to have any more of it.[12]

A 'bounce' confirmed

But 'bounce' it was, as confirmed by Michael Barber, head of the Number 10 Delivery Unit that Blair had set up in 2001 to ensure his priorities were followed through Whitehall. In his memoirs Barber discusses the pros and cons of target-setting in government. The 'cons' involved achieving progress but still being hammered by the media and political opponents for not reaching the targets. The 'pros' involved ensuring dilatory departments were exposed to more media – along with public and political – pressure to up their game.[13] He described 'Blair's out-of-the-blue pledge to halve the number of asylum applications' as an example of the latter.[14] He explained how working with Home Office officials he had made projections of the fall in asylum numbers following the implementation of the Asylum Act 2002 and the closure of the Red Cross asylum-seekers centre near the Channel Tunnel at Sangatte in France.

The projections showed, in Barber's words, 'a deep plunge' during the first six months of 2003 to less than half by the end of the summer. Blair had seen this and was obviously pleased, but it is doubtful whether he gave it any credence: after all, his experience of the IND (the Home Office's Immigration and Nationality Directorate) over several years was of false promises, constant excuses and inadequate results. However, at the height of the public furore over numbers, Blair went on *Newsnight* and announced the halving of applications.[15] Not just a 'bounce' then, but a brave 'bounce'. But Barber was one of Blair's heroes, and Blair's autobiography pays a fulsome tribute to the way the Delivery Unit had improved the effectiveness of government. The projections which Blair had seen may have been using IND data, but they were Barber's work, hence his readiness to embrace the projections. They were not as risky as Barber suggests.

There is a completely different version of Blunkett's reaction to the bounce in his biography by Stephen Pollard, where Blunkett is described as being 'incandescent'. It goes on:

> ... he demanded an immediate meeting with the Prime Minister. In an extremely tense conversation, and doing his best to hide his anger, he made it clear to Blair that

he was not prepared to be crucified over a pledge he himself would never had made and which the projected figures did not support. Managing a reduction was one thing. By giving specific figures, Blair seemed to be doing his best to ruin what little positive press there might be from a reduction, making 'success' dependent on hitting an entirely arbitrary figure conjured out of thin air.... Blunkett was thus presented with a target that he had not agreed, and over which he could have no control. As a result of the meeting, a semblance of agreement was reached, albeit an unsatisfactory one. The damage had been done. Blair would call it a 'firm commitment'; Blunkett would simply say that he was keen to meet it.[16]

Target hit

But for all Blunkett's doubts, the commitment was achieved. Come 27 November 2003, when the September asylum applications figures were released, the numbers had been halved, not least due to the oppressive measures Blunkett had inserted in the 2002 Act: the restoration of a 'white list' of 17 safe countries from which asylum applications would be presumed invalid; a new rule requiring all holders of refugee travel documents to have visas; and a new visa requirement for Zimbabweans introduced in October 2002.[17] The cruel paradox of the UK's asylum processes – that in order to make a perfectly legal application for asylum, more and more potential refugees had to make unlawful entries – continued to widen.

Blair's bounce was not his first initiative in asserting control over asylum. Frustrated by the lack of progress in 2002 – and the level of media hysteria over Sangatte – Blair called a major ministerial meeting for 15 May 2002, which was his first signal of taking personal control of asylum policy. John Denham, who served as Minister of State for policing at the Home Office between 2001 and 2003, conceded that tabloid hysteria had played an important role in raising public concern. But he also emphasised the damage which television coverage of Sangatte had generated. He pointed to the powerful images projected by television news programmes – desperate people trying to jump on and cling to Euro trains before they entered the Channel Tunnel. The numbers were small, but the pictures dramatic. 'They seemed to run night after night on the news.'[18]

All options were open for the 15 May meeting. And all options arrived. The papers were leaked to *The Guardian* and caused an immense fuss. They included linking foreign aid to the readiness of countries to accept refugees; ending cash support for applicants housed in accommodation centres; withdrawing legal aid from manifestly unfounded cases; and deportation to safe havens in the regions that failed asylum-seekers had left.[19] None of these made it into the 2002 Bill, but between 2001 and 2004 there was no subject, with the exception of Iraq, that took as much of Blair's time – 50 meetings, some lasting three hours, over two years, according to Downing Street sources.[20] In his 10 years in office, some six asylum laws were passed.

So what had happened prior to the 2003 bounce?

Britain used to boast (somewhat exaggeratedly) of a proud tradition of providing sanctuary for those fleeing from persecution: from the Huguenots in the 17th century to Jewish people in the 20th. In fact, as Roy Greenslade notes in *Seeking scapegoats*, the refugees were given a rough public reception and Irish and Jewish people in the 19th and 20th centuries had to suffer persistent press hostility.[21] But not only were we no longer proud to offer such sanctuary but by 1997, the Conservative government had created, in the words of the UN Refugee Agency (the UN High Commissioner for Refugees, or UNHCR), the worst asylum procedure in Europe.[22] Labour in opposition deserved credit for refusing to descend to the depths to which Michael Howard sank in playing the race card with his Asylum and Immigration Act 1996. The 1993 Act had already shut most doors and turned thousands of airline staff into immigration officers through tough fines on carriers for every person brought to the UK without proper papers.

Undaunted, Howard was back in Parliament proposing a new round of restrictions. It followed the notorious memorandum on the plight of the Conservative Party written by John Maples, which warned that desperate measures were needed if the party was to be saved. As *The Guardian* argued, the Conservative response was the deliberate politicisation of asylum, race and refugees in a desperate attempt to rally support as their poll ratings plummeted.[23] It was during this time that Amnesty International documented the injustices and inefficiencies of Britain's asylum procedures as 'the culture of disbelief' facing applicants.[24] The only uplifting aspect of these moves were the number of AB voters who were turned off the party by them and the way they reinforced what Theresa May, a later party chair, described as the public perception of Conservatives being members of 'the nasty party'.[25]

Labour's first asylum Bill in 1999 introduced some much needed changes. These included the abolition of the 'white list' of countries from which all applicants were presumed bogus, and an amnesty in all but name for the 30,000 applicants that the Tories had left on the shelf – in order to deal with new applicants – despite 10,000 having been left in limbo for five years and another 20,000 for over two. A third reform was the belated introduction of due process in the detention and vetting procedures, including statutory rules, written reasons for detention and automatic bail hearings within seven days. What was unacceptable was Labour's reform-by-stealth under the cover of a reshuffle; its apologetic approach to these amendments; and the tabloid-tailored changes designed to win populist applause and deter potential applicants.

The party that once vehemently opposed the Tories' decision to deny benefits to half of all asylum-seekers – thus triggering an inadequate patchwork provision of church hall accommodation and soup kitchens – was now planning to remove all benefits and replace them with a notorious system of vouchers. Alongside this was a malevolent proposal to remove the children of asylum-seekers from the protection of the Children Act 1989, which would have allowed them to be taken into care if failed asylum-seekers refused to leave the country. And then there was a no-choice dispersal system around the country, in an understandable bid to relieve the pressure on local authorities such as those around Heathrow, but which threatened to cut off applicants from the meagre support systems of others who shared their language and predicament. What were missing were well-argued and passionate speeches on the importance of protecting human rights. By not seeking even to engage in the argument, Labour allowed their opponents to set the agenda and year by year they adopted more of it.

Within a year of the passing of the Immigration and Asylum Act 1999, Labour ministers were forced to make a last-minute deal with unions, which were opposing vouchers, to head off a resolution demanding their abolition at the annual Labour Party conference in 2000. The government agreed to an immediate review – it was said to be costing £16 million to distribute £26 million – but 10 months later its findings had still not been published.[26] Fortunately the Law

Lords took over this issue, declaring the vouchers unlawful. Instead a second review was set up on dispersal, for which the government had received far too few offers of local authority housing. What was also clear was that it was causing a further nightmare for asylum-seekers, with an application system that started in London but continued 100 or more miles away, often without advisers or interpreters to help fill out the detailed 19-page application form.

Findings of four media studies

There were four key studies of media coverage of asylum in the first decade of this century. The first, *What's the story?* by Article 19, a human rights charity, was published in May 2003.[27] It included an examination of six papers (*The Sun*, *The Daily Mirror*, *Daily Mail*, *Daily Express*, *The Daily Telegraph* and *The Guardian*) for 11 weeks from the beginning of October 2002 and three separate four-week spans of television news bulletins (BBC1, ITV, Channel 4 and Channel 5 for the last session). Of the 308 stories in the press, the closing of the Sangatte camp dominated, accounting for almost one quarter. The Immigration and Asylum Bill 2002 was covered in 36 and the rest were more evenly spread: asylum costs (14), numbers (13), dispersal (11), treatment (10) and crime and terrorism (7).

Using two different criteria, the study found the first, frequency of coverage, ranged from relative silence (*The Daily Telegraph* and *The Daily Mirror*) to intense focus (*Daily Mail* and *Daily Express*). And on the second, impartiality, the coverage ranged from neutrality (*The Guardian*) to extreme prejudice (*Daily Mail*, *Daily Express* and *The Sun*). The asylum-seekers were referred to by 51 different labels, from one-word insults such as 'parasites' or 'scroungers' to 'would-be immigrants'. It went on to note that *The Sun* 'rarely called the group anything other than "asylum cheats" or "illegals", even when referring to them coming with the full approval of the government'. It found the *Mail*, *Express* and *Sun* developed similar themes with respect to Sangatte: thousands of asylum-seekers or illegal immigrants were heading to Britain; the government had lost control of the borders; those who had been granted legal entry to Britain (1,200 on the closure of Sangatte, with France looking after the other three quarters) were 'undeserving'. It added: 'A particularly stigmatizing synonym applied by the *Mail* and *Express* was "inmate", a term usually employed to describe people who are detained as they are a danger to the public'. The *Express* confused its readers further by referring to Sangatte as a detention centre.

Its analysis of television coverage suggested, as other research has done (see Chapter Eight, this volume), that television followed the newspaper agenda. It found that television bulletins repeated newspaper inaccuracies or were guilty of their own. There was one notorious instance when the BBC replicated an *Express* claim that Dover was being 'flooded by asylum-seekers', and its reporter remarked to camera: 'In some streets, everyone we spoke to was a newly-arrived asylum seeker smuggled in, in the back of a lorry.' Like the press, television was criticised for the dominance of politicians, immigration officials and the police and very little of the asylum-seekers themselves, and even less of the background that had prompted them to seek asylum in the first place.

The second report, published a year later in 2004, was commissioned by Ken Livingstone, Mayor of London, to assess the impact of media coverage of asylum on community relations in London.[28] It was produced by the Information Centre about Asylum and Refugees (ICAR), set up at King's College, London, in 2000, and now based at the Runnymede Trust. The study was prompted by the recognition that asylum-seekers were suffering harassment and the concern of community groups that media coverage was adding to tensions.

It took representative samples of national and local London press stories on asylum and refugees collected during August and September 2003. They were analysed by headline and content. Separate focus groups in two boroughs with significant populations of asylum-seekers and refugees explored their view of the media's impact on community relations. There were interviews with local refugee groups, editors of local and regional papers and local borough officials. Refugee community organisations were asked to monitor and record harassment in their area. The study found:

- clear evidence of negative, unbalanced and inaccurate reporting likely to promote fear and tension with communities across

London. Most of this evidence was in the national press, which reported on asylum issues far more frequently than either the local or the black and ethnic minority press;

- the main parties dominated the political sources quoted in news stories. In contrast, there was little reference to legal instruments or to organisations working on behalf of asylum-seekers and refugees;
- the portrayals of allegedly overwhelming but unspecified influxes of asylum-seekers from abroad were likely to bring apprehension to readers' minds while the frequent reporting of criminality among asylum-seekers and refugees was likely to induce fear;
- the language of sections of the press was found to be mainly or frequently unbalanced, negative and in some respects potentially alarming. In some feature articles it appeared that disparate information was welded together in a manner likely to alarm readers;
- local newspapers were more likely than national ones to interpret their role as providing a balanced picture on issues that affected local people.

Its local interviews and local monitoring suggested that harassment and abuse of refugees and asylum-seekers was occurring on a daily basis, much of it unreported and undocumented and therefore unrecognised. Interviews with refugee community groups recorded their fears that the hostile images of asylum-seekers in the press increased the likelihood of local harassment.

The third study was a scathing 40-page report prepared for the Institute for Public Policy Research (IPPR) in 2005, by Roy Greenslade, former *Sunday Times* Managing Editor (News), *Daily Mirror* Editor, and since 1992 *Guardian* media commentator, looking at current coverage of asylum against earlier years. Greenslade argued that for all the many differences between asylum-seekers – ethnic, cultural, religious – the right-wing tabloids had portrayed them as a single separate group:

> They have been made into scapegoats for a variety of society's current ills, or alleged ills, such as the level of crime, the liberalism of the welfare state, the housing

shortage and an apparently overcrowded island. To this end editors have sought to forge a unity of viewpoint between the indigenous white population and second and third generation Afro-Caribbean and Asian immigrants by treating asylum-seekers, of whatever race or creed, as somehow different. They have been cast as interlopers who have little or nothing in common with settled migrant communities. But despite the editors' success in having demonised the concept and practice of asylum-seeking, and turning the very phrase into a term of abuse, the casual misuse of terminology reveals an underlying anti-immigrant mindset. The frequent swapping of the terms asylum-seeker, refugee and illegal immigrant betrays the real agenda: in reality, popular newspapers remain opposed to all immigration.[29]

He looked at the disparity in circulation between the four main proponents of anti-refugee stories (*The Sun*, *Daily Star*, *Daily Express* and *Daily Mail*) and the two papers acting as a counterweight (*The Independent* and *The Guardian*). The four tabloids had a combined daily circulation (in 2005) of 7,500,000 compared to the meagre 630,000 of the latter two. And taking in the generally agreed estimate that three people read each purchased copy, this means that the four tabloids running the most critical copy were read by more than 22 million people.

Greenslade's report – and his *Guardian* columns – helped to give a much higher profile to three of the most notorious examples of tabloid distortions:

- First was a fabricated front-page splash by *The Sun* about a gang of 'callous asylum-seekers' who were catching, cooking and consuming the Queen's swans, on whom a top Scotland Yard team was due to pounce. Scotland Yard denied the entire story, but it took *The Sun* another five months before it printed a mere 60-word 'clarification', tucked away on page 41, with no apology. *The Sun*'s Editorial on the day of the splash would have been better directed at its own behaviour. It declared: 'This sickening behaviour is an insult to our nation's civilised traditions ...'. The Press Complaints Commission (PCC), which had been pushed by a persistent Serbian journalist, Nick Medic, to act, conceded that *The Sun* had been 'unable to provide any evidence for the story', but ruled *The Sun*'s proposed clarification 'constituted sufficient remedial action'.[30]

- One month after *The Sun* 'exclusive', the *Daily Star* followed up with an equally damning fabricated story under the heading 'Asylum seekers ate our donkeys'. Nine donkeys had been stolen from Greenwich Park but local police admitted they had no idea about the identity of the perpetrators or the fate of the donkeys. Undeterred, the *Star* claimed an unnamed police 'insider' as saying 'One of our main lines of inquiry is that they may have been taken by immigrants who like eating donkey meat as a delicacy'. It went on to claim wrongly that donkey meat is a speciality in some East African countries, including Somalia, and that there were 'large numbers of Somalian asylum seekers in the area'. As Greenslade noted: 'On that slight evidence, a community was blamed for a crime despite the local police openly admitting that they had no idea about the identity of the perpetrators.' Once again the PCC dismissed complaints against the story, pointing out it could only deal with discrimination against individuals, not groups. However, on 8 January 2004, the *Star* ran a single paragraph which said it had been asked to make clear that the Muslim religion prohibits the eating of donkeys in such circumstances and 'we apologise for any offence caused'.[31]

- Under a banner headline 'Plot to kill Blair', a front-page splash in the *Express* in the summer of 2004 alleged police had arrested two Lithuanian asylum-seekers linked to al-Qaeda, who were plotting to kill Blair. They had been arrested near to Blair's constituency home in a stolen car. Senior police were so outraged by the falsity of the story that they issued an unequivocal denial calling it 'rubbish' and pointing out that the *Express* reporters had been told in advance that 'no security issues were raised by their arrest'. The paper had proceeded with their unsubstantiated story with the police denial at the very end.[32]

In his summing up, Greenslade produces two powerful and succinct paragraphs:

> There is one overarching point that must be grasped: negative, inaccurate, distorted reporting on a large and frequent scale is bound to awaken feelings among readers that may otherwise have remained dormant. Prejudices amongst some sections of the public towards all incomers to Britain, normally held discreetly, have been aroused. As this paper has demonstrated, there was no widespread public outcry against asylum-seekers prior to a press campaign of vilification which had the effect of legitimising public hostility. In response, editors can argue that they were acting on behalf of their readers and politicians to act [as they did when they appeared before Parliament's Joint Committee on Human Rights (JCHR) on 27 January 2007], the problem then needs to be viewed in terms of the tone of the editorial content in expressing those concerns. Was it balanced? Was it accurate? Was it responsible? On these three criteria the popular press has failed. Much of what has been published has been calculated to inflame a sensitive situation. There has been very little balancing material to explain the plight of asylum-seekers. Worse still, many of the stories have been inaccurate.

He went on:

> This drip-drip-drip of negative stories and alarmist headlines in papers that command the attention of huge swathes of the adult British population cannot but have a negative impact on public opinion. If the only information provided to readers is hostile, one-sided, lacking in context and often wildly inaccurate, how can they be expected to see through the distorted media narrative? The situation is, of course, exacerbated by the fact that the people want to believe what they are reading

because it confirms their prejudices. Repetition is also an important influence on the audience in two ways: it ensures that the message gets across even to the most casual of readers and, for the more regular reader, it is suggestive of the story's significance. I would argue that the repetition on the scale of the popular papers' output on asylum-seekers amounts to propaganda.[33]

Two research reports back up Greenslade's conclusion. The first, by Catherine Rothon and Anthony Heath in *British social attitudes* in 2003, found that overt racism, which had been on a steady decline for 14 years from 1987, rose again in 2002. The authors suggested that the sudden reverse was 'probably' linked to media coverage of asylum and immigration issues.[34] A second study in 2005 by MORI on the attitudes of newspaper readers, *You are what you read? How newspaper readership is related to views*, by Bobby Duffy and Laura Rowden, concluded that of all issues examined, the one on which the press had the biggest impact was immigration and race relations. While over 40 per cent of *Sun*, 46 per cent of *Mail* and 48 per cent of *Express* readers in 2004 MORI surveys placed immigration and race as the most important issue facing Britain, less than half of this concern was found among readers of *The Independent* (20 per cent) and *Guardian* (19 per cent).[35]

The fourth and biggest study was ICAR's 2007 study *Reporting asylum*.[36] It was commissioned and funded by the Home Office and involved a study of all national daily papers and their Sunday equivalents (20 in total), 22 regional and eight ethnic or faith papers, some 50 publications in total over eight weeks between January and March 2005. Over 2,000 articles on asylum were assessed and 18 editors interviewed. There was a sub-group of six national dailies, five tabloids (*Daily Star, The Sun, The Daily Mirror, Daily Express* and *Daily Mail*) and one broadsheet (*The Daily Telegraph*), which had the highest circulations. The report noted public concern with the tone of the political debate, which was described as 'wretched, squalid, shameful and hysterical'. The monitoring period coincided with the run-up to the 2005 election, which included a right-wing speech by Michael Howard, the Tory leader, in which he declared the

Conservatives would withdraw from the 1951 UN Convention on Refugees and introduce a new selection process that would be based overseas, with a ban on any applications being made within the UK.

The study found there had been some improvement since its 2004 report for the Mayor of London, but its coverage had been much wider then, with the regionals and former broadsheets all diluting the venom of the tabloids. There was an interesting contrast between the analysis of the top six selling dailies compared to the national press as a whole. The proportion of the top six describing policy as 'in chaos, out of control, failure, untrustworthy' was three times as high (39 per cent) as the other nationals (13 per cent). Similarly, the proportion of articles discussing health risks from asylum-seekers was twice as high – 10 per cent versus five per cent – a ratio that was repeated with respect to stories suggesting border controls had been handed to the EU.

In terms of inflammatory headlines, the tabloids dominated the top of the table. The *Star*'s were the crudest: 'Spongers face boot' (7 February 2005), 'Kick out this scum' (2 March 2005), 'Asylum HIV fear' (8 March 2005) and 'Migrants on dole cost you £1bn – one in three hasn't tried to find a job' (10 March 2005). But the *News of the World* was just as hostile: 'Asylum crime fear' (30 January 2005), 'Halt this crooked tide' (30 January 2005), 'Shut out this scum' (13 February 2005) and 'We'll boot them out' (13 February 2005).

There were clearly higher standards in the regional papers than the tabloids. One regional editor noted: 'If we produced a racist paper it won't sell in this city. Anything we do we have to live with it, unlike nationals.' There were far more reports in the regionals about communities helping refugees to integrate. Several had joined in campaigns to save individual local asylum-seekers threatened with deportation. Regional editors were consistently more positive about the PCC guidelines on reporting asylum issued in October 2003. One Scottish newspaper executive said 'We are way beyond the PCC guidelines here in Scotland. We have been campaigning for more immigration in Scotland due to our shrinking population.'

The study concludes that the PCC guidelines had helped raise standards, but one national editor admitted, 'In this newsroom and certainly round the rest of Fleet Street they are totally ignored.'

Another national executive added: 'Given the weight of the seriousness of the coverage of this issue, I'm surprised the PCC hasn't taken a more robust view on this.' This view was echoed by an editor of a minority ethnic paper: 'I think some papers need to be stamped on by the PCC so that an example is set. The PCC must make an example of the worst papers.'

In its conclusions the report called on the PCC to widen its remit so that valid complainants were no longer restricted to named individual victims of media misrepresentation, but widened to 'third parties' who wished to protect vulnerable groups. It should also extend the protection against discriminatory reporting in clause 12 of the Editors' Code to asylum-seekers and migrants, as it had recently done for gender. This last proposal had been put to the PCC before, but had been rejected.

Assessing the Labour record

There were three underlying parts to Blair's strategy on asylum:

- To reduce Britain's 'pull factor' to asylum-seekers by reducing benefits, withdrawing them altogether if applicants failed to claim promptly, and curbing legal aid for appeals. In 2003 before the courts declared it unlawful, some 9,415 asylum-seekers were denied any form of government support under the 'promptness rule'. But the 'pull factor' was always exaggerated. Asylum movements are prompted by persecution, ethnic cleansing or wars, not £37.50 a week in cash and vouchers. The top five countries from which asylum-seekers arrived in 2002/03 were testimony to this fact: Afghanistan, Iraq, Sri Lanka, Somalia, and until the imposition of visas, Zimbabwe.
- To ratchet even tighter controls over entry. Hence the restoration of the 'white list' of safe states, from which applications would be automatically assumed to be unfounded.
- And to step up the removal rate of those who failed to receive refugee status.

This latter strand had all-party support, but it was the coercive lengths to which Labour was prepared to go that were appalling – the threat to take the children of failed applicants into state care if their parents failed to leave the country voluntarily. What was sad was the speed with which the honourable resistance that Labour had applied to Howard's Asylum and Immigration Act 1996 evaporated once in power.

Labour policy was being made on the hoof. There were only six lines on asylum/immigration in their 1997 manifesto. As Sarah Spencer, Director of the Oxford Centre on Migration, rightly noted in her study of Labour's policy, there was no clear policy at all in the early years, 'no vision, no policy goals, no third way'.[37] Blair's overriding objective was to convince the public that asylum was under control so as to neutralise the issue. But he made the same mistake as he did with crime, believing tough talk, hyperactivity and multiple Acts of Parliament – six in his 10 years – would reassure the public. They did the exact opposite, with polls showing public concern rising throughout his period of office.

In his autobiography Blair speaks of how out-of-date the asylum system had become since it was created post-Second World War, post-Holocaust. It was understandable for the era it was introduced, but not now. Today the presumption that applicants were in danger of persecution was 'plainly false – most asylum-seekers were not genuine. Disproving them, however, was almost impossible.' He went on:

> The combination of the courts, with their liberal instinct; the European Court of Human Rights with its absolutist attitude to the prospect of returning someone to an unsafe community; and the UN Convention on Refugees, with its context firmly that of the 1930s Germany, meant that, in practice, once someone got into Britain and claimed asylum, it was the Devil's own job to return them....[38]

The idea that it was harder in 2003 to receive refugees when the UK economy was the fourth biggest in the world than it was in the still war-torn economy of the early 1950s was absurd. Even in 2002, when 110,000 applicants and their dependants were in the UK queue, there were five EU states accepting more in proportion to their population. The idea that most asylum-seekers were 'plainly false' was also wrong. True, a majority are rejected, but that is a different story. They include the people rejected for technical breaches, such as the strict timetable, or victims of 'the culture of denial' by case workers or the curb on legal aid preventing appeals. Blair's arguments might have been more persuadable if we had not been made aware by Lance Price and many others (see Chapter One, this volume) of the degree to which policy-making was driven by focus groups, polls and the tabloid press.

Missed opportunities

As the UNHCR told Parliament's JCHR in 2006, Britain suffered from a lack of political leadership in dealing with asylum. It noted some 'attempts to dehumanise asylum-seekers by some sections of the media continue, despite a lessening of frequency since the well documented most vitriolic reporting in 2003'. It went on: 'The numbers of both refugees and asylum-seekers are at their lowest levels for 13 years. In the view of the UNHCR, the UK now has the time and space to take a more rational approach of the management of asylum, and to make a concerted effort to dispel some of the hysteria surrounding the issue.'[39] Alas, the moment was not seized.

In its final report on the treatment of asylum-seekers in 2007, Parliament's JCHR expressed concern about the negative impact of hostile reporting on individual asylum-seekers and its potential to influence immigration case workers, affect government policy and even be linked with physical attacks on asylum-seekers. It noted that the UK was the only one of 192 signatories to the International Convention on the Rights of the Child to have entered a general reservation to the application of the Convention to children who were subject to immigration control. It went on: 'We reiterate our previous recommendation that the Government's reservation should be withdrawn. It is not needed to protect the public interest and undermines the international reputation of the country.'[40]

The all-party committee added an even more startling conclusion:

> Many witnesses have told us that they are convinced
> that destitution is a deliberate tool in the operation
> of immigration policy. We have been persuaded by
> the evidence that the Government has indeed been
> practising a deliberate policy of destitution of this
> highly vulnerable group. We believe the deliberate use
> of inhumane treatment is unacceptable ... the policy of
> enforced destitution must cease.[41]

A sorry tale indeed of aggressive uncontrolled media power prompting a pusillanimous political response. This is one area of policy-making where Lance Price's criticisms (see Chapter One) of Number 10 – spinning stories of very little substance into something bigger than they were – is not true. The degree to which an already coercive system of control over asylum-seekers was tightened and made more intimidating demeaned the Labour government. True, they were under severe media pressure, but it was pressure that they should have resisted.

Notes

[1] 'Blair's asylum gamble', BBC News website, 7 February 2003.

[2] *The Sunday Telegraph*, 9 February 2003.

[3] 'Ministers back down', BBC News website, 10 February 2003.

[4] 'Blair's policy on asylum "muddled"', *Herald Scotland* website, 10 February 2003.

[5] 'Blair "guarantees" asylum figures will halve', *The Independent*, 13 February 2003.

[6] Ipsos/MORI Political Monitor: Long-term trends 2007.

[7] BBC and all national media websites.

[8] Article 19 (2004) *What's the story?*, April, www.article19.org.

[9] Roy Greenslade (200) *Seeking scapegoats: The coverage of asylum in the UK press*, London: Institute for Public Policy Research, May.

[10] Ibid.

[11] Refugee Council/Amnesty poll, carried out in 2003.

[12] David Blunkett (2006) *The Blunkett tapes: My life in the bear pit*, London: Bloomsbury, p 448.

[13] Michael Barber (2007) *Instruction to deliver: Tony Blair, the public services and the challenge of achieving targets*, London: Politico's, p 81.

[14] Ibid, p 81.

[15] Ibid, p 171.

[16] Stephen Pollard (2005) *David Blunkett*, London: Hodder & Stoughton, p 278.

[17] See the BBC and national media websites, 27 November 2003.

[18] Personal interview.

[19] *The Guardian*, 23 May 2002.

[20] Sarah Spencer (2007) 'Immigration', in Anthony Seldon (ed) *Blair's Britain 1997–2007*, Cambridge: Cambridge University Press, ch 16, p 359.

[21] Ibid.

[22] *The Guardian* (1998) Editorial: 'Labour should not be so apologetic', 28 July.

[23] *The Guardian* (1999) Editorial: 'A prime piece of cheek', 25 August.

[24] Ibid.

[25] BBC and national media websites on annual Conservative Party Conference, 7 October 2002.

[26] *The Guardian* (2001) Editorial: 'Repairing a reputation', 14 August.

[27] Article 19 (2004) *What's the story?*, www.article19.org

[28] ICAR (Information Centre about Asylum and Refugees) (2004) *Media image, community impact*, April, www.icar.org.uk.

[29] Roy Greenslade (2005) *Seeking scapegoats: The coverage of asylum in the UK press*, London: Institute for Public Policy Research, , p 5.

[30] Ibid, p 25.

[31] Ibid, p 26.

[32] Ibid, p 28.

[33] Ibid, p 29.

[34] Catherine Rothon and Anthony Heath (2003) 'Trends in racial prejudice', in Alison Park et al (eds) *British social attitudes 2003–2004: Continuity and change over two decades, The 20th report*, London: Sage Publications for the National Centre for Social Research, ch 9.

[35] Bobby Duffy and Laura Rowden (2005) *You are what you read? How newspaper readership is related to views*, London: MORI Social Research Institute.

[36] ICAR (Information Centre about Asylum and Refugees) (2007) *Reporting asylum: The UK press and the effectiveness of PCC guidelines, January to March 2005*, ICAR, London: City University, January.

[37] Sarah Spencer (2007) 'Immigration', in Anthony Seldon (ed) *Blair's Britain 1997–2007*, Cambridge: Cambridge University Press, ch 16, p 341.

[38] Tony Blair (2010) *A journey*, London: Hutchinson, p 205.

[39] House of Lords and House of Commons JCHR (Joint Committee on Human Rights) (2007) *The treatment of asylum seekers, Tenth report of session 2006–07*, London: The Stationery Office, pp 98-9.

[40] Ibid, p 112.

[41] Ibid, p 110.

SIX

Labour's boldest bid: to end child poverty

Several chapters in this book – those on asylum, drugs and crime – describe how politicians bow too much to tabloid populism. This chapter, however, reports on how the 1997–2010 Labour government set out to pursue a crucial reform – the eradication of child poverty – where there was no tabloid pressure for it, and if anything a gut instinct opposed to the idea. But it also shows that, even on 'unpopular issues', where there are vibrant pressure groups, active think tanks and generous donors, the research and activism does get reported, particularly in the more serious media, and does seem to inform and influence public opinion.

Tony Blair's declaration in London's Toynbee Hall on 18 March 1999 was the boldest social policy goal by New Labour in its 13 years in government: the abolition of child poverty within 20 years. It came out of the blue from a party which had been mocked for the modesty of the five pledges – all printed on a single visiting card – on which it had campaigned in the 1997 election. Poverty was not even mentioned. The full manifesto was no better. As *The Independent*'s Political Editor, Andrew Marr, wrote on the day after the manifesto's publication, the only radical element in it was 'the modesty of the promises'.

But there was no disputing the radicalism of the Toynbee Hall pledge. The UK had moved under 18 years of Conservative rule (1979–97) from one of the most equal societies in the world to one of the most unequal. A two-volume report in 1995 drawn up over two years by a commission set up by the Joseph Rowntree Foundation (JRF) set out the devastating facts.[1] Its stark conclusions included the following:

- Income inequality had grown to a greater extent and at a faster rate in Britain since the late 1970s than in any comparable industrialised country.
- The distribution of income was currently more unequal than at any time since the Second World War.
- There was no 'trickle down' of wealth, nor any evidence that the widening income gap had increased economic growth or raised the living standards of the poor.
- In contrast to previous postwar periods, the poorest 20 to 30 per cent of the population had failed to receive any benefit from economic growth.

So not only was Britain in the worst possible position for abolishing child poverty, but not even the more progressive Scandinavian countries had been able to abolish it during this time frame.

What had prompted Tony Blair's speech? It was not a question of him trying to 'bounce' Brown on a social policy reform. It is true, however, that the Treasury confessed to feeling 'miffed' when they first heard about the plan – Brown had a deal with Blair that he would be in control of a large part of domestic policy. But the same officials admitted that the fact that Blair had launched the anti-child poverty programme came in useful when Number 10 became concerned at the rising costs of tax credits. They were able to remind the Prime Minister's Office that ending child poverty was a Tony Blair pledge.

The instigator of the Blair speech was Lord (Robin) Butler, former Cabinet Secretary who had become Master of University College, Oxford, and was organising a series of lectures to celebrate the college's 750th anniversary. Blair was invited to launch the series, speaking on 'Beveridge revisited – a welfare state fit for the 21st century'. The theme had several close links with the college: William Beveridge had been Master of the college when he wrote his magisterial 1942 report that led to the creation of the welfare state. Beveridge had employed as a research assistant Harold Wilson, then a fellow of the college and later Labour prime minister in the 1960s and 1970s. And the prime minister who implemented Beveridge's report between 1945 and 1951, Clement Attlee, was a graduate of the college.

No doubt the success of the Beveridge report may have been an added incentive for Blair. Launched in the middle of a devastating war, it brought a ray of hope to a despondent people with its bold identification of five giants that had to be overcome on the road to reconstruction: want, ignorance, squalor, idleness and disease. The report, 60,000 copies of which had been sold by lunchtime on the first day and which – with the help of a later shortened version – eventually went on to sell 600,000, was a sales record for Her Majesty's Stationery Office (HMSO, the government's printing office). *The Times* declared it 'a momentous document' while the *Daily Express* front page headline declared: 'Beveridge tells how to abolish want'. Column after column in much smaller wartime papers provided detailed summaries while the BBC relayed the news in 22 different languages abroad. A public opinion poll shortly after publication showed 86 per cent in favour and a mere 6 per cent opposed. Perhaps Blair was hoping to catch some of that limelight.

Blair's history lessons

One lesson that Blair and his team drew from this history became his most ambitious challenge in his speech: how to transform welfare from 'a term of abuse' into something 'popular'. The choice of Toynbee Hall for the speech was another bow to history. It was in Toynbee Hall that Beveridge resided as sub-warden in 1903–05. It was founded in 1885 and became the first of many settlement houses that spread across the UK and the US. One aim of the houses, set in poor inner-city areas, was to mitigate class suspicions by placing middle-class graduates into areas of deep poverty to provide help, advice and support to local communities. It was within Toynbee's walls that a succession of progressive groups was launched: Workers' Educational Association (WEA) (1903), Youth Hostel Association (YHA) (1931) and the Child Poverty Action Group (CPAG) (1965).

True to Toynbee tradition there was extensive preparatory work preceding the Blair speech. A dozen leading social policy specialists were invited to submit papers to Number 10 on different topics raised by the title: Beveridge's legacy and his ideas, modern conceptions of social justice, the balance between rights and responsibilities in combating poverty, a critique of the New Right and the Old Left positions and the current state of Labour's reforms since its election in 1997. Ironically, I was turned down when I submitted a FOI media request to Downing Street for the papers that had been used in drawing up the speech and new policy, only to discover that the 12 papers submitted by outsiders had all been incorporated into an excellent book, edited by Robert Walker.[2] A senior Downing Street adviser later confessed that the reason why I was not given access to the inside papers was that there were none.[3] Intriguingly, none of the 12 outside contributions suggested the abolition of child poverty.

The speech writers

So where did the idea for abolishing child poverty come from? I have talked to Peter Hyman, Blair's chief speech writer who wrote the speech, to Carey Oppenheim, Downing Street's special adviser in this area and sundry others. None can remember. They were quite genuine on this issue, pointing out that there had been numerous drafts. It was known to have come as a surprise to senior civil servants and said to have been added late. One Treasury official thought he knew where it had come from.[4] Alastair Campbell leaked the speech to *The Mirror* the day before it was given. He wanted a front-page splash. And how do you get that? By declaring the boldest of goals. It certainly got a splash. On the morning before the speech, *The Mirror*'s front page was able to predict Blair's unequivocal and radical pledge: 'I'll end all child poverty in 20 years.' And there was a fulsome Editorial inside: 'This is a wonderful ambition and is not based on wild promises. Mr Blair does not pretend to have a magic wand which can make things come right instantly. The process will take 20 years, so some children will still suffer. But it is better to be honest than make cruel pledges that cannot be fulfilled.'

If you read the speech, the Treasury's hypothesis is strengthened. If you are going to issue such an audacious target, surely you would not begin with the plan, but instead build up the need for reform and make abolition of child poverty the climax. But if you are trying to convince a tabloid journalist about a good exclusive, then it is better to put it on page one rather than bury it on page 15. There is further evidence that 'abolition' was slotted in late. Shortly after the speech, at a Downing Street policy session to discuss how child poverty could be abolished, Tony Blair confessed to the assembled civil servants that he had not recognised how radical his speech was until he was reading it out.[5]

All of this was finally confirmed in the second volume of Alastair Campbell's diaries, published in late 2010. According to Campbell it was not a long pre-planned leak, but a spontaneous response to a telephone call from Piers Morgan, *The Mirror* Editor, the day before the speech. Morgan had called Campbell for a response to a backbench Labour MP being caught in a massage parlour. The diary goes on: 'I went into my "all you do is trivia" mode and he said well give us something serious and after a bit of toing and froing he agreed to splash on a trail of TB's welfare speech'.[6] Ironically, although this was undoubtedly Labour's boldest social policy, there is not a line about the speech or the launch of the campaign in Tony Blair's autobiography, *A journey*.[7]

Given the scale of what was being attempted, the news columns were subdued. Surely the Prime Minister's opening two paragraphs should have aroused news editors' interests, even if it had already been on the front page of *The Mirror*? The opening paragraphs read:

> Today I want to talk to you about a great challenge: how we make the welfare state popular again. How we restore public trust and confidence in a welfare state that 50 years ago was acclaimed but today has so many wanting to bury it. I will argue that the only road to "a popular welfare state" is a radical welfare reform.
>
> And I will set out our historic aim that ours is the first generation to end child poverty forever and it will take a generation. It is a 20 year mission but I believe it can be done.[8]

The media's coverage

None of the nationals had the story on their front page, but with the exception of a *Daily Telegraph* comment piece by Philip Johnston, the paper's Home Editor ('all things being equal, he's a socialist'), and a critical rant from Auberon Waugh in *The Sunday Telegraph*, the coverage was not hostile. There were only two column inches (fewer than 90 words) in *The Sun* and *Star* and only four column inches in *The Independent* (at the bottom of a quite different story about Gordon Brown's plans to tax child benefit). In the middle market the *Mail* provided 12.5 inches and the *Express* 36, but back at page 17. There were 22 inches in the *Financial Times*, 42 in *The Times*, 62 in *The Daily Telegraph* and 73 in *The Guardian*, which also cleared two pages in the next issue of its *Society* supplement for three of the social policy specialists who had submitted papers to Downing Street to analyse the speech and its implications. There was no news follow-up in the Sunday papers, even though they came out just two days after the daily coverage, and only one comment piece, by Waugh, as already mentioned.

Television coverage was even thinner. The speech made only the fourth item of a mere two minutes' length on ITN's newly revamped early evening news and failed to make the later news. The BBC was even worse, with neither of its two main evening news programmes, BBC 1's *Nine o'clock news* and BBC 2's *Newsnight*, featuring it at all.

The new policy's 20-year deadline caught the most attention in the news columns – who said the media do not like targets? – with much less attention paid to the daunting pledge to lift 700,000 children above the poverty line by the end of the current Parliament, which was three years ahead at the most but turned out to be just over two in practice. This target had still been barely reached 11 years on, let alone two.

True to one of journalism's oldest rules, you cannot get the public to respond to gross national numbers, in this case some four million plus children below the poverty line, so bring it down to the individual. *The Mirror* provided a graphic description of what life was like for Tommy, a 12-year-old in a poor home, under the headline, 'Poor kid':

> He's pale, sickly and underfed. His home is cold, damp
> and squalid. He rarely goes to school. His mother spends
> her time drinking cheap cider. He begins every day
> wandering the streets. He ends each day in despair … the
> saddest fact of all is that Tommy has no idea how much
> better life can be. He has never known anything else….
> Tommy is one of 4.6 million children in Britain who
> Premier Tony Blair pledged yesterday to help in a bid to
> wipe out child poverty within 20 years.[9]

Media critics might rightly add that Tommy's case distorts as much as it illustrates. Yes, there are poor children in dysfunctional families, but there are much larger numbers who have parents in work, who don't drink all day and who don't allow their children to wander the streets at all hours.

The speech reignited the old debate over absolute versus relative poverty. A commentary piece in *The Times* noted: 'The definition of poverty has changed significantly over the last 60 years from having barely enough to eat to having enough to buy cigarettes and a second hand television.' As Peter Golding and Simon Cross noted in their analysis: 'The wistful tone of distaste for this generous redefinition of poverty is unmistakable'.[10] *The Times'* Editorial was more judicious than its comment piece, suggesting there was now 'much to be said in favour of deadlines in life especially when the aim itself may be universally acclaimed as laudable. It is less certain whether that applies when, as in this case, the timescale is so long and the terminology involved distinctly uncertain.'[11]

The *Financial Times* sought perspective, suggesting 'Tony Blair's claim to be heir to William Beveridge, founder of the welfare state, is premature to say the least'. Its Editorial accepted the need for change: 'the social safety net established 50 years ago could hardly be expected to meet the very different needs of the 21st century. There are now far greater proportions of pensioners, single mothers and women at work.'[12] It went on to warn that the use of universal benefits to tackle 'want' had created tax disincentives with even the low-paid now paying tax. The solution, they claimed, was greater concentration on means-tested benefits with tougher conditions. Both could be justified but would involve a high political cost – Housing Benefit, for example, which the Prime Minister had suggested would be the next issue on the agenda, would create large numbers of losers among Labour voters if more toughly tested.

The Guardian, which had supported the way in which Labour had concentrated resources on the most needy through pension and family tax credits, welcomed the move against child poverty, but wanted more clarity:

> Some crucial questions remain unanswered (like which mechanisms will be used? And how will poverty be defined?); several contradictions ignored (both universal and means-tested benefits were embraced); and the toughest decision ducked: you cannot eliminate poverty without embracing the one policy which ministers refuse to acknowledge: redistribution.[13]

Why the sparse coverage in the news columns?

It is fair to say that if the news coverage in many papers was sparse, the editorial columns examined the speech in much more detail, and there are three extenuating circumstances for the circumscribed news coverage. First, it coincided with the height of the Kosovo conflict and, much closer to home, a particularly noteworthy murder in Northern Ireland. Rosemary Nelson, a prominent civil rights lawyer in Belfast, died from a bomb placed under her car. Only the previous month she had led a memorial service for a colleague, the civil rights lawyer Patrick Finucane, on the 10th anniversary of his murder. The two murders bore sinister similarities, chief among them the charge from legal and human rights groups in the UK and the US that British security forces and the local police made them targets by accusing them of sectarian sympathies and may have colluded with Protestant paramilitary groups responsible for their murders.

Second, the leak by Downing Street to *The Mirror* could have been, like many others, counter-productive. The rest of the press may have downplayed it in annoyance that they had not been given the exclusive. For many desks it was now yesterday's news, not today's.

And third, the Prime Minister had set out a vision, but had not said how it was going to be accomplished.

Academic analysis

Peter Golding, Professor of Sociology at Loughborough University, who was an early analyst of media coverage of poverty and social security in the 1970s – and an enthusiastic supporter of this book – believes there are four key 'truths' to media coverage: poverty is not news; poverty policy is rarely news; poverty is insistently understood in popular debate to be absolute not relative; and if poverty policy is to become news, it is only through its contributions to political discord.[14] His own early studies showed the degree to which tabloid papers make scapegoats of benefit claimants. His first three precepts are upheld by the coverage that the Blair speech received. Given the ambition of the speech – and the subsequent coverage down the years as the government struggled to achieve its goal – the speech was poorly reported.

True, there was considerable editorial debate. But that was covered by Golding's second precept: poverty policy is 'rarely' news. This was one of the rare occasions. His third, that poverty is insistently understood in public debate to be absolute not relative, was reflected in *The Times* and the two *Telegraphs* but not elsewhere. And his fourth rule, that poverty policy mainly becomes news only when there is political discord, was reinforced when, only two months after the speech, a row over proposed changes to disability benefits gained far more coverage.

Blair's speech said little about benefits and nothing about income. But he did use the 'p' word and put poverty back on the agenda. In the Thatcher/Major era officials had been banned from using the word. The same had happened in the US where, in the Reagan years, Feifer drew a brilliant cartoon. It showed two 'down and outs' philosophising: 'We used to be poor, then disadvantaged, then deprived, then discriminated against, then socially excluded. We have not got any more money, but we do have a lot of labels.'

Blair's recipe

Blair provided part of the answer to his own challenge to policy-makers: make welfare popular by concentrating the plan on children. Who could be against helping poor children? Not even *The Sun*, it seems. Yet in helping poor children, poorer parents would be helped too. And in helping poorer parents, it would allow some redistribution through tax credits to be introduced in a less threatening way to middle-income voters. It was also clever internal politics, signalling to his critics on the left that New Labour still had Old Labour values.

In his speech Blair was blunt: the New Labour road to reform would be using both universal and means-tested benefits. He asserted that 'the one is not "superior" or "more principled" than the other'. In fact, by the time of his speech, it was already clear that New Labour had dropped the Old Labour preference for a universal approach. Widening income inequalities of the 1980s and 1990s – along with restraints that Labour had imposed on itself – made it financially impossible to rebuild universal benefits in the traditional way. The huge gap between the top and bottom made it even more obvious that the better off did not need many of them. The Conservative spending plans, which Labour had inherited and pledged to follow for its first two years, meant any extra spending had to be concentrated on the poor. Compared to annual average public expenditure increases of 1.9 per cent in the 18 years of Conservative rule (1979–97), Ken Clarke, the outgoing Conservative Chancellor, had set planned expenditure of only 0.4 per cent, almost four fifths less than the previous trend. He would never have followed these plans had he won. Worse still, Blair and Brown, convinced Labour had lost the 1992 election by being branded the 'tax and spend' party, stunned their followers and the country less than four months before the 1997 election by announcing that should they win, they would not be increasing income tax in their first Parliament.

Given these restraints – only made slightly lighter through the one-off windfall tax on the privatised national utilities – the papers from the social policy specialists submitted to Downing Street still found plenty to compliment Labour on for its first two years in office. The New Deal programmes for the unemployed (offering subsidised jobs, voluntary work, training or education all financed from the windfall tax on privatised utilities) were welcomed for recognising that for many people, paid work was 'the best route out of poverty' and 'the main route through which individuals and families gain a sense of dignity, self-respect, and a stake in society'. Policies that had boosted income in work – the minimum wage, working family tax credits and tax changes that had lifted many low-income families out of tax – were also singled out for praise. The Social Exclusion Unit 'at the heart of government' was lauded, as were the government's policies investing in low-income areas through the New Deal for Communities along with Health and Education Action Zones.

The main complaint was the failure of Labour to address the adequacy of existing benefits; its failure to be bolder about redistribution; and its social security rhetoric. Even in the Beveridge speech Blair spoke with pride about cutting the social security budget. (It was a 1 per cent reduction.)

The run-up to 1997

There were three key events in respect of welfare reform that occurred between the 1992 and 1997 elections that changed the political climate. Five months after the 1992 election the pound crashed out of the Exchange Rate Mechanism. 'Black Wednesday', as it became known, demolished the credibility of the Chancellor, Norman Lamont, who had sworn he would never devalue; deeply wounded John Major, given his links to the Treasury; and destroyed the Conservative Party's reputation for economic competence. From there on in, they were on the back foot for a decade-and-a-half.

The second event was Labour's decision, in the wake of the election defeat, to set up a Commission on Social Justice in December 1992. It was designed to be independent of the party with several non-party figures appointed under the chairmanship of Sir Gordon Borrie, former Director General of Fair Trade. But overall there was a clear social democratic majority, with a 28-year-old at the left-leaning IPPR, David Miliband, acting as its secretary. It was prompted by a loss of nerve over the party's traditional support for redistributing some money to the poor and vulnerable. What was promised was a 'new

Beveridge' that would think the unthinkable, review fundamental principles and examine the balance between means-tested and universal benefits. Bryan Gould, who had unsuccessfully run for the party's leadership, had urged the party to reassess the need for universal benefits.[15] He raised a second issue, which came to prominence in the run-up to the 1997 election – the need for Labour to be seen to approve of aspiration, which Blair strongly supported. There were other concerns. A debate that began in the US with the publication of J.K. Galbraith's *The culture of contentment* had spread to the UK.[16] US society, Galbraith argued, had become divided into thirds, with the comfortable and the well-off thirds no longer feeling obligations towards the bottom third. Several commentators saw a similar pattern occurring in Britain.[17]

The most important service of the Commission was making the public much more aware of the depth of inequalities in the UK. It published a succession of 13 issue papers plus two interim reports that fed in to the news and feature pages. Several of its more startling statistics began appearing in comment columns and editorials: the one in five adults dependent on benefits; the one in three children in poverty; the income gap wider than at any time since 1886. A 400-page report was launched at an all-day conference on 24 October 1994, which began with a video introduction produced by the film director, David Puttnam. It was followed by four other sessions involving 16 speakers and numerous discussants.[18] The report rejected two different sets of 'siren voices': the deregulators of the right looking for more privatisation and deregulation 'where the rich get richer and the poor, poorer'; and the levellers of the left, described as pessimists, more concerned with the distribution of wealth to the neglect of its production.

The report set out a 15-year strategy, which contained a host of different proposals aimed at transforming 'the welfare state from a safety net in times of trouble to a springboard for economic recovery'. There were to be multiple changes to benefits, no increases to income tax, but much wider proposals covering pathways to work, a minimum wage, better childcare and a voluntary citizens' service for young people. Learning was to be lifelong, ranging from pre-school education for all to wider A-levels with a vocational option, a graduate tax or student loan system to cover accommodation and part of university tuition costs, and a Learning Bank for adult education. Lone parents on benefits would be expected to return to work when their youngest child was five. Social care – including long-term residential care – would be financed through a new insurance scheme.

A wary Blair

Just three months before the report's launch, Tony Blair had become the new leader of the Labour Party on the sudden death of John Smith, who had been the main driver setting up the Commission. Delivering a keynote address at the report's launch, Blair was full of praise for its diagnosis of what was going wrong – 'the most significant since Beveridge – a remarkable piece of work'. But he recognised several of the proposals would provide targets for the Tories. He got his retaliation in first by noting at the start of his speech that 'Commissions write reports. Parties write manifestos. That is now our task.' Prior to publication he had been reported as being disappointed by the report's recommendations. Yet several of these did emerge when Labour came to power in 1997: the minimum wage, a minimum pension guarantee, student loans, tuition fees and the emphasis on welfare to work programmes. The latter was one that Blair immediately embraced, declaring 'I want to give people a hand-up, not just a hand out.'

There was widespread media coverage of the report, far more than on Blair's address on ending child poverty. Front pages, first leaders, inside pages – three full pages in *The Guardian* and three-and-a-half in *The Independent*, over 300 column inches in each of these papers. Hugo Young, *The Guardian*'s chief political commentator, noted the report's unfamiliar tone of voice:

> It ushers in an age of renewed belief in state inspired solutions to social problems. After two decades of the opposite, this is cultural shock writ long.... Younger readers, in particular, will find the world of Gordon Borrie incomprehensibly optimistic. They have lived in a Hobbesian universe that emphasises the brutishness of

> humanity, redeemable by individual effort alone ... studies
> such as this one, even without socialistic conclusions,
> have become anathema.[19]

Nicholas Timmins in *The Independent* picked out a paragraph in the report, which was later taken up in separate books from Richard Layard, and Richard Wilkinson and Kate Pickett[20]: 'Many people who have the chance to work hard and make themselves and their families better off are insecure about the future, scared about crime, worried about old age and disillusioned with politics. Although nearly three times wealthier as a nation than we were in 1950, we are certainly not three times happier as a society.'[21]

There were mostly welcoming noises from the think tanks and pressure groups. CPAG welcomed the education, childcare and benefit proposals but opposed the tax on higher child benefit for top-rate taxpayers; Age Concern liked the moves to reduce pensioner poverty but criticised the report's failure to demand an official adequacy level; and the Institute for Fiscal Studies (IFS) was impressed by the income-related minimum pension guarantee, which it said had 'strikingly reversed post-war Labour policy'. It went on to say this move to improve means tests rather than ending them 'is an enormous step for the Commission, and an even bigger step if the Labour Party follows'. In terms of social security, that is what it did do from 1997.

JRF Inquiry into Income and Wealth

The third key event was the JRF Inquiry into Income and Wealth that reported in February 1995, some of whose findings were set out at the beginning of this chapter. It was important for several reasons. First it was based on £450,000 of specially commissioned research, which demolished several misconceptions, among them the malevolent idea that widening inequality would help the poor by a 'trickle down' from the top. Second, the report warned that Britain was becoming 'a drawbridge society' in which the affluent were trying to insulate themselves from the bottom third. Britain was becoming the very country John Major had warned against on his first day as Prime Minister – a society not at ease with itself. As the chair of the Inquiry, the widely respected Sir Peter Barclay, JRF trustee and former chair of the government's Social Security Advisory Committee, asserted at the launch: 'We believe the problems of a large and growing minority who have no stake in our future prosperity will rebound on the comfortable majority with heavy economic as well as social costs.' Third, the breadth of the Inquiry group could not be challenged. Its members ranged from the Director General of the Confederation of British Industry (CBI) to the General Secretary of the Trades Union Congress (TUC) with others including the Deputy Chair of British Telecom, a right-wing economist, plus more liberal figures from the academic, think tank and charity world.

Its publication was awaited with eager anticipation in Westminster and Whitehall. Alastair Campbell, Labour's Director of Communications, had sought to secure a leaked copy from JRF. Early copies had been distributed to specialist journalists so they could prepare their pieces properly, but there were none for the partisan. What Campbell ensured did happen was that at Prime Minister's Questions on the day before publication, Tony Blair asked John Major whether reducing inequality was one of the objectives of his government. The Prime Minister snapped back with a one-word answer, 'Yes'.

The first leader in *The Times* on the day after publication must have had Labour squirming with pleasure. Under a main headline 'The new levellers', *The Times* declared: 'If reducing inequality, as an end in itself, were really to be accepted as a major goal of government, the Tories' record since 1979 would have to be judged a dismal failure'.[22] The paper then led with a glass chin, seeking to deny Britain had become more unequal than other countries, an assertion which ignored the findings of other academic studies, listed at length in the two published volumes of the Inquiry. They included work from the OECD, the European Commission and the LSE, along with that of leading Oxford and Cambridge economists. *The Times* did concede Britain had become more unequal, but went on: 'The question for Mr Major is whether he should now promise to "do something" about inequality. Or should he, instead, try reminding Britain that inequality is no vice, provided poverty remains within civilised limits.' *The Times* opted for the latter, asserting – without quoting any evidence – that inequality in Britain remained 'within tolerable bounds: international comparisons suggest that it does'. If only the writer had read an earlier JRF report from 1992 that updated David Piachaud's 1979 pamphlet on *The cost of a child*, which found social security benefits fell 30 per cent below the most basic of living standards, drawn up from a survey of the public.

Nicholas Timmins, a better-informed journalist than *The Times*' leader writer, wrote in *The Independent*: 'with the coolest of language and the coldest of analysis, the JRF today produces a picture of Britain that should make the blood run cold. It is not one of a nation at ease with itself.'[23]

Response from the Sunday papers

The Sunday papers were also divided. *The Observer* Editorial paid tribute to the role of the JRF: 'When royal commissions are as unfashionable as the Royal Family itself, it is good that responsible charities fill the gap in analysis left by the Government.'[24] Under a 'Whitehall blames Tories for poor' headline, *The Sunday Telegraph* front-page splash suggested that the top of the civil service was taking the report seriously. It reported:

> Whitehall's most senior civil servants have blamed Government policy for the growth of an underclass within Britain. They fear it is creating 'islands' of poverty, disaffection, and social division. They conclude that the most deprived have been the least able to take advantage of the drive to widen choice in housing, education and health, with most benefit going to the better off. Their warning was delivered at a meeting of permanent secretaries from eight departments called by Sir Robin Butler, the Cabinet Secretary, in an attempt to raise Whitehall's awareness of the problems caused by Britain's growing social divide.[25]

It added that these fears would dismay ministers, particularly on the Tory right, who the previous week had rejected JRF's report on widening inequality. But inside *The Sunday Telegraph* there was a different view. It cleared two thirds of an inside page to challenge the findings of the report on technical grounds, a somewhat impudent exercise given the expertise of the research team that had carefully gathered the evidence.

Throughout the 1992–97 government, pressure groups were continuing to produce reports. Barnardo's, in July 1994, published a pamphlet by Richard Wilkinson, documenting the devastating effects of relative poverty.[26] Its psychological effects were eroding physical and mental health, education standards, social behaviour and social cohesion. It conceded that crime, drugs, depression, suicide and physical ill health had their own separate causes, but Wilkinson persuasively argued that they could not be seen in isolation because they shared an important common cause: inequality. His pamphlet was filled with correlation charts showing the slowing down of declining death rates in countries with higher inequality rates. He knocked down the new moralists – who blamed it all on the break-up of the family – by pointing to Japan and Sweden, at opposite ends of a spectrum. Japan, with the most traditional two-parent model, and Sweden, where less than half of all children were born to married couples, shared first and second place in international league tables on life expectancy and low crime rates. Their common link was narrow income differentials. He went on to expand the pamphlet in various books, but most famously in *The spirit level* published in 2009 to rave reviews.[27]

Summing up the Thatcher/Major years

To sum up the end of 18 years of Conservative rule: both child and pensioner poverty had accelerated at an alarming rate, child poverty more than doubling after housing costs (from one in seven to one in three children below the poverty line), while pensioner poverty increased even faster, tripling the proportions from 13 to 41 per cent below the poverty line (60 per cent below the median). No European country – and only one developed state outside Europe, New Zealand – suffered such a brutal widening of inequality. Some was due to deep structural changes in the economy, but it was made much worse by top tax rates being cut in half (down from 80 to 40 per cent) and multiple reductions to benefits (via indexing, eligibility rules, time limits). The gap between the rich and the poor doubled in the UK. In 1979 the post-tax income of the top tenth of the population was five times as much as the bottom tenth; by 1997 that proportion had doubled to 10 times as much. Where once the US was the most unequal developed nation, the UK caught up with it. As the 16-strong team of researchers from the LSE who monitored Labour's first 10 years in government documented, Tony Blair inherited levels of poverty and inequality unprecedented in post-war (1945) history. As the first volume of the team reported: 'Unlike every other post war decade, in which the gains of economic growth were shared across income groups, growth in the 1980s benefited the richest most and the poorest least. Indeed, on one measure, the incomes of the very poorest were lower in real terms in 1994/95 than they had been in 1979.'[28] Poverty and deprivation in certain areas reached levels not known since the 1930s. One in five families with children had no earner by the mid-1990s, four times the figure of 1968. But as inequality had widened, so public support for a closing of the gap increased. It was a grim social scene for Labour to inherit, but a promising political opportunity given the public support for a fairer welfare state.

Tony Blair's first term

Rarely has a new government prompted such warm feelings of hope, expectation and pleasure. The Conservatives, as their first female chair Theresa May later admitted to the 2002 annual conference, had come by many to be perceived as 'the nasty party'.[29] But alas Labour's plans for a modernised welfare state faced a year of turmoil. From the beginning it started on the wrong foot. Blair wanted Frank Field as his Social Security Secretary but Brown objected. The worst of all compromises was reached. Harriet Harman, an ally of Gordon Brown, was made Secretary of State but Field, who knew the background intimately, was given a wider brief, Minister for Welfare Reform with a seat on the Cabinet committee dealing with public expenditure. The couple, who were incompatible, worked in separate silos with relations becoming so bad that civil servants would act as lookouts at the end of separate meetings to ensure they would not bump into each other in the corridors.[30] Worse still, there was a third person in this 'dysfunctional marriage': Gordon Brown, who was intent on transforming the Treasury from a monitor of social policy spending to a centre for domestic policy-making. Welfare reform, as far as Brown was concerned, was a central part of his own responsibilities.

Brown's plans completely contradicted Field's. Field wanted to transform the very base of the social security system, transforming its tax base into contributory pension and insurance schemes, delivered through mutual societies and private sector providers, for two reasons: first, because the funds would be more secure from ministerial raids, and second, because the re-creation of a civic society required a more even balance between the state, the individual and voluntary organisations. Brown was much more pragmatic. Given the restraints imposed by the pledge to follow Tory spending plans, he was intent on greater targeting to ensure that what extra money there was in the next two years would be spent on the poor. He was in a much more powerful position to ensure his plan would be implemented. He set up a taskforce under Martin Taylor, chair of Barclays Bank, to examine the idea of an earned income tax credit designed to lift the poor over the poverty line. As early as September 1997, he was already leaking to *The Guardian* that he was going to transform the tax and benefit system in his 1998 Budget. There would be a minimum wage backed up by a new system of tax credits, paid through the pay packet to the less well off.

Ministerial feuds become public

As early as June 1997, Jill Sherman in *The Times* reported that feuding ministers had stalled Blair's plans for radical welfare reform. When in July there was no increase in benefits in Brown's first Budget, Roy Hattersley, a former Deputy Labour Leader, wrote an angry *Guardian* article accusing Labour of 'apostasy' on poverty and equality.[31] By September there were numerous reports in the serious press of splits between Harman and Field. Nicholas Timmins, by now working for the *Financial Times*, reported that Field's 'big bang' welfare reform was proving unworkable.[32] Meanwhile the government was facing a serious parliamentary problem. Two time-bombs that Peter Lilley, the former Conservative Social Security Secretary, had left in the pipeline were primed to detonate. They were seen to be part of Conservative spending plans, but required legislation to implement. One was a cut to Housing Benefit and the other the abolition of lone-parent premiums for new claimants. Brown told Harman that she had to implement one. She chose the lone-parent cut, which led to the first big backbench revolt by Labour MPs voting against the measure, 120 Labour MPs signing a letter in protest to the Chancellor, and mass resignations among ordinary Labour members. A week later, when a letter from David Blunkett, Education Secretary, protesting against planned curbs to disability benefits was leaked, Labour's welfare plans were back on the front pages.[33] Just before Christmas, disabled people chained themselves to Downing Street gates and hurled red paint.

Blair shelved the disability changes and announced he would chair a committee on welfare reform.

Blair's road show on welfare

A 'welfare road show' at nine different venues across the country in the first two months of 1998 was announced. This was designed to help Blair win over party activists on the need for welfare reform. For a brief moment, just before the road show began, it looked as though Blair might go for a radical option. Interviewed by David Frost for the BBC's *Breakfast with Frost* Sunday morning television slot, Blair floated the idea of means testing – or 'affluence testing' as his aides called it – the better off. The basic state pension would become income-related for the rich as it was already in Australia. The more you earned above a certain level, the less basic pension you would receive. Child benefit for the better off would be taxed. Maternity benefit for rich women earners would be gradually withdrawn to help poorer women workers. The television interview was done in Japan, where a pack of political editors on tour with the Prime Minister ensured it was splashed across the front pages the following day. Back in London, Harriet Harman filled out the maternity benefits proposal to *The Times*. There were follow-up pieces the next day, but all were quickly shut down. The headlines had rung panic alarms in Downing Street. 'Middle classes face means test by another name' (*The Times*, 12 January 1998) and '"Affluence exam" for benefits' (*The Daily Telegraph*, 12 January 1998) were seen to be in contradiction to New Labour's intent to encourage aspiration and avoid personal tax increases. This was the year in which Peter Mandelson, Labour's éminence grise, declared 'we are intensely relaxed about people getting filthy rich'.[34]

The main message of Blair's road show can be summarised in two paragraphs:

> Over the last 18 years we have become two nations – one trapped on benefits, the other paying for them. One nation in growing poverty, shut out from society's mainstream, the other watching social security spending

> rise and rise, until it costs more than their health, education and law and order put together.
>
> When I look at the welfare state I don't see a pathway out of poverty, a route into work or a gateway to dignity in retirement. I see a dead end for too many people. I do not believe this is how Attlee or Beveridge intended things to be. I want to clear the way to a new system. Long term, thought out, principled reform is the way forward.[35]

There were two problems. Public expectations were raised far too high. And back on the ground, there was no consensus. There was not just conflict between the two key ministers, but also no agreement between a swathe of competing committees reviewing social policy spending. It was still unclear whether the government had embarked on a moral crusade (work is good, welfare dependency wrong) or a reluctant cost-cutting exercise forced by Labour's imprudent adoption of Tory spending programmes. The result was a mish-mash of conflicting goals and purposes.

The welfare Green Paper

Field's long delayed and many times rewritten Green Paper eventually emerged in March 1998. Although it had a catchy title, 'Work for those who can, security for those who cannot', it received a poor press. There was no 'big bang'. There was no big switch, as he had hoped, to mutual societies and private insurance schemes. The paper had been due the previous autumn. There had been many attempts by civil servants to try and reconcile the Brown/Field proposals, but they were trying to reconcile the irreconcilable. Even the social security staff complained that Field's ideas were incapable of being put into practical form, let alone capable of meeting the 'no cost' rules. The arguments between the two social security ministers did not stop, but in the first government reshuffle in July 1998, both Harman and Field went. They were replaced by Alistair Darling, a wise and experienced former Chief Secretary at the Treasury, who had seen many of the countless welfare reform options in that post.

He brought calm and a reconciliation with the Treasury. The mutual society pathway was ignored and the more pragmatic tax credit route embraced. Thus, when the invitation came from Oxford to deliver the 'Beveridge revisited' lecture in March 1999, Blair had a chance to return to a policy area that was always meant to be at the forefront of Labour reforms.

For the first six years post the 1999 anti-poverty pledge, steady strides were made. Through a combination of tax credits, welfare to work schemes, more widespread childcare and a minimum wage, the number of children below the poverty line (60 per cent below the median after housing costs) fell by 800,000, from 4.4 million in 1998/99 to 3.6 million in 2004/05. This was already behind the target for halving of child poverty by 2010/11. But then, for the next three years, child poverty rose back to 4 million by 2007/08, dropping back to 3.9 million in 2008/09. One reason why it was harder for the government was that Britain was booming, so it was more difficult to keep up with rising median earnings. Another was that the increases were just not big enough.

Redistribution by stealth

Throughout the first six years there had been little publicity about the programme for fear of frightening right-wing horses – it was mostly being achieved by stealth. There was only one mention of the programme in the entire 2001 election campaign and not much more in the 2005 election. Alistair Darling, while in charge of social security, recognised the need for rallying public support, so openly declared in January 2002: 'We should not be afraid to shout from the rooftops about what we're doing to tackle poverty.' Nine months later Tony Blair spoke of the importance of Britain continuing 'to redistribute power, wealth and opportunity to the many, not the few'. But after that, silence returned, and it was not until the success of the high-profile international anti-poverty campaign, Make Poverty History, that the domestic programme began to be given more prominence. Ed Balls, Economic Secretary at the Treasury, told the 2005 Poor Relations conference: 'We need a campaign to surround the Treasury with bells and buggies, demanding an end to child poverty in the UK.' But this coincided, alas, with the beginning of the increase in the numbers of children below the poverty line. Given the media's nose for bad news, what this did ensure was more publicity for the programme. The annual publication of the government's anti-poverty statistics became much more of a media event, with speculative pieces before publication day and wide coverage after it.

Although the tabloids were still running regular stories on welfare scroungers, a host of charitable organisations, pressure groups, independent research institutions and think tanks were producing pamphlets, reports, fact files, press releases and both joint and individual campaigns. My overflowing files – a butt of much internal *Guardian* teasing – still bulge with these reports. These all got some media coverage depending on the paper. The cause was backed by serious think tanks – Fabian Society, IFS, IPPR, Social Market Foundation, The Young Foundation – as well as generous and powerful funders led by JRF. The Campaign to End Child Poverty brought together 150 organisations, many of them with full-time press officers monitoring what was happening and ready to respond and contest inaccurate media or government assertions – they range from well-known names such as Barnardo's, The Children's Society, Church Action on Poverty, Disability Alliance, National Children's Bureau, NSPCC, Oxfam UK, Save the Children, to many medium-sized and smaller groups. Its base is set in the best-known charity of all campaigning against child poverty, CPAG, established by the Quakers in 1965 after the 'rediscovery' of poverty by Professors Brian Abel-Smith and Peter Townsend.

Grim forecasts

There were several significant reports in 2006. The first was by the Fabian Society's Commission on Life Chances and Child Poverty, entitled *Narrowing the gap*, which documented the poor public understanding of child poverty, the progress the government had made and the remaining challenges.[36] The second report was more devastating. JRF had gathered together a panel of the most senior academics and researchers in the field and invited them to submit papers on what would be needed to end child poverty by the target date of 2020. A second advisory group of representatives from child charities and anti-poverty groups was set up. The subsequent report, compiled by the Foundation's most senior writer, Donald Hirsch, shocked the anti-poverty world, including JRF.[37] To achieve the government's halfway target in 2010 an extra £4 billion a year on top of what was currently planned for benefits and tax credits would be needed. This was clearly feasible, requiring a 0.3 per cent increased share of GDP. What was clearly not feasible was the second half of the programme. This was going to require an extra £28 billion spent annually over and above existing programmes from 2010 through to 2020 to achieve abolition. As the JRF summary of the report noted, this was 'an unlikely scenario'. It was not quite as bleak as it looked, however. As Nicholas Timmins noted at the press briefing, reaching halfway would put the UK ahead of Europe, with the exception of Scandinavian states.

Both these reports got coverage, but nothing like the extent of a Conservative policy paper, purposefully leaked to *The Guardian* in November.[38] *The Guardian's* double-front headline on 22 November 2006 declared:

> Cameron told: it's time to ditch Churchill – Polly Toynbee, not Winston, should set Tory social agenda, says adviser.[39]

Toynbee versus Churchill

The paper was drafted by Greg Clark, a former director of policy at Tory HQ who was on the opposition's front bench by 2006 as well as being a policy adviser to the leader. David Cameron, who had only been leader of the party for a year, was due to give the annual Scarman lecture, and as part of his detoxification of the party, had planned to speak about the importance of tackling relative poverty, not just absolute poverty. Clark gave him just the lines that were bound to hit the headlines. The leaked paper suggested that Churchill's belief that the welfare state should be no more than a safety net was all part of 'another outdated Tory nostrum, that poverty is absolute, not relative'. It went on to propose that the bang-up-to-date 21st-century Tories should embrace the 'imagery' of Polly Toynbee, *The Guardian* columnist. He had drawn it from her book, *Hard work: Life in low pay Britain*,[40] in which she depicted society as a caravan crossing the desert, where she warned that the caravan would cease to exist if its weakest and most vulnerable members were left too far behind, or its richest and strongest rolled too far ahead. This required governments to intervene to ensure that the gap between the rich and poor did not become too wide.

The leak, as intended, created a Fleet Street furore. A new Conservative leader was taking up the cause of a *Guardian* columnist, hated by the right, in preference over the views of the most famous Conservative leader in the previous century. It was followed up in all papers and it was not just right-wingers who were splenetic. There were editorials, follow-up news and feature stories, columnists galore having a go, along with collected past quotes by Toynbee and Churchill. Durrants, the newspaper cutting service, identified over 50 national stories in the following two weeks. It had all the ingredients the media likes: a political row, a right-wing backlash, with well-known names, one of whom was known for her ferocious attacks on the *Mail*, Murdoch and other tabloid papers.

The Cameron speech went ahead with a clear reference to Polly Toynbee: 'We understand that a strong society means moving forward together, no one left behind, fighting relative poverty as a central policy goal.' And just to ensure there was no ambiguity about the policy switch, he went on: 'Poverty is relative – and those who pretend otherwise are wrong. We must think in terms of an escalator always moving upwards, lifting people out of poverty.'[41] There was plenty of political analysis of the leak and Cameron's speech. Stephen Glover, eight days after the leak, wrote in the *Mail* about how the Tories were being taken more seriously 'in the progressive media, particularly in the BBC', thanks to Cameron's embrace of various liberal causes. But there was a sting at the end of the column: 'Mr Cameron is a former PR man. His Svengali, Steve Hilton, is in the same line of business. They are forever thinking about "branding", and to the fury of some, and relief of others, they have repackaged the Tory party. But the voters still have very little idea of what lies beneath the glossy packaging, and Mr Cameron is in no hurry to enlighten them.'[42]

Means tests and poverty lines

The speech did not receive serious policy analysis. What was worrying, even by 2006, was news editors' lack of interest in the issue, unless it had a political edge. There are some excellent social affairs correspondents, but they know that their news desks much prefer social change to social security. Yet social security, with by far the biggest budget in Whitehall, used to get more serious coverage. It is a complex area that cries out for explanations. There are covert as well as overt means tests; multiple different poverty lines that can be drawn; and complicated ways in which social mobility can be measured. On each of these fronts, the British public have become increasingly poorly informed. There is no agreed scientific definition of either 'absolute' or 'relative' poverty.

There are three ways poverty lines can be drawn. First, they can chart poverty before or after housing costs. (The government provides both sets. Most researchers prefer using after housing costs because these vary widely between different areas and many low-income families have little choice over changing their place of residence.) Second, the poverty line may use the mean (the national average income) or the median (the point at which equal numbers of people are above or below). In the UK, with its dramatically widening inequality, average pay is much higher than median pay. Third, there is variation in just how far below the line poverty begins: 40, 50 or 60 per cent below. The 'absolute' poverty index in the last decade was based on the 1998/99 poverty line at the start of the campaign (60 per cent below the median), indexed for prices to maintain its real level. The 'relative' poverty line was indexed by earnings to the same 1998/99 base line so that it kept pace with rising public standards of living. One of the big challenges for New Labour in seeking to reduce the numbers in poverty was the large rise in earnings in its first decade that in turn led to a large uplift in the relative poverty line. Some countries, such as Ireland, have used a poverty line based on minimum acceptable social necessities (originally drawn up by

David Piachaud of LSE, but often now established by polling the public on what they think are the minimum necessities).[43] Jonathan Bradshaw, the ebullient University of York analyst, refers to child poverty tripling under the 18 years of Conservative administration, 1979–97.[44] He is right when using the old measure – half average income after housing costs – child poverty rose from one in nine children to one in three. But using the more widely used current measure – 60 per cent of the median after housing costs – the increase peaked at 2.4 times as much.

The Tories made much play, until they belatedly endorsed tax credits in March 2003, of the increased use of 'means tests' by the Blair government. Part of this was pure political linguistics, which far too frequently went by without being challenged. The Tories were talking about tax credits when they accused Labour of 'doubling means tests'. Tax credits, like income tax, are income-related but in the reverse order. The less you have, the more you receive. Nothing could be fairer. What the Tories ignored was that means tests had doubled – from 16 per cent of all benefits to 34 per cent – in their 18 years and, much more seriously, with quite a different purpose. Means tests then were being applied to old benefits to cut public expenditure through poorer indexing, tighter eligibility rules and shorter pay periods. Labour's so-called 'means tests', tax credits, were designed to ensure extra public expenditure was being focused on those most in need, with considerable success in making the UK a fairer place. The sum being redistributed through tax credits alone had soared to £30 billion by 2010. The six bottom deciles all gained in increasing proportions going downwards and the four top tenths all received less in increasing amounts going upwards.[45]

The UNICEF bombshell

Early in 2007 UNICEF – the UN children's organisation – produced a report on children and young people's well-being that was still reverberating three years on in the UK. It looked at 40 different indicators across 21 developed states and concluded that the UK was at the bottom of this league of rich countries.[46] It was the first such study of childhood across the world's industrialised nations. Its remit was to assess 'whether children feel loved, cherished, special and supported, within the family and community, and whether there is support in this task from public policy and resources'. The 40 indicators were grouped into six dimensions. The UK was in the bottom third for five of the six: relative poverty and deprivation; quality of children's relationship with their parents and peers; child health and safety; behaviour and risk taking; and subjective well-being. It ranked higher in educational well-being but overall came bottom of the league. The Netherlands topped the league, followed by Sweden, Denmark and Finland.

Professor Jonathan Bradshaw at the University of York, one of the report's authors, put the UK's poor ratings down to long-term under-investment and a 'dog-eat-dog' society. He explained: 'In a society which is very unequal, with high levels of poverty, it leads on to what children think about themselves and their lives. That's really what's at the heart of this.' It was left to a junior Labour minister in the government, Jim Murphy, to respond. He said that the report was important, but believed some of the data were out of date. He went on: 'Hopefully this report will lead to a wider conversation about what more we can do to eradicate poverty.'

Meanwhile, a perceptive essay by Lisa Harker, a senior figure in Labour's favourite think tank, the IPPR, on hardening public attitudes towards welfare, raised additional doubts about achieving Labour's goal.[47] Using MORI research for the Fabian Society's Commission on Life Chances and Child Poverty to emphasise this point, she was yet another voice calling for the government's redistribution by stealth to stop. Noting that one of the government's most important goals was hardly registering on the public's agenda, she suggested 'the government will not be able to justify additional spending in the absence of public support'. Shortly afterwards she was appointed child poverty tsar, where she wrote the well-received report, *Delivering child poverty: What would it take?*.[48] It concluded that public attitudes had become the greatest obstacle to the anti-poverty programme. It would only be sustainable 'if it is endorsed by the electorate and without a strategy to engage public support for further change, we may already be very near the limits of what can be achieved'.

Indeed the position for Labour was even worse than this. Peter Taylor-Gooby, in the 21st British Social Attitudes survey, showed that the hardening of attitudes had been even more marked within Labour's traditional supporters than other groups. In 1987 those on the right were most likely to believe that welfare benefits 'stopped people standing on their own two feet', but by 2003 it was the left that was most likely to support the proposition. In 1987 there were no significant differences between left, centre and right towards the proposition that welfare recipients did not really deserve help, but by 2003 those on the left were most likely to support this view.[47]

Two media projects

Aware of these concerns, JRF proceeded to fund studies on three separate fronts in 2007, all of which emerged in 2008. On the policy side it funded seven different reports on how to take forward different aspects of child poverty strategy. On public attitudes it funded a series of reports pulling together what could be learned from previous studies and surveys. And on the media front, it funded two different projects. The first was a report from a six-member team at Glasgow Caledonian University which examined the relationship between the UK media and public attitudes towards poverty.[50] It included a systematic content analysis of news content over a week (30 July to 5 August 2007) sampling over 150 newspapers, 100 radio news programmes, 75 television news programmes and a selection of news magazines and a range of new media. Some 372 separate sources of news produced just 297 items on poverty in the UK – less than one item per source, hence the report's finding that the coverage of poverty was peripheral in mainstream UK media. Intriguingly there were more articles on overseas poverty in the week: some 343 items. But this selection was skewed by coinciding with Gordon Brown's first visit to the US as prime minister. There, as well as meeting President Bush, he delivered a major speech to the UN on how the international community was falling far short of meeting its commitments to the Millennium Development Goals, and set out a way for correcting this shortfall.

Not only were there few reports on domestic poverty, but in almost two thirds of the reports identified, poverty was not the main focus. The leading paragraphs dealt with subsidiary issues, such as housing, education, social services or health. People experiencing poverty featured in fewer than one in eight of the reports. Groups with a higher risk of poverty were reported less frequently than those with a lower risk. It was less common, for example, to make references to disabled people than non-disabled, more likely for men rather than women to be covered, and more likely for working than non-working poor people to be mentioned. Almost 50 per cent of poverty stories were found in the news columns, with 10 per cent or less found in feature articles, political columns or readers' letters. There was a tendency for negative reporting of poorer people, particularly in the tabloids. In the 11 focus groups run by the team, there was little public trust or belief in tabloid stories.

The report, like many others, suggested that the international campaign, Make Poverty History, could be influencing public perceptions of poverty at home. The report acknowledged the conflicting research evidence on public perceptions. According to the 2006 British Social Attitudes survey, 55 per cent of people thought there was 'quite a lot of poverty'. In contrast, Castell and Thompson's focus group research in 2006 identified the public's 'resistance and reluctance' to accepting the existence of genuine poverty.[51] It might seem obvious that persuading the public of the hardship generated by relative poverty in Britain was made more difficult in the wake of the pictures, films and stories of people living in absolute poverty abroad. But the Glasgow team's focus groups readily agreed that poverty was widespread in the UK.

The report noted that 'although public attitudes cannot be attributed to the influence of mass media, it is important to acknowledge the media's pivotal role in responding to and reinforcing public ideas about poverty'.[52] It defended Joe Public and called on the media to be more ready to challenge public misconceptions:

> ... the public access media output critically and are not 'cultural dopes' manipulated into believing what they read and see. However, if audiences do not encounter

much coverage of poverty, nor accounts which explain structural causes (ie identify social factors restricting opportunities) they will draw on their existing understandings. The media have the capacity to inform the public about the nature of poverty, there is scope to humanise and politicise poverty. However this possibility is undermined, as poverty is rarely explicitly described or explained.

John McKendrick, the lead member of the Glasgow team, believed one of the most important findings of the study was that, unlike the coverage of domestic poverty, where its structural causes were rarely examined, this was pursued in reports on overseas poverty. There was no reason why it could not be done at home. A second important finding was the scope for better reporting of poverty at local and regional level, where currently it received the lowest amount of coverage. As it was a problem in all regions and most localities, there was an opportunity for local media to provide a local angle. The *Evening Standard* in London, under its new Russian proprietors, Alexander and Evgeny Lebedev, began a series in the spring of 2010 on 'dispossessed London'. Four out of 10 children in the capital were living below the poverty line. It not only raised public attention but also opened a permanent *Evening Standard* Dispossessed Fund for helping small charities and groups working in poor communities.

In the second project, JRF joined forces with the Media Trust and the Society of Editors to run a series of workshops – in London, Glasgow, Manchester, Cardiff and Belfast – in November 2008 on reporting poverty. They drew a wide cross-section of journalists, representatives from anti-poverty groups and voluntary groups working with poor communities. One end product was a well-written 88-page handbook for journalists, by David Seymour, an experienced and respected *Daily Mirror* journalist, on reporting poverty.[53] It included background chapters on poverty, its different dimensions and definitions, five common myths and stereotypes, associated problems (health, housing, education, crime and drugs), along with five pages of contacts and organisations able to provide media guidance. I went to the London event where there was a surprising consensus on the responsibilities of the media. As the media purports to tell us what is going on in society, this should include what is happening to poor people. A democratic society should be aware of what is happening to all its members. There was a place for straight reporting and campaigning, but there were still too many pieces reinforcing existing myths and stereotypes, making poor people more marginal in society.

How banks changed public attitudes

Just as JRF research began emerging in 2008, outside forces were achieving a dramatic change in public attitudes: the financial meltdown in the autumn of 2008 caused by the reckless investment by banks in toxic assets. The National Audit Office estimated in December 2009 that the cost of bailing out the banks had risen to £850 billion – including the purchase of Royal Bank of Scotland and Lloyds shares, indemnifying the Bank of England for its £200 billion of liquidity support, guaranteeing £250 billion of wholesale borrowing by banks and £280 billion for insurance cover for dodgy bank assets.[54] The report noted the full cost would not be known for years. The costs continued to climb through 2010 and 2011, not to mention the economic and social cost of the recession that the financial meltdown triggered.

What did become known quite quickly was how little bank behaviour changed with respect to pay, bonuses, recognition of their culpability in the financial crisis or acceptance of how 'socially useless', to use the words of their chief regulator, Adair Turner, much of their activities were.[55] For all the political declarations of needing to curb bank pay and bonuses, these continued through 2009 and 2010. In February 2011, Barclays announced that the *average* pay per employee in its Barclays Capital branch rose by £45,000 to £236,000 and total bonus payments to £3.5 billion.[56] It also emerged in the same month that despite making a profit of £11.6 billion in 2009, the bank only paid £113 million in corporation tax – about 1 per cent, when corporation tax was 28 per cent.[57]

What was happening at the same time – some of us would say predictably – was growing support for higher taxes on exceptionally high earners. A succession of polls from late 2008 through to 2010 showed that public support for redistribution swelled. Earlier polls in the 1990s had shown public support for helping the poor, but some resistance to achieving this through redistribution. But a new 50p tax rate for the top 1 per cent of the 29 million income tax-payers – a mere 300,000 people earning £150,000 a year or over – was announced by Alistair Darling in his April 2009 Budget, which took effect from April 2010.[58] (A bigger public saving was the curb on tax-free pension contributions, 25 per cent of which was going to the richest 2 per cent.[59]) Even before the 2009 Budget, polls were showing support for a higher top rate. A YouGov poll for the Fabian Society in December 2008 showed 52 per cent supporting a 50p tax rate compared to 28 per cent against.[60] A snap *Times*/Populus poll after the Budget showed the move was supported by 57 per cent compared to 22 per cent against. A YouGov poll in *The Telegraph* that followed just afterwards showed even more support: 68 per cent in favour against 20 per cent opposed.

So much for the urgings of Tony Blair not to abandon the centre ground. A much later poll on 17 October 2010 by Comres in *The Independent on Sunday* showed 54 per cent in support of raising the 50p rate to 60p for people earning £150,000, with 29 per cent opposed. After all, Margaret Thatcher kept a 60p top rate for the first nine years of her administration. Tony Blair and his associates firmly believed their 1997 pledge not to raise income tax had been the foundation of their success. Some serious pollsters disagree. Mark Gill, senior MORI pollster, noted in the 2005 Fabian Review that in MORI's final pre-election poll for *The Times* in 1997, some 63 per cent of voters believed Labour would put up income tax but many still voted for them. By 1999 some 57 per cent wrongly thought their taxes had gone up. Just before the 2001 election, 74 per cent believed Labour would put up taxes despite their pledge. Gill concluded: 'All told, the voters elected Tony Blair with a landslide in 1997, expecting him to increases taxes, and re-elected him in 2001 believing the government had done so and would do so again.'[61]

One of the saddest episodes, as noted in Chapter One, was Gordon Brown's decision to abolish the 10p tax rate in his last Budget as Chancellor in the spring of 2007. It was introduced to finance the cost of reducing the basic rate from 22p to 20p. It duly won the applause of the right-wing tabloids, as intended, only badly to damage Brown's reputation as a progressive, when the media and Parliament belatedly recognised just before implementation in April 2008 that it was going to make five million poor people worse off. Almost as bad as Brown's denial of the effects of the move was his reluctance to remedy it until forced by Parliament.

What did Labour's child poverty campaign achieve?

The final figures for the first half of Labour's 20-year programme to end child poverty emerged on 14 June 2012. They showed that between the announcement of the goal in 1999 and Labour leaving office in May 2010 some 1.1 million children had been lifted above the poverty line.[62] Three factors were involved: more mothers, particularly lone mothers, in work; generous benefit uplifts at the end of the programme; and a dip in the poverty line level with the fall in median pay during the recession. This left 2.3 million children still below the line, which was 600,000 more than the halfway target of 1.7 million, but that is not the whole story. IFS simulations suggest that if the old 1997 Conservative family support system had remained in place – even if uprated in line with inflation – an extra 900,000 children would have been added to the poverty statistics.[63] Mike Brewer, Professor of Economics at Essex University's Institute for Social Research, writing in *The Guardian* in June 2012, described the programme as 'a remarkable achievement, certainly without historical precedent in the UK, and impressive compared with other countries'.[64] Indeed the level of child poverty in May 2010 had dropped to its lowest level for 20 years. And it was not just the bottom tenth who were helped. Thanks to tax credits, the 20 per cent above the poorest 10 per cent had also enjoyed a more comfortable life.

Overseas there was widespread recognition of Labour's achievement. European Union surveys showed the UK was one of only 10 EU states with a reduction in child poverty between 2005 and 2010.[65] The OECD Family Database, set up to provide cross-national indicators on family outcomes across member states, records the UK achieving the largest reduction in child poverty of all 34 states between the mid-1990s and 2008.[66] Jane Waldfogel, a respected academic in America, turned to scrutinise the UK child poverty strategy in her widely praised *Britain's War on Poverty* to persuade her US audience that a sustained, well-resourced and nationally co-ordinated drive to reduce poverty was achievable in Anglo-Saxon democracies.[67] In 2011 Jonathan Bradshaw updated the 2007 UNICEF report on child well-being, which showed startling improvements in the UK. Of the 48 indicators, 36 had moved in the right direction and only four in the wrong direction (all in the area of health – immunisation rates, diabetes, obesity and sexually transmitted diseases). Across a host of other measurements, life for children improved, including: the reduction in poverty, a rise in educational attainment, improvement in housing conditions, a fall in child homelessness, a fall in youth crime and improvement in adolescent mental health and happiness.[68]

Cameron's solemn pledges on poverty

- On his first day as party leader, 7 December 2005, visiting Eastside Young Academy in London: "In the end the test for our policies will not be how they affect the better off, but how they help the worst off in our country."
- In his Scarman lecture on 22 November 2006: "Fighting relative poverty [is] a central policy goal ... I want my party to be in the vanguard of the fight against poverty."
- In a speech in Manchester on 22 March 2007: "Ending child poverty is central to improving child well-being."
- In a comment piece in *The Independent* on 9 May 2008: 'If you care about poverty, if you care about inequality ... forget the Labour Party.'
- In his leader's speech to the annual Conservative Party conference on 8 October 2009: "We can make British poverty history and we will make British poverty history."
- In his closing statement in the final television leaders' debate on 29 April 2010 before the 6 May general election: "There's something else you need to know about me, which is that I

believe the test of a good and strong society is how we look after the vulnerable, the most frail and the poorest. That is true in good times, but it's even more true in difficult times."

- Even in his leader's address to the annual Conservative Party conference on 5 October 2011, when drastic cuts were already being applied: "So who's going to lift the poorest up? ... Who's going to create a more equal society?... It will be us."

Lost promises, forgotten pledges, ignored commitments of the Coalition

The first Coalition Budget in June 2010, along with the October Comprehensive Spending Review, produced a planned £18 billion cut to benefits over the Parliament beginning in 2011.[69] Some 5.7 million families would be made ineligible for child tax credits in the years after 2012. It introduced a new index, the CPI (consumer price index), which was expected to be 1 per cent below the RPI (retail price index) in this Parliament, which meant not only that benefits would not keep pace with earnings but they would be 5 per cent below RPI after five years. This measure was expected to claw back £5.8 billion into government coffers by 2015. It was the failure of the Thatcher/Major governments to allow benefits to rise in line with general living standards that led to the doubling of child and pensioner poverty in the 1980s. In a report in August 2010, the IFS predicted it would be poor families with children and pensioners who would bear the brunt of the Coalition's austerity drive.[70] It calculated that the poorest 10 per cent of families would lose 5 per cent of their income compared to only 1 per cent for non-pensioner households without children in the top 10 per cent. Poor parents having babies in 2011 would receive £1,500 less than they would have received in 2010 due to steep cuts in pregnancy and maternity grants, the abolition of the Child Trust Fund and the squeeze on the baby element of child tax credits. If life under 13 years of Labour ended disappointingly for the poor, life under the Coalition looks much grimmer despite the hard work of its spin doctors. The 2010 Budget was spun as a progressive redistributive budget, but this was only achieved by combining Labour's last Budget with its own. By

Darling's raid on the rich

% hit on income of all pre-announced measures in Labour's last Budget

Osborne's squeeze on the poor

% hit on income of all budget measures in Osborne's first Budget, June 2010

Source: Institute for Fiscal Studies, June 2010

disaggregating the two, the IFS documented just how regressive the Coalition was (see bar charts above).

The Coalition continued to present its budgets, spending plans and welfare proposals as 'fair and progressive'. But on 11 October 2011 the dubious claims were taken apart by the IFS, which documented the severe degree to which the spending plans were regressive. The poorest families with children were losing more than any other group. The planned cuts were far deeper than anything Margaret Thatcher introduced. The IFS forecast that the cuts would increase the numbers of children in poverty by 400,000 by 2015, or 800,000 by 2020.[71] Alison Garnham, CPAG's chief executive, warned: 'Ministers seem to be in denial that, under the current policies, their legacy threatens to be the worst poverty record of any government for a generation. The government must accept that you cannot fight poverty or improve their life chances by making the poor poorer. It doesn't have to be like this.'

It took time for the Coalition's four-year austerity plan to roll out. The big step with tax credits, affecting millions of families, began on 6 April 2012 – Good Friday, relabelled by CPAG as 'Bad Friday' – by which time the £18 billion squeeze had become £20 billion according to Treasury papers.[72] This first year of a four-year squeeze on tax credits involved a £3 billion cut through tighter eligibility rules, shorter back payments, withdrawn elements and tougher tapers. Worse still, contrary to Conservative claims, the Treasury's own analysis in the 2012 budget papers showed that in 2013/14 every household in the bottom half of income tables would lose a larger proportion of their income from tax, tax credit withdrawal and benefit changes than four out of five households in the top half.[73]

Universal Credit – universal concern

The main social security change, which the Conservatives hoped would transform welfare, was to be the creation of a new benefit, Universal Credit. It was due to be piloted in April 2013 in Manchester and Cheshire with the roll-out for the rest of the country taking four years beginning in October 2013. Devised in outline by Iain Duncan Smith when in opposition, the new benefit was designed to bring together multiple disparate benefits which a family can receive in order to remove perversities that can arise when they rub up against each other. The aim was legitimate enough – overlapping means tests spell trouble – but the claims for the benefit were overhyped. No single benefit is ever going to iron out every inherent tension between relieving poverty and rewarding self-improvement. Moreover, it will be less flexible in meeting special needs. But as the months ticked by following the May 2010 election, concern over the cost, timetable and viability of Universal Credit mounted in Whitehall, particularly in the Treasury.

Even more concern was being raised by charities and anti-poverty pressure groups. In September 2012, 70 organisations wrote to the

Commons Work and Pensions Select Committee raising a host of potential objections to the Universal Credit, including doubts about the ability of the government to successfully deliver the necessary IT for such a complicated operation.[74] Various government aides went public over their concern with the legislation. The social security advisory body in charge of monitoring the reforms warned Duncan Smith in the summer of 2012, that elements of his Welfare Bill were 'unworkable and unfair'. They were particularly concerned with provisions requiring part-time workers to raise their number of hours worked from 16 to 24 in the recession or else lose their Working Tax Credit, worth £3,870. Some 210,000 families involving 470,000 children were affected.[75] A commission led by the Paralympics gold medallist Lady Gray-Thompson concluded that half a million disabled people and their families could lose up to £3,016 a year under the Universal Credit scheme.[76]

Another devastating flaw in the Bill, identified by the IFS, concerned Council Tax Benefit, possibly the least-noticed and most widely applied of all means tests. The benefit was paid to 5.9 million households, but in a move to shift some of the blame for cuts, ministers decreed that each of the hundreds of local councils could determine their own means test. This from a government claiming to simplify and unify benefits. From April 2013 the benefit will be cut by 10 per cent. Each local council will receive the sum that was handed out in their area (less 10 per cent) to disperse. They must keep the full benefit for pensioners but will be free to define who is vulnerable. Low-income families in areas with high number of pensioners will be particularly hard hit.[77] By October 2012, it was clear that a significant number of councils had decided not to pursue the poor who refused to pay because the cost, including legal fees, to recover the money would exceed the losses.[78]

Cameron launches a new blitz on welfare

Not content with the £20 billion cuts to tax credits and benefits, the new Universal Credit which will make further cuts, and despite his many pledges on tackling poverty, Cameron launched a new blitz against the welfare state in June 2012, which could add up to a further £10 billion chop. He outlined a further 17 cuts that could be considered. These included: withdrawing housing benefit from the under 25s; making benefits conditional, for example on compulsory community work; setting time limits on welfare; ensuring increases below inflation; and introducing payments in kind, such as food vouchers.[79] The speech didn't even get the support of the Tory tabloids. Under the headline 'Cam on, then', *The Sun* declared: 'Mr Cameron's overall message is spot on: the welfare bill is completely out of hand. The pity is that while he waffles, the bill continues to soar.'[80] The *Daily Mail* echoed the same sentiment: the speech was excellent but two facts became depressingly clear: 'One is that many of the policies haven't been fully thought through. The other is that almost nothing he suggests will happen any time soon. Yet we're in a time of crisis. Right now – not five years hence.'[81] More ominously, Simon Carr, in *The Independent*, noted: 'If that's the return of the nasty party, there'll be an awful lot of nice people nodding along with it.'[82] Too true. By mendaciously selecting extreme examples of welfare beneficence, involving tiny numbers but relayed as though they were widespread and typical, government spin ministers led by Osborne had generated considerable public support for their brutal strategy. The 2012 British Social Attitudes survey showed a serious hardening of attitudes towards Unemployment Benefit. Whereas through the 1980s and up to the late 1990s, 50 per cent of people believed benefits were 'causing hardship' and only 30 per cent that they were 'discouraging work', these positions had reversed, with 60 per cent believing that they 'discouraged work' and just 20 per cent that they 'caused hardship'.[83]

What prompted Cameron's speech? Roland Watson in *The Times* suggested it could have been designed to halt his fall in support on Tory backbenches.[84] The parliamentary sketch writer on *The Times*, Ann Treneman, was more irreverent: 'I am worried about Dave. Indeed I am beginning to see his point that living in public housing – in his case Downing Street – can affect your grip on reality. Yesterday Dave told us about his welfare Utopia ...Transforming lives. Helping people walk taller... (Wow, I had no idea you could get extra vertebrae on the dole.) Dave says we mustn't patronise people on benefits by, er, giving them benefits ...Aspiration is in everyone.

No one is a write-off. Dave's world. Marvellous place. Must visit it sometime – which should be possible at about the same time we can travel to the Moon using our Oyster card.' [85]

Four months on, at the annual Conservative Party conference in October 2012, George Osborne announced there would indeed be a further £10 billion cut to the welfare budget between 2015 and 2017 to help eradicate the country's structural debt.[86] One of the cuts could be withdrawing benefits from jobless parents who go ahead and have more children. The following day, Cameron delivered a leader's speech which was blind to the blight he was inflicting on poor families in Britain. He declared: "Work isn't slavery, it's poverty that is slavery … and again it's us, the modern compassionate Conservative Party, who are the real champions of fighting poverty in Britain today." [87]

It is not just the poor who would have benefited from a much less concentrated attack on the less well off. There are several economic studies which have noted that spending on low-income families has benefited economies in recession because of their higher marginal rates. As even the IMF belatedly acknowledged, transfers to 'hand-to-mouth' and 'credit-constrained' consumers provide higher economic multipliers.[88] A report from the respected Brookings Institution in the US suggested that the economic multiplier for income transfers to low income families is around 1.6. This means for every pound transferred in this way, GDP increases by £1.60.[89] It was put even more plainly by the International Labour Organisation and the Institute for Labour Studies in a joint report: 'During the crisis, social and cash transfers not only assisted those in need, but by putting the cash in the hands of those most likely to spend it, helped to shore up household consumption. For this reason, countries that strengthened the policies towards income transfers managed to recover faster than others.'[90]

The scene at the end of 2012

The Coalition still had another two and a half years to run as this book went to the printers. But what was already clear was that the pledges to tackle poverty made by Cameron over seven years were never going to materialise. What made them even more dishonourable was the trite way they were still being trotted out when it was already clear the government was heading for the most regressive record of all administrations since 1945. By the criterion which he set himself on his first day as party leader – see the first of his pledges in the box on pages 280–1 above – Cameron had lamentably and utterly failed. The Coalition Agreement included a commitment by both parties to the targets set out in the Child Poverty Act 2010. Not only were these ignored from the start but so was the promise that 'the broadest shoulders should contribute the most'.

Of course there had to be cuts, but it was the crude way in which they were constructed, the cocksure manner in which they were presented, and the gross inequalities that resulted which grated. It got worse as it went on, never better illustrated than in Osborne's callous 2012 Budget with its 5% tax cut for the top one per cent on their £150,000+ earnings and £40,000 tax breaks for the six million people earning £1 million+, while five million pensioners faced a 'granny tax', two new taxes were imposed on Cornish pasties and static caravans, together with a cap on tax relief for charitable donations – the last three eventually being lifted in the wake of public and tabloid protests. The shameful way that Liberal Democrat leaders – particularly Nick Clegg – meekly allowed Osborne's regressive proposals to proceed should haunt them to the ballot box. So should their dishonesty over how little goes to the poor from the raised tax thresholds and how much more is funnelled to middle-income and even better-off people.

As for the 'broader shoulders' carrying the weight, the ratio of spending cuts to tax rises was roughly 4 to 1 in 2012, dramatically different from the 1-to-1 ratio that the Conservative government adopted in the recession in the early 1990s.[91] Let the last word go to Professor Alan Walker, a close monitor of social security, who noted in a letter to *The Guardian* on 28 February 2012: 'Out of 27 EU countries, only Estonia has a higher level of poverty among unemployed people than this country. Over the last 40 years unemployment benefit has been cut by 50 per cent as a proportion of average earnings to just 10 per cent. Over the same period the total remuneration of FTSE chief executives rose by more than 100 per cent.' So much for the spin suggesting UK benefits were too generous.

Lessons to be drawn from the Campaign to End Child Poverty

- One possible positive influence of the media was the degree to which the leak to *The Mirror* might have souped up the policy. As noted above, Blair's speech writers cannot recall how 'abolition of child poverty' was inserted in the text. Certainly none of the 12 submissions from academics and practitioners proposed such a course. Tony Blair confessed to a subsequent meeting that he had not realised how radical it was until he was reading it out. Alastair Campbell, in the latest edition of his diaries, confesses to negotiating a front-page splash with *The Mirror*. Front-page splashes in a tabloid need impact.

- The commitment not to raise income tax severely hampered the campaign. As noted above, Labour need not have made such a rod for its own back. Polls showed the public expected Labour to raise income tax, but still voted for them. The polls also showed people were unhappy with the increase in inequality and wanted a fairer Britain. Similarly, the pledge to follow Conservative spending plans for the first two years, which the Tories would never have done, meant some of the post-election goodwill had evaporated by the time the child poverty campaign was launched.

- The fear of frightening right-wing tabloid horses meant that the policy was never properly sold, with only one mention in the 2001 election, and not much more in 2005. By the time ministers had become more emboldened, momentum had been lost and public attitudes towards the poor had hardened. It was Blair's boldest goal but he left it to Gordon Brown to construct the policy. The fact that there is no mention of the speech or the launch of the campaign in his autobiography shows his mind was on other priorities.

- The campaign clearly suffered from the successful and much higher-profile international campaign, Make Poverty History, which reinforced public belief that poverty was something that only happened overseas, where poor people were having to survive on one dollar a day.

- Blair's call in his Toynbee Hall speech for a way of making welfare 'popular' again was indeed a challenge, but he answered it himself

- concentrate on children. Who could be against helping poor children? The public goodwill was there to be tapped.

• The campaign contained three elements that are crucially important in recruiting media pressure: a specific and unambiguous pledge; agreed staging posts – 5, 10, 15, 20 years – where progress could be monitored; and annual public surveys providing clear and hard evidence about the people affected. Indeed, the annual poverty statistics were also used to check progress. Compare this with an almost unknown anti-poverty pledge on housing: 'within 10 to 20 years no one should be seriously disadvantaged by where they live' (see Chapter Nine). No wonder so few people knew about this pledge. It fell down on three fronts: too vague; no clear criteria by which it could be judged; and not subject to annual measurement and monitoring. The child poverty target was well known. Pressure groups did alert the media when publication of the annual statistics were due. There was pre-publication speculation and post-publication analysis, but clearly not enough.

• It is worth remembering that although there was not enough redistribution, the IFS charts, reproduced on page 282, show that there was some significant reshuffling of income. In Labour's last Budget some £30 billion was being spent on tax credits alone. That was in part due to the campaign by charities, funders and research groups that fed the media with the facts and figures needed to maintain pressure on ministers.

Notes

[1] JRF (Joseph Rowntree Foundation) (1995) *Independent Inquiry into Income and Wealth*, York: JRF, 1 February.

[2] Robert Walker (ed) (1999) *Ending child poverty: Popular welfare for the 21st century?*, Bristol: The Policy Press.

[3] Interview with senior Downing Street official.

[4] Interview with senior Treasury official.

[5] Interview with Whitehall civil servant.

[6] Alastair Campbell (2011) *Alastair Campbell diaries, Vol 2, Power and the people*, London: Hutchinson, p 687.

[7] Tony Blair (2010) *A journey*, London: Hutchinson.

[8] For the full text, see Robert Walker (ed) (1999) *Ending child poverty: Popular welfare for the 21st century?*, Bristol: The Policy Press, p 7.

[9] 'Poor kid: harrowing truth behind Blair's poverty crusade', *The Daily Mirror*, 19 March 1999.

[10] See Robert Walker (ed) (1999) *Ending child poverty: Popular welfare for the 21st century?*, Bristol: The Policy Press, p 131.

[11] Ibid.

[12] Ibid.

[13] Ibid, p 128.

[14] Ibid, p 137.

[15] Bryan Gould (1992) *New Statesman*, 15 September.

[16] J.K. Galbraith (1993) *The culture of contentment*, New York: Mariner Books.

[17] See Will Hutton's *Guardian* columns in the early 1990s.

[18] Commission on Social Justice (1994) *Social justice: Strategies for renewal, The final report of the Commission on Social Justice*, London: Vintage.

[19] Hugo Young (1994) *The Guardian*, 25 October, p 43.

[20] Nicholas Timmins (1994) *The Independent*, 25 October.

[21] Richard Layard (2009) *Happiness: Lessons from a new science*, London: Penguin; Richard Wilkinson and Kate Pickett (2010) *The spirit level: Why equality is better for everyone*, London: Penguin.

[22] *The Times* (1995) First leader: 'The new levellers', 2 February.

[23] Nicholas Timmins (1995) *The Independent*, 2 February.

[24] *The Observer* (1995) Editorial, 5 February.

[25] *The Sunday Telegraph*, 5 February 1995.

[26] Richard Wilkinson (1994) *Unfair shares: The effects of widening income differences on the welfare of the young*, Ilford: Barnardo's.

[27] Richard Wilkinson and Kate Pickett (2010) *The spirit level: Why equality is better for everyone*, London: Penguin (paperback edn; hardback published 2009).

[28] John Hills and Kitty Stewart (eds) (2005) *A more equal society? New Labour, poverty, inequality and exclusion*, Bristol: The Policy Press, p 1.

[29] See the BBC and national press websites of the annual Conservative Party conference, October 2002.

[30] Nicholas Timmins (2001) *The five giants: A biography of the welfare state*, London: HarperCollins, p 571.

[31] Roy Hattersley (1997) *The Guardian*, 26 July.

[32] Nicholas Timmins (1997) *Financial Times*, 19 September.

[33] *The Guardian*, 21 November 1997.

[34] On every national media website.

[35] Tony Blair (1998) 'Building a modern welfare state', Speech given to Labour Party members, Dudley Town Hall, 15 January.

[36] Fabian Society (2006) *Narrowing the gap*, London: The Fabian Commission on Life Chances and Child Poverty.

[37] Donald Hirsch (2006) *What will it take to end child poverty?*, York: Joseph Rowntree Foundation.

[38] G. Clark and P. Franklin (2006) 'First principles: Poverty is relative and social exclusion matters', November, Social Justice Policy Group, Conservative Party,

UK; G. Clark and P. Franklin (2006) 'The poorest left behind: Labour's record on poverty', November, Social Justice Policy Group, Conservative Party, UK.

[39] 'Cameron told: it's time to ditch Churchill', *The Guardian*, 22 November 2006.

[40] Polly Toynbee (2003) *Hard work: Life in low-paid Britain*, London: Bloomsbury.

[41] Reported in all national papers, 23 November 2006.

[42] Stephen Glover (2006) *Daily Mail*, 30 November.

[43] Jonathan Bradshaw et al (2008) *A minimum standard for Britain: What people think*, York: Joseph Rowntree Foundation, July.

[44] Jonathan Bradshaw keynote address, 'Understanding and overcoming poverty', JRF Centenary Conference, 13 December 2004, York.

[45] John Hills, Tom Sefton and Kitty Stewart (eds) (2009) *Towards a more equal society? Poverty, inequality and policy since 1997*, Bristol: The Policy Press, p 39, Figure 2.7a.

[46] UNICEF (2007) *An overview of child well-being in rich countries*, York: UNICEF.

[47] Lisa Harker (2006) 'Child poverty', *IPPR Quarterly Journal*.

[48] Lisa Harker (2006) *Delivering child poverty: What would it take?*, London: Department for Work and Pensions.

[49] Alison Park, John Curtice, Katarina Thomson, Catherine Bromley and Miranda Phillips (eds) (2004) *British social attitudes: The 21st report*, London: Sage Publications for the National Centre for Social Research.

[50] J. McKendrick et al (2008) *The media, poverty and public opinion*, York: Joseph Rowntree Foundation, September.

[51] Sarah Castell and Julian Thompson (2007) *Understanding attitudes to poverty: Getting the public's attention*, York: Joseph Rowntree Foundation.

[52] J. McKendrick et al (2008) *The media, poverty and public opinion*, York: Joseph Rowntree Foundation, September.

[53] Media Trust (2008) *Reporting poverty in the UK: A practical guide for journalists*, York: Joseph Rowntree Foundation.

[54] BBC and *The Independent* websites, 4 December 2009.

[55] *The Guardian* website, 27 August 2009.

[56] *The Guardian* website, 15 February 2011.

[57] *The Guardian* website, 18 February 2011.

[58] BBC and national press websites, 22 April 2009.

[59] *Financial Times* (2010) Budget Special, p 10, 23 June.

[60] See Sunder Katwala (2010) 'Next left', Fabian Society blog, 29 August and 17 October.

[61] Mark Gill (2004/05) 'Let's finally talk about tax', *Fabian Review*, Winter.

[62] research.dwp.gov.uk/asd/hbai2011/pdf_files/full_hbai12.pdf

[63] http://www.ifs.org.uk/pr/poverty pr 1011.pdf; full report: http://www.ifs.org.uk/comms/comm121.pdf

[64] Mike Brewer (2012) 'Labour's child poverty effort was exceptional', *The Guardian*, 13 June.

[65] European Commission (2011) *The social impact of the economic crisis and ongoing fiscal consolidation*, Third report of the Social Protection Committee, Luxembourg: Office of the European Union.

[66] OECD (2011) *OECD Family Database*, Paris: OECD, Chart CO2.2.B, www.oecd.org/document/4/0,3746,en_2649_34819_37836996_1_1_1_1,00.html

[67] Jane Waldfogel (2010) *Britain's war on poverty*, New York: Russell Sage Foundation.

[68] See Jonathan Bradshaw (2012) *The well-being of children in the UK*, Bristol: The Policy Press; or the CPAG (Child Poverty Action Group) report from 15 experts examining Labour's record: CPAG (2012) *Ending child poverty by 2020: Progress made and lessons learned*, London: CPAG, p 19.

[69] See national press and BBC websites, 22 June 2010 for the Budget and 20 October 2010 for the Comprehensive Spending Review.

[70] *The Guardian* and *Telegraph* websites, 25 August 2010.

[71] http://www.ifs.org.uk/pr/povertypr 1011.pdf

[72] CPAG (2012) '*Bad Friday': The cuts bombshell hitting low income families on Friday, 6th April 2012*, Press release, London: CPAG.

[73] http://cdn.hm-treasury.gov.uk/budget2012_annexb.pdf

[74] BBC news website (2012) 'Benefit changes: Universal Credit system warning', 9 September.

[75] Daniel Botley (2012) 'Key advisers tell IDS: your welfare bill won't work', *The Observer*, 16 September.

[76] Randeep Ramesh (2012) '450,000 disabled people to lose out under universal credit, study finds', *The Guardian*, 17 October.

[77] Tom Clark (2012) 'Universal credit doesn't knit together', *The Guardian*, 6 June.

[78] Randeep Ramesh (2012) 'Local authorities braced for lost council tax revenue', *The Guardian*, 16 October.

[79] BBC news website, plus all serious newspapers, 26 June 2012.

[80] *The Sun* (2012) Editorial, 'Cam on, then', 26 June.

[81] *Daily Mail* (2012) 'Warped priorities', 26 June.

[82] Simon Carr (2012) 'Cameron: much too nice to lead the nasty party', *The Independent*, 26 June.

[83] British Social Attitudes Survey 2012, National Centre for Social Research, www.bsa-29.natcen.ac.uk

[84] Roland Watson (2012) 'Culture of entitlement has to end, says Cameron', *The Times*, 26 June.

[85] Anne Treneman (2012) 'Tall tales in a marvellous world of self-reliance', *The Times*, 26 June.

[86] Brian Wheeler (2012) 'Tory Conference in £10bn benefit cut row', BBC news website, 8 October.

[87] BBC news website and all national newspapers, 10 October 2012.

[88] Douglas Laxton (2009) *Effects of fiscal stimulus in structural models*, IMF report, www.imf.org/external/np/seminars/eng/2009/fispol/pdf/laxton.pdf

[89] D. Elmendorf and J. Furman (2008) *If, when and how: A primer for fiscal stimulus*, Washington: The Brookings Institution, www.brookings.edu/papers/2008/0110 fiscal stimulus elmendorf furman.aspx

[90] ILO/IILS (2011) *A review of global fiscal stimulus*, EC/IILS Joint Discussion Paper Series No 5, p 15.

[91] UK Treasury (2011) *Impact on households: Distributional analysis to accompany the Autumn Statement*, London: HM Treasury.

SEVEN

Vocational education: the biggest disappointment

The biggest disappointment in my 40 years of watching social policy was the failure to correct one of the oldest defects in our country's culture: a refusal to recognise the importance of vocational education. It was recognised as a failure over 150 years ago and the warnings being issued then are still being heard today. As early as 1855 Lord Playfair, a Scottish scientist and Liberal politician, travelled to the Continent at the request of the Prince Consort to examine technical education and concluded: 'as surely as darkness follows the setting of the sun, so surely will England recede as a manufacturing nation, unless the industrial population become more conversant with science and technical matters'.[1]

This warning was repeated in 1876 when the report of the Devonshire Committee called for a wider development of technical education 'to minimise the danger of our decline'.[2] It had become even more urgent in 1884, when the Royal Commission on Technical Instruction (the Samuelson Report) declared 'we are in danger of being left behind ... much depends on strengthening the base of the pyramid of technical education'.[3] It was this report that led to the Technical Instruction Act 1889 that permitted local councils to levy rates to fund technical instruction. These many reports pointed to Germany and noted how far we had fallen behind Germany's technical education with its trade continuation schools teaching crafts to teenagers and its technical high schools, which were achieving high levels of skills.

Jump forward a century. By then, in the view of Sir Claus Moser, the former Chief National Statistician, Britain was not just limping behind Germany. In a celebrated 1990 presidential address to the British Association, Moser declared that Britain was in danger of becoming 'one of the least adequately educated of all advanced nations'.[4] He ruefully observed that only in Britain would being dubbed 'too clever by half' be seen as an insult. By all the obvious criteria – staying-on rates at school, proportion of GDP invested in education, education standards achieved – England and Wales, and to a lesser extent Scotland, were lagging behind the industrialised world. In the year in which Moser spoke, school inspectors in England and Wales had found almost one third of lessons were 'poor or very poor'. One out of three lessons lacked pace, was over-directed and dominated by worksheets: in plain words, simply too passive and too undemanding.

The vocational deficit

Moser was particularly concerned with the 14–19 age group. His proposals included the need to provide equal status between vocational and academic education; new vocational pathways to higher education; a wider A-level curriculum; and better monitoring of educational standards at all levels. International comparisons at the time were showing that while the average 14-year-old in the UK was one year behind their German contemporaries in maths, the bottom 40 per cent were more than two years behind. Only 39 per cent of 16- to 18-year-olds in the UK were in full-time education compared to 50 per cent in Italy, 66 per cent in France, 81 per cent in the Netherlands, 87 per cent in Japan and 90 per cent in the US. Vocational skills statistics were equally grim: only 18 per cent of the workforce were qualified to craft levels (skilled carpenters, electricians, plumbers), compared to 33 per cent in France, 38 per cent in Holland and 56 per cent in Germany.

Britain was suffering a triple burden compared to its competitors: too few students in full-time education; too few following vocational schemes with recognisable qualifications; and too many parked on undemanding training courses. Moser had called for a Royal Commission into education but Margaret Thatcher did not believe in them – which on this issue was probably wise in political terms. According to the government's school inspectors, two out of three schools in 1990 were in need of urgent repairs, with education in half of them suffering because of run-down conditions. Then there was a 15-year erosion of teachers' salaries that had reduced their pay from 37 per cent above the white-collar average to just 5 per cent above. Nearly half of all colleges and universities were forecasting an aggregated deficit of £50 million.

In the wake of Moser's lecture both main parties began playing a better tune. They both produced new policy papers in the spring of 1991 which recognised three urgent needs: the right of non-academic children to take up high quality and challenging vocational courses after the age of 14; the removal of artificial barriers which prevented pupils following both academic and vocational courses; and ending the unequal status between the two. The framework unveiled by the Conservative government in May 1991 followed the same broad lines of Labour's model one month before: pupils would move from an ordinary diploma at 16 (comprising GCSEs or vocational equivalents) to an advanced diploma at 18 (A-levels and vocational equivalents). Courses would be broken down into modules to allow some switching between streams. Both streams – academic and vocational – would provide direct avenues to a university degree course. Students who left school at 16 would be awarded credits so that they could buy further training. The aim was to ensure that 90 per cent of all 16- to 18-year-olds were in some form of training.[5] But it took another decade before any of this materialised.

A wasted decade

Labour lost the 1992 election. There was no dramatic change for a decade. In this period a National Commission on Education, set up under the auspices of the British Association and funded by the Hamlyn Foundation, acted as the Royal Commission that Thatcher had refused to set up, and provided responses in 1993 to several of Moser's key concerns. Successive reports from Sir Ron Dearing, the Conservative government's favourite troubleshooter, helped keep the need for vocational reform on the agenda. In a January 1994 report on slimming down the National Curriculum, he noted that the needs of the non-academic required a higher profile by policy-makers.[6] In a second report in spring 1996 on the school examination system, he emphasised the need to re-motivate alienated 14-year-olds, something which work-placed and vocational courses could do.[7]

Estelle Morris's legacy

The next big breakthrough came in 2002 under Estelle Morris, the former Schools Minister and a former teacher, who succeeded David Blunkett as Education Secretary of State after the 2001 election. She was extremely popular with teachers and much loved in the department – there were tears when she suddenly resigned in October 2002, declaring she was good at dealing with issues but 'I am less good at the strategic management of a huge department and I am not good at dealing with modern media'. She had been hounded by a series of 'events' – fraud within individual learning accounts the government had set up to give adults the freedom to invest in their own education and training, a grade-fixing A-level fiasco, Blunkett's primary school targets missed, among others – none directly of her doing but as the boss, she 'carried the can' and was subjected to an offensive media onslaught. Once she was wounded, the media hunted in packs to find and concentrate on the most negative events.

What she did achieve was a clear commitment to pursue parity of esteem between academic and vocational courses. In her Green Paper published February 2002, she signalled her intention of creating a matriculation diploma with equal weighting for the twin tracks – a plan which her department had recognised and backed, that would require wholesale reform of the nation's examination system.[8] A year later Charles Clarke, her successor, produced a White Paper saying ministers 'had been confirmed in our view that we need to create a clearer and more appropriate framework for the 14 to 19 phase'.[9] He too anticipated a 'unified framework of qualifications', and formally commissioned Mike Tomlinson, former Chief Inspector of Schools, to find ways of achieving this with a 15-member committee representing all interests.

The interim report

The publication of the Committee's interim report on 15 February 2004 excited even cynical old Fleet Street hands.[9] Representatives of all the interested parties were present at the launch to provide comments after the presentations. Tomlinson had created a plan which united the most unlikely allies – private as well as state schools; classroom teachers as well as their heads; further education colleges as well as universities; not, as yet, the CBI (it wanted more proof the plan would raise standards) but several leading employers as well as craft unions. It was an amazing accomplishment. The consensus produced a real buzz within the press corps as reaction quotes that were being swapped began to show just how wide the consensus had become.

Just how little Britain had advanced since Moser's 1990 lecture was set out in the report. It pointed to a 2003 OECD survey which showed only three of its 30 member states had fewer 17-year-olds in education or training – Mexico, Turkey and Greece. Half of all

16-year-olds were failing to achieve a C grade or above in GCSE maths, and 44 per cent in English. One quarter of all pupils had abandoned learning by the age of 17.

The report tackled the two most serious problems facing secondary education head on. The first was the degree to which brighter students were failing to be stretched by A-levels, making it more difficult for universities to make appropriate higher education selections from the 20,000 students who were getting three A grades at A-level. To the delight of the universities, the report proposed adding two extra grades to the top of A-levels: an A plus and an A double plus. At the other end, the committee found new ways in which not only to engage alienated non-academic 14-year-olds into the education process, but also to restructure the 5,000 vocational qualifications, which left pupils, schools and employers totally confused.

Tomlinson's new framework provided for a diploma at four levels of ability, with a twin-track system giving students from the age of 14 a choice of academic or vocational courses, or even some of both. It not only would have bridged the divide but would have also opened up links to the rapidly expanding modern apprenticeships – by then numbering 250,000 – as well as an avenue to higher education. It also aimed to condense the 5,000 qualifications into 20 broad pathways. What was winning applause from employers, who had been complaining about the lack of literacy and numeracy of young people recruited, was the proposed new set of functional tests – in maths, English and information technology (IT) – pupils would be required to pass before being awarded a diploma.

The main criticisms in February 2004 were from the right wing. True to her tradition, Melanie Phillips in the *Mail* was scathing. Under the banner headline, 'Another reform, another betrayed generation', she declared that the report 'does not even begin to address the meltdown in education standards'.[11] The *Mail* Editorial was no better, but then remember that the *Mail* rejected A-levels when they were first introduced in 1952, only to become an ardent supporter later on. Ruth Lea, Director of the Centre for Policy Studies, was equally damning in *The Telegraph*: 'When I read the report my heart sank. This is not the way to go'.[12]

The final report

On the eve of the final report all looked serene. The two main opposition parties – Conservative and Liberal Democrat – had signalled that they would not play politics with its proposals. In pre-publication briefings by the Education Department, the media were told that the Education Secretary would be welcoming the report. Liz Lightfoot, in *The Telegraph*, reported just that on the morning of the launch. True, the *Mail* did not wait to read the report, but published its Editorial on the morning of the launch under the headline 'For our children's sake, bin this exam report'. No surprise there, then, but the language was more upmarket although with syntax problems. It declared the report would not solve the problems in education but 'is more likely to presage the destruction of the important concept of examinations and of education itself'.[13] There was some nervousness from some interests about 'cherry picking'. David Hart, General Secretary of the National Association of Head Teachers, was quoted in several papers urging ministers to give their full backing to the package and avoid 'fudge'.

There were no real surprises of either timing or content in the report.[14] One of the benefits of the Tomlinson Report was that all three components of the education system – curriculum, assessment and qualifications – were looked at together. It was still being seen as a 10-year plan – evolution as much as revolution. And in addition to the interest groups already backing the plan, it had the support of two key players: the Chief Inspector for Schools and the head of the Qualifications and Curriculum Authority (QCA). Tomlinson had already signalled in the interim report an ambition for GCSEs and A-levels to be absorbed into an overarching diploma that would also embrace restructured vocational qualifications. These signals were just made more specific in the final report, which documented the need for a reduction in some of the unnecessary burdens of the current exam system. A typical A-level student was completing 40 separate public examinations in just over two years with a considerable amount of course work on top. The final report suggested that over the long term these problems could be solved by restricting external exams to core skills at 16 – maths, literacy and IT – and when a proper system of teacher-led assessment had been rigorously tested, to use this for most of the other levels. It noted that once the proportion of 18-year-olds in education or training had risen from 50 to 80 per cent, external tests at 16 would have far less relevance.

At the press conference launching the report, Tomlinson was asked by the BBC education reporter whether he was worried that his report might be 'cherry-picked'. He expressed his hope that it would be accepted as a coherent whole. Alas, it was not to be. Responding in the Commons in the afternoon, the Education Secretary declared that 'rigorous, trusted and externally marked examinations' would continue at both 16 and 18, as would league tables. In other words, as the Prime Minister made clear in a speech to the CBI in the evening, both GCSEs and A-levels would remain untouched.

Chopping down the cherry tree

I got a telephone call from David Miliband, Schools Minister, on the afternoon of the launch asking what I was going to say in the paper's editorial the next day. I had only just begun writing so I read out roughly my first three sentences: 'There was concern yesterday that the government would "cherry pick" the Tomlinson report. They haven't. They have chopped down the cherry tree.'[15] He protested, but only half-heartedly. He knew, I knew, how much he had pushed for the reform, going back to the early 1990s when he was a researcher in this field at the IPPR. He did not speak publicly about Blair's veto on the plan until over five years later, during his unsuccessful bid for the Labour leadership in the summer of 2010. He visited his old secondary school in North London where he told the audience that Blair's refusal to embrace Tomlinson's plan was 'an historic error'.[16] He described the decision as 'the biggest political frustration' of his political life (he had not lost the leadership race at that point), and made clear that reintroducing Tomlinson in some form would be high on his agenda.

What caused the 'historic error'?

How did the decision on Tomlinson go so wrong at such a late stage? The government, which provided the secretariat, knew well in advance what it was going to produce. Indeed, it had steered the process from the beginning, with Estelle Morris's Green Paper. Miliband's support for the project as Schools Minister was well known. Yet it was only at the last minute that it was vetoed. Why?

It was a mixture of politics and media. The politics involved timing. The final report was due in the summer of 2004; by being delayed until mid-October it was becoming dangerously close to a 2005 general election date. A 'phoney' election was already under way. Michael Howard, the Conservative leader, was in difficulty with the polls and desperate for issues. Despite earlier pledges to keep the issue out of politics, Tomlinson's proposals for moving away from external assessment and replacing it with internal teacher-led assessment – even though this would have been over time – gave him an opportunity to bang the traditionalists' iconic drum: 'save our gold standard exams'. They were far from even gold-plated. Due to address the Society of Editors on launch day, Howard ensured that their news desks also received early copies of his highly political speech on educational standards. He did not just defend the need to keep GCSEs and A-levels, but declared he would go backwards and restore the 'norm referencing' system of grading in A-levels. Under this procedure, the number of A grades would be restricted to a small fixed proportion, a system which was abolished by the Conservatives in the 1980s. It was replaced by the fairer 'criterion referencing', under which students who achieved the set standards for a grade, would get the grade.[17]

Then there was Tony Blair. His popularity had plummeted given the bad news in Iraq. His attention had been more concentrated on overseas than domestic issues. He was known to believe Miliband had become too close to the department. And a peep at his background would have shown that Blair was always an A-levels man. One of his first tasks as Labour leader in July 1994 was to launch a discussion document on the party's education policies, including a recommendation to scrap GCSEs and A-levels in favour of a diploma.

Ignoring these recommendations Blair emphasised that A-levels were safe with Labour – and that was what the next day's headlines carried.[18] On Labour's sweeping victory in 1997 the three options outlined by Dearing in his 1996 report were still open for adoption: retain and improve existing qualifications; introduce an overarching certificate that could be achieved by both academic and vocational routes; or replace the multiple different awards – both academic and vocational – with a diploma. Only the first two were put out for consultation and it was the first that won Blair's approval.

Blair would have been alerted by his political aides to the speech Howard was making. He was well aware of Howard's skill (see Chapter Three, this volume) – of winning over worried middle-class voters. He was also aware – as a senior civil servant told me at the time – of how forcefully the two newspapers read by those voters, the *Mail* and *Telegraph*, would be campaigning to defend GCSEs and A-levels. It was not difficult for him to insert a riposte in the speech he was delivering to the CBI that day. He backed Tomlinson's proposals for stretching the most able, improving vocational education and introducing basic literacy and numeracy tests. But he went on: 'Let us be clear that the purpose of the reform will be to improve upon the existing system, not to replace it.' [19]

Reshuffles and another White Paper

Eight weeks after Tomlinson, Charles Clarke was moved from Education to the Home Office when David Blunkett resigned as Home Secretary in December 2004. Significantly, David Miliband was not promoted to Education Secretary but moved across to the Cabinet Office to draw up the Labour Party's manifesto for the 2005 election. The new Education Secretary, Ruth Kelly, was a clever economist who had worked at *The Guardian* and Bank of England before winning a parliamentary seat in 1997. Four years later she was promoted into the Treasury, first as Economic Secretary and then Financial Secretary, where she had done well. But she had no background in the intricacies of education politics or policies, and was the youngest and least experienced Cabinet minister. She was now in charge of drawing up a White Paper in response to Tomlinson.[20]

Blair's will was bound to succeed, although close associates of Kelly suggest her own views were rather similar.

Just a week before the White Paper was published, a *Times/Winmark* poll in February 2005 suggested almost half of headteachers in England had lost confidence in A-levels and GCSEs. About one in four said they would prefer to follow the broader-focused International Baccalaureate than A-levels, if given a choice. *The Times* noted: 'The findings point to a showdown after unions gave warning yesterday that teachers will be "in despair" if Mrs Kelly rules against large parts of the proposed Tomlinson diploma, which envisages the scrapping of A-levels and GCSEs.'[21]

Kelly was undeterred. Indeed she (or more likely Downing Street) ensured her White Paper had a pre-publication puff in *The Sunday Telegraph* revealing, unsurprisingly, 'A-levels are here to stay'.[22] GCSEs also remained 'safe', leaving the new diploma restricted to promoting vocational education through 14 new, broad, work-related lines of learning. This was completely at odds with a government consultation exercise that followed Tomlinson, which had asked whether retaining independent GCSE and A-levels examinations within a 'wrap around' diploma was an appropriate way forward. Over 90 per cent of responses rejected the idea. Similarly the headteachers of the top 100 schools in the GCSE league table also thought the White Paper was wrong.[23] A Press Association questionnaire on Kelly's White Paper sent to these headteachers gave it just four out of 10 marks. Six out of 10 said she was wrong to reject Tomlinson's proposals. Three quarters said she would fail in one of her key aims of improving the status of vocational education.

Developing the diplomas

It turned out that 2005 was an appropriate year to begin drawing up a major restructuring of vocational qualifications. It coincided with the Interim Report of the Leitch Committee on skills, which echoed those warnings of 150 years earlier, of the danger of the UK falling behind internationally because of a chronic shortage of skilled workers.[24] The message was reinforced a year later when the final report suggested that by 2020 there would only be 500,000 low-skill jobs in the country, compared to the then two million. But there would be 2.4 million more jobs requiring high level technical and science skills.[25]

Initially the plan was to phase in the 14 specialised diplomas over five years, beginning with pilot schemes involving five diplomas in 2008/09. It was recognised from the start that a single school would not have the capacity to offer 14 different specialised diplomas, so consortia of schools, colleges and employers were set up. By March 2005, 145 consortia covering 97 local authorities had been formed and a further 197 given provisional approval for starting in 2009. Each consortia was being offered £30,000 for each type of diploma on offer. Inevitably there were ups and downs. Momentum was not helped in March 2007 when Alan Johnson, Education Secretary, confessed at the annual conference of the Association of School and College Leaders that 'things could go horribly wrong, particularly as we are keeping A-levels and GCSEs ... that does mean there is a danger of the diplomas becoming if you like the secondary modern compared to the grammar'.[26] Later that year Ed Balls, who took over as Education Secretary when Gordon Brown became Prime Minister, announced three extra diplomas in academic subject areas – science, languages and humanities (history and geography) – in a bid to improve the status of the diploma. He declared that over time they could replace A-levels as the 'qualification of choice'.[27]

Over this period there was a mix of good and bad headlines. In 2006 further education colleges were worried by the vocational element being watered down, that led to a 'New diploma "sink course" fear' headline on the BBC website.[28] In 2007 the QCA Chief Executive, Ken Boston, reported misgivings by leaders of industry and exam boards about lack of clear management that generated 'wide concern over diplomas'.[29] And in April 2008, just 14 weeks before diploma courses were due to begin, under a *Guardian* front-page headline, 'Exam chief: rival to A-level in disarray', the head of Edexcel, one of the leading exam boards, said serious flaws still needed correcting: teachers not having had adequate training; schools not knowing how new features should be taught; and a fear that the qualification would be too demanding for pupils, leading to more pupils ending up without qualifications.[30]

But the Universities and Colleges Admissions Service (UCAS) reported in May 2008 that 100 higher education institutions had provided statements backing the new diplomas.[31] And three months later Ofsted (the education inspectors) produced its first report on the diplomas. It was a mixed message. It was worried about the teaching of functional skills and found work on construction was 'no better than satisfactory'.[32] But the other four subject areas were better than this. Equally importantly it found that in 19 of the 23 areas visited, the number of young people not in education, employment or training had gone down.[33] A government-funded University of Exeter survey in 2008 found the design of the diplomas being used were 'well aligned' with undergraduate teaching, but found tutors at the most competitive universities were being 'quite cynical' and 'cautious' about the academic rigour of the qualification. The 19 institutions surveyed would accept the diploma but all but two would need at least one A-level as well.[34]

The pilots begin

The pilot schemes began, as planned, in 2008/09. Initially it had been hoped to have 40,000 pupils on the courses, but only 11,500 pupils signed up. There were five options to choose from: construction, engineering, IT, media and health and social care. Media proved the most popular. Each diploma had three levels of accomplishment: level one (broadly similar to lower GCSE grades) attracted 2,000 pupils; level two (broadly equivalent to five good GCSE grades of C and above) won 8,000; and level three (equivalent to three A-levels) had 1,400 entrants. In September 2009 a further five diplomas were added to the options and the final four introduced in September 2010. By then 40,000 students had begun a diploma course, far fewer than the Labour government had wanted. Even so, there was encouraging news from UCAS in September 2009 when the first statistics on access to universities through the diploma were released. Some 743 applicants with the Advanced Level had applied, with 89 per cent receiving at least one offer and 65 per cent taking up a place. Putting this in perspective, UCAS officials noted there were only 5,000 applications from candidates with the International Baccalaureate, an examination that had existed for 20 years in the UK. Looking ahead, UCAS said 232 higher education institutions would be ready to accept applications from students with the diploma in 2011.[35]

The Conservative response

The Conservatives had initially kept a low profile on diplomas, but at a CBI Education Summit in September 2008 Michael Gove, then Shadow Education Secretary, declared a Conservative government would abolish Ed Balls' three new academic diplomas. He said Labour were only introducing the academic diplomas in the hope that they would overtake A-levels, but the Conservatives wished to 'preserve and enhance' A-levels.[36] He said he would like to see the 14 specialised diplomas succeed, but there were a number of worrying indications that the exams were not rigorous enough and their assessment would not be externally monitored effectively.

Following the 2010 general election and the emergence of the Conservative–Liberal Democrat Coalition, much worse happened. Gove became Education Secretary. The academic diplomas due to start in 2011 were abandoned. So also was a plan for an 'extended diploma' and an 'entitlement' for all pupils to be able to choose a diploma course. Worse still for an exam which is more expensive to teach than other subjects, the funding for the diploma was one of the hardest hit in the Department for Education's spending cuts. On top of a series of cuts for the 14–19 age group – abolition of regional advisers and a range of 'efficiency savings' – there was a £13 million cut for the support funding for delivering the 14–19 reforms.[37] Gove said he was concerned about vocational education, but instead of recognising the potential of the specialised diplomas, which had by then won the support of the CBI, he announced yet another inquiry into the issue.

Wolf's inquiry

Professor Alison Wolf, an academic specialising in educational skills, was appointed to carry out the inquiry. Like all her predecessors, she found a long list of baleful facts. She estimated that between a quarter and a third of 16- to 19-year-olds were currently getting 'little to no benefit from the post-16 education system'.[38] Worse still, one of the reasons for such large numbers taking courses which would not lead to a job or higher education was the 'perverse incentives' of the current funding system. As some vocational qualifications were worth four GCSEs, guiding pupils to these courses helped schools rise in the GCSE league table. She suggested funding should be per student, not per qualification, as currently.

Some of her other proposals were less well aimed. She suggested that students should mainly follow academic subjects until they were 16. If they did not get a good GCSE in English and maths by that age, they should be required to keep trying, however often they failed. What she ignored was the fact that even students who do get good grades are still found by employers to have too little functional literacy and numeracy. That was why Tomlinson drew up his functional skills programme, which has won praise from employers and approval from the CBI. Wolf's suggestion that no student aged between 14 and 16 should spend more than 20 per cent of their time on a vocational specialism opened another wound in the diploma programme.

The crumbling gold standards

Ironically, the first serious blow to hit what had been regarded as Conservative gold standard exams was provided by a newspaper which had campaigned for their retention: the *Daily Telegraph* on 8 December 2011. It was a brilliant piece of investigative journalism which exposed just how defective some exam boards had become. Under a seven-column-wide, two-line front page splash headline 'Cheating the system: how examiners tip off teachers', the newspaper disclosed that teachers were paying up to £230 a day to attend seminars with examiners to gain secret advice on how to improve their schools' GCSE and A-level results.[39] Undercover reporters from the paper went to 13 meetings organised by exam boards and found that 'teachers were routinely given information about future questions, areas of the syllabus that would be assessed and specific words or facts which students should use in their answers to win marks'. It went on: 'The advice appears to go far beyond "guidance" and opens up exam boards to accusations that they are undermining syllabuses by encouraging "teaching to the test".' Films and audio recordings of examination board officials revealing content of future test papers were made by the newspaper. One chief inspector who was recorded telling teachers which questions their pupils could expect declared: 'We're cheating. We're telling you the cycle [of the compulsory questions]. Probably the regulator will tell us off.'

The following day there was another equally damning front page splash headlined: 'Chief Examiner is filmed boasting about how easy her GCSE geography paper is'. The senior Edexcel examiner told the *Telegraph* undercover reporter, posing as a teacher who was considering using the test, 'you don't have to teach a lot' and that there was a 'lot less' for pupils to learn than with rival courses. She later told the reporter there was so little content in the geography paper 'we don't know how we got it through [the exam regulators]'. *The Telegraph* commented: 'Today's disclosures of the covert remarks made by Edexcel examiners are the first indications that exam boards are actively boasting about the ease of their courses in an attempt to try to secure valuable business'.[40] The paper noted that the attraction for schools of lower exam standards was the prospect of higher league table positions. The attraction for the highly competitive exam boards was higher customer numbers and profits.

There were widespread follow-ups by the rest of Fleet Street. Michael Gove responded by declaring the revelations 'confirm that the current system is discredited'. He set up an immediate official inquiry into the exam boards.

A bid to resurrect O-levels

Six months on, the future of the diplomas suffered a further major setback, with what the *Daily Mail* described as 'the most radical shake up in school exams for 30 years [that] will see dumbed-down GCSEs scrapped and rigorous O-levels brought back'.[41] It would mean a return to end-of-course exams in traditional academic subjects and the slashing of continuous assessment, coursework and resits. The paper's exclusive turned out to be true. It had seen the new Gove plans. The minister, who was summonsed to the Commons, shamelessly confirmed the report's accuracy. Not only was there no mention of the diplomas in the plan, but there was hardly any detail of what would happen to less academic pupils. It simply stated 'less intelligent pupils will sit simpler exams, similar to the old CSE'. Ironically, it had been under Margaret Thatcher's rule in 1986 that the merger of O-levels with the CSE exam had rightly taken place to create the GCSE. Both older exams had passed their sell-by date. The O-level, introduced in 1951 for the 20 per cent most able pupils and the CSE introduced in 1965 for the next 40 per cent of the ability range were doing nothing for the other 35 per cent.

Gove's plan won plaudits in the *Mail*'s Editorial – 'There are days when Michael Gove seems the only true Tory in the cabinet' – but little support in the serious daily press.[42] The headlines all pointed a downturned thumb to the idea. In the *Financial Times*, the Editorial under 'Gove reforms do not pass the test' explained: 'Relegating 14-year-olds to a lesser qualification could brand them as under-achievers and drain both students and schools of any incentive to push for higher standards. Yet a third of children who score in the bottom 25 per cent at the age of 11 break out of that grouping by the age of 16' (10 June 2012). *The Independent*, under the headline 'Not enough just to scrap GCSEs', argued in its Editorial: 'In order for less academic pupils not to be abandoned by the system, more effort must go into providing high quality vocational training'. The *Guardian* Editorial, 'Failing the test', noted that 'the actual content of the new CSE was a half-formed afterthought to the nostalgic boast of restoring an imagined O-level gold standard'. It also observed that Gove's insistence on 'all-or-nothing written tests in silent school halls' had dubious foundations. It explained: 'Barring Mr Gove's own chosen career of newspaper columnist, there are few vocations where the defining ability is wielding a pen under panic conditions' (9 June 2012).

There was even a thumbs-down from Kenneth Baker, a former Conservative Education Secretary under Margaret Thatcher, who declared in a column in *The Independent*: 'The problem that my predecessor Keith Joseph found with the old CSE – which Mr Gove wants to reintroduce – was that it had become a valueless piece of paper. Employers didn't rate it but students who obtained it were led to believe it was a passport to jobs and success. It wasn't. So don't resurrect a failure.'[43]

In the end the crude, badly thought-through idea was defeated. Furious that they had not been consulted, the Liberal Democrats vetoed a return to a two-tier exam system at 16. Indeed, several questioned whether there was a need for an exam at 16 at all. Lord Baker, for one, reminded policy-makers that O-levels and GCSEs were introduced to coincide with the end of formal schooling.[44] This was no longer true. By 2012 only six per cent of those aged 16 left school to find work. In 2013 the school leaving age rises to 17 and in 2015 to 18.[45] David Miliband wrote a similar piece in *The Times* pointing out that the UK was one of the last developed nations to have exams at 16, which meant school children faced three manic years of exams at 16, 17 and 18.[46] There was one constructive proposal that emerged. Gove announced on 16 September 2012 that a single exam board would preside over each subject, bringing to an end the dumbing down to get more customers that *The Daily Telegraph* had exposed. The exam boards would be able to compete with each other to offer qualifications for each subject, but only one would be selected.[47]

The Alliance compromise

Three months on from the June shenanigans Gove produced the alliance compromise on 17 September 2012.[48] Once again it was leaked early to the *Mail*. The GCSE would be replaced by the English Baccalaureate (EBacc), designed to drive up standards and prevent schools 'teaching to the test'. The overarching exam would be initially in English, maths and the option of three separate sciences from September 2015 for examination two years later. It would be extended to history, geography and languages in 2016 for examination in 2018. The new qualification would end continually assessed coursework based on modules, worth half the marks in some GCSE subjects, replaced by an examination at the end of a two-year course, with limited resits. There would be no alternative exam for less academic children, so there would, in effect, be a two-tier system. Pupils who failed to sit exams at 16 would get a report card with a 'statement of achievement' outlining their strengths and weaknesses and a chance to take the EBacc at 17 or 18. Under GCSE one per cent – 6,000 pupils – failed to get a single pass and a further seven per cent – 42,000 pupils – failed to get more than one grade C. Given the emphasis on making the new exam more challenging, this proportion of non-achievers looked likely to grow.

Once again the needs of the vocationally minded were mostly ignored. Gove claimed the new exam could be a foundation for further vocational training. But delaying vocational work until 16, 17 or 18 would be too late for many bright but alienated young people. The best age to begin vocational training is at 14, when children are more likely to know what they want to do post school, and have not become disillusioned. As *The Telegraph* noted, for the Gove plan to work 'academies and free schools must start placing as much emphasis on the vocational as on the academic'.[49] There was no recognition of this at the September launch of the new system. Nor was there any mention of using the existing diplomas to fill this vocational gap. *The Times* too was concerned. In an Editorial, 'Making the grade', it noted that 'while the desire to set high expectations for all children is admirable, it leaves a gap for those who are not academically minded. The Government's reforms must be judged on what they do for this group as well as those at the top.'[50] At the time of this book going to press, there was nothing to cheer the vocational movement in the Gove plan.

But he was forced to announce on 7 February 2013 that he was abandoning his new English Baccalaureate certificate following damning criticism of the plan by the Conservative-chaired Select Committee on Education ('too much, too fast' and could threaten exam quality); the opposition of teachers, employers and universities; and a serious warning from the chief exam regulator, Glenys Stacey, that his ambition for the new exam 'may exceed what is realistically achievable through a single assessment'. GCSEs were restored but would move away from their modular structure and continuous assessment towards 'a single assessment' of a final exam after two years' study. The single exam board per subject was dropped on legal advice that it could run counter to EU rules on public service contracts.

Two non-government vocational initiatives

There were, thankfully, two modest new non-government vocational initiatives that had attracted support from local authorities and universities. The first was a Young Foundation enterprise, Studio Schools, which in the three years up to 2012 had established 16 schools with a further 16 in the pipeline. These schools have been devised for 14- to 19-year-olds of all abilities to bridge the gap between the skills and knowledge that young people require to succeed and those that the current education system provides. They seek to teach through enterprise projects and real work. Working closely with local employers the schools offer a wide range of academic and vocational qualifications. The schools cater for up to 300 pupils, providing a 9am to 5pm working day and feel more like a workplace than a school.

The second venture, promoted by Lord Baker, is special technical colleges for 14- to 19-year-olds, teaching engineering and technical skills that employers need. They each have links with local companies and local universities, providing master classes and access to university facilities. Hence their name: university training colleges. Five were due to be opened by the end of 2012, another 14 in 2013 and 15 in 2014. Students spend three days a week on academic subjects – maths, English, science, foreign languages – and two days a week learning practical and technical skills.[51]

But to catch up with our continental competitors, the English system must also create serious challenging vocational courses in mainstream schools. The diplomas are there to be seized and built on. At the October 2012 Labour Party conference, hopes were raised by a leak to *The Guardian* that Ed Miliband was going to pledge a commitment to 'the forgotten 50 per cent' who do not go to university in his leader's address.[52] True to the leak, the section on vocation – like the rest of speech all spoken without script or prompt screen – began encouragingly. 'We cannot succeed if we have an education system which only works for half the country. I want ours to be a country where kids aspire not just to go to Oxford and Cambridge, but to excellent technical colleges and elite vocational institutions.' He declared that Labour would develop 'a clear vocational route to a gold standard qualification'. Businesses would be involved in designing the courses, which would be 'rigorous and high quality, so that they are no longer seen as a second-class option'. But there was no mention of using or developing the existing diplomas. At the time of this book going to press, all three main parties seemed content to let the diplomas 'wither on the vine'.

There has always been ambivalence on the left and right about recognising the academic/vocational divide. But the divide is real, not artificial. Refusing to separate sheep and goats can be as damaging as giving the separate flocks unequal status. The solution is not to ignore differences but to build a structure to accommodate both. The diploma would have achieved that if Blair had pressed the 'go' button in 2004 when it had such widespread support. David Miliband was right – Blair made an 'historic error', an error partly on his own prejudices and partly on his perpetual worries about retaining the support of *Mail* and *Telegraph* readers. Another victory, alas, to a prejudice-based media campaign.

One final word on this issue. A report from the CfBT Education Trust, an international charity, in June 2010, drawn from interviews with former education ministers and their civil servants about three decades of initiatives, concluded that schools policy had 'more to do with media than evidence'. Worse still, it was the short-term interests of the media that had 'disproportionate influence', making it difficult for both Conservative and Labour governments to develop effective long-term strategies. The researchers suggested that education policy-makers needed a more effective way of evaluating ideas and policy proposals similar to the way that the National Institute for Health and Clinical Excellence (NICE) provides independent evidence-based guidance on health. The report called for an independent chief education officer to give objective advice.[53] Alas, even if there had been one, Michael Gove would have been quite ready to ignore him/her. The Education Secretary did have an independent panel of education experts on the reform of the national curriculum, but chose to ignore their advice and listen to a more ideologically sympathetic shadow group he had set up to bypass the real experts.[54] He lost one of Whitehall's most effective permanent secretaries, Sir David Bell, and the next two most senior people in the department. He was more interested in policy-based evidence than evidence-based policy.

Notes

[1] Lord Playfair (1855) *British eloquence: Lectures and addresses*.

[2] Devonshire Commission (1876) *Report of the Royal Commission on Scientific Instruction and the Advancement of Science*, p 45.

[3] Report of the 1884 Royal Commission on Technical Instruction, known as the Samuelson Report.

[4] Presidential address to the British Association by Sir Claus Moser, 3 September 1990.

[5] *The Guardian* (1991) Editorial, 'Two streams merging', 9 February.

[6] R. Dearing (1994) *The National Curriculum and its assessment*, January, London: SCAA.

[7] R. Dearing (1996) *Higher education in the Learning Society*, Norwich: HMSO.

[8] DfES (Department for Education and Skills) (2002) *14–19: Extending opportunities, raising standards*, Education Green Paper, February, London: The Stationery Office.

[9] DfES (Department for Education and Skills) (2003) *The future of higher education*, Cm 5735, January, Norwich: HMSO.

[10] Working Group on 14–19 Reform (2004) *Interim report of the Working Group on 14–19 curriculum and qualifications reform*, February, London: DfES.

[11] Melanie Phillips (2004) 'Another reform, another betrayed generation', *Mail* online, 28 February.

[12] Ruth Lea (2004) *The Telegraph*, 23 February.

[13] *Daily Mail* (2004) Editorial, 'For our children's sake, bin this exam report', 18 October.

[14] DfES (Department for Education and Skills) (2004) *Final report of the Working Group on 14-19 Reform* (Tomlinson Report), October, London: The Stationery Office.

[15] *The Guardian* (2004) Editorial, 'Much needed reform', 19 October.

[16] *The Guardian* online, 27 June 2010.

[17] *The Daily Telegraph* (2004) 'Howard says Tories would restore the currency of the exam system', 19 October.

[18] See A. Smithers (2005) 'Education', in Anthony Seldon and Dennis Kavanagh (eds) *The Blair effect 2001–5*, Cambridge: Cambridge University Press, ch 16, p 267.

[19] *The Daily Telegraph*, 19 October 2004.

[20] Department for Education and Skills, *14–19 Education and Skills White Paper*, Cm 6476, February, Norwich: The Stationery Office.

[21] *The Times* (2005) 'Schools give low marks to exam', 14 February, p 10.

[22] *The Sunday Telegraph*, 20 February 2005.

[23] *The Daily Mail* online, 3 May 2005.

[24] Lord Leitch (2005) *Skills in the UK: The long term challenge*, Interim report of the Leitch Committee, 5 December, London: HM Treasury.

[25] Lord Leitch (2006) *Prosperity for all in the global economy: World class skills*, Final report of the Leitch Committee, 5 December, London: The Stationery Office.

[26] BBC website, 9 March 2007.

[27] BBC News (2007) 'Diplomas "could replace A-levels"', 23 October (http://news.bbc.co.uk/1/hi/education/7058015.stm).

[28] BBC website, 22 November 2006.

[29] BBC website, 5 January 2007.

[30] *The Guardian* front page, 17 April 2008.

[31] National press and BBC websites, 21 May 2008.

[32] BBC website, 25 August 2009.

[33] National press and BBC websites, 17 August 2008.

[34] BBC website, 25 August 2009.

[35] Mike Baker (2010) 'Anger grows as diploma support wanes', BBC News, 25 September (www.bbc.co.uk/news/education-11407563).

[36] Mike Baker (2008) 'Tories would scrap some Diplomas', BBC News, 19 September (http://news.bbc.co.uk/1/hi/education/7625483.stm).

[37] Mike Baker (2010) 'Anger grows as diploma support wanes', BBC News, 25 September (www.bbc.co.uk/news/education-11407563).

[38] Alison Wolf (2011) *Review of vocational education – The Wolf Report*, London: Department for Education.

[39] Claire Newell and Holly Watt (2012) 'There's so little content we don't know how we got it through', *The Daily Telegraph*, 12 September.

[40] Ibid.

[41] Tim Shipman (2012) 'Return of an O-level: Gove announces radical plan to scrap GCSEs', *Mail Online*, 8 June.

[42] Ibid.

[43] Kenneth Baker (2012) 'Please do not turn back the clock', *The Independent*, 22 June.

[44] Ibid.

[45] Ibid.

[46] David Miliband (2012) 'Why fuss over exams at 16? No else does', *The Times*, 20 September.

[47] Saran Hams (2012) 'The day that Gove put rigour back into school exams', *Daily Mail*, 16 September.

[48] All national newspapers, 18 September 2012.

[49] *The Daily Telegraph* (2012) Editorial, 'An exam system that passes the test', 18 September.

[50] *The Times* (2012) Editorial, 'Making the grade', 18 September.

51 Kenneth Baker (2012) 'At last schools for getting your hands dirty', *The Times*, 29 May.

52 Patrick Wintour (2012) 'End of elitism: Miliband vows to prepare teenagers for work', *The Guardian,* 2 October.

53 CfBT Education Trust (2010) *Instinct or reason*, London: CfBT. See also Sean Coughlan, BBC education correspondent (2010) 'Schools policy "more to do with media than evidence"', BBC website, 2 June.

54 Daniel Boffey (2012) 'Gove's own experts in revolt over curriculum shake up', *The Observer*, 17 June.

EIGHT

Health and social care: the most expensive breakfast in history

This case became known to health service watchers as 'the most expensive breakfast in history'. It involved Tony Blair's pledge on the sofa of the Sunday morning television show *Breakfast with Frost* on 16 January 2000, that the UK's spending on health would meet the EU average within five years. This is perhaps the most common form of media influence: cases in which a continuous run of bad but genuine news stories push politicians into a position they were ultimately going to take, although probably not as promptly or as generously, because of the public fuss generated by newspapers and broadcasters. It is followed in this chapter by case studies showing the media not just distorting policy but changing human behaviour in a harmful way.

The Blair pledge came at the end of a troublesome year for the NHS in 1999. Two years of pursuing Tory spending limits – as Labour had pledged itself to do – had hit the NHS hard. It had, in fact, got slightly more than the limits, as the Tories would have done too, but it was not nearly enough. The financial squeeze on the service, allied with Conservative suggestions that other forms of funding in place of taxation should be found for the NHS, left only three national dailies (*The Guardian*, *Financial Times* and *The Daily Mirror*) still believing a tax-funded health service was the most efficient by the autumn of 1999. Others had switched in favour of a more richly fed, juicier-looking apple in the continental orchard: social insurance. Not only was this alternative more costly, but it relied on existing employers more heavily. As a result, some of these models were already discussing, indeed switching to, tax-funded systems. Supporters of tax funding were later vindicated by a study from the World Health Organization (WHO) Observatory on Health Care Systems. It was commissioned by the Treasury-based Wanless Review, and examined alternative forms of finance used in Europe.[1]

The news columns in the second half of 1999 were filled with stories of critical bed shortages, long trolley waits, cancelled waiting list operations, a threatened flu outbreak, a pressure group report on elderly patients being starved and an East Anglian hospital being forced to hire a freezer truck because its morgue was full. The BBC had an 'NHS crisis' logo running above its NHS bad news stories. Then two individual cases broke. They are always more powerful in media terms because they humanise dry statistical returns. First came Mrs Mavis Skeet, a brave 78-year-old lady with throat cancer, who had four successive planned operations cancelled and by the fifth opportunity the tumour was so large and the patient so weak, it was too late to operate. There was widespread coverage of her plight.

The second individual case broke in the New Year after a Christmas week in which a grave shortage of critical care beds had been prominent. It began when the 87-year-old mother of the best-known doctor in Britain, Lord Winston, had to go into hospital. Lord Winston is not just a leading infertility specialist who has appeared regularly on television and radio medical programmes, he is also a Labour peer and known to be on friendly terms with the Blairs. Unfortunately the treatment his mother received was abysmal, so bad in fact that Lord Winston gave a searing interview to the *New Statesman*.[2] He spoke of her 13-hour trolley wait in casualty before she was transferred to a mixed-sex ward where drugs were not given on time, meals were missed and one night she had fallen out of bed and not been found until the morning staff came on, by which time she had caught an infection. He described such a catalogue of failure as 'normal', and added, 'the terrifying thing is they accept it!' He accused Labour of being deceitful over abolishing the internal market and claimed UK funding was not as good as Poland's.

Bad news spreads

The story was picked up and splashed in the Friday and Saturday editions and followed up in the Sundays. Although not all Winston's facts were right, he won the support of the presidents of the two most eminent and powerful Royal Colleges – the Physicians and the Surgeons. And it was on that Sunday that the Prime Minister went to his long pre-arranged David Frost interview. Frost told me at that point in the political cycle he was getting two interviews a year with Blair and had not expected anything momentous,[3] but in fact there had been media speculation about the interview and the crisis in the health service was the top item.

There are two versions of what happened on the show. Nicholas Timmins, the *Financial Times* reporter, in his excellent biography of the welfare state *The five giants*, suggests it was a 'bounce' by Blair (egged on by Alan Milburn, Health Secretary) on Brown.[4] With the NHS due to celebrate its 50th birthday, there had been hints from Milburn and Blair that the NHS would receive 'lots of money' in the government's second Comprehensive Spending Review. There was still a lingering embarrassment over the first three-year Comprehensive Spending Review, in which, at its launch in 1998, Gordon Brown had aggregated the increases in health spending over the three years to a grossly exaggerated £21 billion. It would have meant a 50 per cent increase in spending when the rise in real terms was only 5 per cent a year. It had initially been welcomed with awe by health managers ('beyond our wildest dreams', said their leader, Stephen Thornton[5]), but then with anger when the deception was exposed.

The negotiations on the second Comprehensive Spending Review had not been completed when Blair met Frost. No final decision had been made on health spending but it was a fait accompli by the end of the interview. A specific pledge had been made, not on a Downing Street sofa but publicly on a television studio sofa: a commitment to increase NHS spending to the European average. There was an initial flurry of questions about the precise words used by the Prime Minister. Both Number 10's health adviser, Robert Hill, and the Health Secretary's adviser, Simon Stevens, were at their desks to advise journalists on its implications. The Chancellor's aides were not. This all supports the deliberate 'bounce' interpretation and Timmins' contacts were impeccable. Another factor could have been Brown's 'bounce' on Blair on 17 December 1999, when he announced he was writing off all third world debt owed to the UK on the BBC's *Nine o'clock news*.[6]

A slightly alternative version

Clive Smee, the respected Chief Economist at the Department of Health, believes it could not have been that well planned in advance.[7] He was at home at midday when he received a call from Number 10 asking how much extra per year would be needed to reach the European average within five years. Fortunately for Downing Street, his eldest daughter's boyfriend had come to lunch with a compound interest function on his calculator that allowed them to make the complicated calculations needed for the press release that Number 10 was sending out. There were many to-and-fro conference calls with on duty Treasury officials asking if their boss was on board and Number 10 declaring it was now a public pledge. A furious Brown was reported to have barged into 10 Downing Street the next day accusing Blair of stealing his 'f...ing budget'.[8] But in his spring Budget, pre-empting his second Comprehensive Spending Review that was not due until July, Brown announced that NHS spending would rise on average by 6 per cent a year for five years in real terms – double the real terms average of the previous 20 years, providing over the five years from 1999 a cash increase of 50 per cent and a real terms rise of a third.

It can be persuasively argued that the health service got too much. It was education that was supposed to be Labour's top priority (Blair's pre-election mantra on priorities was 'education, education, education'), but health ended up with much more (see Chapter Two, this volume). A health service, which historically had learned to be lean, made serious mistakes in distributing its new riches (see below) while social housing, poor neighbourhoods and support for poor students in higher education could have made much better use of some of the funds.

Herceptin, the wonder drug

This is a tale of how media hype – and corporate public relations (PR) – helped a relatively obscure drug rise to become a cancer 'wonder drug' in just a few months, severely damaging one of Labour's most important innovations: NICE (the National Institute for Health and Clinical Excellence) which was set up to advise on what was and was not cost-effective spending. The story began in May 2005 at the American Society of Clinical Oncology conference in Florida. The annual meeting attracts the top scientists in the world in this field of medicine to come and hear the latest advances in the treatment of cancer. In 2005 oncologists learned that new tests using Herceptin on women who had just completed chemotherapy for early stages of breast cancer had reduced the risk of recurrence by 50 per cent in some cases. In the words of Professor Ian Smith, Head of the Breast Unit at the Royal Marsden Hospital and a lead investigator in the trial: 'This is the biggest treatment development in breast cancer, in terms of magnitude of its effect, for at least 25 years, perhaps as big as anything we've seen.'[9]

The drug was already being used for advanced breast cancer in the UK, but it had not even begun the dual process of approval for the early stage of the disease. This required a licence from the regulatory authority checking the safety of the drug and a cost-effectiveness assessment by NICE. Indeed, Roche, the manufacturer, had not even applied for a licence, but its PR firm went into overdrive to recruit women who would benefit from the drug. One of the first people to be approached was Lisa Jardine, Professor of Renaissance Studies at Queen Mary College, University of London, and a well-known television presenter.[10] She was recovering from early-stage breast cancer and was asked during a newspaper interview what she thought about Herceptin. She had replied that there ought to be a choice. But by the time she received the call from the PR firm, she had already decided she did not want the drug. Undaunted, the PR company wondered whether she would like to help promote the drug for which there would be a fee. Outraged by the offer, Jardine did go public, not to promote the drug but to expose the PR company's marketing strategy.

But it was not difficult for the company to find other women patients. Stirred by the widespread media coverage, women with early-stage breast cancer were taking to the streets to publicise their cause, turning to the courts for their right to obtain it, and travelling to 10 Downing Street with a petition signed by 35,000 people demanding the drug be approved. The patients and their lawyers knew how to feed the media with emotional material, referring to the 'death sentences' being imposed by NHS trusts that were refusing to fund the drug until approval had been given from the licensing authority and NICE. There was only one breast cancer story around in the summer of 2005: Herceptin.

Some 41,000 women were being diagnosed with early-stage breast cancer at the time. Herceptin only works for women who are HER2 positive, about one fifth of the group. About half of this group would have some form of heart or other problems which would rule them out from taking the drug. This left about 5,000 potential beneficiaries. The 50 per cent reduction in recurrences was not quite what most of the media and public thought it to be. What it meant was that 9.4 per cent of women on the drug found cancer returned compared to 17.2 per cent for women who were not taking it.

Pressure on the Health Secretary

As public pressure on Patricia Hewitt, Health Secretary, to do something continued through the summer and was still building in the autumn, she intervened. It was in November 2005 after the North Stoke Primary Care Trust (PCT) refused to fund the drug for Elaine Barber, a mother of four, that Hewitt caved in. She asked to see the evidence on which the decision was taken, and within a day the PCT had reversed it. She issued new guidance that PCTs should not refuse to prescribe solely on the grounds of cost. Other PCT chief executives complained (but with requests for no attributions) that North Stoke had been left with 'no option and has left all PCTs toothless if patients come forward in the future demanding the drug'.[11]

Early in 2006 the clinical director of NICE joined in the debate on costs in an article in the journal *Lancet Oncology*. The cost of treatment was reported to be £20,000 per patient. Re-analysing the trial data, the article revealed that 18 patients would have to be treated to save one life. It went on: 'For every 100 suitable patients prescribed tastuzumab (Herceptin), 94 will have been exposed to the side effects without any benefit, at a cost of £400,000 per recurrence prevented.'[12]

On Sunday, 5 February 2006, BBC *Panorama* examined whether 'the hype may have overtaken the hope' of Herceptin. It pointed to an Editorial in the respected *Lancet* medical journal that questioned how much was known about Herceptin. The journal raised concern about the limited data that existed. The trials had been stopped early, on the grounds that early results were so good that it had become unethical not to give the drug to women on the trial instead of giving them a placebo. *The Lancet* Editorial concluded: 'The best that can be said about Herceptin's efficacy and safety is that the available evidence is insufficient to make reliable judgments.'[13] The programme also noted that the survival data, which was normally collected over at least five years, showed no statistically significant improvement at the one-year stage. Professor Ian Smith, whose effusive appraisal was quoted earlier, had since conceded that, on the key question of survival, the proven benefit of the drug was currently only marginal.

Decisions of the courts

The next week in the lead case before the High Court, the lawyer of Ann Marie Rogers told the judges that his client had written out a statement, which in part explained 'with my prognosis, waiting for the cancer to return is like waiting on death row'. Her lawyer argued that it was wrong to deny a patient an effective drug. But this is what health managers and medics have to do every day. The case was lost in the High Court[14] but reversed by the Appeal Court nine weeks later.[15] Ironically, it was because Swindon PCT followed Hewitt's instructions that they should not refuse to permit prescribing solely on the grounds of cost, that Swindon lost its case. (Mrs Rogers continued to receive Herceptin but died on 5 March 2009.)

In the wake of the Appeal Court decision in April 2006, the licence for the drug and the NICE review of its cost-effectiveness was fast-tracked by June 2006. By then there had already been an

11-page article in *CancerWorld* declaring: 'Herceptin may turn out to be the biggest advance in treating breast cancer since Tamoxifen. But if we are to prevent soaring drug bills eating up our health budget or barring Europe's poor patients from the latest therapies, cancer professionals will have to wrest back the debate from the unfettered hype of the mass media.' [16]

Near the end of that same year, three doctors writing in the *British Medical Journal* (*BMJ*) complained that NICE had capitulated to 'high profile patients, media bias, industry support and political gaming' by approving its use. The article argued that the £1.7 million cost of treating 75 patients with Herceptin at the Norfolk and Norwich University Hospital would prevent 355 patients with other cancers being treated with cheaper alternatives. One of the doctors, Ann Barrett, said: 'We will be the ones to tell them that they are not getting a treatment that has been proved to be effective, which costs relatively little, because it is not the treatment of the moment'.[17]

Summing up

Media hype had helped push a Labour Health Secretary to seriously undermine one of Labour's most important innovations: NICE's rational approach to assessing new drugs. It had forced NICE itself to override its own rules. By its own statistics, spending £400,000 for preventing one recurrence of breast cancer was too high a price to pay. Once more, an intervention by the courts in social policy rationing decisions demonstrated they were unable to recognise that upholding one individual's rights could create far wider problems for many more people denied access. The more the courts – and the lawyers – are kept out of such decisions, the better.

There was one other loser in this saga: the reputation of medical charities. They are not as independent as they look. Drug companies in the UK are forbidden from promoting their products direct to patients, but they are not barred from giving grants to patient charities which can carry out their PR for them. Sarah Boseley, in her 2006 *Guardian* article 'The selling of a wonder drug', disclosed the close links between pharmaceutical companies and medical charities.[18] Just five out of 24 charities were not receiving funding from drug companies. It became even clearer two years later when the UK National Kidney Federation (NKF), an umbrella organisation of kidney patient groups, described NICE's decision to turn down four kidney cancer drugs as 'barbaric, damaging and unacceptable'. Jeremy Laurance, Health Correspondent of *The Independent*, disclosed that NKF was receiving half its £300,000 budget from pharmaceutical or kidney-related commercial companies.[19] NKF made no mention in its press releases of the excessive charges the companies were applying to the four drugs – some £3,363 for just one 30-capsule packet. Professor Sir Michael Rawlins, Head of NICE, in an *Observer* article,[20] estimated kidney cancer drugs could be made for one tenth of the current charge. As Laurance noted: 'The way in which NICE is pilloried by patient groups, while drug companies are ignored, suggests a reluctance to bite the hand that feeds them.'[21]

MMR, measles, mumps and rubella

The fears whipped up by the media – particularly the *Mail* – over the risks posed by the MMR vaccine for young children have been described at length in Tammy Boyce's *Health, risk, and news: The MMR vaccine and the media* and by my *Guardian* colleague Ben Goldacre in the last chapter of his book, *Bad science*.[22] But as it is one of the worst examples of over-hyped journalism – and the damage it can cause – it has to have an entry even if in truncated form. Any idea that the media does not change human behaviour is scotched by this case.

It all began when one maverick scientist, in a trial involving only 12 children, suggested during a press conference in 1998 that MMR jabs might cause autism and bowel disorder. The press conference had been called to coincide with the publication of a paper in *The Lancet* on this issue. Written by a team of doctors, the paper was cautious, noting the small number of children involved and emphasising that the study did not prove for certain that there was a link. But Andrew Wakefield, a gastroenterologist and the key figure in the saga, was far less ambivalent. He told the reporters present at the press conference that it was 'a moral issue' and he could no longer support the continued use of the three-in-one jab. He believed it would be safer to use single vaccines for the three diseases. This was clearly a story, given the widespread use of the MMR jab – over 400 million doses in 90 countries at that time with the unequivocal backing of WHO. *The Guardian* and *The Independent* ran it on their front pages, the *Mail* at that point buried it in the middle of the paper and *The Sun* ignored it.

The response in the UK was immediate. Government medical officers, senior scientists and public health doctors all defended the jab. Within a month the Medical Research Council had drawn together a panel of 37 experts to examine *The Lancet* paper and its arguments and found there was no evidence to indicate any such link to autism or bowel disorder.[23] And just one month later, in April 1998, a 14-year study by Finnish scientists involving three million children who had received the MMR vaccine found no such links.[24]

Undaunted, Wakefield joined forces with Professor John O'Leary, Director of Pathology at Coombe Women's Hospital in Dublin, and presented evidence to the US Congress in April 2000, reporting that tests on 25 children with autism revealed 24 had traces of the measles virus in their gut. O'Leary claimed this was 'compelling evidence' of a link between autism and MMR.[25] The Department of Health responded by saying the research did not show that the virus caused the autism and proved nothing.

Stories spiral

It was not until 2001 that the interchanges began to spiral. For the first three years MMR stories were running at about 150 a year in national newspapers, but that leaped to 750 in 2001 and over 1,250 in 2002.[26] The issue had become political. In the run-up to the 2001 election the Conservative Party had argued for widening choice by the provision of separate vaccinations for each of the three diseases. Public health doctors pointed out that this would require six separate injections – two visits for each disease – and make it much more likely that some would be missed, losing the protection that they would have provided. The Labour government insisted on sticking to the MMR strategy, but then towards the end of that year, Tony Blair came under pressure first from tabloid papers and then by a Conservative MP in the Commons to say whether his 18-month-old son had been given an MMR jab. He refused on the grounds it would invade his son's right to privacy but made it clear that he supported the strategy. *The Sun* reported in late December that Leo had not an MMR jab because it had been delayed by a mild cold;[27] *The Independent* reported he had received the jab in early February 2002,[28] which Downing Street refused to confirm but was finally verified in Cherie Blair's autobiography run in *The Times* in 2008.[29]

While all this was going on various new expert studies were being published which could find no evidence of a link between the vaccine and autism. One was published in the *BMJ* in February 2001;[30] another in September by the Institute of Child Health which examined all the studies published on MMR;[31] and a third in December 2001 by the Medical Research Council reviewing the research for the Department of Health.[32] All found no link. None of this deterred the *Mail* and *Telegraph* building Wakefield up as a heroic figure, a modern-day David taking on the Goliath of the British scientific establishment, the WHO, and sundry distinguished international medical bodies. JABS, an active support group for parents who believed the autism of their children had been caused by MMR, was at close hand to provide the British media with these live and emotional stories.

But all too slowly – thanks to the support he was getting from some parts of the media – the wheels turned against Wakefield. In February 2002, a team from the Royal Free Hospital, London – where Wakefield carried out his original research – published a study on the *BMJ* website saying there was no link between MMR and autism.[33] In 2003 *The Lancet* announced it should not have published Wakefield's paper, which was seriously flawed. In February 2004, Brian Deer, *The Sunday Times* investigative reporter, alleged Wakefield had a conflict of interest as he was also being paid by the Legal Aid Board to find out if the parents who claimed their children had been damaged by MMR had a case.[34] He was also alleged to have pursued unethical research practices, which triggered a General Medical Council (GMC) investigation. Both allegations were upheld in the GMC inquiry. And in 2005, Japanese researchers provided perhaps the strongest evidence that there was no link between MMR and autism. Japan had stopped the MMR jab in 1992 only to see the autism rates almost double by 1996.

Catastrophic fall in protection

For those who are sceptical about the media changing human behaviour, it is worth looking at the catastrophic fall in the use of the MMR vaccine. From a peak of 92.5 per cent of all children under two in 1995, the immunisation rate fell to 78.9 per cent in 2003 and to as low as 60 per cent in some parts of London. Herd immunity requires 95 per cent. By 2008 there were about three million people aged 18 months to 18 years who had missed being properly vaccinated. The warnings from public health doctors proved true. There was an increase in measles, from 56 cases in 1998 to 449 in the first five months of 2006.[35] Mumps moved from tiny numbers to become an epidemic, with 5,000 notifications in the first month of 2005.[36] Mumps and measles rose in 2006 at rates of 13 and 37 times as much respectively as 1998 levels.[37] And in 2008 measles for the first time since 1994 was declared endemic in the UK.[38]

The King's Fund, a think tank in London which carried out a study of the media coverage of health in 2003, was refused an interview with the editors of the *Mail* but found a *Mail* contact ready to defend the paper: 'It is not our job to promote group immunity. If some of our readers' kids might be affected as individuals – even if that is a remote chance – then we have to report it and will continue to do so'.[39] The *Mail* contact conceded that they ran scare stories, 'but if they have a certain basis in science, they make news ... of course in empirical [sic] terms we do go over the top from time to time – and there might be all sorts of reasons for that – but if people didn't like the paper's coverage they wouldn't buy it'.[40] The BBC did not emerge from this report with much glory either. Challenged by the authors on why they had followed up the anti-MMR stories in the *Mail*, Mark Popesco, Editor of BBC *Ten o'clock news*, said he was obliged to consider stories that widely read newspapers had initiated. MMR would continue across the media as long as the *Daily Mail* kept running the story. He added: 'Strictly on the level of risk, we probably over-reported MMR, but I am not just governed by that cold calculation. I am also governed by whether there is a public debate going on ...'.[41]

What makes it worse is that television can have much greater influence on people's attitudes than press reports. Watching a filmed interview with a mother and her autistic child in her home explaining how autism had emerged very shortly after the MMR jab has much more impact on a viewer than a scientist explaining to camera that there is no such link. Another study funded by the ESRC found most people wrongly believed that doctors and scientists were equally divided over the safety of MMR as both sides were getting a fair hearing on television news. Less than one quarter were aware that the overwhelming bulk of the evidence favoured the vaccine.[42] So much for the difficulties of balanced reporting.

The GMC inquiries that began in 2004 ended in May 2010 when Wakefield was struck off the medical register.[43] He was found guilty of multiple charges, which included acting 'dishonestly and irresponsibly' in conducting his research; carrying out invasive tests on vulnerable children against their best interests; and failing to disclose he had been paid to advise solicitors representing parents who believed their children had been harmed by MMR. (A libel case, which Wakefield started and then dropped against a Brian Deer television documentary, disclosed he had received over £400,000 from legal aid.) He was found to have brought 'the medical profession into disrepute' by behaviour that constituted 'multiple separate instances of serious professional misconduct'.[44] Wakefield was no longer living in the UK, having moved to the US in 2004, and set up a autism centre founded on his theories.

Ben Goldacre, in *Bad science*, believed the MMR scandal should not be laid at the door of a single man. He declared:

> The blame lies instead with the hundreds of journalists, columnists, editors, and executives who drove this story cynically, irrationally, and wilfully onto the front pages for nine solid years ... they extrapolated from one study into absurdity, while studiously ignoring all reassuring data, and all subsequent refutations. They quoted 'experts' as authorities instead of explaining the science, they ignored

the historical context, they set idiots to cover the facts, they pitched emotive stories from parents against bland academics (who they smeared), and most bizarrely of all, in some cases they simply made up stuff.[45]

While acknowledging all that, I should add that it was an investigative reporter, Brian Deer, who triggered the GMC investigations and there were other papers, *The Guardian* and *The Independent*, that questioned and refuted the Wakefield line.

Management

There is one group of workers that both the media and opposition parties dislike: bureaucrats. There are always too many of them, with calls for cuts concentrated on them. The Conservative Party particularly dislikes them. Both in opposition and in government. One of the proudest boasts of Andrew Lansley, the architect of the 2011 health plan, was of the thousands of bureaucrats who would be stripped out of the NHS. Some 24,000, if you believed the *Express* headline on 20 January 2011. Yet ironically the architect of the current system of NHS management was Margaret Thatcher. It was her most important contribution to improving the NHS.

It was designed by Sir Roy Griffiths, Managing Director of Sainsbury's, who Thatcher brought in to government in 1983 as a part-time adviser on NHS management, which was non-existent in those days. As he said in his short report to her: 'If Florence Nightingale were carrying her lamp through the corridors of the NHS today, she would almost certainly be searching for the people in charge.'[46] What he proposed required 14 different drafts of the implementing circular but eight months after delivering his proposals, managers replaced administrators, doctors were given budgets, targets were set and cost improvement programmes introduced.

Two decades on, in January 2004, Michael Howard, as the leader of the Conservative opposition, pledged to slash NHS management, which at the time was said to be 4 per cent of the overall cost. Even if the true figures were two-and-a-half times bigger, a 10 per cent saving on 10 per cent would only achieve a 1 per cent saving.

He would have done better, as we said in *The Guardian*, to look at the huge variation in the work rates of doctors. One study for the Department of Health by Alan Maynard, Health Economist at the University of York, across five surgical specialties found 80 per cent variations in work rates between the top and the bottom clinicians. The range in some specialties was even greater. The most active trauma and orthopaedic surgeons completed three times as many consultant episodes (1,500) as the least active (500).[47]

The Daily Telegraph was quick to spot one lacuna in the 2011 health plan. Under the headline, 'Seven in 10 health managers will just shift jobs after the shake up', it reported that the redundancies would not be as big as the *Express* had suggested.[48] An impact assessment attached to the plan noted that although 15,800 staff would be made redundant, between 50 and 70 per cent would be transferring to the new structures.[49] And many of the services contracted out would also need managers, but these would not, of course, be included in the NHS workforce surveys. A King's Fund report in April 2010 reported that there were 42,509 managers in the NHS, which employs 1,400,000 people. Management made up 3.6 per cent of the workforce, much smaller than most big organisations.[50]

Public health

A three-member team assembled by The King's Fund in 2000 set out to assess how the media covered health.[51] One of the members, Anna Coote, Director of Health Policy at The King's Fund and a former journalist, was already aware of the difficulties of engaging journalists in stories about improving health, preventing illnesses and reducing health inequalities. Another, Roger Harrabin, was on leave from the BBC, where he had been correspondent with the Radio 4 *Today* programme and founding presenter of *Costing the Earth*. They first interviewed health professionals and policy-makers, who complained about the undue prominence which relatively low risk health scares – such as SARS and MRSA – were being given in the media compared to the proven health risks of tobacco, alcohol and obesity. They also complained about too much focus on the NHS system, too little on the health of the nation.

The team then carried out a one-year study of three key BBC news programmes (BBC 1's *Ten o'clock news*, BBC 2's *Newsnight* and Radio 5 Live's 8am news) in the year up to September 2001, and three national newspapers (*The Daily Mirror*, *Daily Mail* and *The Guardian*) for 80 days. Intriguingly the newspapers appeared to provide a broader agenda than the BBC news programmes. The BBC was dominated by NHS-in-crisis stories, and ethical issues, followed by health scares. '"Serious proven risk stories" rarely made an appearance.' In the newspapers the biggest category of news stories was also the NHS, but there was a smaller proportion of health scares than the BBC, and a higher proportion of news on treatment and diseases along with 'proven health risks'.

There were large differences between the coverage of the three papers. The *Mail* carried 493 health stories, of which 72 involved some form of crisis – three times more than *The Mirror* and five times more than *The Guardian*. *The Mirror* ran 98 stories on alcohol, three times those of the other two. *The Guardian* had the broadest agenda, running 456 stories on health including 58 on mental health (compared to the *Mail*'s 13) and 47 on HIV/AIDS (compared to the *Mail*'s six). Interviews across a range of journalists provided two reasons for health prevention measures being under-reported. First, journalists liked to tell stories through the experience of individual victims – while preventive health concentrated on people avoiding becoming victims. And second, the three main health threats – tobacco, alcohol and obesity – were not new.

Tobacco and alcohol

But it was not just the media downplaying public health issues. So were ministers. There was the fiasco over the tobacco advertising ban.[52] It was promised in Labour's 1997 manifesto, widened to include sponsorship after the election, and then suddenly amended on the order of the Prime Minister to provide an exemption for Formula One racing events. The purported reason was that this would prompt Bernie Ecclestone, the owner of Formula One, to move abroad, losing 50,000 hi-tech jobs in the UK. What subsequently occurred following intense media scrutiny was that Ecclestone had given

Labour a £1 million donation in January 1997, the size of which both Ecclestone and Labour had not wanted divulged. It ended up with the donation having to be returned and the exemption lasting for only two years.

In July 2000, when Labour produced its 10-year plan for health, public health was demoted to Chapter 13. And yet, by the end of Labour's 13 years, not only was there a tobacco advertising and promotion ban in place, but three other reforms had been enacted: the first banning smoking in public places, a new regulation banning cigarette vending machines from September 2011 and a third reform requiring shops to keep cigarettes under the counter rather than on prominent display. The latter is being implemented, under a delayed timetable, by the 2010 Coalition government. The debate that this legislation generated helped widen the message that tobacco remains the single greatest cause of illness and premature death in Britain, killing some 86,000 a year. If The King's Fund trio had delayed their survey by a decade, they would have found a much improved scene. Smoking has fallen from almost one half of all adults in the 1970s to almost a fifth (21 per cent) today. It is, of course, much higher in deprived areas, but the new government is committed to reducing the overall rate to 18.5 per cent by 2015. A victory for medics, nurses and ASH (Action on Smoking and Health), the indefatigable pressure group for preventive medicine.

There is more mixed news on alcohol. Drinking in Britain has been falling for a decade, according to the Office for National Statistics. The average consumption of young men aged 16–24 has had a dramatic fall, from 26 units a week on average in 1999 to 15 units in 2009.[53] But this ignores the huge increase in people being treated for alcohol misuse, which has doubled in eight years – one of the largest rises for any medical condition. Medical campaigners are equally unhappy with the Coalition government's reluctance to make more use of pricing to curb consumption. There is also criticism of the government's 'voluntary approach' to the drink manufacturers and retailers. All but three of the health groups that initially joined the government's voluntary 'responsibility deal' project with the drinks industry walked away before its formal launch in 2011.

The industry's claim that the issue was only about a small minority of 'problem drinkers' was sounding increasingly hollow in light of reports such as the National End of Life Care Intelligence study showing a rising number of alcohol-related deaths of people in their 40s.

Belatedly, in March 2012, David Cameron announced that the Coalition would introduce legislation setting a minimum alcohol price of 40p per unit in England – enough to add £135 to the annual bill of a heavy drinker but not as high as medical colleges and health charities wanted. Even so it was billed by Downing Street as the biggest public health intervention since the Labour government's initiatives on tobacco set out above. Cameron also pledged to stop the sale of multi-buy discount deals in supermarkets. The strategy followed months of Whitehall in-fighting over the legality, effectiveness and politics of imposing a minimum price.[54]

Cameron, who intuitively would have been expected to oppose such an intervention, was persuaded by evidence from crime and health experts on the damaging social and medical impact of alcohol. Downing Street estimated that a 40p a unit minimum price would mean 50,000 fewer crimes each year and 9,000 fewer alcohol-related deaths over the next decade. The Prime Minister overruled the objections of Andrew Lansley, the Health Secretary, who consistently lined up with the industry against unit pricing. Lansley refused to accept the evidence of a Sheffield University study which found raising prices was an effective way of reducing drinking. The research showed that a 50p minimum unit price would cause consumption to fall by 5.7 per cent, or 7.8 per cent if combined with a promotion ban. It was Lansley's rejection of this evidence that led to the BMA, the Royal College of Physicians and the British Liver Trust walking away from the alcohol panel that was negotiating with the government and the drinks industry.

The Commons Select Committee on Health, chaired by Stephen Dorrell, a former Conservative health minister, was also unimpressed with Lansley's strategy on drink. Its report raised many questions, but as a *Guardian* Editorial noted, the 'real attack is reserved for the government's responsibility deal – less passing the buck than dropping it. The committee has joined major health organisations to dismiss the idea that Andrew Lansley's vaunted project is any substitute for government policy. Committee reports are rarely game-changing, but this one certainly puts another ice cube in the Health Secretary's drink.'[55]

In late November 2012, when the government's consultation documents had still not been published, the BMA and Royal College of General Practitioners wrote to *The Sunday Times* urging that the unit price should be set at 50p. They believe this could prevent 98,000 hospital admissions and 3,060 alcohol-related deaths a decade. Strong drink would be the hardest hit.[56] A two-litre bottle of Sainsbury's Basics Cider, which costs £1.18, would cost £8.40 at 40p a unit, and £10.50 at 50p. A bottle of Sainsbury's Basics Vodka, currently £6.41, would jump to £11.20 at 40p or to £14 at 50p. The drinks industry is almost united in opposition to the proposals, but three supermarkets – Asda, Morrisons and Sainsbury's – are in favour, with Tesco opposed.[57]

The government finally announced in late November 2012 that it would seek a minimum price of 45p per unit of alcohol and also wanted to introduce a ban on supermarket 'buy one, get one free' offers to curb binge drinking. A 10-week consultation period was set. The drinks industry was expected to challenge any implementation of such a price in the courts under EU competition laws.

Chronic care

Another way in which the media distorts reality is in its focus on acute hospital care, which only accounts for a small proportion of the one million people treated by the NHS every 36 hours. To their credit, the Department of Health and the NHS Confederation, the managers' organisation, did try to change the focus through private briefings. Unlike patients on the waiting list for elective surgery, chronic patients will never be cured, but with proper medical management they can live full and rewarding lives. They never receive much attention from most of the media – which prefers the glamour of acute patients, who can be cured rather than cared for – but they absorb by far the largest proportion of NHS resources. Their numbers run to 17.5 million people, ranging through angina (1.4 million), diabetes (1.5 million), asthma (3.4 million), arthritis (8.5 million), to mental health, the biggest category of all. Some people have more than one of these disabilities. They account for about 60 per cent of GP consultations and more than 60 per cent of hospital beds.[58]

Studies within the Department of Health suggest that 5 per cent of patients, all with chronic conditions, account for 42 per cent of hospital inpatient days. At the other end of the spectrum, 55 per cent of patients, nearly all elective surgery, account for only 10 per cent of overall inpatient days. Chronic disease does not just affect the old. Indeed, in aggregate numbers there are far more patients below the age of 65 – some 13 million including 1.5 million children. But it is old people, often with multiple conditions, who absorb beds, resources and staff time. One elderly woman was referred to her local accident and emergency department 51 times in one year. The good news, however, is that self-management is growing. Once patients achieve this, there are fewer demands on GPs, less spent on drugs and a stricter compliance with prescribed medicines. So why don't these community treatment programmes get more coverage? Niall Dickson, the former BBC Social Affairs Editor, explained why television prefers acute hospital care over community care: 'There is everything there for the viewer – people in white or coloured coats, some wearing stethoscopes and with high tech machines behind.'[59]

Treatment of elderly patients

Reports on the poor treatment of elderly people in hospital go back a long time. And there has been a succession of reports in the last dozen years: Department of Health (1998), Help the Aged (1999), the Royal College of Nursing (2008), Healthcare Commission in its annual reports on inspections (particularly 2009 and 2010), and the Health Service Ombudsman in 2011. The government chose older people to be the first patient group to have a National Service Framework, setting down the required standards of care in 2001. Ministers launched a Dignity in Care Campaign in 2006. And yet still complaints flood in. About one fifth of the 9,000 complaints the Ombudsman received in 2010 were about the care of older people.[60] She selected 10 cases to set out in more detail their harrowing experiences. These repeated similar experiences to earlier years, of patients being left in soiled or dirty clothes, and being given little or no help with food or water. But one case concerned the discharge of a confused 82-year-old woman, who, unsure of how to get home asked a nurse to call her daughter, only to be told 'that's not my job'.

Some changes, even for something as big as the NHS, can still happen surreptitiously. One of the biggest changes between 1988 and 1993 was the withdrawal of free NHS beds for long-term dependent patients. No one announced the change. There was no public debate. No new regulation or Act of Parliament, but a survey by *The Guardian* in 1993 found 43 per cent of long-stay beds in two of the 14 health regions had been closed in the previous five years. The Alzheimer's Society, which looked at 56 districts, found a 56 per cent reduction in three years in 1993. The 1996 JRF Inquiry into Continuing Care found it had accelerated, further breaking 'an implicit contract between the citizen and the state'.[61] Little of this gained much attention.

The media and older people

The media prefer children to older people. Here are two examples. First, compare two similar cases of abuse. Victoria Climbié, aged eight, died in 2000 from severe abuse, neglect and multiple injuries – including burns and scalds – inflicted by her great aunt who had brought her to England from Sierra Leone. Her death generated massive media coverage, including 303 news and features stories, 237 in national newspapers. One year later, Margaret Panting, aged 78, died from similar severe abuse, neglect and multiple injuries – burns and razor cuts – within five weeks of being moved from sheltered accommodation to the house of her son-in-law. Her death generated just five news stories, only two of them in the nationals.[62]

Second, in February 2006 senior ministers from three departments held a press conference to launch *Sure Start to Later Life*, a 120-page report from the Social Exclusion Unit documenting the inequalities older people suffered.[63] The government was proposing to launch a series of Sure Start schemes for older people on similar lines to the pre-school schemes for children.[64] There were some obvious parallels between the two groups. Both rely on multiple services, for individuals with diverse needs. Like the pre-school schemes, the Sure Start to Later Life projects were planned to be locally owned, responsive and economically effective. They could also go one better than Early Years and engage the clients, older people, in the design.

From all points of the older people's lobby, praise could be heard. Tribute was paid to the shift from crisis intervention to preventive care; the move beyond social services to creating new opportunities in education, leisure, housing; the promise to make more moves to reduce isolation, loneliness, ageism and poverty, which millions of older people suffer. There were eight journalists present at the launch but only one – myself – who got a decent slot in a national newspaper. So what prompted the yawns on the news desks? Older people are still not seen as interesting copy.

The media and social workers

The media are also not very fond of people who look after older people and children in need: social workers. Compare the media's excoriating coverage of social workers involved in child death inquiries with the absence of almost any coverage of deaths from medical mistakes. Social workers have to tread a perilous path along which on one side they will be damned for taking children away from families without good cause, and on the other for failing to take away children who were at serious risk of harm. The NSPCC used to estimate that there were between one and two child deaths each week from abuse or neglect in the home. Ofsted's annual report for 2007/08 covering its first full year of responsibility for protecting children estimated there were three deaths a week. All child deaths, where public services have been involved, require a serious child review. The more serious prompt public inquiries, and there have been 70 since the Children Act 1948.

Now consider the investigations into the injuries or deaths from mistakes by doctors known in the profession as 'adverse incidents', which get little media coverage. A working party for the Chief Medical Officer in 2000 suggested that there were 850,000 'adverse incidents' in the NHS in a year. That would be 1 in 10 of the 8,500,000 hospital admissions a year. The study suggested that in one third of the cases there was serious harm and in 8 per cent the error contributed to the patient's death. These proportions suggested 280,000 permanent or moderate injuries and 68,000 deaths.[65] A later study in 2003 by Sir Brian Jarman, medical member of the inquiry into the deaths of children undergoing heart surgery in Bristol, suggested a lower figure of 28,000 avoidable 'adverse incidents' deaths.[66]

It was the way in which there was so little known about these 'events' that led the Chief Medical Officer, Sir Liam Donaldson, to introduce a new procedure under which staff would be encouraged to put up their hand when they had made an error so that the organisation could learn from the mistakes.[67] This had been standard practice for air traffic controllers for some years. A new National Patient Safety Agency was set up to be at the heart of the new experiment. It was abolished in the cull of quangos that the new Coalition government of May 2010 introduced.

The 2012 Health and Social Care Act

On 12 July 2012 just 60 days after the Coalition government had been formed, Andrew Lansley, the new Health Secretary, published the government's White Paper on the NHS.[68] It was the fastest produced White Paper of any new government, much of it having been drafted by Lansley in the six years he had spent as Shadow Health Secretary in opposition. Within its 50 pages it repeated the mantra that David Cameron had used repeatedly to 'detoxify' his party's poor reputation on health: 'We will stop the top-down reorganisations of the NHS that have got in the way of patient care.' Yet, as a shocked nation discovered, the policy document contained a detailed top-down plan for the biggest reorganisation of the health service in its 63-year history.

The existing super-structure of 10 Strategic Health Authorities (SHAs) and 152 Primary Care Trusts (PCTs) was to be abolished. GPs would take over the commissioning of hospital and community health services overseen by a national commissioning board. A new economic regulator would promote patient choice that would drive competition and widen NHS care to more 'willing providers' from the private and voluntary sectors. Health and well-being boards would be set up to bring together GP commissioners with local councillors to promote greater integration of care. The Health Protection Agency would be absorbed into the Department of Health, with a chunk of its public health budget transferred to local authorities. And Health Secretaries would no longer be able to micro-manage the service, but instead concentrate on setting outcomes for the national commissioning board to achieve. This latter, long-needed, provision was aimed at ending the never-ending NHS restructuring – 20 reorganisations in the previous 38 years – to promote more stability.

As Nicholas Timmins set out in a comprehensive but succinct 145-page report on the 2012 Act, neither the media nor NHS workers should have been surprised by this content.[69] Much of it had been laid out by Lansley in a speech in 2005 to the NHS Confederation and reworked in more detail in a 2007 Conservative report that was cheekily labelled: 'White Paper on NHS autonomy and accountability, proposals for legislation'. Certainly it was no surprise at the

Department of Health, which in the run-up to the 2010 election was preparing policy papers for all eventualities. As one official said, the proposals were 'one of the most closely pre-advertised plans in history'.[70] The media might have been better informed if they had not by 2007 been slashing their specialist staff. Launching the report at their annual party conference, the Conservatives guaranteed it would be seen only by political reporters, who would not have been much interested in its content. That suited Tory election strategy, which was to be 'radical' on education but 'reassuring' on health. Cameron was concentrating on consolidating his 'detoxification' campaign, which by 2006 had for the first time for a decade in a Populus poll in *The Times* placed the Conservative leader ahead of Labour's on whether they 'believed in the principles of the NHS and want to improve it'.

There was little debate about the NHS in the 2010 election. The Conservatives had pledged to provide special protection of the NHS with their pledge to maintain a real-terms increase in funding. Labour realised that it could not outbid that pledge, although in reality the Tory increase turned out to be just 0.1 per cent. All three main parties recognised that there had to be cuts in the face of the 2008 financial meltdown and rising national debt. All three manifestos focused on cutting management costs and achieving efficiency savings. All three were ready to widen NHS services to private and voluntary providers. Labour promised an 'active role' for the independent sector. Patients requiring elective care would 'have a right in law to choose from any provider who meets NHS standards and quality at NHS costs'. The Conservatives pledged to give 'every patient the power to choose in health care providers that meet NHS standards within NHS prices'. The Lib Dem health spokesman, Norman Lamb, pledged that NHS patients 'should have the right to go private at NHS expense if the service failed to treat them on time.'

Lansley's poor use of media

Health hardly featured in the five-day talks that led up to the Coalition agreement. The next 10 days were spent producing a much more detailed 'programme for government'. Health was raised near to the end of this process when party differences became glaringly apparent: the Conservative emphasis on markets to raise efficiency; the Lib Dem priority of elected health boards along with a stronger local authority voice. The result was a bizarre plan to reform PCTs with a mix of part-elected and part-appointed members. As one Liberal Democrat described it, 'a half horse/half donkey' policy.[71] This plan was dropped when it subsequently became clear that with the commissioning of hospital and community services being transferred to GPs together with the transfer of public health duties from PCTs to local councils there was nothing left for PCTs to do. Timmins discovered that there was a paragraph in the first civil service draft of the White Paper that noted how the proposals were a continuation of Labour policies: competition and choice; a focus on outcomes; practice-based commissioning; getting all hospitals to foundation trust status; making more use of the private and voluntary sectors. But this was deleted by Lansley.[72]

This was a major tactical error by Lansley, as was his refusal to seek to achieve his reforms through administrative change, as his civil servants offered, rather than legislation, as he belatedly conceded would have been possible. Both moves, as Timmins notes, would have removed the full-throated legislative battles from the front pages, which so wrecked Conservative poll ratings.[73] Given the technical details of the changes, they would have been lucky to make even an inside page. News editors believe public service restructuring is a boring issue which will not interest readers. No wonder at least one aide in Downing Street wanted Lansley shot.[74] Instead, most of the coverage was left in the hands of political reporters, not health specialists, and inevitably became more black and white: Coalition in favour of more private providers in the NHS; Labour opposed. This, of course, ignored the manifesto pledges above, and the fact that Labour remained split on the use of the private sector: with Blairite ministers such as Alan Milburn in favour, while a successor, Andy Burnham who served as Health Secretary under Gordon Brown, opposed.

A second way the media distorted the picture was the degree of coverage concentrated on the long drawn-out parliamentary battle, thus obscuring the more immediate problem facing the NHS of achieving £20 billion of efficiency savings over four years. This was needed to meet the rising demand generated by demography along with new and rising drug and equipment prices. What was required was a 4 per cent efficiency saving every year for four consecutive years – a challenge which no health service in the developed world had ever achieved. It was, of course, madness to engage in such a massive restructuring exercise while at the same time pursuing the biggest ever efficiency savings operation. The first exercise has been calculated to cost up to £3 billion, which does not include the huge diversion of management time. True, the first exercise also involved a 45 per cent cut to NHS managers – some 30,000 employees – but as new layers upon new layers of boards emerged as the Health and Social Care Bill progressed, many of these redundant people were needed to man the new boards.

The Bill was published on 19 January 2011 with 22 schedules, 280 clauses and some 550 pages – three times the size of the Bill that set up the NHS in 1948. The Bill took eight months to pass through the Commons and a further six-and-a-half months in the Lords. It generated 1,000 amendments – many of them simple name changes but some much more substantial – that led to 100 divisions and the longest committee stage for a decade. Rarely can a Bill have received such widespread criticism from all sides. Just to take Conservative criticism: Lord Tebbit, former Thatcher minister and a hero figure of Lansley's, spoke out against the Bill's unfair playing field, with private hospitals not being required to pay for the training costs of doctors;[75] Stephen Dorrell, former Conservative Health Secretary, was opposed to absolving his successors from accountability for what happens in the service;[76] the Commons Health Committee, which Dorrell chaired, was concerned about the lack of accountability of GP commissioning bodies; and most surprising of all, Reform, the pro-market pressure group, expressed doubt over whether GPs would have the necessary skills.[77]

Within the medical world, the BMA and the Royal College of Nursing called for the Bill to be withdrawn in January 2012, while the Academy of 20 medical Royal Colleges came within one College of agreeing to declare their inability to support the Bill in its current form. Partly through the use of social media, a succession of emergency meetings of other medical groups – radiologists, public health doctors and physiotherapists – called for the Bill to be withdrawn. And in an unprecedented move three key health journals – the *BMJ*, the *Health Service Journal* and *Nursing Times* – ran a joint Editorial condemning the Bill as 'an unholy mess'. There was an eight-week hiatus in the Commons, when Downing Street set up four working groups, from which the private sector was barred, to examine possible compromises given the breadth and depth of the opposition. Working under the umbrella of Future Forum, several of their proposals were accepted, including: requiring a change in the brief of the role of Monitor (the regulator) from promoting competition to being a watchdog on anti-competitive practices; and the relabelling of GP consortia as clinical commissioning groups, no longer comprised solely of GPs but still GP-led with a hospital doctor, nurse and possibly others to widen their perspective. The Lords should have been more daunting, given the specialist knowledge among members of the House, but unlike Lansley, the Health Minister there, Earl Howe, was a gifted communicator and ready listener. Shirley Williams worked tirelessly in the Lords, making the Liberal Democrat leadership more assertive in changing the more egregious clauses, holding over 60 meetings with health experts on questionable proposals before submitting a raft of key amendments.

Uncertainty remains

Yet for all the 20 months of debate, key parts of the Bill remain unclear to both the public and health service workers. Take Monitor, which has been landed with multiple responsibilities – a duty to promote integration, create a level playing field, identify failing hospitals – but there is still no consensus on their duty with respect to competition. Liberal Democrats believe it is no longer to promote competition; Labour believes it is still a primary purpose. The issue is made more complex by European law, but fatally the Act allows hospitals to seek to raise private income – so long as it does not disadvantage NHS patients – up to 49 per cent of their budgets. That includes income from shops in hospitals foyers, and from overseas earnings as well as private patients in the UK. For most hospitals, whose private earnings are as low as 3 per cent, this will have little effect. But for the more famous, world-leading institutions – such as the Royal Marsden cancer hospital and Great Ormond Street children's hospital for which some say it was defined – this has created a red flag around which opponents of any competition can rally. Ironically, privately raised income at the Marsden only accounts for 24 per cent of its budget. The two should have been given an exemption and a much lower level set.

What will be the result? The main changes do not begin until April 2013. There will be much partisan point scoring until then. Andy Burnham, Labour's Shadow Health Secretary, declared in October 2012 that contracts for almost 400 NHS services – worth a quarter of a billion pounds – were signed resulting in the 'biggest act of privatisation ever seen in the NHS'. Sounds a lot, but in a service with a £100 billion budget that amounts to just 0.25 per cent of the budget.[78] Sir David Nicholson, the Chief Executive of the NHS, who will chair the new national commissioning board, was publicly blunt about the restructuring from the beginning, telling the NHS managers that 70 per cent of big change programmes 'don't work: they fail – a real possibility in these circumstances'.[79] He was later to say someone had said 'it is the only change management system you can see actually from space – it is so large'.[80]

What went wrong? First, Lansley was allowed to work it all out by himself without any oversight. Worse still there were no health specialists within Downing Street. Cameron foolishly disbanded the Number 10 Policy Unit, the Cabinet Office's Strategy Unit and the Prime Minister's Delivery Unit. As one Health Department official told Timmins, 'by the time they [the centre of government] woke up to what was happening, it had gone too far'. Lansley's poor communication skills were another factor, including his inability to express clearly what he thought was wrong with the NHS and why what he was doing would make it better. Then, unlike Labour and its major NHS plan in 2000, he failed to even try to corral the key players behind it before publication. None were signed up when it was sprung on them. Ironically, when the 'programme for government' was unveiled in May 2010, Cameron and Clegg made special mention of the NHS changes, hailing them as 'a united vision for the NHS that is truly radical'. A wiser head in the Health Department told Timmins that it was 'a disaster' – 'almost impossible to conceive a worse piece of policy making, really'. Currently it looks as though history will probably show the health official right and the political antennae of Cameron and Clegg abjectly awry.

Social care

A survey released by the Association of Directors of Adult Social Services in April 2011 reported that only 22 out of 148 local authorities were now ready to provide social care to people with moderate needs, such as help with making meals or having a bath.[81] Some 50 councils were now restricting care to those with 'substantial needs' and six to 'critical needs' only. I chaired a JRF inquiry into the help which older people were receiving in their homes in 2005/06.[82] We discovered the number of hours of help had doubled over the previous three decades, but the number of people helped had fallen by 60 per cent. What began as a low-level home help support service to carry out minor tasks had become a high dependency service to keep seriously disabled or ill people out of residential care. While this was an admirable goal, we concluded that a little bit more help upstream could help delay some of the high dependency help needed downstream.

Like the NHS, social care involves more than a million workers. Unlike the NHS, the social care budget did not double in seven years. Unlike the NHS, two thirds of the social care workforce is in the voluntary or private sector. And unlike the NHS, the 1.3 million employees in social care are mostly unqualified and distributed across 26,000 employers. Yet the two systems are umbilically linked. Many of the people in the NHS's biggest client group – the 17 million suffering from a chronic disease – also have social care needs. But the current system of care is riddled with outrageous anomalies: unequal charges, unacceptable variations in standards and indefensible different approaches to different diseases (free care for cancer and coronary patients but means-tested care for those with Alzheimer's and Parkinson's). There has been a Royal Commission report (1999), a national commission (Wanless Report for The King's Fund, 2006), a 2006 JRF report on *Paying for long term care*, Green and White Papers, pilots and partnerships, some integration between health and social services, but still no agreement on how it should be funded. 'Now is the time for bold reform,' declared Labour's White Paper on 30 March 2010.[83] And what did that reform consist of? 'At the start of the next parliament we will establish a commission to help reach a consensus.' So that is what the new government did, and the well-known economist Andrew Dilnot, its chair, reported in July 2011. Dilnot, a former director of the Institute for Fiscal Studies, produced a clever rebalancing of financial responsibility for funding long-term care for the frail elderly and disabled, currently numbering one million. He lifted the current limit of £23,250 for assets a person may hold before being barred from state help to £100,000. People would still be liable for the costs of accommodation and food in a care home, but this would be limited to £10,000 a year. On top of that he proposed a cap of £35,000 on the amount any individual should have to pay towards their lifetime care costs.[84]

The package would add an additional £1.7 billion to government spending, rising to £3.6 billion in 2025. But Dilnot noted that this was the equivalent of a mere 0.25 per cent of public spending. He described it as 'a price well worth paying' to take away people's fear of having to sell their homes and spend all their wealth on care. It should reduce the number of such cases, estimated to number 20,000 in 2010. The government's reaction was cautious, promising further consultation. It welcomed the report but noted that the new costs would need to be considered against other financial priorities and calls on constrained resources. A White Paper previously promised for the end of the year was put back until spring 2012. To his credit, Ed Miliband offered cross-party talks to explore whether a consensus could be achieved. This was a generous act given the Tories had disgracefully sunk a belated Labour plan that had been gathering cross-party support — the introduction of compulsory contributions to finance a national long-term care service – by falsely dubbing it 'a death tax' just before the 2010 general election.

Dilnot's plan was widely welcomed by many charities and welfare groups, but Stephen Burke, Chief Executive of United for All Ages, noted that the proposals were regressive because richer families would benefit disproportionately. Just how vulnerable the present system is was dramatically demonstrated one week after publication of the

Commission's report. Southern Cross, the UK's largest operator of care homes, threw in the towel. Southern Cross, which at an earlier stage had sold its homes and then rented them back, found it was unable to meet the rent levels. It suspended its shares – down from 600p in 2007 to just 6p in 2011 – on 11 July 2011, declaring it would be wound up in the next few months.[85] This left 31,000 residents and 44,000 employees facing an uncertain future. Southern Cross's 750 homes were spread across 80 landlords. An estimated 130 homes were thought not to be commercially viable. As Patrick Butler wrote in *The Guardian's* Society section, the last rites of this toxic symbol of all that can go wrong once profit usurps social mission coincided with the Prime Minister's launch of a White Paper on public service reforms promoting new ways in which the private sector can engage.[86]

For the next 12 months, ministers sucked their thumbs while charities, policy-makers and pressure groups continued to press for some clarity. Finally in July 2012 Andrew Lansley declared that Dilnot would be shelved because its £2 billion cost had been declared unaffordable by the Treasury. But, just one month after that bombshell, the front pages ran with a more positive U-turn from Cameron: 'PM pledges to end heartbreak of elderly forced to sell homes: A £35,000 cap on care bills', proclaimed the *Daily Mail*. It reported that Cameron 'has had a dramatic change of heart and is determined to press ahead with the plans'. It went on to say Cameron and Clegg would use the Government's Care and Support Bill to ensure that the reform was introduced by 2017. The paper added: 'It means the Conservatives and the Lib Dems can turn round in 2015 (election year) and say – we sorted out social care ... that's a pretty big achievement and would appeal to both sets of voters ... such a move would make it more difficult for Labour to object since they have also called for a deal'.[87]

The front page of *The Independent* also ran with the same story: 'Affordable old age: U-turn on money for the elderly'. It noted that the plans had yet to be formally signed off, but suggested they would closely follow Dilnot's proposals. The Cabinet had been informed just before Parliament went into summer recess. A Number 10 spokesman told the paper: 'I wouldn't deny the Prime Minister wants to secure the big future of social care. It's one of the big, long-term issues that the Coalition wants to solve. We want to do it and get it right.'[88] Its Editorial added that the July move to shelve the reform 'was a catastrophic failure of leadership ... that was rightly attacked by charities for the elderly as a betrayal of Britain's older people'.[89] The Prime Minister, it concluded, had been right to overrule Lansley and reverse his decision. Jeremy Hunt, appointed Health Secretary in September 2012, expressed his support for the Dilnot plan, but there was still no timetable for it or commitment to the £35,000 cap at the close of 2012. Specialists feared the reform could still face serious delays.[90]

Notes

[1] D. Wanless (2002) *Securing our future health: Taking a long-term view*, Wanless Report to the Treasury, March; published alongside Anna Dixon and Elias Mossialos (eds) (2002) *Health care systems in eight countries: Trends and challenges*, London: European Observatory.

[2] *New Statesman*, 12 January 2000.

[3] Personal interview.

[4] Nicholas Timmins (2001) *The five giants: A biography of the welfare state*, London: HarperCollins, p 595.

[5] Personal interview.

[6] Alastair Campbell (2011) *The Alastair Campbell diaries, Volume 3*, London: Hutchinson, trailed in *The Guardian*, 4 July 2011.

[7] Personal interview.

[8] Andrew Rawnsley (2000) *Servants of the people: The inside story of New Labour*, London: Hamish Hamilton, p 338.

[9] John Thynne (2006) 'Is Herceptin a "wonder drug"?', BBC News, 3 February (http://news.bbc.co.uk/1/hi/programmes/panorama/4678430. stm).

[10] Sarah Boseley (2006) 'The selling of a wonder drug', *The Guardian*, 29 March.

[11] Nick Triggle (2005) 'Hewitt "has left NHS toothless"', BBC News, 10 November (http://news.bbc.co.uk/1/hi/health/4422662.stm).

[12] John Thynne (2006) 'Is Herceptin a "wonder drug"?', BBC News, 3 February (http://news.bbc.co.uk/1/hi/programmes/panorama/4678430. stm).

[13] *Lancet* (2005) 'Herceptin and early breast cancer: a moment for caution', vol 366, 12 November.

[14] BBC News (2006) 'Drug refusal a death sentence', 6 February (http://news.bbc.co.uk/1/hi/health/4677086.stm).

[15] BBC News (2006) 'Woman wins Herceptin court fight', 12 April (http://news.bbc.co.uk/1/hi/health/4902150.stm).

[16] *Cancer World* (2006) 'Beyond the Herceptin hype', March/April, pp 14-24.

[17] A. Barrett, T. Roques, M. Small and R.D. Smith (2006) 'Rationing: how much will Herceptin really cost', *BMJ*, vol 333, 23 November.

[18] Sarah Boseley (2006) 'The selling of a wonder drug', *The Guardian*, 29 March.

[19] Jeremy Laurance (2008) 'Are patient protests being manipulated?', *The Independent*, 1 October.

[20] Gaby Hinsliff (2008) 'Health chief attacks drug giants over huge profits', *The Observer*, 17 August.

[21] Jeremy Laurance (2008) 'Are patient protests being manipulated?', *The Independent*, 1 October.

[22] Tammy Boyce (2007) *Health, risk and news: The MMR vaccine and the media*, Oxford: Peter Lang Publishing; Ben Goldacre (2008) *Bad science*, London: Fourth Estate.

[23] 'MMR research timeline', BBC website, 27 June 2006.

[24] Ibid.

[25] Ibid.

[26] See the chart in Ben Goldacre (2008) *Bad science*, London: Fourth Estate, p 289.

[27] *The Sun*, 24 December 2001.

[28] *The Independent*, 2 February 2002.

[29] *The Times*, 12 May 2008.

[30] 'MMR research timeline', BBC website, 27 June 2006.

[31] Ibid.

[32] Ibid.

[33] Ibid.

[34] Brian Deer (2004) 'Revealed: MMR research scandal', *The Sunday Times*, 22 February.

[35] P. Asaria and E. MacMahon (2006) 'Measles in the United Kingdom: can we eradicate it by 2010?', *BMJ*, vol 333, 26 October.

[36] R.K. Gupta, J. Best and E. MacMahon (2005) 'Mumps and the UK epidemic', *BMJ*, vol 330, 12 May.

[37] Health Protection Agency, 22 April 2007.

[38] Eurosurveillance 13/European Centre for Disease Prevention and Control.

[39] R. Harrabin, A. Coote and J. Allen (2003) *Health in the news: Risk, reporting and media influence*, London: The King's Fund.

[40] Ibid.

[41] Ibid.

[42] *BMJ* (2002) 'Media misled the public over the MMR vaccine', 24 May.

[43] Nick Triggle (2010) 'MMR doctor struck from register', BBC News, 24 May (http://news.bbc.co.uk/1/hi/8695267.stm).

[44] Ibid.

[45] Ben Goldacre (2008) *Bad science*, London: Fourth Estate, p 274.

[46] Nicholas Timmins (2001) *The five giants: A biography of the welfare state*, London: HarperCollins, p 407.

[47] Malcolm Dean (2004) *Guardian Society*, 21 January.

[48] M. Beckford (2011) *The Daily Telegraph*, 20 January, p 14.

[49] Ibid.

[50] The King's Fund (2010) *How many managers are there in the NHS?*, London: The King's Fund, 16 April.

[51] R. Harrabin, A. Coote and J. Allen (2003) *Health in the news: Risk, reporting and media influence*, London: The King's Fund.

[52] Andrew Rawnsley (2000) *Servants of the people: The inside story of New Labour*, London: Hamish Hamilton, Chapter Six.

[53] James Morgan (2011) 'Why is alcohol consumption falling?', BBC News, 15 February (www.bbc.co.uk/news/magazine-12397254).

[54] Patrick Wintour (2012) 'Coalition to set minimum alcohol price', *The Guardian*, 23 March.

[55] *Guardian* (2012) Editorial, 'Alcohol abuse: Dry matter', 19 July.

[56] Sarah-Kate Templeton (2012) 'Doctors seek huge rise in price of drinks', *The Sunday Times*, 18 November.

[57] Simon Goodley (2012) 'Drinks industry refuses to swallow government line on alcohol pricing', *The Observer*, 4 November.

[58] Malcolm Dean (2004) 'Progress by pre-emption illness', *The Guardian*, 21 April.

[59] Personal interview.

[60] 'Care and compassion', BBC and national media websites, 15 February 2011.

[61] JRF (Joseph Rowntree Foundation) (1996) *Meeting the costs of continuing care*, Findings 36, York: JRF.

[62] Paul Cann and Malcolm Dean (eds) (2009) *Unequal ageing: The untold story of exclusion in old age*, Bristol: The Policy Press, pp 10-11.

[63] Social Exclusion Unit (2006) *Sure Start to later life*, London: Cabinet Office.

[64] Malcolm Dean (2006) 'New approach to an age old problem', *The Guardian*, 8 February.

[65] *The Guardian* (2001) Editorial: 'Medical massacre: admitting error', 5 March.

[66] Malcolm Dean (2004) 'Adverse events', *Guardian Society*, 18 February.

[67] Malcolm Dean (2002) 'Organisations with memories', *The Guardian*, 5 June.

[68] Department of Health (2010) *Equity and excellence: Liberating the NHS*, White Paper, www.dh.gov.uk/prod_consum_dh/groups/dh_digitalassets/@dh/@en/@ps/documents/digitalasset/dh_117794.pdf.

[69] Nicholas Timmins (2012) *Never again? The story of the Health and Social Care Act 2012*, London: The King's Fund/Institute for Government.

[70] Ibid, p 22.

[71] Ibid, p 47.

[72] Ibid, p 64.

[73] Ibid.

[74] Ibid, p 111.

[75] Ibid, p 95.

[76] Ibid, p 70.

[77] Ibid, p 68.

[78] Randeep Ramesh (2012) 'Labour raises alarm on "biggest act of privatisation" in NHS history', *The Guardian*, 4 October.

[79] Sir David Nicholson (2010) Speech to the NHS Confederation, 25 June.

[80] Nicholas Timmins (2012) *Never again? The story of the Health and Social Care Act 2012*, London: The King's Fund/Institute for Government, p 74.

[81] 'Councils cut back free adult social care', BBC website, 16 April 2011 (www.bbc.co.uk/news/uk-13102559).

[82] JRF (Joseph Rowntree Foundation) (2006) *The Older People's Inquiry into 'That little bit of help'*, York: JRF.

[83] HM Government (2010) *Building the National Care Service*, London: The Stationery Office.

[84] Commission on Funding of Care and Support (2011) *Fairer Care Funding*, Final report of the Commission on Funding of Care and Support, July, London: Department of Health.

[85] Simon Mundy (2011) 'Southern Cross admits defeat', *Financial Times*, 12 July.

[86] Patrick Butler (2011) 'The reform agenda is fast losing allies', *Guardian Society*, 13 July.

[87] Tim Shipman (2012) 'A £35,000 cap on care bills', *The Daily Mail*, 16 August.

[88] Oliver Wright (2012) 'Affordable old age: U-turn on money for elderly', *The Independent*, 16 August.

[89] *The Independent* (2012) Editorial, 'Time to cap the costs of care for the elderly', 16 August.

[90] 'Viewpoints: care for the elderly', BBC website, 26 October 2012.

NINE

The disappearance of the housing correspondent

Housing is a good example of how governments can still dictate the media's agenda. Almost five years into the New Labour administration a much-quoted JRF study in March 2002 produced an astounding statistic: the completion rate of public and private housing had reached its lowest level (outside the Second World War) since 1924.[1] It went on to set out a catalogue of grim facts: the gap between demand and supply was widening by as much as 56,000 a year; while London and the South accounted for 70 per cent of rising demand, only 50 per cent of new homes were being built there; and unless the current rate of building dramatically increased, there would be a shortfall of a million homes by 2022.

One reason why the statistics were such a shock was that there were no longer full-time housing correspondents in Fleet Street. As housing fell further and further down successive government agendas, so the media lost interest in reporting what was happening. Four decades ago, when there were fewer specialist posts, housing was a prized post for an ambitious journalist. Yet almost two decades ago there were none left in the main newsrooms of the national press or the BBC. It was left to city and personal finance journalists to report on the growing wealth of its home-owning readers. Social housing dropped out of sight despite the millions living there and the huge changes taking place. A whole host of stories were being ignored: the growth of suburbs and their new self-sufficiency in terms of jobs as well as houses; the rise of housing associations and the fall of council housing; the stock transfers from councils to housing associations which the House of Commons Public Accounts Committee reported were bad value for taxpayers; and the emergence of a virulent anti-housing lobby led by the Campaign to Protect Rural England.

Instead, what monopolised coverage were the regular releases of house price rises by Halifax or Nationwide as the media helped push what became Labour government policy in 2004, the politics of aspiration, set out further below. The higher the rise in prices, the better it was reported to be. A doubling of house prices in five years and a near tripling in just over 10 years in some parts of London before the 2008 recession was regarded as a bonus for all. The problem which first-time buyers were facing received far less attention, and the lessons of the property crash just a decade earlier were totally ignored. Yet still living in the country were two million households who had learned from bitter experience about the capricious character of housing investment in the early 1990s. By 1995 one million house buyers were still suffering from negative equity (holding a mortgage which exceeded the value of their home), 250,000 were at least six months in arrears with their payments and 300,000 had suffered an even worse fate: their homes repossessed.

At the other end of the housing spectrum, run-down housing estates and homelessness were ignored by most papers. In April 2004, Shelter launched what it billed as the largest campaign in the homeless charity's 40-year history.[2] It had been carefully prepared, based on studies commissioned from Alan Holmans, former chief housing adviser to several governments. It was presented in a media-friendly 18-page document with graphic pictures and dramatic sound bites. Astutely, the focus was on children, the one million living in unfit homes to the detriment of their health, education and life prospects. There was early notice of the launch, an appropriate launch pad, the Institute of Child Health, and yet at the London press conference – a second one was in Glasgow – there were no national reporters present. The next day there were 800 words in *The Guardian*, 600 in *The Daily Telegraph*, just 50 in *The Times*, nothing in *The Independent*, a short piece in the *Daily Express*, with only *The Mirror* giving it real space: a two-page spread. One paper that had worked with Shelter to prepare a large spread pulled it for a lifestyle story on how to recognise upcoming districts.

The campaign was initiated by the pressure group's director, Adam Sampson, who took over from Chris Holmes, a director whose long-term service in the field had given him easy access to all the key corridors. Sampson, who came from the Prison Reform Trust (PRT), soon concluded that the dire state of housing investment required a return to the proactive campaigning tactics that put Shelter on the map under Des Wilson in the 1960s. What went wrong? One reason was the political climate. Poll surveys were suggesting that the public was totally disillusioned with politics and political campaigns. Wilson was lucky. He too was operating when there was widespread dissatisfaction with a Labour government, but was able to divert large numbers of young disillusioned people away from mainstream politics into a single issue campaign. Bad housing was a news story in the 1960s, but not in 2004. Unlike the 1960s, there were no housing correspondents to put pressure on news desks to run with it. Thatcher's children were not thirsting for a cause.

Shelter had timed its report to influence Gordon Brown's Comprehensive Spending Review, due in July 2004, which would set departmental budgets for three years. It did not work. Labour's housing investment in its first eight years was, in real terms, below the levels of the early 1990s, less than half the levels of the 1970s and a third of the level of the 1960s.[3] The Treasury already had its own review – the Barker Report[4] – that called for large increases in house building, but Holmans' report to Shelter said this would still fall short of what was needed. For a media more interested in politics than policy, this was too esoteric. Kate Barker's report, which did get reasonable coverage because of her respected name in economic circles, was wide-ranging. It called for an extra 120,000 public and private homes per annum – on top of the current 140,000 – to meet demand and to curb prices. It was roughly what Gordon Brown called for when he became prime minister in 2007. But Barker went much wider than just numbers. She condemned under-skilled builders for taking twice as long as Danish constructors, Byzantine planning procedures and the squeeze on social housing as key structural problems that had driven up house prices twice as fast as the European average.

Analysing the problem

No one could accuse Labour of failing to analyse the problem. Amid a welter of documents two stood out: the Barker Report and an earlier report produced by the government's Social Exclusion Unit (SEU) within 16 months of the 1997 election.[5] The SEU report examined the plight of the four million people living in the nation's 3,000 worst housing estates. Eight different national programmes to rehabilitate Britain's most disadvantaged urban areas had been launched in the previous 30 years. Yet deprivation was worse, social disadvantage more concentrated and the gap between these communities and the comfortable majority even wider. This deepening inequality had multiple dimensions – housing, health, education, crime, employment, income, anti-social behaviour and quality of public services. The report led to the setting up of 18 Policy Action Teams, which in turn led to the National Strategy for Neighbourhood Renewal in 2000, covering the 88 most deprived local authority districts in England. Among its multiple projects were the New Deal for Communities with a £50 million regeneration programme in each of 39 areas of around 4,000 homes and then Sure Start, which began with a budget for 500 pre-school centres for children and parents living in 500 poor districts, but eventually grew to 3,500.

Conservative and Liberal Democrat spokespeople, concerned by the amount of redistribution needed to reduce poverty, frequently accuse Labour of a one club approach to attacking poverty – redistributing money through benefits and tax credits. This could not be more false. Sceptics should look at the two volumes produced by a team of 16 academics at the LSE who scrutinised Labour's multi-dimensional anti-poverty programmes in Blair's 10 years of administration.[6] The conclusion on the New Deal for Communities, one of several different neighbourhood renewal projects, was positive:

> Progress in services was significant, beyond the general service gains under New Labour. Resident satisfaction with areas as places to live rose significantly and the gap in satisfaction between the targeted areas and the average closed. The gains in the New Deal for Communities areas were significantly higher than control areas or the national average. Nonetheless, although the gap closed by 11 percentage points between 2002 and 2006, the New Deal areas were still 16 percentage points behind the average in 2006.[7]

In pursuit of aspiration

The politics of aspiration was put back on Labour's agenda in the run-up to the 2005 election. Alan Milburn, the ex-Labour minister charged with coordinating the party's manifesto, was unequivocal, even borrowing a Conservative slogan: 'As we advance towards the next election, our task is to rebuild the New Labour coalition around "one nation politics" that recognises that, while life is hard for many, all should have the chance to succeed'.[8] He suggested that widening ownership of assets, most important of all housing, could make 'the biggest contribution' to boosting social mobility and reducing poverty. Changes in the housing market were opening up the widest gulf: the child of London home-owning parents stood to inherit, on average, £250,000; the classmate in a rented social home would inherit nothing.

The proportion of people owning their own homes was one of the biggest social revolutions of the 20th century – up from 10 per cent at the start to 70 per cent at the end. But in a league table of 19 nations by the OECD, seven nations had higher proportions than the UK: Spain, Greece and Italy all had over 80 per cent and Hungary had 92 per cent. The fact that Eastern European communist states had higher proportions of owner-occupiers always used to incense Margaret Thatcher. But several prosperous social democratic states had less than the UK: not just Scandinavia and the Netherlands, but France (55 per cent) and Germany (42 per cent) too. It was not quite as simple as Milburn made out. One third of children living below the poverty line were in owner-occupied housing; half of all adults in poverty were also there; and two thirds of homes not coming up to 'decent housing standards' were owned by people without the resources to improve them.

The queen of aspiration

Milburn was, in fact, 'playing catch up'. As noted earlier in Chapter Two, Margaret Thatcher got there first with her council house sales policy. Council house sales to tenants began under the Conservative government of Edward Heath in 1970–74 at a modest level. There were even some Labour councils, such as Islington in London, that engaged. Indeed, one of the big beasts of the Labour Party, Anthony Crosland, wrote a *Guardian* article in 1971 criticising councils for displaying some of the worst traits of 'landlordism'. Too many were deciding 'what repairs are to be done, what pets may be kept, what colour doors will be painted, what play areas there should be ... the tenant is not consulted. He has no right to appeal. He has far less freedom than the owner occupier.' [9] He did not propose council house sales but did advocate that councils should build houses for sale along with a tenants' charter and the promotion of housing associations to end the council monopoly of rented social housing.

The right for council tenants nationally to buy their rented homes appeared in the 1974 Conservative manifesto, an election which they lost. But when they returned to power in 1979, Michael Heseltine was there to implement it. In the 1970s the Conservatives justified the policy on the grounds that the funds raised would allow new homes to be built 'for the aged, the disabled and those on waiting lists'. All that changed in the 1980s. Councils were prohibited from spending most of the revenue raised from sales. They were told instead to pay off their large debts as part of the drive to reduce public expenditure. In the 1970s house building continued alongside council house sales. In the 1980s, council house building was reduced by more than half, even though some 500,000 council houses were sold by 1983. Labour was divided between those totally opposed to council house sales and a smaller less vocal group who thought sales should continue but only as long as proceeds from sales were spent on new social houses. The first group won. Labour's 1983 election manifesto was pledged not just to end the Right to Buy, but that councils would be given the authority to buy back council homes on their first resale. As Nicholas Timmins noted in his *The five giants*, it provided votes for the Tories in places they had never had before, hugely reinforcing the change in the political map of England and Wales.[10] By 2010 some 2.8 million council houses in the UK had been sold under the Tory Right to Buy initiative – almost a quarter of them in England being bought under New Labour's administration.

What else got reported?

It required a major report (such as the final report of the Urban Task Force in 1999), or a major switch in policy (John Prescott's massive expansion of housing in the South East), or a controversial speech for housing to win any space in the news columns. Tony Blair caused a stir with a speech in December 1999 challenging one of the most widely held perceptions – the North/South divide.[11] Some of his arguments were indisputable: the extraordinary prosperity to be found in parts of even the poorest regions; the pockets of poverty in the most prosperous. Where *The Guardian* disagreed with him was his assertion that 'the disparity within regions is at least as great as that between them', and his suggestion that there should be 'a more even handed debate'.[12] The first ignored the depth and spread of deprivation in the North, while his even-handed debate posed the threat of even-handed help that would only widen the divide.

In the following 18 months a succession of academic studies were published disputing Blair's claims. *The Guardian* commissioned Professor Brian Robson, a long-standing government adviser based at the University of Manchester, for a response at a *Guardian* North debate in March 2001. In his words, 'the disparities are undeniable and their roots are systemic and structural'. Merseyside, Tyneside and Sheffield had continued to lose jobs and people; Manchester had stood still; only West Yorkshire, reflecting a regenerated Leeds, had expanded. Yet even within half a mile of prosperous Leeds and Manchester, already boasting penthouses, restaurants and smart boutiques, lay surrounding rings of dilapidated and unsaleable property.[13]

New homes for a new South

John Prescott's sustainable communities paper in February 2003 sparked a fierce debate.[14] It took a 30-year forward look at housing needs, raising the numbers in the South East even higher than his 15-year look in July 2002. Then he had wanted 200,000 new homes in four growth areas in the South East. By 2003 this had increased to 1,100,000: 30,000 in Ashford, 200,000 in Thames Gateway, 370,000 in Milton Keynes and 500,000 in the London-Stansted-Cambridge corridor. As *The Guardian* noted, a Cabinet stuffed with northern MPs signalled that it would not just protect the current North/South divide but actually dramatically increase it.[15] The one spectre threatening the great engine of Britain's economic growth – the shortage of affordable housing in London and the South East – was being robustly addressed. Some of it made sense; some of it did not. In January 2004 the planned expansion of Milton Keynes was made even bigger – doubling its current size. Sir Richard Rogers, architect and chair of the 1998/99 Urban Task Force, had already made his position known in a *Guardian* feature long before the added expansions.[16] Although most of Milton Keynes' new homes were for private owners, the public purse would be spending a further £40,000 for each house, providing roads, schools and expanded health services. Was this sensible when 50 miles north of Milton Keynes stood Birmingham, with empty houses, spare land and attractive canal sites still losing its population?

Density

The low density of UK developments was another hotly disputed issue. Two members of the 1998/99 Urban Task Force clashed on this issue when the team published a six-year audit on their proposals in November 2005. Sir Peter Hall, town planner and foremost geographer of his generation, felt the follow-up report was pushing density and brownfield development too far. Writing in *The Times*, Hall declared:

In 1999 we all agreed that something was wrong. Our great cities – Liverpool, Manchester, Newcastle – were shrinking. Vast tracts of brownfield land close to city centres lay vacant, while families moved in droves to surrounding towns and villages. Throughout England most new housing was built at low densities – less than 30 homes to the hectare (2 acres), too low to support bus services. People were being forced to buy and use cars. So we advised the Government to ensure that 60 per cent of all new housing development was on brownfield land at 30 homes (plus) per hectare. We all signed up to that. Now my colleagues want to raise that brownfield quotient to 75 per cent and minimum densities of 40 per cent. This could prove disastrous.

Already the brownfield percentage has risen from 56 per cent to 68 per cent; our cities are coming back to life. You could say this is heartening; it confirms we were right in 1999. But a second look raises doubts. Despite a 33 per cent increase in brownfield completions and a 20 per cent decrease in greenfield, we built just 9 per cent more homes in 2004 than in 1999. This is nowhere near enough ... the truth is that these policies mean more – and smaller – flats and fewer houses with gardens. The percentage of flats to total completions has doubled in five years; 16 per cent in 1999, 34 per cent in 2004. In Yorkshire and Humber, the proportion has quadrupled. And room sizes are shrinking – by 10 per cent since 1980 ... homelessness statistics show an urgent need for family homes [to avoid] a potential disaster for families with children.[17]

Anne Power, an LSE academic, member of the Task Force and prolific writer, had set out her views in a succession of *Guardian* articles:

The UK is one of the most densely populated countries in Europe, yet its urban areas are among the least dense ... on average we build 23 homes per hectare (roughly the size of a football pitch), yet we need 50 to support a local school, shop, policeman and bus stop ... we do not have to live with the triple legacy of detached private estates around every country town and village; depopulating, decayed inner cities; and broken down social structures ... the higher density of many European cities leads to a stronger street presence of door porters, super caretakers and wardens than our low density houses support. More people on the streets mean safer streets ... by building at 50 dwellings per hectare, double our current average, we could achieve 100 per cent of all new building on brownfield sites. Semi-detached, three- and four-storey, spacious Georgian-style houses with gardens and attractive Cornish villages are both at this density.[18]

The rise of housing associations – and the fall in council housing

The media likes to portray itself as a watchdog on government irregularity. But the media had a two-decade-long sleep while one of the more questionable changes in social policy was pursued by successive governments from 1988. It was Parliament that exposed the questionable practice, not the press shorn of any housing correspondents. The governments were right to break the council monopoly of social housing, right to promote housing associations and co-ops, and to provide tenants with more say. But the MPs were right that ministers had gone a step too far.

It began following the 1987 election when the Conservatives were already thinking of a new and separate way in which the state could be curbed. William Waldegrave, the new Housing Minister, declared: 'The next big push after the right to buy should be to get rid of the state as landlord.'[19] He had been listening to his leader, who had made it clear she wanted the state to withdraw 'just as far and as fast as possible' from the building, ownership, management and regulation of housing. The Tories took up Crosland's 1971 idea of promoting housing associations to end the councils' monopoly of social housing. There were some incentives for local authorities to participate. Starved of cash and facing a cumulative £19 billion backlog of maintenance and repair bills, transfers of council housing to non-profit housing associations raised large capital receipts for local authorities and offered a better opportunity for the estates being upgraded. Crucially the housing associations, guaranteed revenue from rent underwritten by Housing Benefit from the transfers, were also given the right to raise private finance to help do up the estates. It began with small streams – bundles of 5,000 houses or so – in the late 1980s and ended up just over 20 years later in 2009/10 with housing association stock (2,614,000) exceeding local council numbers (2,365,000). At its peak in 1979, council housing in the UK numbered over five million homes, accounting for over 30 per cent of total housing units, compared to about 2 per cent for housing associations.

Table 1: UK housing by tenure, 2009/10 (in 000s), compared to 1983

	2009/10 (*n*)	2009/10 (%)	1983 (%)
Owner-occupiers	18,480	69.5%	59%
Privately rented	3,659	12.4%	11%
Housing association	2,614	9.7%	2%
Local authority	2,365	8.4%	28%
All dwellers	27,110	100%	100%

Source: CIH 2009/10 statistics; J. Hills in H. Glennerster and J. Hills (1998) *The state of welfare*[20]

Much of this housing transfer happened with very little media coverage. Clearly many local councils had mismanaged their stock. Estates had become too big. Management was too remote. But the anti-local council consensus, shared by the two main parties, went too far and created an unfair playing field – not all councils should have been tarred by the brush of the worst. The Conservative government had not tried to hide its ambition to remove the state from any aspect of housing provision; New Labour was more circumspect. It declared in a Green Paper in 2000 that it wanted to separate strategic housing management from the day-to-day management of local authority stock.[21] The first, strategic management, could be left to local councils; but the second, day-to-day management of housing stock, should be given to housing associations, arm's-length management organisations (essentially local council management teams, known as ALMOs), or PFI (private finance initiative) schemes. The Green Paper asserted that this would strengthen the separate roles and make them more effective.

Parliamentary committees challenge the policy

In March 2003 the powerful Public Accounts Committee, a watchdog on government spending, published a report on housing transfers. It concluded that they had 'led to the under valuation of the houses transferred so far, resulting in a greater contribution from the taxpayers than was necessary to deal with, for example, the backlog of repairs'.[22] It went on to assert that despite the millions spent on housing after transfer, there had only been a slight increase in tenant satisfaction – up by 3 per cent from 78 per cent before transfer to 81 per cent post transfer. Satisfaction with repairs had gone down (from 68 to 63 per cent). The financial shortfall was reported in some papers. *The Guardian*, for example, noted:

> The Government's policy of transferring council homes to housing associations is costing the taxpayer billions of pounds and delivering questionable benefits, MPs said today ... faulty assumptions in the complex calculations of how transfers are valued has meant that the Government has under-estimated the price of the policy to the taxpayer.[23]

In 2004 the Commons Select Committee responsible for monitoring housing held hearings on the government's 10-year programme to raise all social housing to a prescribed 'Decent Homes' standard by 2010. During this hearing it examined the benefits of splitting housing strategy from day-to-day management. Two key expert bodies provided evidence: the Audit Commission, which had a remit to monitor and inspect local government services including housing, and the Chartered Institute of Housing (CIH), the professional organisation for housing managers. Both expressed scepticism about the benefits of splitting the functions. The Audit Commission declared: 'There is no indication that the 90 authorities which had sold their stock were better at strategic management than the ones which had not ... there is no evidence that splitting the roles guarantees better performance.'[24] The CIH came to the same conclusion, arguing that 'there is no theoretical or practical reason why local authorities cannot handle both the strategic management of housing policy as well as managing a portfolio of council housing at ground level'. The CIH conceded that while local authorities had not been good at handling both tasks in historical terms, 'with proper guidance there was nothing to stop them from doing both tasks well in the future'.[25] I could find no other newspaper account of this important report in computer searches.

But the Select Committee's criticisms did not stop there. It went on to document a serious change in policy. Initially New Labour had signalled that the huge sums involved in the Decent Homes renovations programme would be available to all social housing, whether tenants had opted for local council management or a stock transfer to an outside body. But this approach was abandoned in 2001. The government was, in effect, said the Committee, using Decent Homes funding to lever local authority housing out of direct local authority control or even ownership. (The amount of money was huge – subsequent reports showed some £33 billion was spent between 2001 and 2008. The renovations included 550,000 new bathrooms, 700,000 new kitchens, 700,000 homes rewired and one million provided with central heating.[26]) Unless local authorities were able to fund renovations out of their existing funding streams – which very few were – they were obliged to transfer their stock to an outside body for their housing estates to get the upgrading funding. Tenants were made aware of this prior to ballots being held on their wishes. The 2004 report concluded that the government was using the Decent Homes programme 'as a Trojan Horse ... in a dogmatic quest to minimise the proportion of housing stock managed by local authorities'.[27]

The government remains unmoved

The reports did not change the strategy. Nor did successfully passed resolutions at four successive Labour Party conferences – pushed by local council delegates and trade unions – calling for a level playing field in the provision of social housing. Why didn't more of this get reported? News desks never like stories on restructured services. They need specialist reporters to explain the importance of the story. The second handicap in housing was the fact it was a local government service. Local government is as unpopular in Fleet Street as it is in Downing Street. Specialist local government correspondents disappeared even before housing correspondents.

Five years on, the Select Committee on Housing issued a second report in March 2009.[28] By then 170 local authorities had transferred their stock to a registered social landlord (housing association or housing co-op); 66 councils had established ALMOs; 14 were using, or planning to use a PFI scheme; and 112 were still running their own estates. One serious anomaly the report highlighted was the problem faced by local councils which had wanted to transfer their stock in order to benefit from Decent Homes funding, but which had been turned down by the tenant ballots that were needed before transfer. Birmingham had spent £12 million on trying to persuade their tenants of the benefits of transfer but was turned down. The London Borough of Camden was another example. Even in these cases there was no extra funding for the councils to carry out the necessary renovation to meet the minimum standards.

Audit Commission evidence in the 2009 report documented that local councils that had retained their housing stock were delivering a considerably worse service than housing associations or ALMOs.[29] Only three out of 34 councils inspected were providing a good/excellent overall service, compared to 39 out of 113 housing associations. ALMOs on different criteria scored 42 out of 56. But, as the Committee noted, the local authority-managed estates had not received the extra funding that housing associations and ALMOs had enjoyed. They found it 'difficult to separate out with confidence the causes of the problems'. They concluded: 'Rather than take day to day management of housing off the hands of these councils, the

Government should establish a mechanism to incentivise housing departments to improve their performance in order to receive additional funding. This would put these local authorities on an equal footing.'[30]

One way councils have improved their housing management

Anne Power, LSE academic, who launched the Priority Estates Programme in 1979, documented the degree to which even the most run-down of council estates – 20 of them spread across Britain, nearly all with dreadful reputations – could be turned around. Her recipe included involving the tenants, introducing locally based, intensive, hands-on management in permanent estate-based offices and reintroducing caretakers and neighbourhood wardens to tackle one of the most serious complaints of tenants in low-income estates – too few people to keep property maintained and the area tidy and friendly. There were clear benefits: lettings, rent arrears and cleaning all improved noticeably, with repairs improving 'to some extent'. Vacated flats were relet quickly, ending large numbers of empty properties and the vandalism they can attract. Even though the poverty of the tenants increased over the next 15 years – with the numbers unemployed rising up to 34 per cent – the tenants expressed a significant increase in satisfaction. The story is told in Power and Tunstall's *Swimming against the tide: Polarisation or progress on 20 unpopular council estates: 1980–1995.*[31]

New spinner takes over

Nowhere in the new administration that moved into Whitehall in May 2010 was the use of spin and manipulation more prevalent than in the Department of Communities and Local Government, which was in charge of housing strategy. Even New Labour might have been embarrassed by its blatancy. On Monday, 21 November 2011, over 18 months after becoming Prime Minister, David Cameron donned boots and appropriate clothing for a visit to a muddy new housing site accompanied by television cameras and newspaper photographers. The visit was to launch his 'unashamedly ambitious' housing strategy for England with, among other things, 'hundreds of thousands of affordable homes'.[32] These included an increase in the subsidy available to developers under the 'Affordable Homes Programme'; and rule changes to accelerate council house sales to finance further houses. It received reasonable coverage plus a parliamentary debate. A day later, the government quietly slipped out how many affordable homes had been built in the six months since April. The answer was 454 compared to 12,482 in the same period two years previously under Labour.

This staggering figure missed many news outlets but not Mark Easton, home editor for BBC News. His story on BBC Online was appropriately headlined 'Building trust in building statistics'. He explained: 'Housing matters hugely to people and yet the subject does not have the political bite to keep it at the top of the news agenda. The launch of England's housing strategy was a rare opportunity to consider the state of the crisis and the political solutions on offer. When the housing figures were published the very next day ministers could have expected there would have been little media appetite to return to the topic. In that sense a cynic might think it was "a good day to bury bad news".'[33] The department sought, unconvincingly, to deny there was a cover-up. Their readiness to ignore the Code of Practice for Official Statistics was blatant and obvious. It states that ministers must 'ensure that no statement or comment – based on prior knowledge – is issued to the press or published ahead of the publication of the statistics' and reminds them of their duty 'to promote trust and maximise public value' of official data.

The spin did not stop there. Seven months on, Grant Shapps, the housing minister later promoted in 2012 by Cameron to become chair of the Conservative Party 'for his communication skills', was full of pride for the new 'impressive' Affordable Homes Programme. He proudly announced on 12 June 2012: 'Far from the predictions of the doom merchants, today's figures show work has started on over 15,000 new affordable homes since last September – a massive increase on the previous six-month period. This is clear evidence that our efforts to get Britain building are starting to yield impressive results.'[34] Far from it, as the BBC's online headline accurately put it: 'Housing crisis deepens'. The statistics released were the annual housing statistics. In them was a table giving numbers of affordable houses built in the three years ending in March 2012. They ran as follows: in the last full year of the Labour government (2009/10): 54,303; in the first year of the Alliance (2010/11), numbers fell to 49,363; and in the current year under the Alliance (2011/12): a mere 15,698. This was hardly surprising given the 63 per cent cut imposed on the housing capital budget by the Alliance in 2010.[35]

A party which was once wedded to a 'home-owning democracy' found itself presiding over a housing crisis affecting all three main sectors: owner occupiers, social housing, and spiralling rents in an ever-expanding private sector boosted by large numbers of buy-to-let landlords. Annual total house construction had fallen to just over 110,000 a year, a figure that had not been seen – with the exception of the Second World War – since the early 1920s. Eric Pickles, the Secretary of State for Communities and Local Government, had arbitrarily removed 200,000 from the pipeline on entering office in 2010. The National Housing Federation was forecasting that home ownership, which peaked at 72.5 per cent in 2001, was likely to fall to 63.8 per cent by 2021. Every £100 million cut in house building loses 2,500 jobs and 1,650 homes.

Labour's housing targets, labelled 'Stalinist' by Shapps, were replaced by a 'New Homes Bonus' scheme. Shapps boasted that it represented 'a powerful incentive' for new housing with the aim of turning 'nimbys' – not in my backyard – into 'yimbys' (yes, in my back yard).[36] The incentive was a pledge to match the additional council tax collected on people in new homes with a government grant. Alas a survey by *Inside Housing* magazine suggested that less than a quarter of local councils were going to invest the bonus back into housing. Some were using the bonus to plug the deep cuts to other services. Others, like Kensington and Chelsea, were exploiting the scheme by redesignating single occupied homes into multi occupied so that all extra tenants were paying council tax.[37] The north was hit by a sub-clause under which any housing demolished must be subtracted from the total new homes.

Housing becomes a saviour of no growth

Belatedly as growth failed to materialise from the severe austerity programme, the Alliance turned to extra housing as a means of boosting the economy. Vince Cable, the Liberal Democrat Business Secretary, was an outspoken supporter and spoke about how a massively increased housing programme in the early 1930s lifted a recession. Figures from Get Britain Building, a coalition of organisations in the struggling construction industry, suggested that for every £1 spent on construction the government gets back 56p in reduced welfare payments and an increase in tax income. The first serious step by the Alliance was a radical change in planning laws in 2011. Some 1,200 pages of planning guidance were reduced to 52. There were several ticking bombs inside it. Devolving planning decisions down to local councils was likely to become a 'nimby charter', despite Shapps' New Homes Bonus. Even more contentious was the proposal that the presumption in favour of development should be a 'default yes'.

The Commons Select Committee on Communities urged the government to make several changes including the open door being given to development. The green lobby pulled all its known strings. *The Daily Telegraph* took up the cause and launched a 'Hands Off Our Land' campaign. Dame Fiona Reynolds, the director general of the National Trust, took the unprecedented step of writing to all 4 million members asking them to join in a highly political campaign against key proposals, such as the 'default yes' position on development.[38] And at the last moment some 45 MPs (37 Conservative and eight Liberal Democrats) in a letter organised by Zac Goldsmith, former environmental adviser to Cameron in his period as Opposition leader, asked for the restoration of the principle of building on brownfield sites before the countryside.[39] Just days before the new rules were due to come into operation Cameron conceded. In late March 2012 an amended National Planning Policy Framework, which emphasised that town centres and brownfield sites should be considered for development before green fields, was published.

Six months later this U-turn was reversed. The zigzag led the *Telegraph* front page on 3 September 2012: 'Cameron in an assault on green belt'. There were to be new curbs on residents' ability to protest against new developments. Councils were to be encouraged to allow building on green land. Rules which allowed this to happen by redesignating other land would be streamlined.[40] George Osborne went on the BBC Sunday morning *Politics Show* to declare: "It is absolutely ludicrous that it takes years to get planning decisions in this country. You can get much faster decisions on the Continent, let alone countries like China."[41] In a newspaper article Cameron took on 'nimbyism': 'The nations we're competing against don't stand for this kind of paralysis and neither must we.' Then, ignoring his own hesitations and double U-turns, he vowed to end the 'dithering' and 'paralysis' that was holding back Britain's economy.[42] Three days later Cameron announced an emergency year-long free-for-all in house extensions, allowing home owners to build up to eight metres into their gardens without council planning permission. The move doubled the amount of space home owners and businesses could build on and also freed conversion of lofts and garages from regulations.[43] To cap the week Eric Pickles, in a government supposedly committed to decentralising decisions to the local level, declared that local councils would be stripped of their planning powers if they indulged in slow decision-taking. Their powers would be handed to a centralised planning inspectorate. The inspectors would be able to override all agreements between councils and developers enabling developers to reduce the required number of affordable homes, making development more profitable and hence more likely to be built. The department was perfectly clear about the purpose of the threats. They were designed to force councils living in 'an economic la-la land' to allow more house building.[44]

What all these ministers ignored was that developers were already holding 'land banks' of more than 200,000 plots with planning permission, which they were not using. They were not building on the plots, because they could not sell houses they had already built, owing to the difficulty of obtaining mortgages. Lending was still two thirds below the 2007 peak. It was not a simple problem. Developers were not free from blame. An IPPR study was told by one shameless developer: 'Our focus is to rebuild our margins'. Why not build more? 'We'll double in size, but halve the margins, so what's the point.'

Given the subsidies which developers still receive from diminished government schemes – 'Get Britain Building' and 'Build Now, Pay Later' – perhaps Eric Pickles should be looking at their performance to see how he could threaten them to up their game.

To sum up: housing remains the least popular and most frail arm of the welfare state. It does not get anything like the media attention that it deserves. Look at the intermittent coverage that the house-building schemes or planning changes received, compared to the scrutiny – reports, analysis and comment pieces – on the restructuring of the NHS. Housing is a classic example of the media following the agenda of governments. Successive governments have demoted its place on the Whitehall agenda. Something similar happened to local government correspondents, who disappeared as Thatcher, Major, Blair, Brown and Cameron governments all kept local councils under their thumb through central financial controls. A true democracy needs specialist reporters monitoring all arms of the welfare state.

Notes

[1] J. Barlow et al (2002) *Land for housing: Current practice and future options*, March, York: Joseph Rowntree Foundation.

[2] Shelter (2004) *No room to play: Children and homelessness*, April, Shelter's submission to the Treasury's 2004 Comprehensive Spending Review.

[3] Chris Holmes (2006) *A new vision for housing*, London: Routledge.

[4] Kate Barker (2004) *Review of housing supply: Final report* (Barker Report), March, London: HM Treasury.

[5] SEU (Social Exclusion Unit) (1998) *Bringing Britain together*, London: The Stationery Office.

[6] J. Hills and K. Stewart (eds) (2005) *A more equal society? New Labour, poverty, inequality and exclusion*, Bristol: The Policy Press; and J. Hills, T. Sefton and K. Stewart (eds) (2009) *Towards a more equal society? Poverty, inequality and policy since 1997*, Bristol: The Policy Press.

[7] J. Hills, T. Sefton and K. Stewart (eds) (2009) *Towards a more equal society? Poverty, inequality and policy since 1997*, Bristol: The Policy Press, p 122.

[8] Malcolm Dean (2004) 'Home untruths', *The Guardian*, 24 November.

[9] *The Guardian*, 16 June 1971; see also A. Crosland (1972) *Socialism now*, London: Jonathan Cape, pp 129-33.

[10] Nicholas Timmins (2001) *The five giants: A biography of the welfare state*, London: HarperCollins, p 378.

[11] National press and BBC websites, 6 December 1999.

[12] *The Guardian* (1999) Editorial, 6 December.

[13] *The Guardian* (2001) 'Northern renaissance', Editorial, 1 March.

[14] CLG (Department for Communities and Local Government) (2003) *Sustainable Communities Plan*, London: CLG.

[15] *The Guardian* (2003) 'Unbalanced Britain', Editorial, 6 February.

[16] Richard Rogers (2002) 'Cities reborn', *Guardian Society*, 30 October.

[17] Peter Hall (2005) 'Public opinion', *The Times 2*, 29 November, p 3.

[18] Anne Power (2002) 'Cities reborn', *Guardian Society*, 30 October.

[19] Nicholas Timmins (2001) *The five giants: A biography of the welfare state*, London: HarperCollins, p 433.

[20] John Hills (1998) in Howard Glennerster and John Hills *The state of welfare: The economics of social spending*, 2nd edn, Oxford: Oxford University Press.

[21] CLG (Department for Communities and Local Government) (2000) *Quality and choice: A decent home for all*, London: CLG.

[22] House of Commons (2003) *Improving social housing through transfers*, March, London: Public Accounts Committee.

[23] *The Guardian* website, 24 July 2003.

[24] ODPM (Office of the Deputy Prime Minister) Select Committee (2004) *Decent Homes*, 7 May, London: The Stationery Office.

[25] Ibid.

[26] ODPM (Office of the Deputy Prime Minister) Select Committee (2009) *Beyond Decent Homes*, March, London: The Stationery Office.

[27] ODPM (Office of the Deputy Prime Minister) Select Committee (2004) *Decent Homes*, 7 May, London: The Stationery Office.

[28] Ibid.

[29] Ibid.

[30] Ibid.

[31] Anne Power and Rebecca Tunstall (1995) *Swimming against the tide: Polarisation or progress on 20 unpopular council estates: 1980–1995*, York: Joseph Rowntree Foundation.

[32] Affordable homes cover three types of social housing rents (new homes where rents can be 80% of market rate; older homes where rents can be as low as 30% of market rate; and intermittent) plus shared ownership schemes.

[33] Mark Easton (2011) 'Building trust in building statistics', BBC website, 23 November.

[34] Mark Easton (2012) 'Housing crisis deepens', BBC website, 12 June.

[35] Homes and Communities Agency National Housing Statistics, 2011–12, Table 1a, Housing starts on site by tenure, England, published 12 June 2012.

[36] Peter Hetherington (2012) 'Plans for new housing are built on sand', *The Guardian*, 22 February.

[37] Ibid.

[38] Cole Moreton (2012) 'Middle England goes to war', *The Sunday Telegraph*, 1 April.

[39] Christopher Hope (2012) 'Planning reforms must be rewritten, 45 MPs tell Cameron', *The Daily Telegraph*, 15 March.

[40] Ibid.

[41] Ibid.

[42] Patrick Wintour (2012) 'Growth plan gets an extension', *The Guardian*, 6 September.

[43] Patrick Wintour (2012) 'Hopes for building boom – but fears recession is here to stay', *The Guardian*, 7 September.

[44] Polly Toynbee (2012) 'Housing is hanging off its hinges. Build, build, build', *The Guardian*, 22 June.

TEN

Subverting democracy (1): seven sins of the reptiles*

The parable of the pastor and his ass

The pastor trained his ass to run, and the beast turned out to be a winner, coming first in his first local race. *The Daily Mirror* covered the story under the headline, 'Pastor's ass out in front'. The bishop, angry and embarrassed by the headline, demanded the pastor put an end to it. The pastor withdrew the beast from any more races, leading to a headline in the *Mail* 'Bishop scratches pastor's ass'. The bishop was further enraged and sent Sister Mary in from the nunnery to get rid of the animal completely. She took it to a farmer and traded the beast for a tenner. *The Sun* reported 'Nun sells ass for £10'. Angrier still, the bishop demanded that Sister Mary stopped the story going any further. She bought the animal back from the farmer and let it go in the countryside. The *Express* reported 'My ass runs wild and free, says top Nun'. Only *The Times* reported the bishop's death from a heart attack the next day. And the moral? The more you worry about how the press defines your ass, the worse it gets.

This chapter looks at the seven different ways the media's sins can damage and erode the democratic process. They are a mixture of the old and new, but even the old are now perpetrated in a much more pernicious and malign manner, generating deeper and more damaging wounds to the democratic process. Ironically, but perhaps appropriately, this book was being written at the same time as Jon Stewart, the ebullient US talk show host and comedian, was organising the 'Rally to Restore Sanity' which attracted over 200,000 people to Washington's famous National Mall in 2010. The rally was,

---

* Denis Thatcher's waspish word for journalists.

in part, a response to the coarse, abrasive, over-heated mid-term election with its ever-more vicious and expensive attack adverts. But it was aiming at the US media as much as the politicians, urging them to turn down the volume and to adjust the tone. As one billboard declared: 'I support reasonable conclusions based on supported facts'. Or, as Jon Stewart told the rally: 'If we amplify everything, we hear nothing.' This is an echo of Alastair Campbell's complaint in Chapter One (this volume): 'a lot more noise, but there is less understanding by the public on what's actually happening'.[1]

It is sad to note that US newspapers – as against right-wing radio jocks or the proudly right-wing Murdoch television channel, Fox News – were a much more conscientious and reliable source of information than the British press. Many of Tony Blair's criticisms highlighted in Chapter One, particularly in respect of the tabloids, but not only them, were accurate: the hunt for impact, the need to get noticed, the search for scandal and sensation, the lack of balance or context, the black-or-white vision that admits no grey and the demand to generate heat rather than light.

One unusual defender of the British press is the Norwegian sociologist, Stein Ringen, of Green College, Oxford, who acknowledged that British newspapers were often sloppy, inaccurate and short on dignity, failings not helped by their self-regulator, the PCC, but these factors should not blind people to the collective role Britain's vibrant press have played. With respect to this last criterion, he thought it 'simply brilliant'.[2] He suggested that the British media may lack the monopolistic monotone of the *New York Times* and *Le Monde*, but its competitive plurality rendered it 'independent, irreverent, often funny, and, thank God, intrusive'. The diversity of its whole was more crucial than the shortcomings of its parts. The weakness of this analysis is that, unlike people with access to college common rooms or club libraries, the vast majority of British newspaper readers do not have access to all of the five more 'serious' papers or their five 'popular' cousins. They usually only read one.

In Chapter One we learned that even a politician as powerful as Prime Minister Tony Blair was wary of a frontal attack on a powerful tabloid paper. He picked out *The Independent*, rather than his real target the *Daily Mail*, in his speech on the media because 'he feared what the paper would do to him and his family should he have targeted it'.[3] Later in this book we learn that there was a much wider group of MPs who were scared to challenge a different and even bigger media organisation, Rupert Murdoch's national newspapers, over the allegations of widespread hacking of MPs' mobile voicemail by the *News of the World*. This is in a category of its own, because what is alleged – and confirmed with convictions in the case of two employees, the arrest of several more and the belated admissions of the Murdoch Group – went beyond morality, ethical journalism and even sin. It involved a blatant breach of criminal law (see Chapter 11 and the Afterword).

Sin one: Distortion

The first need in a democracy is the supply of unbiased and fairly set-out facts. In Britain newspapers are under no obligation to do this; only broadcasters are legally obliged to seek balance. There is, of course, the PCC, with its Code of Practice, drawn up by editors, that is unambiguous about the standards with which all editors are expected to comply. The first sub-clause of clause one of the Code states: 'The press must take great care not to publish inaccurate, misleading or distorted information, including photographs.' Not only is this regularly ignored by both the media and the Commission, so is sub-clause two of the first clause: 'A significant inaccuracy, misleading statement or distortions once recognised must be corrected, promptly, and with due prominence, and – where appropriate – an apology published.'[4]

From the case study chapters, particularly the coverage of asylum, drugs, crime and welfare, readers will have found plenty of examples of such distortions. They can, of course, be generated just as much by selective reporting of the facts as by reporting totally fictitious events. Both happen, and the first more often than the second. But the extent of both has become so routine it no longer shocks. It is no wonder that only 10 per cent of the public trust what they read in the tabloids, and trust in the serious papers has also fallen. As the Phillis Report (see Chapter One) noted, only 6 per cent of respondents regarded newspapers as the most fair and unbiased source of news, compared to 70 per cent for television.

In the wake of the many weaknesses of the PCC, the emergence of media commentators in the last two decades has been beneficial. Several have proved important watchdogs. There is a coterie of former editors turned watchdogs: Peter Preston in *The Observer*; Peter Wilby among others in *The Guardian*; Brian MacArthur at one time in *The Times*. But the doyen of them all is Roy Greenslade, who, as a journalist, worked for the *Mail*, *Star*, *Express* and *Sunday Mirror* before becoming Assistant Editor of *The Sun* (1981–86), Managing Editor (News) at *The Sunday Times* (1987–90) and Editor of *The Mirror* (1990–91). In 1992 he became *The Guardian*'s chief media commentator and still has a regular blog on *The Guardian*'s Media website as well as being Professor of Journalism at City University, London.

Asylum

In a series of columns and reports Greenslade has documented a succession of distortions by the tabloid press. He was particularly watchful of the coverage of asylum. He noted in a report prepared for the IPPR in 2005 the false links which tabloids draw between asylum-seekers and issues of public concern: 'There is hardly a social ill – welfare scrounging, council home queue-jumping, prostitution, working in the black economy – that has not been laid at their door.'[5] He was particularly vigilant over two of the most notorious cases, a three-page spread in *The Sun* accusing asylum-seekers of stealing, killing and eating the Queen's swans in July 2003, and a follow-up in the *Star* the following month, falsely alleging they were doing the same thing with donkeys in Greenwich Park. Worse still, of course, was the fact that the PCC, which had noted the lack of evidence supporting the stories, still refused to censure these papers[6] (see Chapter Five, this volume).

A column in 2004 was typical of Greenslade's steely approach. It was in response to a *Sun* front page blasting the British National Party ('Bloody Nasty People') and its leading article declaring them 'a collection of evil, hate-filled moronic thugs ... wicked men ...

criminals who should be locked up'. Greenslade reminded *The Sun* of its own record on racism:

> In the past couple of years the *Sun* has run stories, some of them false, some far-fetched, many full of distortions, which are guaranteed to stimulate its readers' latent – and, all too often, manifest – racism ... the *Sun* has been in the press vanguard in stoking up concern about Britain being 'swamped' by asylum seekers, relying for its scare stories on dodgy figures supplied from unofficial sources.
>
> Even when the National Audit Office issued a report in May, which concluded that the government's asylum data and statistics were 'in most respects reliable', the *Sun*'s news report accentuated the negative ... nor has the paper cared about delineating who it is talking about. For the *Sun* there appears to be no difference between asylum seekers, refugees and immigrants. They are all the same: foreigners 'our people' don't want. In other words, the paper has echoed the views of the BNP. For the *Sun* has taken every chance to attribute Britain's social problems on incomers, as a classic headline last November illustrated, 'HIV soars 20%: Migrants blamed for rise'. In fact, the report on which the story was based by the Health Protection Agency, laid greater emphasis on the increase in HIV transmission by homosexual and bi-sexual men.[7]

Health

Chapter Eight sets out two separate serious distortions of facts by the media with respect to drugs: the over-promotion of one drug, Herceptin, which led to a health secretary undermining the rigorous vetting procedure her own government had set up with the creation of NICE, and an even more disgraceful subversion of another drug, the MMR vaccine, which resulted in three million people aged between 18 months and 18 years without proper protection against measles, mumps and rubella.

Crime

Chapter Three documents the degree to which the penal populist war, in which both major parties engaged and were eager to be seen as the toughest on 'law'n'order', pre-empted a more serious debate. In the words of Professor Ian Loader to a Downing Street seminar on civil rights:

> It is as if – on this issue – you have lost confidence in the capacity of government to engage in a dialogue with the people, to point out some facts (about resource limitations, the effects of prisons, or the constraints on what can be done to tackle crime in a liberal democracy), to put another view, to be a voice for reason and restraint rather than a conduit or cheer-leader for longer sentences and more punishment.[8]

There was a cringe-making example of the distortion of crime statistics revealed on Steve Hewlett's BBC Radio 4 programme, *The Media Show*, on 29 September 2008. It examined how the latest crime statistics – including the first knife crime figures – had been reported. *The Telegraph* Home Affairs Editor, Christopher Hope, was put under scrutiny for downplaying the fall in violent crime and for suggesting that knife crime had spread from city to town and village. The statistics could not show a trend because it was the first time that they had been collected. Hope replied:

> The problem with the official police record statistics, as opposed to the British Crime Survey figures, is that they do not reflect what our readers see on the streets every day. You can try and cut it any way you want. We try and get a picture which reflects what our readers are seeing every day ... some of us would say, our readers see this lawless Britain in some part of their life, they do not want to be told by the government that violent crime is falling.

Here was a specialist reporter saying that his readers did not want to hear the accurate national statistics about crime, but preferred to rely on what they saw and witnessed themselves. Were they ever asked by *The Telegraph*? MORI surveys in 2004 found that the public placed crime as the fifth most important issue facing the country. It reported, '*Telegraph* readers are most concerned at 27% (despite being more likely to live in the relatively low crime East and South East), with *Guardian* readers least concerned at 15% (despite the fact that a third of all *Guardian* readers live in higher crime London).' Could *The Telegraph* be responsible for some of this disparity? And *The Guardian* too?

As Chapter Four records, the 2007 report from the RSA Commission on Illegal Drugs, Communities and Public Policy severely censured the media – and politicians – for demonising drugs and drug-taking, making it impossible to have a rational debate: 'Demons are diabolical, evil spirits and are therefore to be slain. In our view, using such language and thinking in such terms is childish, if not mediaeval. It stifles rational and realistic debate and makes it harder, not easier, to deal with the very serious matters at hand.'[9]

How scapegoat reporting distorts public perceptions

There is another good example of how scapegoat reporting – tabloids on their scrounger-bashing beat – can distort public perceptions, set out in the British Social Attitudes survey for 2002/03 with respect to welfare.[10] Opinion surveys found there was widespread recognition that social security benefits were now the biggest item in public expenditure, but found completely wrong perceptions on how this money was spent. The public believed 44 per cent of social security spending went on the unemployed when it was, in fact, only 6 per cent; and 13 per cent on lone-parent families when it was less than 1 per cent. Few recognised the biggest beneficiaries were pensioners, accounting for over 50 per cent.

There is an equally interesting study on public perceptions on health conducted by Ipsos MORI in 2006 for the NHS Confederation, the health management body, comparing public perceptions of health services with patients' experiences of them.[11] Here is another survey suggesting malign media influence and a distortion of reality, this time by concentrating on the negative. (See also 'Sin seven' below.) Ask the public for their sense of satisfaction with respect to NHS services and the returns are low: inpatient services (47 per cent), outpatient services (54 per cent), walk-in centres (30 per cent) and NHS Direct (36 per cent). There is one exception, GP services, which get 80 per cent. Why is this? This is the one service most of the public will have visited, so they can use their own experiences to evaluate it. For the other services, the public have to rely on media reports and hearsay. But when the same question is put to patients about the satisfaction they experienced with the same group of services, the answers could not be more different, always 33 per cent higher and sometimes twice as high: inpatient services (74 per cent), outpatient services (70 per cent), walk-in centres (69 per cent) and NHS Direct (71 per cent). GPs scored 81 per cent, but for the reason explained above, that was almost identical to the public's response.

Broken Britain

It is worth looking in more detail at the three-year long 'Broken Britain' campaign run by David Cameron in the run-up to the 2010 election. The tabloids, particularly *The Sun* and *Mail*, loved it, as no doubt his Director of Communications, Andy Coulson, the former Editor of the *News of the World*, would have told him. The catchphrase became a dominant pre-election theme. With its bundle of disparate issues – dysfunctional families, welfare dependency, youth crime, teenage pregnancies and anti-social behaviour – the theme provided the Conservatives with an armoury of social missiles to fire at the Labour government. But it was not just broad issues that were wilfully distorted, but a series of heart-stopping, isolated and atypical events that were seized and portrayed as clear proof of Britain's fractured and morally bankrupt society, rather than being set in context.

Case by case they were taken up by the media. And not all turned out to be what was originally reported. A splash in *The Sun* in February 2009 revealed the UK's youngest father: Alfie, an East Sussex boy, a mere 13 years old. In the eyes of *The Sun* this demonstrated the degree to which Britain was receding into a Dickensian society.

In fact, three months later, after the media fuss had died down, the Broken Britain bandwagon temporarily lost a wheel when it turned out that the boy was not the father of the child.

But it is hardly surprising that in a society of 60 million people, over a three-year period, terrible cases of inhumanity and abuse happened. They rightly received extensive media coverage, but the conclusions drawn by the tabloids were almost always too sweeping and simplistic. Three cases which helped the Tories to reinforce their Broken Britain mantra involved:

- Baby 'P', who died aged 17 months after suffering more than 50 injuries – including a broken back, his finger tips sliced off and nails pulled out – who had been placed back in the care of his mother and her boyfriend in Haringey, London, in August 2007, after having previously been taken into care.
- Fiona Pilkington, a mother who killed herself and her severely disabled daughter, by setting her car on fire in October 2007. A depressed and timid single parent with borderline learning difficulties herself, she gave up her life after continuous and horrific harassment by local youths. Stretching back years she had made 33 calls to the police that had failed to lead to any arrests or proper protection from the hate crime she was suffering.
- The South Yorkshire brothers, aged 10 and 11, who had been taken into care and placed with foster parents, who lured two other young boys, aged 9 and 11, to a secluded spot near Edlington on 4 April 2009. There the victims were subjected to 90 minutes of sexual humiliation and harrowing violence with knives, a brick and a burning cigarette that left one near to death.

The first and third cases involved criminal trials, and all three prompted serious inquiries into different public services – social services, health and the police – that kept the cases in public headlines. Is it any wonder that a Populus poll in *The Times* in February 2010 found that 70 per cent believed British society was broken, and some 64 per cent thought Britain was heading in the wrong direction? The Conservatives pre-released the 'Broken Britain' chapter in their forthcoming election manifesto early, to coincide with the sentencing of the Edlington boys on 23 January 2010. Both *The Observer* and *The Economist* took Cameron and his manifesto to task. Under a 'Cameron tells us Britain is broken – but not how to fix it' headline, *The Observer* suggested: 'The Conservative leader is right to identify a systemic cultural and economic malaise in parts of Britain. But this does not mean society as a whole is broken ... it does not need to be couched as a denunciation of national mores.'[12]

The Economist was even tougher. It produced a long special supplement analysing 'How broken is Britain?' accompanied by a long leader.[13] The Editorial conceded that Britain was far from perfect, with its binge-drinking youth, serious drug abuse and teenage pregnancies higher than most European countries. But it went on:

> The broken Britain of legend is one where danger stalks the streets as never before. In the real Britain, the police have just recorded the lowest number of murders for 19 years. In mythical Britain, children are especially at risk. Back in real life, child homicides have fallen by more than two-thirds since the 1970s. Britain used to be the third biggest killer of children in the rich world; it is now 17th. And more mundane crimes have fallen too: burglaries and car theft are about half as common now as they were 15 years ago. Even the onset of recession has not reversed that downward trend so far.

But, rightly, they did not stop with crime. They went on:

> Teenage pregnancy is still too common, but it has been declining, with the odd hiccup, for ages. A girl aged between 15 and 19 today is about half as likely to have a baby in her teens as her grandmother was. Her partner will probably not marry her and he is less likely to stick with her than were men in previous generations, but he is also a lot less likely to beat her. In homing in on the cosier parts of the Britain of yesteryear, it is easy to ignore the horrors that have gone. Straight white men are especially vulnerable to this sort of amnesia.

The weekly journal placed part of the blame for such amnesia 'on a dominant national press that tends to report the grotesque exceptions not the blander rule'.[14] But it also indicted politicians for conniving in it. Labour was not blameless, but it was the Tories who were heading to be the next government. Cameron was wrong in pandering to his right wing to suggest society had suffered a comprehensive breakdown. 'The story of broad decline is simply untrue ... it is clear that by most measures things have been getting better for a good decade and a half. In suggesting the rot runs right through society, the Tories fail to pinpoint the areas where genuine crises persist. The broken-Britain myth is worse than scaremongering – it glosses over those who need most help,' it concluded. Game, set and match, I would suggest, to *The Economist*.

Cameron's Broken Britain campaign was an attempt to emulate a similar strategy of Tony Blair. He first came to prominence in 1993, when in a widely publicised speech he blamed the horrific murder of a two-year-old, James Bulger, by two 10-year-old Merseyside boys, on a general breakdown in society under Tory rule. Ironically, in his 2010 memoirs, Blair belatedly admitted he had drawn a 'flawed conclusion' in 1993. Society had not broken down, only a part. 'The problem was real, the analysis was faulty.' He added that it was only at the end of his premiership in 2007, that he finally realised his mistake and saw the remedy was to directly target out-of-control and lawless youngsters.[15]

From broken Britain to Great Britain

Broken Britain also illustrates the erratic, intermittent and fitful media coverage that social issues receive in the UK. Compare the bleak Broken Britain coverage in the run-up to the 2010 election with the reporting of the much more dire social and economic conditions two years on. By August 2012 Britain was mired in a double-dip recession which, as the Bank of England Governor had predicted in 2011, was producing 'the most prolonged fall in living standards for more than 80 years'.[16] A combination of frozen or falling pay; rises in VAT and duty taxes; spiralling rises in food, energy, and oil; and cuts to tax credits and other benefits meant average family earnings showed the sharpest annual decline since 1981.[17] For the increased number of unemployed, under-employed and young people unable to find work the position was even worse. Even though by August 2012 only 20 per cent of the Coalition's £18 billion reduction in the social security budget had been applied, this £3.6 billion cut was already hurting on several fronts while the Treasury signalled that a further £10 billion of cuts to welfare on top of the £18 billion would be needed in the next four years.

The number of shops closed down since the start of the recession in 2008 rose to one in seven nationwide, with places like Margate suffering as many as one in three. New charitable food banks, not seen for decades in most places, were mushrooming. The Trussell Trust, the biggest charity in the field, was operating 200 food stalls and opening two new ones a week yet still not meeting demand. Despite £325 billion of quantitative easing funds provided by the Bank of England (40% of the benefits of which went to the richest 5%[18]), mortgages and loans to small businesses were still difficult to obtain, bank bonuses were still running at £13 billion, and a succession of other financial offences by the big banks had plunged their reputations to new lows. These included toxic payment protection insurance schemes for mortgages and loans that courts had condemned, requiring banks to pay back over £9 billion; the five-year-long rate-rigging scandal of the Libor – the daily interest rate used as a benchmark for the cost of borrowing for households and businesses round the world – under which Barclays, which was fined £290 million and lost three top executives in July 2012, was only the first of a cabal of banks facing serious sanctions; and the London-based HSBC found guilty by a US Senate committee of massive money-laundering operations for Mexican 'drug kingpins', and 'rogue nations' such as Iran.

Inequality was being brutally widened by a succession of Coalition moves, not least by George Osborne's disastrous 2012 Budget, under which 4.4 million pensioners had their age-related tax allowance frozen or axed losing them £285 a year while the 300,000 richest families came in line for luxurious savings by the top tax rate being cut from 50p to 45p. Indeed, the 8,000 people earning more than £1 million became eligible for a minimum tax cut of £40,000. The

Budget prompted widespread protests, damaging front-page banner headlines (such as '"Granny tax" hits 5m pensioners' – *Telegraph*, 22 March 2012), and a spectacular plunge in the Coalition's public support in opinion polls. It responded by introducing three further U-turns adding to the 31 previous reversals of policy in the preceding two years. Two proposed taxes – on Cornish pasties and static caravans – were dropped and a proposed cap on tax relief for charitable donations lifted. Even the Prime Minister later conceded the March Budget's mistakes had left the government 'ploughing into a brick wall'.[19] The main thrust of the Budget, however, remained rigidly regressive. The government's claim that its austerity programme was being applied to all – "We're all in this together" – was exposed as a sham.

More serious than all of this was the failure of the government's economic plan to provide any progress towards its growth and debt reduction targets. Martin Weale, director of the National Institute for Economic and Social Research, declared in August 2012: "Not only are we not making any progress, we are not growing at all".[20] A month later, when the government's public finance figures for August were released, the debt programme looked even grimmer. The government's aim was for the deficit to fall by 4 per cent in 2012–13 but in the first five months it had risen by 21 per cent with no sign of a growth uplift. Public sector net debt by the end of August reached £1,039 billion, equivalent to 66 per cent of GDP. *The Times* reported: 'Citigroup has predicted that the debt ratio could rise to 90 per cent by 2015–16, torpedoing the Chancellor's goal of putting it on a downward path.'[21]

So how much gloom were these dire developments producing in the media at the time. All too little. All papers, left and right, popular and serious, were speaking about how 'great' Britain was in August 2012. Front pages, multiple inside pages and editorial columns were all talking about 'Dream GB'. *The Sun* declared on its front page: 'We're world beaters' (13 August 2012). *The Star* responded: 'It's GREAT Britain'. The *Express*, like the other two a Broken Britain advocate, had changed its tune, with a resounding Editorial on the same day: 'Too often we are liable to put ourselves down ... concentrating on the superficial rather than that which has made us truly great. Britain has a long record of rigour, excellence, and an incorruptibility in all walks of life.' Compare that to the pre-2010 drip, drip of Broken Britain.

What caused this tsunami of positive reporting? Britain's success in the London Olympics. Even Jeremy Paxman, the notoriously cynical anchor of *Newsnight*, the BBC's late night news analysis programme, wrote in *The Sunday Telegraph* on 12 August 2012:'Who thinks Britain is rubbish now?'. He declared that the Olympics had 'exploded the myth that we were a country best suited to basic failure'. Even more encouraging was the recognition of how much the success was due to having a multi-ethnic team. Jessica Ennis, chosen as the face of London 2012, a beautiful and brilliant athlete who won gold in the pentathlon, was the daughter of a Jamaican father and white mother. Mo Farah, who came to the UK from Somalia as a refugee aged eight unable to speak English, won both the 10,000m and 5,000m gold medals to the acclaim of the whole country and the sporting press. A practising Muslim, his double gold had been achieved by only six men in the previous century. Asked whether he would have preferred to have been representing Somalia, he replied:"Not at all, mate. This is my country."

Even the *Mail* backhandedly recognised the ethnic contribution in an Editorial:'Inevitably everybody wants to claim the overwhelming success of the Games for themselves, with the Left presenting it as a victory for multiculturism. In fact they are a victory for British pride and patriotism, supportive families, shared loyalties and common values, whatever our ethnic backgrounds.'[22] Yasmin Alibhai-Brown was more effusive in a *Mail* online column on the same day: 'These two weeks have been a watershed of true significance. There has been a visceral reaction among black and Asian Britons ... For some, it has been perhaps the first time they have really felt a part of this country. For others, the promise of tolerance and integration has come true.'[23]

Middle Britain

Another absurd distortion is generated by the right-wing papers' definition of the middle class. The 'death tax' campaigns to abolish or curb inheritance tax by the *Express*, *Telegraph* and *The Sunday Times* were waged as though they were on the side of middle

Britain. But only 6 per cent of estates were paying the tax when the *Express* launched its campaign in 2006. It still continues, even though currently married couples, with each partner having a transferable £325,000 threshold, can pass on £650,000 of assets before their estate pays any tax. Where once British society was a pyramid with a tiny elite, a larger middle class and a vast working class, it is now more like a diamond. Manual occupations have shrunk from 75 per cent of the workforce in 1911 to 28 per cent in 2000. Not many of the 350,000 readers' names the *Express* collected on its 'Great Inheritance Crusade' petition will be paying the tax.

It happened again in September 2010, when it was announced at the Liberal Democrat conference that the new Coalition government had instructed tax inspectors to scrutinise the returns of people earning over £150,000. There are just 275,000 people out of 31.7 million taxpayers in this category – just under 1 per cent – but *The Telegraph* led its story: 'Middle class professionals could be subjected to ...'.[24] No, they are not middle class; they are decidedly top income people. Median pay in the year ending April 2009 was £25,428. That means that there were 15.85 million of the 31.7 million income tax payers above this level and 15.85 million below. Dividing all taxpayers into fifths, as the Department for Work and Pensions has done, the lifestyle of the middle fifth is very far from the media's idea of middle class. They are not worrying about private school fees or the inheritance tax their children will have to pay on £700,000 homes. Some 6 per cent of this group could not afford to send their children swimming once a month, 9 per cent had too few rooms to be able to put over-10s of the opposite sex in separate bedrooms, and almost a quarter could not afford a week's family holiday away from home.

As Margaret Thatcher understood, and Philip Gould, the Labour Party pollster got New Labour to recognise, the key middle-class groups are the C1s (lower white-collar workers) and C2s (skilled manual) who make up half the population of Britain. The top two categories, A and B, make up another quarter, and the poorest two, D and E, make up the last quarter. It is the C1s and C2s who are the most likely to be swing voters. One reason why MPs may have been late in picking up the importance of the C1s and C2s is because of

MPs' salaries. With annual incomes of £65,738, MPs are not middle class but in the top 4 per cent of income tax payers.

Daylight Saving Campaign

There was a fascinating item on how newspaper coverage can distort final decision-taking in the BBC Radio 4 programme, *Costing the Earth*, on 25 October 2010, referring to a new 'Daylight Saving Campaign'. One of the researchers of the 1968–71 trial, under which summer time was two hours ahead of Greenwich Mean Time (GMT) and winter one hour ahead, was interviewed and, disclosed the Commons, under pressure from farmers and Scottish interests, voted against its continuation even before all the evidence had been collected. She reported that every serious road accident or death in the darker early mornings was widely covered in the press, but none of the accident-free lighter afternoons. No accidents meant no story. But when the final tally was concluded – and after the Commons had vetoed its continuation – the trial period was found to be far safer.

Jeremy Paxman's complaint

The BBC *Newsnight* presenter Jeremy Paxman spoke about a different form of distortion in television news in his MacTaggart lecture in August 2007: the 'expectation inflation' caused by 24/7 news. He confessed that on some days he felt if he was being truly honest he should start the programme by saying: 'Not much has happened today, I'd go to bed if I were you.' He spoke of the not-wrong-for-long syndrome – the pressure to get the story first, if wrong, was greater sometimes than the pressure to get it right, if late. He went on:

> The story needs to be kept moving, constantly hyped. So the pavement-standers in Downing Street or wherever have to pretend to omniscience, even though they've spent so long on the end of a live link that they've had no chance to discover anything much ... in this context, the very slightest development, which might give some

sense of movement to a story, is fallen upon as if it were a press release for a Second Coming.

Blair's complaint

Then there is Tony Blair's genuine complaint set out in Chapter One of the media's distortions through its obsession with impact; its insistence on seeing the world as black or white; the hyping of events, criticised by Paxman above, so that a problem is 'a crisis', a setback is a policy 'in tatters' and a criticism is 'a savage attack'. All true. All needing to be addressed.

False wars

Finally there have been the frequent declarations by Conservative spokespeople of ending 'the war on the motorist'. Philip Hammond, Transport Secretary, repeated it again on the eve of the 2010 Conservative Party conference. But what war was he referring to? He could not have been using his own civil servants' figures, which showed that the cost of motoring fell 14 per cent between 1997 and 2009, even while rail fares went up by 13 per cent and bus and coach ticket prices by 24 per cent. It could not have been Gordon Brown's increase in fuel taxes in the early Labour years because they were abandoned after the lorry drivers' blockade. By 2010, fuel duty, after inflation, was 11 per cent lower than it had been in 1999. Could his distortions have been trying to exploit motorists' skewed memories, always remembering tax rises but forgetting their reductions?[25]

Sin two: Dumbing down

Let a man who has worked on almost all the tabloids speak first:

> Popular newspapers have forgotten what journalism is about. They have become organs of entertainment instead of organs of information. Even that old halfway house – infotainment – is no longer an appropriate description of what they purvey in their meretricious diet of glitz,

tits, and naughty bits. Celebrity is no longer an aspect
of the popular press agenda: it is now its raison d'être.[26]

Yes, Roy Greenslade again, this time in his inaugural lecture as
Professor of Journalism, at City University, London.

I worked shifts on *The Daily Mirror* between 1964 and 1966 while
I was putting myself through Ruskin College, Oxford. In those
days *The Mirror* used to have four pages devoted to serious national
issues every day, called *Mirrorscope*. It looked at the issue from all
angles, set out the background and interviewed specialists about
what could be done. It was brilliant popular journalism, exploring
in simple language the pressing issues of the time. Ideal for a healthy
and thriving democracy – keeping its citizens well informed. Alas
this section, along with much more admirable work, was dropped
following the takeover of *The Sun* in 1969 by Rupert Murdoch. The
serious but dull broadsheet was turned into a tabloid. Both sex and
the sensational were used to promote sales. The topless page three
girl began alongside serialisation of erotic books, and features on such
themes as 'The way into a woman's bed'. Circulation was regarded as
the only criterion of success. In 1978 *The Sun* overtook *The Mirror* in
sales and switched from supporting Labour to backing the Tories. *The
Mirror* stuck with Labour but, alas, it dumbed down its content in an
unsuccessful attempt to halt its circulation decline. Meanwhile *The
Sun* became ever brasher, coarser and more vitriolic in the 1980s. In
1984, when Tony Benn was standing in the Chesterfield by-election,
it interviewed a well-known US psychiatrist claiming Benn was
'insane', with the psychiatrist discussing parts of his pathology.[27]
The psychiatrist subsequently denounced the story and the quotes
attributed to him as 'absurd'. The paper had apparently fabricated
the whole story. In the 1987 election, still backing the Tories, *The
Sun* ran a mock editorial entitled 'Why I'm backing Kinnock' by
Joseph Stalin.

Back at *The Mirror*, in the wake of the September 11, 2001 terrorist
attack on the twin towers in the US, Piers Morgan, *Mirror* Editor
between 1995 and 2004, declared to much public approval he was
taking the paper upmarket to tackle more serious issues than its
current obsession with celebrity news. It was not long, however,

before he switched 'back to the froth because he and his owners feared a dramatic fall in sales if he continued with his mission to inform. Like it or not, they felt they must give in to the supposed demands of their audience.'[28]

The new opium of the people

Greenslade suggested in a lecture at City University, London, that it is celebrity rather than religion that is now the opium of the people. He believes it has led the media into being 'hoist by its own petard'. The media:

> … act as both the conduit for the would–be famous and the stage for the already famous. They also make profits from showing off the famous to the non famous. But they

have been subordinated by the fame game because their survival now depends on satisfying the appetite they've stimulated so successfully among their audiences. They are now forced to go on producing and reproducing the famous. They have become the drug pushers and the drug addicts. They can't control the system in which they play such a vital role because as perpetrator and victim, they cannot stop the world and get off. Piers Morgan's reluctant acquiescence to the wishes of his celebrity-obsessed readers is a case in point, though most editors have never bothered to question their role. They have grown up in a journalistic environment which has made a virtue of the cult of celebrity, absorbing it so thoroughly that they cannot conceive of producing papers any other way.[29]

Just how celebrity-obsessed this world has become was brought home to me with a shudder at a recent conference. I was in a group of six, talking together between sessions, where a researcher was describing what she had experienced in speaking to different small groups of primary-aged children. The first thing the children wanted to know was whether she was famous. The second was how much she earned. Deeply disappointed by her answers, the children declared their own aspirations were to become famous and earn 'loads of money'. The era of doctors and nurses – let alone train drivers – being played out in the primary classroom corners has apparently disappeared.

The mid-market pursuing the down-market

There was a period in late 2004 stretching into 2005 when the *Mail* was clearly seeking to overtake *The Sun* as the highest-selling national daily. In that period the *Mail*'s headline sales were running at 2,380,000 copies a day, while *The Sun* was selling 3,260,000. But on Saturdays, when the *Mail* provided a fat package, the difference between the two narrowed to 750,000. And on one Saturday in December 2004, the gap became as narrow as 400,000, due largely to a CD giveaway by the *Mail* and a simultaneous absence of promotions by *The Sun*. In mid-2005, the *Mail* pocketed two prizes which *The Sun* would have liked to retain: it poached back *The Sun*'s most popular columnist, Richard Littlejohn, and outbid *The Sun* for the second serial rights of a book by Jools Oliver, the wife of the celebrity chef, Jamie Oliver.

Greenslade wrote about the contest between the two papers in June 2005:

> In its determination to knock the *Sun* off its perch, the *Mail* has emerged as a chameleon, changing its colours to attract the widest possible readership. While it affects to tempt the readers of the *Times* and *Telegraph* with its strident politics and right wing, middle-class columnists such as Simon Heffer, Melanie Phillips and Stephen Glover, it also aims to woo readers of the *Sun* with a range of celebrity material that it would once have scorned. Long gone are the days when the *Mail* featured only A-list stars or purveyed only genuine stories of the rest. Now the *Mail* is getting down and dirty with all manner of tittle-tattle about the C-list crowd.
>
> The ups and downs of the Beckhams are regular *Mail* fare nowadays with unashamed follow-ups to *News of the World* tales about the pair. The adventures of a variety of soap stars and *Big Brother* contestants get big headlines. Even more surprising, given the *Mail*'s much vaunted family values philosophy, is the space given to the activities of Abi Titmuss and Rebecca Loos, women famous only for their sexual high jinks. Much of this material is illustrated by sneaky pictures taken by the paparazzi whom the *Mail* once pledged to boycott. Indeed, the *Mail* has been so eager to incorporate the *Sun*'s agenda into its own that it has begun to 'borrow' ideas from the latter, adding a touch of the magpie to its chameleon. Did the *Sun* not run with various features about chavs – posh chavs, A-Z of chavs, chav jokes – before the *Mail*? Was a *Mail* feature entitled 'How to conduct a perfect affair' not run originally in the *Sun*?

> How clever was it for the *Mail* to run the feature 'Heart
> scan that could save your life' on April 12, just five days
> after it first appeared in the *Sun*?[30]

But it was not to be. The *Mail* was striving for far too wide an appeal.
The more it went towards *The Sun*, the more it lost its middle market
readers – you can't attract *Telegraph* readers and bid for *Sun* supporters
at the same time. Five years on, both had lost circulation, but the gap
between the daily editions had not changed much: a gap of 775,000,
with the *Mail* selling 2,129,000 and *The Sun* 2,904,000.

Dumbed-down broadsheets

What Greenslade and other media commentators have not ignored
is the degree to which the old broadsheets have also been dumbed
down. They too follow celebrity television events, just like the
tabloids, although not in quite the same obsessive manner. And, as
the BBC's Andrew Marr has noted, celebrity journalism has infested
other parts of journalism, not excluding current affairs, with political
reporters concentrating on the human drama of who is 'up' and who
is 'down' to the exclusion of context and detail.[31]

But it is more serious than that. In a lecture on 'What are
newspapers for?' in 2005, Alan Rusbridger broke the 'dog does not eat
dog' rule of journalism with a blunt analysis of what was happening
to newspapers.[32] It ranged over *The Sun*'s abandonment of serious
news on its front pages; media awards which seemed more concerned
with trivia than serious reporting; the rise of apathetic readers; and
the losses being suffered by former broadsheet newspapers – *The
Guardian* (–£6.2 million), *The Independent* (–£15 million?), *The
Times* (–£20 million?) – compared to the profits of the tabloid *Mail*
(+£120 million). He then looked at the techniques used by the *Mail*
– punchy front pages, opinionated copy, views before news, picture-
led layout, headlines with attitude – and how these had infiltrated
The Independent and *The Times*. His slides showed the similarities
between *The Independent* and *Mail* front pages on big news stories,
such as the publication of the Hutton and Butler reports on different
aspects of the Iraq war. He pointed to the period when *The Times*

was producing both broadsheet and tabloid versions: '... it was easy enough to demonstrate that the two papers were markedly different. Different in tone, priority, prominence, news values, story length and so on. But through it all the paper refused to budge from its public assertion that the two products were exactly the same!' Rusbridger went on to suggest that the starting point of any discussion ought to be a frank acknowledgement that things have changed. The old broadsheets were no longer what they were. But, by and large, the media commentariat had gone along with *The Times'* claim of no change. They did not want a debate.

I am obviously biased, but I believe *The Guardian's* 'Berliner' format, midway between tabloid and broadsheet, has helped the paper escape the worst traits, although it is by no means innocent. I was glad to see Harry Evans, who wrote a brilliant book on newspaper design while editing *The Sunday Times*, make this same point about the advantages of a middle format in his interview with the *Press Gazette* in 2006. *The Telegraph*, with an infusion of former senior *Mail* journalists, has not just got rid of some of its best reporters; it has also introduced the opinionated copy and headlines with the attitude of their former employer.

The *Financial Times* has steadfastly kept up its serious standards, although even it, as my *Guardian* colleague Polly Toynbee spotted, was woeful in its reporting of the government's proposed new £30,000 tax levy on non-doms (non-domicile foreigners living in the UK).[33] In her words – and she is a well-known fan of the paper – in the eighth week after the announcement she protested at the 'page after page, day after day, of spurious, unsourced, unchecked campaign coverage, reporting "many planning to relocate all or part of their operations to countries with lower tax rates".' The *Financial Times* Editor, Lionel Barber, cried 'foul', declaring the paper's editorial line favoured reform of the tax treatment of non-doms but not the Treasury's 'rushed and botched' plan. It was not the editorial line she was criticising, but the reporting that was neither fair nor 'without favour'. It was biased in its balance, full of favourable quotes from rich non-doms and hopeless in persuading these so-called 'exit candidates' to identify themselves in public.

Sin three: More interested in politics than in policy

This is an old sin, but still operating even after specialist reporters rapidly expanded between the early 1970s and mid-1990s. It was an era when education, health and crime climbed up the political agenda in alignment with opinion polls, putting them at the top of the public's priorities. Even so, policy is complicated, and news desk editors don't like too much complication. Some *Times* specialists were specifically told to concentrate on more human interest stories in their areas rather than policy.[34] Criminal justice Bills, welfare reform, pension restructuring all require pages to cover in detail. Chapter Six (this volume) reports how stricter eligibility rules for disability benefits received many times as much coverage as the government's pledge to abolish child poverty. Why? The disability plan had become political, with Labour rebels able to stage the biggest – although still unsuccessful – backbench revolt in the first two years of Blair's government. Political reporting through a bi-focal lens can produce a more simplified story: who is for and who is against.

Then there is the old Whitehall trick of leaking policy proposals to political reporters, some of whom are not as up to date as specialist reporters, so are more likely to run it not knowing it has already been announced – indeed, on some occasions, policies that have not only been announced but announced several times before. Dressed up as a scoop, it is all too tempting for the less well informed to accept being spoon fed.

Robin Cook's indictment

Robin Cook, former Labour Leader of the House of Commons, in a radical speech on the reform of Parliament to the Hansard Society in May 2002, set out the problems which the media generated by its addiction to personalities and politics, and disdain for social policy:

> The challenge to the Commons is whether we can adjust to the less tribal society, which we are supposed to represent. And it is a real challenge. We may know that the public outside want to see a Commons that

is more concerned with the public interest than with scoring party political advantage. But we also know that what will get reported in the media is not the serious, and mildly boring, business of scrutinising social policy. What we will get reported in the media is a good bout of party political mud wrestling. We are stuck with the conundrum that we cannot restore respect for Parliament without airtime, but we cannot get airtime without displays of the partisan aggression that in the long-term lowers respect for the parliament.

When I first came to Parliament in 1974 there was only one BBC microphone within half a mile of the chamber. It was literally in a garden shed attached to Abbey Gardens. The place is now awash with microphones and cameras. There are now 30 accredited BBC journalists. I am sure they all work jolly hard and many of them are extremely likeable people. Nevertheless, Parliament was more often in the bulletins 30 years ago, when we had one microphone, than it is today when we have 30 BBC reporters.

I don't wish to single out the BBC for the present ambiguous relationship between Parliament and the media. The print media must also accept their responsibility, especially the allegedly serious print media. Every nation has its version of the tabloid press. What makes Britain unique is that our broadsheet press now faithfully tracks the agenda of the tabloid press. Politics is reported as a soap opera of personality conflict, which puts the spotlight on the process of decision-making by these personalities rather than the outcome of policies for the nation. This makes it difficult for the press to cover serious social issues.[35]

He pointed to the 'virtual abolition' of long-term youth unemployment in the previous five years, which had helped in the reduction of crime but which had gone 'virtually unremarked' in the media. He went on: 'Both press and Parliament now are handicapped by a culture of political reporting that is too introverted and too little about what is going on in the lives of readers and electors.'

And he added:

> Political reporting reinforces the public impression of a self-preoccupied 'Westminster village'. It is dominated by the issues about which Lobby journalists and MPs like to gossip to the exclusion of the issues which are pressing upon the lives of the public beyond Parliament Square. Jonathan Freedland [*Guardian* columnist] pointed out recently that, if newspapers were edited by plumbers, they would give prominence to disasters about blocked drains and street floods. As they are edited by journalists, they give prominence to stories about spin-doctors and press officers.... It is strange that a media, which keeps offering itself as an example of a highly competitive industry, is so blind to the real interests of the market.

Michael Crick's response

One journalist who disagrees with Robin Cook's analysis is Michael Crick. The highly respected BBC *Newsnight* Political Editor, Crick is the author of numerous books on politicians including Jeffrey Archer, Michael Howard and Michael Heseltine. He is renowned for digging out new facts and uncovering new scandals, a genuine investigative reporter, whose biography of Jeffrey Archer, *Stranger than fiction*, is now in its fourth edition. With over 25 years in serious political journalism – he was a founder member of the *Channel 4 News* journalist team in 1982 – he defends the new focus by the media on the personalities of the politicians rather than just their position on the political spectrum. He points to the serious overlap on policy positions of the three main political parties in England as they have all moved to the centre. This was before the creation of the Conservative–Liberal Democratic Coalition in 2010, which would strengthen his case. He argued that in such a fluid political situation, it was even more important for voters to understand the characteristics of the people they were voting for – their honesty, persistence, readiness to compromise and ability to persuade. As the policy differences narrowed, it had become even more important to judge the character of the people running for office.[36]

My 'yes, but' response to this argument was that there are still significant differences between the parties on policy that the media do not do enough to set out and elucidate. A more policy-oriented media might have helped reduce the huge U-turns in health policy under Blair – from creating the most centralised system in the history of the NHS, to theoretically the most decentralised, with the transfer of 80 per cent of the budget to PCTs. A more policy-focused media would have done more to expose the huge holes in Blair's tough law and order policies. The irony of Blair's penal populism is that it did not work. As noted in Chapter Three, the main results of his tough rhetoric, hyperactivity and continuous criticism of the criminal justice system was that the public believed crime was continuing to climb, which was totally untrue. A 2006 survey showed two thirds of the public wrongly believed that crime was still going up and blamed the government; one third rightly believed it was going down, but gave the government no credit for this fall. Quite right too, because according to even Blair's own Strategy Unit, the record fall in crime was not caused by his penal populism – it estimated that prison accounted for just 20 per cent of the fall – but rather a host of other factors: better security of cars and homes, falls in the value of electrical goods, a sharper police focus on persistent offenders, more investment in drug schemes and economic stability.

Hyped claims

A media with a better balance between policy and politics would have been more ready to challenge the wild claims by political parties. The centrepiece of the Liberal Democrat manifesto in 2010 was its £10,000 personal tax allowance, which the party claimed was a tax cut for struggling families aimed at 'lifting those on low incomes out of tax'. In reality some three million households in the poorest quarter of the population – low-paid, part-timers, unemployed, pensioners – would not gain a penny because their incomes were already below the existing tax threshold. But much worse, as the IFS documented in March 2010, only £1.5 billion of the £17 billion cost of the tax cut went to the poor, with most of the rest going to the comfortably off. Unlike Labour's progressive tax credits, which gave most to the poorer half of the population, the Liberal Democrat tax cut was regressive, giving most to the richer half.

Complicated policies

The more complicated the story, the worse the reporting becomes. Social mobility is a complicated story. Not even the sociologists who measure it are in agreement. And LSE researchers, who produce work for the Sutton Trust and use an income measure, believe that there has been a serious silting up. The longer-standing Oxford group, who use class, dispute this finding. But there is one basic fact that a competent reporter should be able to grasp and apply. If in measuring what is happening to social mobility social scientists look at the position of a 30-year-old male and compare his position (either by income or class) with the position of the father 30 years earlier, then the result of that study has nothing to do with the existing government. The crucial period will have taken place during the 30-year-old's early years together with schooling and possibly further and higher education. And yet the reports of the silting up of social mobility in the UK have been used by the tabloids (and, it has to be said, by Conservative, Liberal Democrat and even some Labour MPs too) to lambast the Blair/Brown governments. Yet the first children born under New Labour will not reach 30 until 2027. It is only then that social scientists will be able to say whether Labour's large investments in setting up 3,500 Sure Start schemes for pre-school children, school improvement programmes and anti-poverty schemes between 1997 and 2010 have improved social mobility.

It is true that both the LSE and Oxford researchers show a surge in social mobility between the 1960s and 1980s, with the growth in white-collar jobs and the dramatic shrinkage in blue-collar work, but only the LSE researchers record a silting up during the 1990s. The measurements are taken from four British longitude studies that track cohorts of babies born in one week in 1946, 1958, 1970 and 2000. Collectively they are known as the National Child Development

Study (NCDS), and are one of the crown jewels of social research, looked on with envy by overseas researchers. We would have been better off still if the Thatcher/Major governments had funded studies in 1982 and 1994 to maintain their 12-year cycle, but these administrations despised social science and were not keen to have their own records that closely monitored. There was a 30-year gap until Labour restored the programme with the Millennium Survey.

The 1958 study, for example, involved 17,000 babies, surveyed from birth, through childhood and adolescence, into adult life. These surveys showed there was considerable social mobility for this generation. It also discovered women who smoked had smaller and sicker babies. It was with the 1970 survey cohort, whose results began appearing under New Labour as they reached the age of 30, that silting up began. But it was not New Labour's fault – they were already 27 when New Labour came to power.

In a study for the Sutton Trust, which campaigns for a fairer educational system for children from low-income families, the LSE researchers looked at eight European and North American states and found the UK and the US at the bottom of this social mobility league table, doing considerably worse than the other six. It was right that it received wide media coverage, but wrong to consider it a fault of the Labour government. The study was using the 1958 and 1970 cohorts.

A much longer report in November 2008 from the Prime Minister's Strategy Unit raised some new hopes. It suggested that family background seemed to have become less significant in determining GCSE performance for children born in 1990 and 1991 and who took their exams in 2006. With education known to be one key effect on life chances, Liam Byrne, the Cabinet Office minister, suggested: 'Things look like they are starting to improve.' Yes, maybe, but the children were still 14 years away from their 30-year-old earning level. As Professor Paul Gregg, a leading researcher in the field at the University of Bristol, admitted, the findings were encouraging, but he warned: 'GCSEs are only the beginning of the story of life chances and earnings. If more and more people are getting good GCSEs – and they are – then GCSEs may be less important than they were as the key to future chances. It is a little like literacy, which was a huge influence 200 years ago but became less so as more and more people could read.'[37] Predictably the 2008 report, with some possible good news, did not get anything like the media coverage of the 2005 report, with old bad news.[38]

The squeeze on specialist staff

In the last decade, as editorial budgets have been squeezed with the downturn in advertising and reduction in sales, there has been an accelerating trend of cutting specialist reporters. Most tabloids no longer have specialist education reporters. Broadsheets that used to have two now have only one. There is no longer a full-time social security specialist, even though the benefit system has become ever more complicated. And the old-style housing specialist, who covered social and private housing, has disappeared, as outlined in Chapter Nine.

Sin four: Group think – hunting in packs

Again, this was not a new vice, but one that strengthened as the specialist groups emerged. Where once there were three main beats – politics, police and labour (industrial relations) – now there are multiple numbers, even as industrial reporters on most papers have been replaced. Health is now divided between medical and administrative. Science was a burgeoning field, with specialist sections as well as specialist reporters, until the budget cuts began. Environment was belatedly expanded but also cut back in the financial crisis.

Nearly four decades ago Timothy Crouse persuaded *Rolling Stone* magazine that there was an interesting story to tell about how the press corps was operating during the 1972 presidential election campaign of Richard Nixon. He coined the phrase 'pack journalism'. Later his columns were expanded into a famous book, *The boys on the bus*.[39] The press became a story and has remained one.

Here in the UK a familiar scene takes place once a social policy departmental briefing has concluded. As the minister leaves, the journalists get together. Sometimes in one group, sometimes – at the

Home Office – in at least two: tabloid and old broadsheet. They swap and check quotes with each other and then discuss 'what's the story?'. It is driven by two factors: the intense competition between papers, together with the insecurity of journalists. They don't want an 11pm call from their night news desks asking why they are leading with story A, when all the other papers have opted for story B. Within the groups there are often pairings – particularly when the specialists have held their posts for some time. They might even tip each other off when they have a scoop, with the agreement nothing is done until the first editions break. There are, of course, some singular journalists who do not join in. And there are some briefings so straightforward no group gathering is necessary.

Some of this is inevitable and can be productive. A big White Paper or new Bill will have multiple different angles that could be covered. Senior press officers on these big occasions will often stay behind to fill out answers already given, or take questions that were not called.

Where it has become perverse is when ministers run into trouble, which is when Tony Blair's 'feral beast' begins to hunt. This has become worse as papers have become more hostile to politicians. Hugo Young, *The Guardian*'s chief political columnist who died in 2003, noted:

> Sitting in government, watching quite a lot of political journalism chasing itself in a downward spiral of propaganda, innuendo and competitive truth-stretching, in a context that assumes the worst motive for every political act or speech, or alliance, could anyone disagree that every prime minister will need an Alastair [Campbell], to fight back on their behalf?[40]

The lust for blood has been fed by the succession of ministers brought down during the Major and Blair governments. Tony Blair, in his farewell speech on the media, made a fair point in how the tone of criticism has changed: 'Attacking motive is far more potent than attacking judgement. It is not enough for someone to have made an error. It has to be venal.'[41] Not all papers go this far, but too many are falling in line with the motto of Lord Rothermere, the *Daily Mail*'s founder: 'Give the readers a daily hate'.

Sin five: Too adversarial

One of the drivers of this sin of being too adversarial was the perception that Parliament had become too enfeebled in the face of Labour's massive majorities in the 1997 and 2001 elections. There is some truth in that, but the press has always been partisan. What is different is that the press has become more anti-government and anti any authority. The Major government was attacked by right-wing papers – partly because it was being insufficiently anti-Europe – almost as ferociously as the last Labour government. The comment from Trevor Phillips, quoted earlier, from *The Guardian*'s survey of leaders in public life, has resonance: 'Journalists do now seem to believe that the person in charge is always wrong.'[42]

Take the tabloids' – particularly the *Mail*'s – persistent attacks on NICE. This was one of Labour's most important reforms. It was set up as a key cog in the drive for evidence-based medicine, with its remit to bring together evidence of good practice, then to promote and diffuse it. It was responsible for laying down standards and determining the criteria for the use of new drugs on the basis of both clinical and cost-effectiveness. Previously, when left to clinicians, there had been huge and wasteful variations in practice. NICE was also a much stronger buffer against the hard sell of the drugs industry, requiring them to show what was new and more effective with new drugs. By 2005, NICE had made over 100 rulings so there had been plenty of 'rationing' decisions for the tabloids to get cross about before the Herceptin drug story broke that year.

Read Chapter Eight on health to see how a PR agency for Roche, the pharmaceutical firm, was working with the help of medical charities and the media to build up public support for the drug Herceptin even before the manufacturer had applied for a licence for it to be used for early-stage breast cancer. Then see how the Health Secretary, Patricia Hewitt, buckled under intense tabloid pressure and intervened, undermining her own government's creation, NICE. In the same chapter, there is a succinct summary of the *Mail*'s campaign against the MMR vaccine, which has led to a catastrophic decline in the use of the vaccine, leaving three million people aged 18 months to 18 years not properly protected from measles, mumps and rubella.

NICE was also under attack in the run-up to the 2010 election. David Cameron was reported in the Conservative election campaign as saying: 'I have a man in my constituency with kidney cancer, who came to see me with seven others. Tragically two of them have died because they could not get the drug, Sutent, that they wanted.'[43] The *Daily Mail* on 9 April 2010 had published an article claiming that 15 cancer drugs had been rejected by NICE. In fact, 10 out of the 15 had been approved by NICE, including Sutent. On the same day the article appeared, the head of NICE wrote to the campaign heads of the three main political parties pointing out the *Mail*'s error. Somehow the message did not get through.

Finally, it is the *Mail* that provides clear and unequivocal evidence to uphold the complaint by Trevor Phillips that 'journalists do now seem to believe that the person in charge is always wrong'. As Ben Goldacre documented in a column in April 2009, the *Mail* seemed to be in two minds over the use of a cervical cancer vaccine.[44] In England, where there was a free cervical vaccine under the NHS to cut cancer, the *Mail* ran numerous hostile stories under scary headlines: 'Revealed: the serious health concerns about the cervical cancer jab'; 'Alert over jab for girls as two die following cervical cancer vaccination'; 'Twelve year old girl paralysed "after being given cervical cancer jab"'; and 'How safe is the cervical cancer jab? Five teenagers reveal their alarming stories'.

But in Ireland, where the Irish government was refusing to fund the vaccine, the *Daily Mail* was vigorously campaigning for the jab under various bold headlines: 'Join the Irish *Daily Mail*'s cervical cancer vaccination campaign today'; 'Europe will shame FF into providing Ireland's life-saving cervical cancer jabs'; 'Health campaigners in Ireland take fight for cancer jabs to Washington'; and 'Cervical cancer vaccine for Ireland's girls: online poll slams decision to pull funding'. So much for the *Mail*'s consistency.

Sin six: Too readily duped

A classic example of being too readily duped is set out in Nick Davies' *Flat earth news*:[45] the millennium bug. It was first tentatively raised in the back pages of a Toronto paper, the *Financial Post*, in May 1993. By 1999 the world's media was in over-drive: all mortgage, insurance and pension records could be wiped out; computer-guided elevators, security systems and fire alarms could cease to function; many ageing computers in Eastern Europe may crash; US military defences, including its nuclear arsenal, could be disabled; power stations faced meltdown; and planes could drop out of the sky.

Diverse interested parties were ready to push the story: office managers wanting new IT systems; companies making millennium bug kits selling at £30 a time; publishers of books on *How to survive the bug* and assorted titles. What had been created was an echo chamber in which media cries led to louder cries. So what happened on 1 January 2000? Well, a computer system in the weather station in north Scotland did crash, but that was as a result of mice nibbling a connection. In fact, all the dire predictions proved wrong. So what was the media's response? Simple; just quietly drop it. The UK government claimed to have helped 58 other countries and was reported to have spent over £400 million. The US bill came to something similar. Neither Italy nor Russia made serious efforts to confront the bug, and they had no more trouble than the UK or the US. Was this reported? No.

In the opening of Chapter Three (this volume) I report on how Tony Blair insisted on parcelling up a progressive five-year strategy on the criminal justice system with a hard-line wrapper about 'the end of the liberal consensus' to divert media attention, most of which took the bait.

No one has done more to monitor, record and expose the many ways in which the media are misled, duped or deliberately misreads science and health studies than Ben Goldacre in his weekly 'Bad Science' column in *The Guardian* on Saturdays. A qualified doctor, scientist and holder of a Master's degree in philosophy, Goldacre has been writing his column since 2003. Both erudite and witty, his targets are not confined to journalists but also include pharmaceutical

PR agents, pseudo research units, 'quacks', cosmetic companies, homeopaths and nutritionists. He has divided his collection of media howlers into three broad categories: whacky stories, scare stories and breakthrough stories. There are now about 500 of them, and some of the best have been republished in his book, *Bad science*,[46] released in autumn 2008 to rave reviews. He has his own blog, where readers forward their own findings.

Goldacre has taken on and punctured stories in virtually all national newspapers as well as from the BBC, exposed the way medical research can be skewed to mislead and debunked a wide range of seasonal chestnuts. With surgical skill he has documented in detail the degree to which many journalists – such as Melanie Phillips in the *Mail*'s campaign against MMR – totally misunderstand both the scientific method and basic epidemiology. Science does not do certainty, which some commentators have found difficult to comprehend. He writes with verve and memorable phrases: 'health scares are like toothpaste: they're easy to squeeze out, but very difficult to get back in the tube'. He has won a string of awards for his writing, from the Association of British Science Writers, the Medical Journalism awards and the Royal Statistical Society, and he still works as an NHS doctor. He was described in *The Telegraph* as 'one of the few out and out good eggs' in journalism, and even the *Mail* online has shown grudging respect.

Sin seven: Concentrating on the negative

This seventh sin is the most serious one. Critics who make such a charge get their arguments distorted by an army in the trade, ready to rush in and deny it. But how do you maintain a liberal democracy if the public is systematically being misinformed? Geoff Mulgan, former head of the government's Strategy Unit, confessed in 2005: 'The government's worst nightmare is not that its policies will fail, rather that they might succeed but no one would believe them because of the chronic distrust of statistics on hospitals, schools, police.'[47]

Of course what is going wrong needs exposing. Take the NHS in recent years: *The Observer*'s campaign against poor maternity services was taken up by the Healthcare Commission; the *Express*'s concern for patient dignity was included in the Darzi plan, which will be used to assess hospitals; *The Times* punctured GP claims that patients didn't want longer opening hours by commissioning an opinion poll; *The Independent* maintained a long campaign for improvements to mental health services; and *The Guardian* exposed various drug company scams.

But where are the good news stories about the NHS, of which there are many? As David Bell, the former Ofsted chief noted (see Chapter One), a lack of coverage of positive stories can create the impression of a system in a perpetual state of crisis that is simply untrue. With 25,000 schools it is not hard to find some poor ones. The inspectors identify them, along with the much larger group of excellent schools that get ignored. The Healthcare Commission, which inspects NHS work, would echo a similar sentiment. With a million people seen by NHS staff every 36 hours, it is not hard to find people who have been inappropriately treated. But there have been huge improvements in NHS services, as testified by the independent surveys of patient satisfaction ratings.

Departmental press briefings

At the various briefings from Whitehall departments and the different inspectorates that now examine public services – they numbered 12 until recent mergers – it has been intriguing to watch the assembled journalists searching desperately for the bad news in the fat annual returns. The poor old home affairs correspondents have had a bad decade – although you would not know it from the stories they write – as the dramatic decreases in crime continue in an ever wider number of categories: domestic burglary, commercial burglary, theft, fraud, car crime (both theft of a vehicle and theft from a vehicle); even violent crime, their old standby, is now decreasing, including firearms offences and murder.

When I was grumbling to Howard Glennerster, the social policy guru at the LSE, about this trend in negativity, I was surprised by his response. It was, he said, the same in academia. The best way young researchers could get their research published was to concentrate on what was going wrong. So it is not just my trade that needs to take a look in the mirror. A new research study from the LSE, released in September 2008, based on a survey of 1,100 RSA fellows, found them more cynical about politics than anything else: 51 per cent viewed politics cynically, 37 per cent the media and 30 per cent business.[48] More seriously, it found cynicism was the most important factor in prompting people to opt out of voting.

The US Senator Daniel Moynihan once said: 'If you go into a country and all you see in the papers is good news, then you know all the good people are in jail.' But to go into a country and find that all you can see is bad news is equally disturbing. Robin Cook, in his Hansard Society Lecture in May 2002, noted that Philip Gould, Labour's main pollster, had observed the previous week that the ratio of negative to positive stories had increased, from 3:1 in 1974 to 18:1 in 2001. David Bell paid tribute to the specialist education reporters but pointed to the increase in commentators, 'fact-free and prejudice-rich who witness the casual slandering of state education that permeates our newspapers'.[49]

One paradox is the time that all the serious papers now spend on ensuring there is something lighter or funny to lift readers' spirits from the grim events on modern news lists. But the uplifting events rarely include positive stories about public services. They are much more likely to be related to some sort of celebrity piece, whimsical event or forthcoming television programme.

Minor media moves to more cheeriness

There are intermittent moves within the media to shift the current negative/positive balance. There was a plea from the Queen for more good news in the media in her 1985 Christmas message. And there was a call from Martyn Lewis, the television presenter, in 1993, for a better balance between negative and positive news items on television.[50] Contrary to his detractors, he was not calling for a happy–clappy good news service, nor a Soviet-style nothing is wrong. What he did do was compare the balance that BBC reporters apply to individual stories with the huge imbalance of negative-to-positive stories decided by the editors of the news programmes. He had a list of interesting positive stories that had been dropped. What he wanted was a small shift in the balance, from 5 per cent positive to perhaps 10 to 15 per cent. He got some support from a trustee and a manager, but his campaign failed, and he was dropped as one of the principal readers of the BBC's main evening news, which in those days, was at nine o'clock.

Early in 2008, Channel 5's news programme announced a restructuring that would reject the 'doom and gloom' of rival bulletins and search for the positive – something that Martyn Lewis had specifically ruled out.[51] But the relaunch was disrupted by the pregnancy of the channel's new name, Natasha Kaplinsky, the *Strictly Come Dancing* star, who took maternity leave from the UK's highest-paying news reader post very shortly after she began the £1 million job.

There have also been intermittent initiatives by the press. For one day in 2007 the *Edinburgh Evening News* tried out an *Edinburgh Evening Good News*. Fortunately for them it was a day without any big bad news stories. Executives on London's *Evening Standard* issued a memo in 2007 calling for calmer, cleverer and cheerier stories, declaring readers did not want to be 'coshed by doom and disaster stories on the way home'. The *Times Educational Supplement* also followed suit, with managers requiring the Editor to draw up weekly counts of 'positive' and 'negative' headlines – and to redress the balance in favour of the former. Peter Wilby, former Editor of *The Independent on Sunday* and later the *New Statesman*, commenting on the last two moves above in his *Guardian Media* column in 2007, described how he was banned from writing his educational column on a Monday in the *Evening Standard* in the 1990s by Max Hastings, its then Editor.[52] Hastings believed readers needed to be cheered up at the beginning of the working week, and no education story could possibly do that.

Wilby went on:

> Is it true that readers want cheerier newspapers? This view emerges from the focus groups so beloved of managements, where readers also say they want smaller, more manageable papers. It has been shown repeatedly, however, that the more pages and sections a paper can add, the more copies it will sell. Similarly, any editor

knows disasters sell and the bigger the disaster, the bigger the sale. Nobody buys a paper to learn how many aircraft took off and landed safely the previous day. The *Daily Mail*, the most successful British daily paper of the age, is also the gloomiest, dwelling on rising crime, plunging school standards, imminently falling house prices, cancer threats and a country rapidly going to the dogs.

My answer to that is yes and no. Take sport. Sales of morning papers after an evening victory by England in a World Cup match are bigger than when they lose. Hastings was wrong to believe that an education story had to be a downbeat read. With 26,000 schools in the country, there are all manner of successful pilot schemes that could cheer up parents, teachers and ordinary readers. His comment, however, reminded me of a tongue-in-cheek column by the fastidious Peregrine Worsthorne, who once argued that there was more truth in advertising columns than in news columns. In advertising columns aircraft did take off and land safely every day, Italy was a land of beautiful hill towns surrounded by vineyards and Buckingham Palace was a splendid tourist attraction; whereas in news columns aircraft only appeared when they caught fire or crashed, Italy when it was hit by an earthquake and Buckingham Palace when the Queen woke up and found a burglar in her bedroom.

Doom and gloom still dominate the papers, even when violent crime goes down and the NHS improves. The morning and evening freebies in many big cities now are more cheerful – they depend on advertising and advertisers do not like bad news. But they also demonstrate that being cheerful is not enough – they are thin, jejune, unintelligent giveaways with little journalistic merit. With the launch of the redesigned *Guardian* on 12 September 2005, the Editor insisted that the third editorial of each day should be about something positive, which could be praised rather than condemned. It was not popular with some of my colleagues. And at the beginning, it was intriguing to discover how difficult it was sometimes to find a positive story to fill the 'In praise of ...' slot. But it still continues six years on.

One last reason why editors should address negativity is the degree to which it tilts papers into seeing events as either black or white.

Life is more complicated than that, and it is time news was treated in a more adult manner.

Notes

[1] Alastair Campbell (2002) 'It's time to bury spin', *British Journalism Review*, vol 13, no 4, pp 15-23.

[2] Stein Ringen (2007) *What is democracy for?*, Princeton, p 275; or Stein Ringen (2003) 'Why the British press is brilliant', in *British Journalism Review*, vol 4, no 3, pp 31-59.

[3] Adam Boulton (2008) *Memories of the Blair administration: Tony's ten years*, New York: Simon & Schuster, p 180.

[4] See PCC website (www.pcc.org.uk).

[5] Roy Greenslade (2005) *Seeking scapegoats: The coverage of asylum in the UK press*, May, London: IPPR.

[6] Roy Greenslade (2003) 'Dead meat', *The Guardian*, 1 December.

[7] Roy Greenslade (2004) 'How to beat up racism', *The Guardian*, 19 July.

[8] See website of Ian Loader, Oxford criminologist.

[9] RSA (Royal Society of the Arts) Commission on Illegal Drugs, Communities and Public Policy (2007) *Drugs – Facing facts*, London: RSA Commission, March.

[10] Peter Taylor-Gooby and Charlotte Hastie (2003) 'Support for state spending', in Alison Park et al (eds) *British Social Attitudes: The 19th report, 2002/03*, London: Sage Publications, ch 4, p 87.

[11] E. Edwards (2006) *Lost in translation: Why are patients more satisfied with the NHS than the public?*, London: NHS Confederation.

[12] *The Observer*, 24 January 2010.

[13] *The Economist* (2010) Main Leader: 'How broken is Britain?', 4 February.

[14] Ibid.

[15] Tony Blair (2010) *A Journey*, Hutchinson, pp 56–7, 204.

[16] FS press release 'Biggest one year fall in middle incomes since 1981', 15 June 2012 (www.ifs.org.uk/pr/hbai2012.pdf).

[17] Robert Winnett (2011) 'Bank of England chief Mervyn King: standard of living to plunge at fastest rate since 1920s', *Daily Telegraph*, 25 January

[18] Larry Elliott (2012) 'Britain's richest 5% gained most from quantitative easing – Bank of England', *The Guardian*, 23 August.

[19] Patrick Wintour (2012) 'Cameron: budget errors left government "ploughing into brick wall"', *The Guardian*, 3 June.

[20] Philip Aldrick (2012) 'Britain isn't in recession, it's just not growing, says Bank rate-setter', *Daily Telegraph*, 17 August.

[21] Sam Fleming (2012) 'Falling tax revenues put pressure on Chancellor as borrowing rises again', *The Times*, 22 September.

[22] *Daily Mail* (2012) Editorial: 'Olympics that prove UK can deliver', 13 August.

[23] Yasmin Alibhai-Brown (2012) 'Mo's joyful embrace of Britishness and why these Games mark a truly historic watershed', *Mail* online, 13 August.

[24] *The Daily Telegraph*, 20 September 2010.

[25] *The Guardian* (2010) Editorial, 2 October.

[26] *Guardian Media* 26 January 2004.

[27] *The Sun* (1984) 'Benn on the couch', 1 March.

[28] Roy Greenslade (2004) *The Guardian*, 26 January.

[29] Roy Greenslade (2004) 'Do these people have a right to privacy?', *The Guardian*, 26 January.

[30] Roy Greenslade (2005) '*Mail* domination', *The Guardian*, 5 June.

[31] Andrew Marr's lecture to the Political Studies Association's Media and Politics Group, published in *Parliamentary Affairs*, 2005.

[32] Alan Rusbridger (2005) 'What are newspapers for?', Inaugural Hugo Young Lecture at the University of Sheffield, 9 March.

[33] Polly Toynbee (2008) 'To throw the enemy the chancellor's head would be utterly in vain', *The Guardian*, 15 February.

[34] Private conversation with *Times* correspondent.

[35] Robin Cook (2002) 'A modernised parliament in a modernised democracy', Hansard Society Lecture, 22 May.

[36] David Butler (2008) Seminar at Nuffield College, Oxford.

[37] *The Independent* (2008) 'Can do better in the social mobility class', 4 October.

[38] PMSU (Prime Minister's Strategy Unit) (2008) *Getting on, getting ahead. A discussion paper: Analysing the trends and drivers of social mobility*, November, London: PMSU.

[39] Timothy Crouse (1973) *The boys on the bus*, Random House.

[40] Hugo Young (2003) 'Every prime minister must have an Alastair Campbell', *The Guardian*, 29 July.

[41] Tony Blair (2007) 'Blair on the media', 12 June (http:\\news.bbc.co.uk/1/hi/uk_politics/6744581.stm).

[42] *Guardian* Media Supplement Survey of leaders in public life, 10 January 2005.

[43] Ben Goldacre (2010) 'Evidence based voting', *The Guardian*, 24 April.

[44] Ben Goldacre (2009) 'Cancer jabs: good or bad? The *Mail* in two minds', *The Guardian*, 18 April.

[45] Nick Davies (2008) *Flat earth news*, London: Vintage Books.

[46] Ben Goldacre (2008) *Bad science*, London: Fourth Estate.

[47] Geoff Mulgan (2005) Foreword in Ipsos MORI, *Who do you believe: Trust in government information*, London: Ipsos MORI.

[48] Caroline Davies (2008) 'Cynicism can damage democracy's health', *The Observer*, 14 September.

[49] *Guardian* Media Supplement Survey of leaders in public life, 10 January 2005.

[50] Martyn Lewis (1993) 'Not my idea of good news', *The Independent*, 26 April.

[51] *Times* Online, 7 February 2008.

[52] Peter Wilby (2007) 'Good news – but not for the papers', *Guardian Media*, 12 November.

ELEVEN

Subverting democracy (2): serious crimes of the reptiles

Privacy invasions before hacking

Illegal media invasion of privacy did not start with hacking. It happened in virulent form before mobiles were widely distributed. The most notorious case was the Motorman investigation in 2003 by officials of the Information Commissioner's Office (ICO), the watchdog protecting individual privacy and promoting public access to official information. In a raid on just one private investigator, Steve Whittamore, ICO investigators revealed it was being done on an industrial scale. Whittamore had created a thriving information acquisition business through a network of blaggers (people adept at sounding like senior officials who had a right to the information they were seeking on the phone), along with illicit contacts within the police, telephone companies, DVLA and other government agencies. It was generally believed there could be up to 12 private investigators working for the media. (A later inquiry in 2012 by the Commons Home Affairs Committee, examining whether the burgeoning number of private investigators should be put under statutory regulation, heard there could be between 5,000 and 10,000 of them. Over 50 per cent are retired police officers, who have gone into private practice.[1])

The raid on Whittamore's office took away a large cache of handwritten records documenting 17,000 requests – both legal and illegal – for information from journalists. Whittamore along with another private investigator plus a police communications officer and a retired police officer all pleaded guilty in 2004 to conspiracy to commit public misconduct in public office. All four received two-year conditional discharges. Other members of Whittamore's network were due to stand trial but the case collapsed. No journalist was prosecuted. Two reports by the Information Commissioner, Richard Thomas, followed in 2006; both the first *What Price Privacy?* in March, and the second *What Price Privacy Now?* in December were presented to Parliament. The 17,000 requests were boiled down to 3,750 requests involving over 300 journalists from 31 newspapers and magazines. The second report listed some of the key nationals involved. The *Daily Mail* topped the list with 952 requests from 85 journalists and the *Mail on Sunday* came third with 266 requests from 33 journalists. Almost all nationals were involved. The *News of the World*, *Sunday People* and *Daily Mirror* were the others in the top five.

The second ICO report came with a press release in which the Information Commissioner noted that he had requested the Editors' Committee, which controlled the Press Complaints Commission (PCC) Code of Practice, to insert guidance into the code 'to make it clear that it is unacceptable without an individual's consent, to obtain information about their life by bribery, impersonation or subterfuge' unless there was a clear public interest. The committee was chaired by Les Hinton, chair of News International, who replied this request had been rejected. All of the three transgressions set out in the proposed guidance were found in Whittamore's files. The likelihood of a large proportion of the requests passing a public interest test looked low given the work summaries that Whittamore listed on his weekly pay claims: bonking headmaster, lonely heart, dirty vicar, Street stars split, Miss World bonks sailor, judge affair, royal maid, witch doctor, footballer, TV lovechild, junkie flunkie, orgy boss, BBC gardening blunder, Hurley and Grant.

The 17,000 requests were collated on spreadsheets by the ICO containing a wealth of information on commissioning journalists' names, their targets, personal details, types of information sought (criminal records, court judgments, mobile phone numbers) and the substantial fees invoiced by Whittamore. None had been officially released, but copies were sent to the Leveson inquiry. Sir Brian, the chair, allowed 'core participants' in the inquiry to receive copies under strict conditions of confidentiality before deciding whether they should receive wider release. The newspaper lawyers (one set of 'core participants') produced multiple arguments against wider release: too long ago; would cause 'reputational damage'; information was available legally elsewhere; public interest defence. Counsel for the victims of hacking argued that publication was essential 'to demonstrate the prevailing and continuing culture, practice and ethics of the press'. He felt it important for the media to explain the subsequent rewards and career trajectories of journalists named in the Motorman files, as well as the lack of disciplinary action and the fact that at least a number had been promoted to senior editorial positions.

Leveson sides with the victims

Leveson agreed that these were 'potentially relevant considerations' and made short shrift of the arguments of the media's counsels. He declared: 'When I saw the identity of some of those who had been targeted and the nature of the information sought, it seemed to me clear not only that much information had been obtained in breach of the Data Protection Act 1988 but also that the potential to deploy the statutory (public interest) defence was limited in the extreme.' However, he said he had been reluctant to disclose the details, not least because of the consequent publicity, probably unwelcome, to the targets who would suffer a further invasion of privacy. But having talked to some of the victims, he would accept any further information from any of them that might be able to provide information about current journalists, who are listed in the files, particularly if there was any recent evidence of potentially illegally obtained numbers, addresses or other details. Perhaps most important of all, the lesson he drew from Motorman was that it provided better evidence of distorted media ethics than his own inquiry, in that 'it undeniably extends beyond one title'. He also suggested that the press had been slow or reluctant to learn any lessons from Motorman – one newspaper group even continued to employ the services of Whittamore after his conviction.

As a former employee – and trust member – of the *Guardian/Observer* group, I should also note that *The Observer* came ninth in the ICO's list, with 100 Whittamore requests. This was later raised to 200 when the ICO revised its figures. These figures were released to *The Observer*'s independent ombudsman, John Willis. He found that 80 per cent of the cases did have sufficiently clear information about names and stories, and would have had a public interest defence. In the other 20 per cent it was impossible to know because it was unclear who the person was or what the story was about. The 16-page report is on *The Observer's* website.

In 2010 Sharon Marshall, a presenter on ITV 1's *This morning* and former reporter for the *News of the World* and other tabloids, wrote about being a tabloid journalist in her book *Tabloid Girl*. Some called it 'quit-and-tell' showbiz journalism, where you leave the tabloid and are free to say what the job was like. She wrote: 'You will find yourself in the oddest positions, doing the oddest things. You will have to lie, scheme, cheat, secretly tape, con, and beg to get stories. You must crash weddings, funerals and lives and try not crash and burn yourself in the process.' She described how one journalist had 'shadowy contacts with mobile phone firms who could hand over phone records for anyone you wanted'. And then went on: 'This wasn't the only trick you could pull with a mobile phone. Dial any mobile number, enter one of a series of numerical codes and you can listen to all the voice messages which have been stored on the phone.'[2]

The *News of the World* hacking saga

In August 2006 Scotland Yard raided the home of private investigator Glenn Mulcaire, who was under the employment of the *News of the World* (NoW), which led to his conviction of intercepting the voicemail of eight people. Two of the stories involved Prince William, written by Clive Goodman, the NoW's Royal Editor. Goodman admitted conspiring with Mulcaire to hack into the mobile phone messages of the Royal Family and their aides. He was sentenced to four months in prison in January 2007; Mulcaire, who pleaded guilty to illegal interceptions against eight people, was given six months. They were told by the judge, Mr Justice Gross, that the case had nothing to do with the freedom of the press – 'it was about a grave, inexcusable and illegal invasion of privacy'.

Andy Coulson, Editor of the NoW, denied any knowledge of the phone hacking but resigned as the man in charge. He described Goodman as a 'lone rotten apple' on the paper's staff. Two months later, Murdoch executive Les Hinton told a Commons Select

Committee Inquiry that after a 'rigorous internal investigation' the company had found no evidence of widespread hacking at the paper. The PCC reached the same conclusion on 15 May 2007. Two weeks after that, David Cameron made Coulson his Director of Communications at the Conservative Party.

After a pause and then some indefatigable digging by Nick Davies on *The Guardian*, it appeared there was a lot more going on. Civil suits by celebrities – named as victims in the 2006 trial papers – produced new lists of people including MPs and ministers (John Prescott and Tessa Jowell) who had allegedly had their phones hacked. Parliament became upset. The civil cases were threatening to expose other NoW journalists who were involved in hacking. In April 2008 James Murdoch, who had become Chief Executive of News Corp's European and Asian operation in December 2007, agreed to a £700,000 payment to Gordon Taylor, Chief Executive of the Professional Footballers' Association, to settle a phone-hacking claim against NoW. The deal included a gagging clause preventing Taylor from discussing his case. (Murdoch acknowledged this signing in July 2011 but said he 'did not' have a complete picture of the situation in 2008.) Details of this payment were revealed by *The Guardian* on 8 July 2009. The next day the Assistant Commissioner of the Metropolitan Police (the Met) John Yates, announced that after 'the most careful examination by experienced detectives' no further investigation was needed. On 21 July 2009, *The Guardian* revealed that up to 3,000 people may have had their voicemail hacked by NoW journalists. In February 2010, at reopened Commons committee hearings, NoW executives were accused of 'collective amnesia' and 'deliberate obfuscation'.[3]

In a debate in the Commons in September 2010, criticism was expressed about the inadequacy of the initial police investigation. There was also concern about how fearful some MPs were about 'media barons' retaliating. Tom Watson, member of the Commons Media Committee, declared in the debate:

> The barons of the media, with their red top assassins, are
> the beasts in the modern jungle. They have no predators;
> they are untouchable. They laugh at the law; they sneer

at Parliament. They have the power to hurt us, and they do, with gusto and precision, with joy and criminality. Prime Ministers quail before them, and that is how they like it. That, indeed, has become how they insist upon it, and we are powerless in the face of them.[4]

In January 2011 a new Scotland Yard investigation was launched into the hacking allegations, and the Crown Prosecution Service began a review of all the material held by the police. Coulson announced his resignation as Director of Communications at Number 10 on 21 January, saying that the drip, drip of hacking claims meant he could not give 'the 110 per cent' the job needed. Three further NoW journalists, the chief reporter and two former news editors, were arrested for questioning. In the same month, the NoW published a public apology for the interception of voicemail that its reporters had carried out. The Murdoch Group announced it was setting up a compensation fund, signalling it was ready to accept liability in certain civil cases and would be ready to provide compensation of up to £100,000, although it had paid much higher sums to Gordon Taylor, as discussed above, and Max Clifford, the PR agent (Clifford was reported to have got 10 times that amount). Several civil litigants insisted they wanted to continue with their suits. On 15 April 2011 the High Court selected 4 out of 20 pending cases to provide a framework for the other 16.

Murdoch meltdown

As described in Chapter One, it was the NoW hacking of the phone of murdered schoolgirl Milly Dowler that triggered widespread media coverage in early July 2011. This in turn ignited public anger of such sustained force that within three days Rupert Murdoch agreed to shut down the paper. In the days that followed there were seismic shifts of power within and between three institutions: Parliament, the press and the police. A succession of revelations, resignations, summonses, arrests and sackings, all interacting with each other, was being logged daily, sometimes hourly. It was not until the end of the third week, with Parliament in recess and the Oslo bomb and slaughter at the youth camp, that the story dropped down the news agenda. By then Murdoch had shut down his biggest-selling newspaper, lost his BSkyB bid, had financed full-page advertisements in the national press apologising for 'serious wrongdoing' at the NoW, had seen his two closest executives – Les Hinton and Rebekah Brooks – resign, was facing investigation by both the Justice Department and the FBI in the US and multiple inquiries in the UK, and had been required, after initially refusing, to appear before a Commons select committee with his son James and Brooks to account for by then belatedly acknowledged widespread hacking by the NoW but still disputed who-knew-what-when. In the three-hour hearing, which was screened worldwide, Rupert Murdoch described the NoW hacking as 'sickening and horrible'.

The front page headlines the next day (20 July 2011) set out one story: 'Murdoch eats humble pie' (*Telegraph*); 'The most humble day of my life' (*Financial Times*); 'Murdoch's humble pie' (*The Guardian*). The subheadings and cross-stories told another story: 'Murdoch pleads ignorance' (*Financial Times*); 'The people I trusted have betrayed the company and betrayed me' (*The Times*); 'From ruthless boss of his media empire to frail octogenarian' (*The Independent*). The general consensus was that Rupert Murdoch looked frail, tended to ramble, and was forgetful, but produced sharper replies than his son. He told the MPs that NoW was only one per cent of his business. Tom Watson, Labour MP, was picked out as the best questioner. A key quote: 'Don't you think it's incredible that you were chief executive of the company and had no idea of what was going on?'

What was clear in the run-up to the hearing was how much the elder Murdoch had lost his political touch. Just days before the hearing in his first press interview – in *The Wall Street Journal*, his own flagship paper in the US – he insisted, against all the evidence, that his company had handled the July crisis 'extremely well in every possible way', making just 'minor mistakes'. If he thought this would not be reported in the UK he could not have been more mistaken. It was given widespread coverage and withering comment in the UK press.[5] In an interview 12 days later on BBC Radio 4's *The Media Show*, James Harding, Editor of *The Times*, described the handling of the July crisis initially by News International as "catastrophic".

He said that following the Milly Dowler story both paper sales and subscriptions to the digital version of *The Times* fell: 'There were some people who were not just disgusted with the *News of the World* but wanted to express that anger in any way.'[6]

Rhidian Brook, the writer and broadcaster, provided the most succinct summary of the first 10 days on BBC Radio 4's 'Thought for the day':

> the scandal enveloping News Corp is playing like a drama that is hard to categorise: it's blockbuster, soap opera, morality play, family saga, political theatre and police story all rolled into one. It is gripping for all kind of reasons and not all of them noble: shocking, brazen, unsubtle, spiced with hubris, schadenfreude, revenge and justice. And it seems all the more dramatic because no one saw it coming, even though some of the writing had been on the wall for months, even years. If it is about one thing it is about power: who has it; how much should they have; and what are they going to do with it.[7]

Police resignations

On the same day as the parliamentary inquisition of the Murdochs, the two most senior officers of the Metropolitan Police, who had both just resigned largely for relations with members of the press that were thought inappropriate, were giving evidence to a separate Commons select committee. The revelation that the Met had hired Neil Wallis (the former NoW deputy editor under Andy Coulson when the tabloid was alleged to have been engaged in large-scale phone hacking), to be a temporary but senior PR consultant to senior officers, was one reason the two chiefs resigned. It had been almost as big a shock as the hacking of Milly Dowler's phone that a former deputy editor of a suspect tabloid could have been placed in the heart of Scotland Yard to advise the Commissioner and his senior colleagues on public relations; it was only after Wallis had been arrested for alleged phone hacking by the new Met team investigating

NoW activities the previous week, that his one-year post at the Met became known. Sir Paul Stephenson, former Commissioner, initially was unapologetic but later resigned shortly after a *Sunday Times* claim that he had accepted up to £12,000 in luxury hospitality from one of the country's leading health spas following a serious operation.[8] Stephenson told the MPs that the Met had approached Wallis to perform the role and that he had been consulted. He explained: 'Neil Wallis was known to me. When his name came up I had no concern.' Wallis was given his two-day-a-month contract, worth £24,000 a year, in October 2009 when the Met was still under pressure to reopen the investigation into the NoW. John Yates, former Assistant Commissioner, also knew Wallis and helped approve his appointment. Yates told the Home Affairs Committee that it was not just the police who had failed, but News International too, for failing to hand over evidence to detectives which showed that phone hacking at NoW was more widespread than just one rogue reporter. He told the committee that there should be other resignations at News International, which was interpreted as a reference to James Murdoch, given that Rebekah Brooks had already resigned.[9]

Scotland Yard in crisis

The hearing was held just after another bombshell had hit Scotland Yard. Both Stephenson and Yates, along with two other retired senior officers, Andy Hayman, former Assistant Commissioner, and Peter Clarke, former Deputy Assistant Commissioner, were referred by the Metropolitan Police Authority (MPA) to the Independent Police Complaints Commission (IPCC) on 18 July 2011. The MPA cited concerns about their handling of investigations into the phone-hacking story. Scotland Yard was reported to be reeling in the wake of the unprecedented referral of four top police officials to the country's main police watchdog.[10] Theresa May, the Home Secretary, in a move to restore stability, cancelled a trip to the US to make an emergency statement in the Commons. After setting out new temporary postholders before new appointments to replace Stephenson and Yates could be made, she announced she had set up three other separate inquiries: one by Elizabeth Filkin, former

Parliamentary Commissioner for Standards, on the ethics that should underlie the relations between the Met and the media; another by the police inspectorate into the general state of corruption in the police; and third on whether the IPCC needed wider powers, including the power to question civilian witnesses.[11]

The Home Affairs Committee released its report on hacking on the same day that it questioned the senior officers. It concluded News International was guilty of attempting to 'deliberately thwart' the original investigation.[12] The police were criticised in the same report for 'a catalogue of failures', including having 'no will' to investigate.

James Murdoch was back on the front pages on 22 July 2011 when he was accused of misleading the parliamentary committee that had questioned him earlier in the week. He had told the MPs that when he authorised a payment of £700,000 to Gordon Taylor, he was 'not aware' of an email about hacking which appeared to implicate the newspaper's chief reporter. But according to a statement released by two NoW executives – Colin Myler, former Editor, and Tom Crone, the paper's legal manager – this was untrue. In a joint statement, they each said they had personally drawn this to his attention. Under a bold headline 'Wapping at war as former allies turn on James Murdoch', *The Independent* made it their main news story of the day. The email is believed to be 'the smoking gun' in the saga. If the email had become public in a full-blown court case, it would have blown a hole in News International's claim that only one rogue reporter was involved.

There were also foreboding developments overseas. Judicial screws in the US appeared to be tightening in late July. The US Justice Department was reported by the *Wall Street Journal* to be preparing to subpoena News Corp to help with the Department's investigation into whether the company had broken anti-bribery and hacking laws on both sides of the Atlantic.[13]

The Guardian even got a hidden tribute from *The Times* in its first leader at the end of the third week. Writing on the affair, the Murdoch paper noted that even the Office of the Prime Minister had a central role in the drama through the decision to employ a former Editor of the NoW as director of communication, but went on:

The full story will have to wait the outcome of the inquiries that have now been established and the criminal investigations by the police. But what has already emerged is to the credit of investigative journalism. The paradox is that if journalism is in the dock, it was at least journalism that has put it there. At its heart this is an investigation into the use and abuse of power. It has raised the question of whether people who seek to investigate on behalf of the public have, in discharging that privilege, lost sight of their public purpose.[14]

It even went further, raising the question of 'whether such a powerful media company can be held to account by politicians and the police who have sought to curry favour with the purveyors of publicity'.

In the emergency debate on hacking on the last day in Parliament before the summer recess, Cameron finally admitted for the first time that hiring Coulson was a mistake and apologised to MPs for the furore that it had caused. Distancing himself from his former adviser, he said if Coulson had lied about not knowing anything about the hacking he should face 'severe' criminal charges. He added: 'If it turns out I have been lied to that would be a moment for a profound apology, and in that event I can tell you I will not fall short'.[15]

A moment to savour

The end of the July Spring was a moment to savour: the most powerful media man in the West had been curbed; British politicians had recovered their nerve to help cut him down; the prospects of a more effective and pro-active newspaper regulator to monitor media standards looked promising; the insidious symbiotic relationship between tabloid press, police and politicians (see Chapters Three, Four and Five) was exposed and undergoing even further forensic scrutiny; proper order in a genuinely democratic state was being restored.

The degree to which News International executives obstructed police investigators from uncovering criminality was already emerging – from the Commons Home Affairs Select Committee report in July 2011 – with much more to come. The blatant reluctance of Scotland

Yard to pry too closely into the 'black arts' of NoW journalism had seemingly shocked the Prime Minister. As noted in Chapter Two, scandal has historically been the biggest driver of police reform. In his Commons statement in the emergency debate on hacking on 20 July, the Prime Minister hinted about changing the entire culture of the police. He spoke of allowing people from other backgrounds to be eligible for late-entry senior positions, short service commissions, and different entry levels. It had been raised before but never in the wake of such a scandal.

The Leveson hearings begin

The Leveson hearings began on 22 November 2011. They were to last eight months with 650 witnesses testifying in person or in writing, generating 6,000 pages of evidence. There were 97 days of sittings. The Bell Yard entrance to the Royal Courts had a four-tiered stand to accommodate the large army of photographers who turned up on the days celebrities were giving evidence. But it was the stories of ordinary people, whose lives had been callously ruined, that had the greatest impact on the packed courtroom. Sally and Bob Dowler, parents of the murdered schoolgirl Milly Dowler, were the first people to give evidence. They explained how the hacking of their daughter's phone had given them false hope that she was still alive. Tribute was paid by the sketch writers to the dignified and honest way they described the effects of being at the centre of a media frenzy. There was Mary-Ellen Field, who told the inquiry that her own story was 'like a B movie'. So firmly convinced had her employer, Elle Macpherson, become that the highly personal information that routinely appeared in the press originated from Field selling stories that she persuaded her bewildered former adviser to enter a psychiatric-facility in the US for 'an adjustment disorder'. Later she was sacked before Macpherson learned the leaks had been achieved by phone hacking.

Then there were non-hacking cases, stories of distorted news coverage that led to further tragedies. Margaret Watson came to tell how her son Alan killed himself after reading false and derogatory stories about his murdered sister. The first ran in a Glasgow paper, then a similar story was published by *Marie Claire* the following year. Shortly afterwards, the couple's 15-year-old son, their only other child, killed himself. He had a copy of the magazine's article in his hand. Christopher Jefferies, the retired teacher and Bristol landlord of Joanna Yates, suffered a frenzied media campaign 'to blacken his name' when he was taken in for police questioning about Yates' murder. He deservedly collected a large amount of libel damages that followed his release.

'Lives casually ruined'

Then there were the relatives of well-known people who suffered. Max Mosley's 39-year-old son, a drug addict, hadn't killed himself over the press coverage of his father's sex life, Mosley was careful to say, but 'the *News of the World* story had the most devastating effect on him. He really couldn't bear it. He went back on drugs.' Alexander Mosley died in 2009. Garry Flitcroft, the former Blackburn Rovers captain, spoke about the savage tabloid attacks he had received. As Esther Addley wrote in *The Guardian*, philandering multi-millionaire footballers do not naturally attract the greatest sympathy – and yet, as Flitcroft continued his evidence, it became clear why he had asked to address the inquiry. As the taunting in the stadium, fed by relentless negative press stories, became worse, his father who suffered from depression, felt unable to watch. 'His life was coming and watching me play football ... and that took him out of his life.' His father killed himself in 2008. His death came a long time after the tabloid assault, Flitcroft conceded, 'but all I can say is, it affected him a lot'.[16]

There were other families who through no fault of their own found themselves at the centre of media attention. Gerry and Kate McCann, whose daughter disappeared on holiday in Portugal, urged the inquiry to introduce tougher press regulations. A halting Kate described a succession of blows she had suffered: reports that said 'we stored her body in a freezer'; photographers jumping out of bushes and shaking their car to get a startled look; and how she felt 'totally violated' when the *News of the World* published her personal diaries without permission. The paper was forced to pay £125,000 in damages, while Richard Desmond, owner of the *Express* and *Star* papers, was forced by the courts to pay the couple £550,00 for a series of 100 stories in four months, of which at least 38 involved gross and egregious inaccuracies. (Late in January 2012, Desmond was reminded by Robert Jay QC, counsel to the inquiry, 'your papers were accusing the McCanns on occasion of killing their daughter'. He asked him to describe his papers' approach to ethics and morals. Desmond replied: 'Ethical? I don't quite know what that word means, perhaps you will explain. We don't talk about ethics or morals because it is a very fine line and everybody's ethics are different.')

The celebrities

There were only limited reports on these people in the tabloids but more when the celebrities appeared. Hugh Grant, the actor turned campaigner against press intrusion, told the inquiry that hacking was not confined to the Murdoch press. He said his mobile could have been hacked by the *Mail on Sunday*, leading to a ferocious response from the *Mail* stable the next day accusing him of 'mendacious smears'. The paper's response was criticised by Leveson. The counsel to the inquiry, Robert Jay QC, noted: 'There is a critical difference between a right of reply and a right of attack.' More endearingly, Grant told the inquiry how he had turned the tables on Paul McMullan, former features editor of *News of the World*. He had gone to a pub run by McMullan in Kent and secretly taped him describing how tabloids worked, including a claim that the *Daily Mail* had been involved in phone hacking. Grant said he would not submit the recording to the inquiry, but would allow its lawyers to listen to key sections. 'I feel like I did a revenge number on Paul McMullan and that's the issue closed with him. Two separate police inquiries have asked me for the tape and I've refused – it seems too harsh. I don't want to be sending Paul McMullan to prison.[17]

J.K. Rowling told how she felt 'a sense of invasion' when she found a note from a journalist in her daughter's bag when she returned from primary school. 'It's very difficult to say how angry I felt that my five-year-old's school was no longer a place of complete security from journalists.' She objected to the publication of her properties that were clearly identifiable. 'The attitude seems to be utterly cavalier.

Indifference. "What does it matter? You're famous. You're asking for it."' Sienna Miller, the actor, whose phone was hacked by the *News of the World*, told the inquiry: 'I would often find myself at midnight running down a dark street on my own with 10 big men chasing me. The fact that they had cameras made it legal.' Steve Coogan was in the first batch of civil litigants to win damages in the civil courts. The actor, writer and comedian said he was representing a lot of celebrities who felt they could not speak out for fear of reprisals from the tabloids. He had been subjected to hacking, blackmail, entrapment and a series of false stories. He noted there had been so many persistent intrusions in to his personal life, that the press had effectively made him immune from further attacks as his 'closet is empty of skeletons'.

The Commons committee on the media inquiry

In a separate part of London the Commons committee on the media (the Culture, Media and Sport Select Committee) was assembling evidence in its inquiry into News International, which eventually reported in May 2012. Records obtained from the company's former solicitors, Farrer and Co, included emails, billing files and handwritten notes which showed the development of a cover-up of the *News of the World*'s hacking. Julian Pike, the Farrer and Co lawyer handling the negotiations with Gordon Taylor, the chief executive of the Professional Footballers' Association whose phone was tapped, testified that he believed James Murdoch personally authorised the £500,000 pay-off as the price of Taylor's silence. This coincided with the publication of a counsel's opinion commissioned by News International on the phone-hacking scandal. In it, Michael Silverleaf QC spoke of damaging documents unearthed: 'to have this paraded at a public trial would, I imagine, be extremely damaging to [NI's] public reputation', he wrote in June 2008. 'There is overwhelming evidence of the involvement of senior journalists in the illegal inquiries ... There is a powerful case that there is, or was, a culture of illegal information access.'[18]

Surrey Police expose *News of the World* interference

The extent of the *News of the World*'s interference in the Milly Dowler case was exposed in a report published on 23 January 2012 by Surrey Police. Based on the force's logs from 2002, it depicted a news organisation ready to try and bully detectives, already over-burdened in their desperate search for clues about the missing girl, into backing the tabloid's own misguided theories. The report asserted that NoW reporters – there were five of them – were so confident of their own power that they openly admitted the paper had obtained tapes of the voicemail from Milly's phone. One message was from an employment agency in northern England, which had led the paper to believe she was still alive. Reporters raced up to the agency claiming they were working in full cooperation with the police, which was a lie, to demand more details of the job offer. The agency, which said they had had no contact with Milly, complained to the police they were being harassed by the tabloid for more details. On 13 April 2002, the Surrey Police heard from a senior NoW journalist directly. He told them that the recruitment agency had telephoned Milly's mobile and left a message with an offer of a job. Initially the Surrey force dismissed this news as a hoax, but later discovered it was 'a pure coincidence ... of no evidential value' – the company had dialled a wrong number. Undaunted the paper still ran a strong story on 14 April claiming the police were 'intrigued' by the alleged lead. It quoted verbatim from three messages on the phone and implied they had been retrieved by the police, which they had not. After protests from the police, the final edition altered the story to suggest that it was a hoax.[19]

Civil courts

In a third corner the High Court was working towards the conclusion of the first batch of civil compensation claims. Lawyers for the victims were describing how the hacking of their clients had damaged their lives, sometimes causing them to wrongly suspect relations or friends of betraying them. The settlement of the first 37 claims was announced in the New Year when Mr Justice Vos, the judge presiding over the civil claims, said the Murdoch-owned company behind the

News of the World, News Group Newspapers (NGN), had made 'an admission of sorts' that it had engaged in a deliberate cover-up of evidence relating to phone hacking. He said he had seen evidence which 'raised compelling questions about whether you concealed, told lies, actively tried to get off scot free'. He ordered the company to search a number of computers which could contain evidence that its executives had deliberately tried to destroy evidence of phone hacking. He said he had seen emails that showed how, days after Sienna Miller wrote to the company asking it to retain emails which might relate to hacking her phone, 'a previously conceived plan to conceal evidence was put in train by NGN managers'. NGN refused to admit the allegations but agreed that damages paid to the victims could be assessed 'on the basis of the facts alleged'. Similarly, NGN had earlier refused to admit its former directors and senior executives had presided over a cover-up , but agreed that 'aggravated damages' could be calculated 'as if' the allegations that they had lied, obstructed police and destroyed evidence were true. The Murdoch subsidiary said it had made the concessions solely in 'the interest of prompt and efficient determination of the claims'.[20]

The publisher paid a seven-figure total in aggravated damages to settle 37 phone-hacking claims brought by victims. They included some well-known names, including MPs, actors, footballers and rugby players, such as John Prescott, George Galloway, Dannii Minogue, Ashley Cole, Sara Payne, James Hewitt, Gavin Henson and Ulrika Jonsson. Jude Law's damages of £130,000 were some of the highest. He had been subjected to repeated and sustained physical surveillance over several years including blagging that led to 16 articles being published. *The Times* reported that Law's damages included a number of 'similar intrusive articles in *The Sun*', thus widening the shadow over the Murdoch groups.[21]

In a separate piece in *The Times*, Ben Webster reported that the damages awarded ranged from £25,000 to £200,000. He went on to note that the company had set aside £20 million for damages but the total cost of settling claims with up to 800 hacking victims could be more than double that figure once legal costs of both sides were included.[22] In his media column in *The Observer*, Peter Preston wrote: 'In one bizarre sense, News International may have done us all – and Lord Justice Leveson – a service. Look at some of the 37 names who settled their phone-hacking claims with Murdoch last week: Paul Dadge who heroically tended the 7/7 injured on the streets of London; Sara Payne, mother of a murdered child; Shaun Russell, grieving husband of a murdered wife; Christopher Shipman, a shell-shocked son whose father killed and killed again. In sum Milly Dowler's parents were not alone. All these men and women, thrust into the news by tragedy, became victims twice over as they switched on their mobile phones.'[23]

Three weeks later the Murdoch company reached a settlement with another 21 victims, who included Steve Coogan and the Liberal Democrat deputy leader, Simon Hughes. With News International having agreed to meet claimants' legal costs, the first group of 37 were estimated to have cost £10 million and the extra 21 payouts some £5 million. Hugh Tomlinson QC, counsel for hacking victims, told Mr Justice Vos that 50 fresh cases were in preparation.[24] Coogan, who had previously promised to have his day in court, told *The Guardian* that, having run up legal bills of £400,000, it was no longer worth the risk to fight on when a legal action with others had already contributed to 'turning up the heat against News International'. Coogan, in common with other litigants, made a settlement that would ensure that the evidence obtained would feed into any future criminal cases and a future phase of the Leveson inquiry. Charlotte Church, the singer, and her parents settled for £600,000 in damages at the end of February 2012. She had been subjected to persistent harassment from the age of 16 in 2002 and her mother bullied into giving details of her own private medical condition for no other reason than that she was Charlotte's mother. Church said she had decided not to go ahead with a trial because her mother would have had to relive too many painful memories.

Civil war at *The Sun* as police arrests rise

The activities of News Corporation's management and standards committee (MSC), set up in the wake of the hacking scandal by Murdoch's global HQ in New York, were causing trouble in *The Sun* newsroom. This powerful unit, housed quite separately from

News International executives and newsrooms, was chaired by Lord Grabiner QC and overseen by Will Lewis, the former editor of *The Daily Telegraph*. The unit, which reported back directly to New York, was helped by an army of lawyers as well as 20 police detectives, searching through *The Sun*'s email archive to find evidence of wrongdoing that could be handed over to the police. The fact that its investigations had led to the arrest of 10 *Sun* journalists on suspicion of corrupt payments within its first four months, demonstrated how far-ranging News Corp's clean-up campaign was this time. It was an important defensive move to protect the American-based company from prosecution under the US Foreign and Corrupt Practices Act.

There had been several arrests of former *News of the World* journalists by the police squad pursuing hacking, but then the separate police team pursuing illegal payments to public officials began making arrests at *The Sun*. The first arrest of four *Sun* journalists was quickly followed by the arrest of five senior journalists at the paper on 11 February 2012. *The Sun* went into revolt, with a front-page splash declaring 'Witch-hunt has put us behind ex-Soviet states on press freedom'. It was written by the paper's most senior writer Trevor Kavanagh, a close confidant of Rupert Murdoch. It opened robustly: '*The Sun* is not a swamp that needs draining. Yet in what would at any other time cause uproar in Parliament and among civil liberties and human rights campaigners, its journalists are being treated like members of an organised gang. They are subject to the biggest police operation in British criminal history – bigger even than Pan Am Lockerbie murder probe. Major crime investigations are on hold as 171 police are drafted to run three separate operations.' True to *The Sun*'s tradition, most of those facts were wrong. There were roughly 170 officers pursuing the serious criminal allegations of hacking and corrupt payments, but no major investigations were on hold. And far from being more than for the Lockerbie murders, which had 1,000 officers in its early days, or the 5,000 used in the G20 event, or the 16,000 officers on the streets of London on the third night of summer riots in 2011, Kavanagh could not have been more wrong.

He went on: 'Instead of being called in for questioning, 30 journalists have been needlessly dragged from their bed in dawn raids, arrested and held in police cells while their homes are ransacked.

Wives and children have been humiliated as up to 20 officers at a time rip up floorboards and sift through intimate possessions, love letters and entirely private documents.'[25] The bloggers had fun, Richard Wilson chronicling Kavanagh's own past cheering for police excess and his widespread disrespect for due process, while Full Fact documented many inaccuracies in the splash. But the best response came from Brian Cathcart, former journalist, now professor of journalism at Kingston University and founder of the Hacked Off campaign. He wryly noted: 'Setting facts and consistency aside (a useful *Sun* device), the very idea of a bullyboy, dish-it-out, don't care newspaper dressing itself up as a tragic victim is enough (as *The Sun* might write) to make us choke on our cornflakes. "Boo hoo", the headline might say and we would all laugh.'[26]

Undeterred, Kavanagh took to the airwaves to tell BBC Radio 4 that 'there is unease about the way that some of the best journalists in Fleet Street have ended up being arrested on evidence that the MSC has handed to the police'. In another interview on BBC Radio 5 Live, he accused 'certain parts of the company' of 'boasting that they are sending information to the police that has put these people into police cells'.[27]

Kavanagh had also defended payments made by *Sun* journalists to obtain stories, suggesting it had always been 'standard procedure' for all popular papers. These payments had unearthed stories, opened closed doors: 'there is nothing disreputable about it. And, as far as I know at this point, nothing illegal'; he got that wrong, too.

What Kavanagh ignored was the fact that Murdoch had very little choice but to get rid of senior journalists who may have helped cover up the seriously illegal corrupt payments to public officials or hacking to protect his much more important and profitable US parent company from American investigations after Mr Justice Vos's rulings in the first round of the civil settlements. There was a real fear in the *Sun* newsroom that Murdoch intended to close it. Instead he came back to the UK and announced that he would not only keep it going but there would be a *Sunday Sun* in place of the *News of the World* as well. This emerged on 26 February 2012. He also lifted the suspension of the 10 arrested *Sun* journalists 'until or whether they are charged'. The civil war subsided.

'Power, corruption and lies'

One day after the new *Sunday Sun* was launched, Sue Akers, the deputy assistant commissioner of the Metropolitan Police in charge of its three separate investigations of News International (alleged hacking, bribery, and computer tampering), made a dramatic appearance at the Leveson inquiry. She was clearly intent on correcting Kavanagh – and three Fleet Street titles, *The Telegraph*, the *Mail* and *The Times* – who had weighed in on the excess numbers of police involved in the investigation. She set out how *The Sun* had established 'a network of corrupt officials' and created 'a culture of illegal payments'. There were 'multiple payments' by *The Sun* to public officials, with one individual receiving £80,000 in alleged corrupt payments over a number of years. One *Sun* journalist drew more than £150,000 over the years to pay sources. She said the *Sun* reporters were largely publishing 'salacious gossip' on the back of the information they were receiving. The cases her team were investigating were not ones involving the 'odd drink and meal' with public officials, but regular payments using an internal system designed to hide the identity of those allegedly receiving money illegally.[28] Akers said that although she was dependent on News Corp's MSC to turn over incriminating emails, the cooperation was working well and the MSC was independent of News International. She said the investigation into bribes was following Crown Prosecution Service advice to focus on cash payments and not on 'more general hospitality such as meals or drinks', which were specifically excluded. Her testimony contradicted claims by some *Sun* journalists that they were being prosecuted merely for buying lunch for contacts. She also emphasised that the MSC was handling police requests for information 'in a manner that seeks to protect legitimate journalist sources at all times. Our aim is to uncover criminality. It is not to uncover legitimate sources.'[29]

In other developments on the same day, Murdoch is understood to have studied Akers' incendiary testimony and issued a short statement a couple of hours afterwards. He said: 'As I've made very clear, we have vowed to do everything we can to get to the bottom of prior wrongdoing in order to set us on the right path for the future. That process is well understood. The practices Sue Akers described at the

Leveson inquiry are one of the past and no longer exist at the *Sun*. We have already emerged a stronger company.'[30]

The Daily Telegraph report of the same hearing suggested internal police logs showed that the Metropolitan Police knew almost immediately that hacking went wider than one reporter at News International but they failed to widen the scope. Police collusion with News International was laid bare in disclosures showing that the company paid thousands of pounds to a network of serving officers and had a mole in the original hacking investigation. Brian Paddick, a former deputy assistant commissioner, told the inquiry that there had been a 'revolving door' between the Met and News International, with the former commissioner Lord Stevens and the former assistant commissioner Andy Hayman both employed by the company when they left the force.[31]

The heir apparent loses his crown

James Murdoch's resignation on 28 February 2012 made many front pages the next day. *The Times* reported that the resignation had come just weeks before the publication of a report by MPs that was expected to criticise his handling of the phone-hacking scandal. It noted it came in a week in which News International had been subjected to damaging allegations at the Leveson inquiry into media ethics. He remained, at the age of 39, as News Corporation's deputy chief operating officer, the third most senior position in the parent company. He would be based in New York, but would return to London regularly in his role as Chairman of BSkyB.[32] A headline inside summed up his work in the UK: 'Newspaper scandal casts a shadow over Murdoch's achievements at BSkyB'. A senior News Corp executive told *The Times*: 'James loves journalism but he's less in love with the business model of newspaper. TV is what everyone thinks he's good at and that's what he will focus on.'

Michael Wolff, a biographer of Rupert Murdoch, wrote in *The Guardian*: 'What's done is done – even if they don't yet acknowledge that it is 100 per cent done. James Murdoch, hopelessly tarred by the phone-hacking story exits his position as chairman of News International ... he has not existed as a force since the meltdown of the *News of the World* last summer. And there is no possibility that he will inherit the top job.'[33] The *Financial Times* reported: 'It might look like a relief for him to leave the last of his London roles apart from the chairmanship of BSkyB. But it would do very little to insulate him from the spreading scandal and it represented a further dismantling of the power base he had built in London.'[34]

Brooks and husband arrested

The Daily Telegraph front-page headline succinctly summed up the dramatic event: 'One minute they were off racing, the next they were under arrest'. Rebekah Brooks, former chief executive of News International, was arrested at dawn on 13 March alongside her husband, the racehorse trainer Charlie Brooks, on suspicion of conspiracy to pervert the course of justice. They had both been planning to be at the Cheltenham races. Instead they were taken to separate police stations in Oxfordshire and Buckinghamshire and held for 12 hours. The two were released on bail along with four others, also granted bail. Two of the four were News International employees. *The Telegraph* noted that conspiracy to pervert the course of justice charges, which all six might face, were far more serious than charges of hacking or corrupt payments. While hacking and corrupt payments can carry prison sentences, the offence of perverting the course of justice can include a life sentence in exceptional cases. Of the 44 arrests made before the six on 13 March, only three had been arrested on suspicion of perverting the course of justice.

Charlie Brooks was not even married to the former *News of the World* editor at the time the hacking was allegedly going on, but he came to the attention of the police when his laptop was handed in to the police the day after his wife's first arrest in July 2011. A cleaner at the Design Centre apartment complex in Chelsea Harbour where the couple have a London home found a bag containing a computer, a phone and some paperwork in an underground car park and dumped them in a bin, where they were found by a security officer. Brooks said his briefcase had been dropped in the car park but he had forgotten to pick it up because he was glued to Sky News. He said it was all to do with his personal information and nothing to do with his wife.[35]

Meanwhile, on the same day at the Leveson inquiry, Dick Fedorcio, Scotland Yard's communications chief, was, in the words of *The Independent*, revealing 'incestuous' Murdoch ties. He acknowledged that the teenage son of the former Met Commissioner, Sir Ian Blair, was given a work experience placement at News International and his own son was given a valued place at *The Sun*. A tendering process organised by Fedorcio handed a lucrative consultancy to Neil Wallis, a former deputy editor of the *News of the World*. But he denied a suggestion from the inquiry's leading counsel, Robert Jay, that the force's relationship with News International was 'incestuous'.[36]

Rupert Murdoch's blackest week

In the last week of April 2012, Rupert Murdoch went through his blackest seven days. It opened with a two-day appearance before the Leveson inquiry beginning on 25 April, where he uttered his most complete apology yet for his shortcomings over the hacking affair: 'a serious blot on my reputation'. It ended six days later with the damning conclusion in a report from the Commons Select Committee on the Media that he was 'not a fit person to exercise the stewardship of a major international company'. This was only the second time – the first before MPs in 2011 – that the Murdoch dynasty had been required to account for itself in public. This time the questioning was more informed, skilful and penetrating than before the MPs. There were only two interrogators – the chief counsel and the chairman – rather than a whole committee. It was therefore more systematic and better able to control deliberate diversions. It needed to be given the succession of denials, several repeated more than once, made by the western world's most powerful media mogul: 'I've never asked a prime minister for anything in my life.... we have never pushed our commercial interests in our papers ... I don't know many politicians'. And that was only on the first day.

Murdoch's aim was to deconstruct the 'myth' that he ever exercised undue political power, or that he traded the allegiance of his newspaper for political favours. Just in the month before Murdoch appeared before Leveson, newly released files from the Thatcher archive in Cambridge contained details of a secret Chequers lunch on 4 January 1981 between Thatcher and Murdoch. It took place just weeks before her government decided his bid for Times Newspapers did not need to be referred to the Monopolies and Mergers Commission (MMC). The sealing of the bid allowed Murdoch to become the dominant media force in the UK with almost 40 per cent of national newspaper sales. For the next 30 years neither Thatcher nor Murdoch would acknowledge the lunch had taken place. Thatcher instructed that the memorandum of the meeting should not be disclosed. Murdoch failed to inform the historian writing his paper's official history of the event. The memorandum noted that at the lunch Murdoch had set out his plan for making the papers profitable: taking on the unions, introducing new technology, reducing the workforce by 25 per cent.

Robert Jay quoted an item recorded in the diary of Woodrow Wyatt MP, who once told Murdoch: 'Margaret is very keen on preserving your position'. Murdoch produced his standard denial 'I didn't expect any help from her, nor did I ask for any' – and then found himself accepting that while *The Sun* supported her, she had delivered a series of decisions which were extremely helpful to him, allowing him to own both *The Times* and *The Sunday Times* without referring his bid to the MMC. He now no longer denied that there had been any contact between himself and Thatcher during the period of the bid and referral was up for discussion. He said the lunch meeting on 4 January 1981 had been at his request. It was merely to inform her of the proposed purchase of 'a great iconic asset'. He insisted no favours were asked of Mrs Thatcher. Responding, Jay put it to him that he would not have needed to be so 'cack-handed'. Murdoch responded with his mantra: 'I have never asked a prime minister for any help'. The interchange prompted Harry Evans, former editor of first *The Sunday Times* and then *The Times*, to write in *The Guardian* that had this event emerged at the time, it would have destroyed Murdoch's chances of acquiring the papers.[37] Then there was the exemption, under the Thatcher government, of BSkyB from the regulations of the 1990 Broadcasting Act that had generated huge profits for his company.

There was similar parrying over Murdoch's relationship with Tony Blair. He was hazy on the detail of their courtship, nor could he recall Blair pledging not to tighten up the media ownership rules, as recorded in Alastair Campbell's diaries.[38] He batted away a suggestion by Leveson that surely he was 'reassured' that, unlike in the previous election of 1992, there were no cross-media ownership proposals in the 1997 Labour Party manifesto. 'I don't even remember noticing it', he responded.

Michael White, *The Guardian*'s sketch writer, summed up the first day rather succinctly: 'In one of the tighter corners of his corner-cutting career, the media mogul repeatedly insisted that he enjoys little political influence, let alone charismatic authority over prime ministers. Sun King? He was trying to sound like Burger King. Tony Blair's ingratiating 1997 *Times* article? "I didn't read it." Gordon Brown's pyjama party? "Just a bunch of women," he loftily explained. Actually the performance was even more ruthless than that. Time and time again, Murdoch contrived to sound rather likeable, his self-deprecating humour far from tycoon pomposity. People laughed.'

The second day's hearing

Nick Davies, the *Guardian* journalist who had first exposed the wholesale hacking at *The News of the World* three years earlier, was there to watch:

> This is a man who is used to getting his way. He is not used to being confronted by people who have power, the skill and the simple effrontery to challenge him. On Wednesday morning he walked in with all the protection that his advisors could give him in the previous days of detailed briefings and rehearsal. By yesterday, there were times when he had lost the script, lost the plot and he simply sat there, with nobody to help him and no way out. Just after 11.30am there was one riveting and typical exchange, in which he tried all the manoeuvres that would normally have allowed him to create some

diversion to avoid answering a question. And all of them failed.'

The question involved was a moral one. At least one *News of the World* journalist had threatened to expose the identity of a prostitute unless she cooperated in the paper's exposé of Max Mosley, in which case she would receive a payment. A judge in the case had described it as blackmail. Murdoch tried to dismiss this as a journalist doing a favour for the prostitute. At which point Leveson intervened 'I ought to be very clear to you I find that approach somewhat disturbing, because I don't think Mr Justice Eady is using too strong a word if he described this as blackmail. And therefore, if it is the culture and practice of the press that this is acceptable, I would like to know that. I really would.' Davies concluded: 'So it was that this most powerful man was compelled to agree that he would go off and read the judgment, which he claimed not to have read; and to submit in writing his view about whether or not it is acceptable for reporters to engage in blackmail.'[39]

Other key points were:

- On the hacking cover-up: Murdoch admitted there had been a cover-up, but said he and other executives had been 'shielded' from the truth. He blamed 'two very strong characters' on the paper for not alerting management. He recognised hacking was 'against the law, quite apart from the ethical side. It was totally wrong, and I regret it and I've said it's going to be a blot on my reputation for the rest of my life.'
- On shutting down the *News of the World*: 'I'll say it succinctly. I panicked, but I'm glad I did. And I'm sorry I didn't close it years before and put a *Sun on Sunday* in. I tell you what held us back: *News of the World* readers. Only half of them read *The Sun*. Only a quarter regularly.'
- On trading favours with politicians: He said it was a myth, but in an unguarded moment, he admitted that he saw trading favours as normal behaviour. 'It's a common thing in life, way beyond journalism, for people to say, "I'll scratch your back if you scratch my back".' Robert Jay responded: 'But it's interesting that you say

that's no part of the implied deal in your relations with politicians over 30 years, Mr Murdoch. Is that right?' A hesitant answer: 'Uh … yes. I don't ask any politician to scratch my back.'

- On his relations with his editors: Jay read from an article by David Yelland, a former editor of *The Sun*, in *The Independent*: 'Most Murdoch editors wake up in the morning, switch on the radio, hear that something has happened and think: what would Rupert think about this? It's like a mantra in your head, it's like a prism. You look at the world through Rupert's eyes.' Murdoch: 'It's nonsense and I think you should take it in the context of Yelland's autobiography, when he said he was drunk all the time he was at *The Sun*, which we didn't notice.'

- On the future of newspapers: Murdoch urged the government not to regulate the press out of existence. He said newspapers may have only 10 years as a printed product because of the competition from the internet. 'Every newspaper has had a very good run … it's coming to an end as a result of these disruptive technologies. I think we will have both (web and print news) for quite a while, certainly 10 years, some people say five. I'd be more inclined to say 20.'

To sum up, Tim de Lisle, editor of *Intelligent Life* magazine and former arts editor of *The Times*: 'Rupert Murdoch's evidence to the Leveson inquiry was like one of his tabloids: a lively mixture of accurate and inaccurate reporting, one-eyed comment and total fantasy. It was hard to say which of his statements provoked the most incredulity. There was his declaration that *The News of the World* was a "campaigning newspaper". There was the idea that the great Harry Evans, while editing *The Times*, knocked on Murdoch's door and asked what line to take … as Harry Evans has shown, it is when Murdoch hotly denies something that we need to be most suspicious.'[40]

Commons committee condemns Murdoch

Murdoch was lucky his Leveson appearance preceded the Commons report rather than followed it, as even he would have found it difficult to worm out of some of its indictments: unfit to run an international corporation; wilful blindness; lack of curiosity; contempt of Parliament. The headlines were blunt and accurate about the report. 'Murdoch not fit for global role, says report' in the *Financial Times* would have ensured many influential people overseas were made aware. Only *The Times* headline indicated it was not unanimous, 'MPs split on whether Murdoch is "fit" to run his empire'. The editorials were more nuanced. The FT noted that few would be surprised by the findings 'with the stream of arrests and legal cases over the past year, as well as the evidence being unearthed almost daily by Lord Leveson's inquiry, it has become evident that not only was there wrongdoing at News International but also a serious and persistent effort to cover up. Nonetheless, the report's verdict will add up to a sense of siege at News Corp.... All this challenges the idea – which Mr Murdoch put out at the Leveson inquiry – that the cover-up was confined to executives at the now defunct Sunday tabloid.' But it added a strict caveat; 'The report's force was, however, blunted by a partisan decision from Labour and Liberal Democrat members to insert observations that Rupert Murdoch "was not a fit person to exercise the stewardship of a major international company". As a result, Tory members refused to put their names to it. Given that such a judgment is clearly beyond the investigation's remit, this can only be construed as an attempt to sway shareholders and regulators in the US, who are watching the UK investigations into News Corp closely.'

The *Mail* concluded: 'There *was* a phone hacking cover up at *News of the World* ... senior executives *did* mislead Parliament ... Rupert Murdoch is "not a fit person" to run a major international firm ... the findings were brutal ... were they fair and impartially reached? Regrettably, with regard to Mr Murdoch, the answer is No.' Dan Sabbagh, *The Guardian*'s media editor, said Murdoch would be able to bat away the committee's 'not fit' finding because of the partisan vote underpinning it, but it might not prove so easy for him to swat away the other findings concerning corporate governance. 'MPs concluded by 9 votes to 1 that it was "simply astonishing" that Rupert and James Murdoch did not realise "that one rogue reporter line was untrue" until December 2010. There was a 7 to 3 vote in support that News International and News Corp had exhibited "wilful blindness" for which its directors should take responsibility.

There was a 7 to 2 support for "questions of competence" raised by some of James Murdoch's decisions.'

Milly's phone: the truth may never be known

The full truth about the extent of hacking into Milly Dowler's phone may never be known, police admitted in a report to the Leveson inquiry on 9 May 2012. It confirmed that the *News of the World* had hacked into her phone after her death but concluded 'it is not possible to state with any certainty whether Milly's voicemails were or were not deleted'. Detective Chief Inspector John Macdonald of the Metropolitan Police said two voicemail messages appeared to have been removed, but because the full technical call data was missing, 'reaching a definitive conclusion is not and may never be possible'.

Gill Phillips, the lawyer representing *The Guardian*, told the inquiry: 'In April 2002, Surrey police made a connection between the apparent deletion of Milly's messages and the *News of the World* ... *The Guardian*'s story of 4 July 2011 was based on multiple sources and the state of knowledge at the time. Our error – as we acknowledged and corrected last December – was to have written about the cause of the deletions as a fact rather than as the belief of several people. We regret that.' She was referring to a *Guardian* report that had said the *NoW* had hacked the phone and deleted some messages.

Anthony White QC, representing the *News of the World*, apologised for the paper's behaviour. He added that the deletions were likely to have been caused by automatic dropping-off of voicemails after 72 hours and that had led to to Sally Dowler's 'false hope moment'.[41]

The story of a Cameron spin doctor

Andy Coulson, who appeared before the Leveson inquiry on 10 May, in his first public appearance since his resignation from Number 10 and his subsequent arrest, was not cross-examined about phone hacking at the paper to avoid any risk of prejudice to any future trial. But he did say that the only time he was asked by Cameron about phone hacking at the paper was before his initial appointment as the Conservative Party's communications director in May 2007. It was not raised in July 2009, when *The Guardian* reported that hacking at his paper was far wider than one reporter. He conceded he may have had unsupervised access to top-secret papers while he worked for Cameron in Downing Street, even though his security vetting had been at a lower level than his predecessors and his successors in the post. His vetting status only became known in the summer of 2011, which prompted a series of official freedom of information requests to the Prime Minister on the issue. It fuelled suggestions that Cameron had failed to take proper steps to check allegations that Coulson had been involved in illegal behaviour at the *News of the World*. Coulson admitted that he had failed to declare £40,000 shareholding in News Corp while at Number 10, but had only come to realise it could have been a conflict of interest after he had resigned.[42]

The 'Brooks' Six' are charged

Rebekah and Charlie Brooks, along with four current or former employees of News International, were formerly charged with conspiracy to pervert the course of justice on 14 May. The charge related to allegations of concealing evidence from Scotland Yard's phone-hacking team in the last days of the *News of the World*'s existence and the weeks that followed. Rebekah Brooks and her husband gave statements to a small invited audience of television crews, which *The Daily Telegraph* described as 'already becoming a public relations battle with prosecutors'. The couple announced the charges five minutes before the scheduled Crown Prosecution Service briefing formally opened. Charlie Brooks described the charges as 'an attempt to use me and others as scapegoats, the effect of which will be to ratchet up the pressure on my wife'. Rebekah Brooks said: 'Even News International's harshest critics cannot wish to see today people with no involvement with the central issues being treated like this'. She is charged with three counts, between 6 July – two days after the hacking of Milly Dowler's voicemails became known – and 19 July 2011, four days after her resignation as Chief Executive of News International and two days after her first arrest for suspected hacking.

The Daily Telegraph noted: 'The charging of two good friends of the Prime Minister means that the scandal threatens to dominate David Cameron's entire first term ... police have already budgeted for the investigation carrying on until 2015.'[43]

The BBC Newsnight anchor's lesson on hacking

Jeremy Paxman, the BBC Newsnight presenter, appearing on 23 May, described how Piers Morgan, then Editor of the *Daily Mirror*, had described in detail how to hack a mobile phone at a lunch held at the paper's HQ in September 2002. At the lunch Morgan had teased the TV presenter, Ulrika Jonsson, saying that he knew about her private conversations with Sven-Goran Eriksson, the England football manager with whom she had had an affair. Choosing his words carefully, Paxman went on: 'Now I don't know whether he was repeating a conversation that he had heard or he was imagining this conversation. In fact, to be fair to him, I think we should accept both possibilities, because he probably was imagining it.' Morgan, who was working in the US, took to Twitter the same day with a response: 'Right – that's the last time I'm inviting Jeremy Paxman to lunch.'

Previously when asked in December 2011 whether he had advised Jonsson to change her mobile security code at the same lunch, Morgan said he could not recall what had happened. There had been speculation that the *Mirror* broke the Sven–Ulrika affair story with the help of phone hacking, but this was strongly denied by Morgan and Trinity Mirror. James Hipwell, a former financial reporter at *The Daily Mirror* who was jailed for two months for insider trading, told the inquiry that phone hacking had been widespread at the paper.[44]

The saga of a Murdoch 'cheerleader'

Running parallel with the inquisition of Murdoch was an investigation by Leveson of Jeremy Hunt's handling of the BSkyB bid. Hunt had been given the job of Secretary of State for Culture, Media and Sport after it had been removed from Vince Cable, who had been recorded telling two undercover *Telegraph* reporters purporting to be constituents that he was 'declaring war on Murdoch'. Hunt had never tried to hide his support for Murdoch, even labelling himself a 'Murdoch cheerleader' on his own website. But once given responsibility for supervising the bid on 10 December 2010, he told MPs that he had followed a due process approach in his quasi-judicial new role. On Murdoch's first day before Leveson, the headlines were dominated by the previous day's witness, Frédéric Michel, James Murdoch's aide and chief lobbyist on the BSkyB bid.

To coincide with his appearance, Murdoch's News Corp had released 160 pages of text messages, emails and notes on phone calls between Michel and Hunt's office. They exposed both the close and intimate contact that Michel had built up with Hunt's special adviser, Adam Smith, and the extraordinary degree to which the company was able to lobby for its cause. In the 13 months from June 2010, when News Corp announced its intention of buying the remainder of the BSkyB shares and July 2011 when the bid was withdrawn after the *News of the World* scandal broke, Michel made 191 phone calls, wrote 158 emails, and sent 799 texts to Hunt's office, the vast majority to Adam Smith. He in turn texted Michel 257 times between November 2010 and July 2011. Later, Smith admitted he had had no contact at all with the large coalition of newspapers opposing the bid.

There were several explosive emails in the package. One much used by all the media was a message that Michel had sent to James Murdoch claiming to have details of what Hunt would say to Parliament the next day on the BSkyB takeover, noting that it was 'absolutely illegal' for him to obtain such information. Another reported a plea from Hunt to the Murdoch team for help 'to try and find as many errors as we can' in an Ofcom report on the public interest implications of the BSkyB bid. A third, dating back to January 2010, reported Hunt's belief that it would be 'game over' for opponents of the takeover once plans to spin off Sky News into a separately listed company were announced. Michel went on: 'He [Hunt] said we would get there at the end, and he shared our objectives.'

The headlines following this evidence had two themes: 'Murdoch's revenge' (*The Independent*), 'Murdochs turn the tables on Cameron and Hunt' (the *Financial Times*), 'Revenge of the Murdochs' (the *Daily Mail*), or 'Hunt in frame over handling of BSkyB deal' (*The Times*), 'Minister for Murdoch (*The Guardian*). The front-page splashes all talked of a minister who was fighting for his political life in the face of Labour calls for his resignation. *The Times* Editorial declared: 'Judging from the published emails, his [Hunt's] office was too close to News Corp. At best, his office was providing a running commentary on a deal on which Mr Hunt was supposed to be adjudicating. At worst, he was betraying the confidences in government, offering market-sensitive information to the bidder and helping to frame remedies that would help secure the bid. These are questions which Mr Hunt must now answer'.[45] The *Daily Mail* Editorial complained that his role as adjudicator of the bid 'always carried a bad smell'. It explained: 'After all, the Culture and Media Secretary has gone on record to fawn that Mr Murdoch had "done more to create variety and choice in British TV than any other single person"! Now, however, devastating emails released by the Leveson Inquiry have revealed Mr Hunt was not merely a sycophant; he was apparently prepared to give the Murdoch empire utterly improper access to the inner sanctum of the Cameron government.'[46]

Cameron refuses to refer Hunt to independent adviser

Calls for Hunt to be referred to the Independent Adviser on Ministers' Interests, Sir Alex Alan, to examine whether the ministerial code had been broken were rejected by the Prime Minister on the ground that Hunt would be appearing before Leveson to examine Michel's evidence. But Leveson intervened to say his remit was to inquire into 'the culture and practices of the press', not the practices of Hunt. But Cameron, supported by his deputy, Nick Clegg, still refused to make a referral. Leveson refused to advance the date that Hunt was due before the inquiry but on 31 May he duly appeared. He admitted to the inquiry that he had continued to communicate privately with James Murdoch despite having been advised at least twice by his officials that he should not do so. On one occasion he cancelled a meeting but they had talked by mobile phone. Despite his admissions, a defiant Downing Street cleared Hunt of any wrongdoing within minutes of the conclusion of his six-hour cross-examination.

In its Editorial the next day, *The Daily Telegraph* criticised Hunt on two grounds. The first was that he had misled MPs in his earlier statement to Parliament in which he had implied that he had engaged as much with the opponents of the bid as with Murdoch. In fact there had been only one communication with opponents. The second criticism was that he had made no attempt to disguise his support for the takeover. It went on: 'Such callow behaviour is unacceptable in a senior minister. In a rather sheepish performance, Mr Hunt even admitted texting Mr Murdoch during the bid process over which he was presiding, which makes a nonsense of the concept of a quasi-judicial relationship.' The day before he appeared before Leveson, Professor Vernon Bogdanor, one of Britain's foremost constitutional experts (and Cameron's tutor at Oxford), wrote a scathing article on Hunt's behaviour, pointing out that under the ministerial code he was fully accountable for the behaviour of his special adviser. He thought it 'implausible that Hunt was unaware of what his special adviser was doing. But even if he was unaware, that does not make him innocent. It makes him guilty of gross incompetence.'[47]

Summing up what had been learned from Hunt's day at the inquiry, *The Guardian* noted: 'First that Mr Hunt was as biased in favour of News Corp's bid as Vince Cable was prejudiced against it and that Mr Cameron knew it. Second, that Mr Hunt does not have a consistent view of due process.' The need for a referral to the independent adviser on the ministerial code rumbled on. Liberal Democrat MPs refused to vote against a Labour motion calling for a referral on 13 June, but the motion was still defeated. Hunt survived, finally moving to become Health Secretary in the September 2012 reshuffle.

Lessons from history

Stephen Dorrell, who as Heritage Secretary in the 1990s had responsibility for media policy, described to the inquiry on 23 May what happened to the last report that had tried to reform the regulation of the press: the second Calcutt report in 1993. It proposed outlawing doorstepping, bugging and long-lens photography as part of a bid to curtail what was seen as an increasing invasion of privacy by the press. John Major, the Prime Minister at the time, thought it would backfire horribly and provide editors with a chance to be 'martyrs', which they would love. In a confidential memo from Major to Dorrell, which was shown to the inquiry, the former Prime Minister said a spell in prison for an editor would 'do wonders for their paper's circulation and be worth a fortune in free publicity'. A memo from Dorrell to Major noted the depth of hostility to statutory regulation and forecast 'a major press row'. A Cabinet committee was convened on 15 June 1993, attended by Lord David Hunt, now the Chairman of the Press Complaints Commission, drawing up a substitute for the PCC, where it was agreed that they would adopt a 'do nothing' strategy and not proceed with the proposal.

The political implications of Leveson

By the end of May 2012 commentators were noting how an inquiry which was meant to put the media in the dock had placed the government there too. None was more powerful than Andrew Rawnsley's *Observer* column on 27 May. He wrote:

> Originally designed to shine a pitiless light on the sins of the press, Leveson has turned into an inquisition into the ethics and conduct of the Tory leader and some of his closest friends. As a result of the inquiry, the cabinet career of Jeremy Hunt hangs by a thread that grows thinner with each new piece of evidence brought into the public domain. The inner workings of Number 10 are being subject to hideous, from their point of view, exposure. Worst of all from Downing Street's perspective, the integrity and judgment of the Prime Minister are being put in the dock. Little wonder that one senior Conservative calls Leveson '... an unmitigated disaster ... yet another spectacular own goal'.

Comparing the scrutiny that Cameron was undergoing with Blair's during the inquiry into the Iraq war, Rawnsley suggested:

David Cameron is now being subject to similar punishment by daily revelations, though in his case much earlier in his premiership – two years in, rather than two terms in – as a result of the release into the public domain of thousands of pages of texts and emails between Murdoch operators and senior government figures across multiple departments.

We have learned, to much cringing at Number 10, of the intimate relationship between Mr Cameron and Rebekah Brooks, the former editor of *the Sun* and the *News of the World*, who has been charged with perverting the course of justice. I am not sure which disclosure is worse for the Prime Minister: that he signed off his chummy texts to her with 'lol' or that she eventually had to tell him that the abbreviation stands not for 'lots of love' but 'laugh out loud. I do know this: there are not a lot of laughs inside Number 10 at the moment.[48]

Blair's relationship with Rupert Murdoch

In a rare UK public appearance Tony Blair told the inquiry on 29 May that he had taken a strategic decision to 'manage' but not confront the media. If he had chosen confrontation, he would have had to put off other reforms such as healthcare and education. 'It would have been a huge battle with no guarantee of winning,' he said. But now was the time to address regulation and it was 'really important that people don't play politics' with the recommendations that emerge. 'It is the draining of the poison from that [media] culture that is the real challenge.' Blair defended his 'working relationship' with Rupert Murdoch, insisting that it was a bond based on power but denying he had struck a deal with the media baron. 'I find these relationships are not personal. They are working [relationships] to me.' After he had left office, 'I got to know him [Murdoch]. It's different – not the same.' It was only then that he became a godfather to one of Murdoch's children.

Questioned about Labour's changed position on media cross-ownership, he said it had been done for 'sound and objective' reasons and not as the result of any deal 'with Rupert Murdoch or indeed anyone else, either expressed or implied'. He conceded: 'it would be fair to say that had we kept to the original policy, there would have been a problem with the Murdoch press' (see Chapter One, p 6). In the 2003 Communications Act, a 'Murdoch clause' would have allowed the media baron to buy Channel 5 or take a large stake in a company like ITV, by relaxing foreign ownership restrictions. Blair responded by saying that there was a clause allowing the Trade and Industry Secretary to order a public interest test if there was a threat of concentration of the media. He went on to argue that he had made more decisions against the wishes of News International than in its favour, and listed six. These included the boost to the role of Ofcom, the broadcasting regulator; raising the BBC licence fee; granting the BBC new channels; and stopping BSkyB's bid to take over Manchester United.

He criticised a section of the media, particularly the Mail group, for waging 'personal vendettas', one of which had targeted his wife, Cherie. 'What I think is wrong is where sections of the media – and again I emphasise it is a section – where powerful people say, "Right, we are going for that person". And then what happens is they go for you. And, as I say, it is full on, full frontal. That's not journalism. In my view it's an abuse of power.' He said his wife, who is a barrister, had taken or had considered taking legal action about media reports more than 30 times between 2006 and 2011. The *Daily Mail* complained Blair had been given 'a terribly lame interrogation' and had not been questioned on a succession of key issues. Stephen Glover, its media commentator, wrote: 'A stranger to our shores watching Tony Blair at the Leveson inquiry yesterday would have got the impression of a reasonable and decent man, who had unaccountably been abused and mistreated by a – his word – "feral" press. If I had not lived through the Blair years and seen the way in which newspapers were manipulated and sometimes lied to by his formidable press machine, I might have been persuaded by this suave and confident performance.'[49]

Cameron enters 'the dock'

An early indication of his final decision came on David Cameron's appearance before the Leveson inquiry on 14 June 2012. He declared it would be 'much better' if the newspaper industry reformed itself without Parliament having to intervene. He partially resisted suggestions from the Lord Justice that a new system of regulation would require statutory underpinning. He said: 'It can't be self-regulation, it has to be independent regulation ... and seen to be independent, you can't opt out of it. It has to have real teeth in terms of penalties and the ability to get out and find out what happened rather than just deal with self-reported problems ... where mistakes are made and bad practice happens there are real penalties as a result.' He said he had looked carefully at what Lord David Hunt, the chair of the Press Complaints Commission, had drawn up and thought there were 'some very good ideas there'. (Robert Jay, a month later, in an inquisition of Lord Black, the main author of the plan, documented how many shortcomings there were, too.) Cameron suggested he would favour a robust form of self-regulation as long as it passed the 'Dowler' test – that is, that it won the support of key victims of the hacking – when Leveson reported.

He was loathe to express any sense of pleasure over the curbing of Murdoch's power. He was twice asked about whether his reaction to the media's 'July Spring' in the summer of 2011 was similar to Ed Miliband's, the Labour leader:

> Robert Jay: 'Would you agree with Mr Miliband's view that the events of July last year were liberating, to use a word, in the sense that, I paraphrase, Mr Murdoch's power had already been substantially weakened.'

> Cameron: 'I think I would put it in a slightly different way, that I think because of all the issues that it has raised, in terms of press conduct and the relationship between politicians and the media, that some of the distance and better processes that are required are already being put in place.'

Jay tried again: 'I think what he [Miliband] might have meant, that whereas before some politicians were operating in a self-imposed constraint, that they were not prepared to speak out against News International, the chains have come off and now everybody feels they can. Would you agree with that?'

Cameron: 'I would just put it my own way of saying, that the debate that needs to take place about how we regulate the press, including News International and all those titles, is now properly being had.'

The 87-word text from Rebecca Brooks

It was a difficult day for the Prime Minister with his close personal as well as professional relationship with Rebekah Brooks revealed in texts obtained by Leveson lawyers under the Inquiries Act 2005. A gushing text from Brooks on the eve of Cameron's speech to the annual Conservative conference in 2009 won the most attention. It spoke of 'Let's discuss over country suppers' (their country houses in the Cotswolds were quite close, Charlie Brooks being one of Cameron's oldest friends from Eton) and 'OE (old Etonian) charm' but the killer sentence that was highlighted in all the papers was: 'I am so rooting for you tomorrow not just as a proud friend but because professionally we're definitely in this together! Speech of your life? Yes he Cam!' Quentin Letts in the *Mail* described what happened when the text was read out at the hearing: 'Mr Jay did permit a tiny note of relish to enter his voice as read aloud Madam Brooks' oh-so-familiar billet-doux. "Country suppers?" enquired the QC ... Mr Cameron pinked, stiffened, stalled. It was the only moment he looked shifty. He would not say how frequently he and Mrs Brooks chummed up at week-ends.' Cameron returned after the lunch break to say he had rung his wife, who had checked their diaries, and found it was once every six weeks. To which Leveson replied: 'The great value of wives.'

Rarely has one text received such extensive media analysis. There was agreement that there was much there to make Cameron squirm. *The Times*, which noted that the initial part of the text had been redacted, thought 'Mr Cameron may have cause to be thankful for small mercies'. Its headline read 'In just 87 words, the text speaks volumes about the nature of power'.[50]

Cameron had been quite open at the hearing as to the importance he had placed on establishing good relations with the media once having been appointed leader of his party in December 2005. In the next four-and-a-half years leading to the 2010 election he had had 1,404 meetings with media people – an average of 26 meetings every month. They included 10 with Rupert Murdoch, 15 with James Murdoch, and 25 with Rebekah Brooks. He also told the inquiry he would forever be 'haunted' by his decision in 2007 to hire Andy Coulson as his communications chief. The Prime Minister said that 'with hindsight' he would not have hired him.

Leveson versus Gove

In a 20-minute opening statement on 25 June 2012, Leveson made a robust defence of his inquiry, denying he had any 'hidden agenda' to inhibit the press. He also denied he had tried to 'gag' Education Secretary Michael Gove, following a speech in which the minister warned about the inquiry creating a 'chilling atmosphere' towards freedom of speech. (Gove, a bumptious right-winger and former columnist on *The Times*, was another open cheerleader for Murdoch.) The judge confirmed that he had made a call to the Cabinet Secretary, Sir Jeremy Heywood, in February following Gove's speech, to question whether Cameron still supported the judicial inquiry he had set up. He was concerned by comments made by Cameron at Prime Minister's Question Time in the Commons, which indicated that he supported Gove. Cameron had said that Gove had made 'an important point', adding 'Even as this inquiry goes on, we want to have a vibrant press that feels it can call the powerful to account, and we do not want to see it chilled'. Leveson was responding to a story in *The Mail on Sunday* on 17 June headlined 'Leveson's threat to quit'. He did not deny or confirm this aspect of the story, but said *The Mail on Sunday* had made 'very serious allegations'. Explaining why he had made the call to Sir Jeremy, Leveson said: 'It seemed to me at the time that ... the PM's response was open to the interpretation that he was indeed agreeing with Mr Gove's views ... of greater concern to me was the question whether what he said had become the government's position to not just the effects of the inquiry, intended or otherwise, but also that there was a danger that I had an interest in taking over as arbiter of what a free press should be.' He added that he thought it 'necessary and appropriate' to make the call to Heywood. 'I received the assurance that no fixed view had been formed,' he said.[51]

Snow versus Associated Newspapers

On the same day (24 June) Jon Snow, the Channel 4 news anchor, appeared before the inquiry and launched a scathing attack on Associated Newspapers, publishers of the *Daily Mail* and *The Mail on Sunday*. He claimed they had a 'pernicious' and sometimes 'mendacious' agenda to undermine people in public life. He thought they were worse than the News International titles and had an agenda that undermined politicians and others. He went on: 'There is something more insidious about Associated Newspapers and very possibly they will go after me for saying so. I believe they have an agenda for trying to undermine or wreck the careers of individual people in public life and I think that is unhealthy.' Snow added that the private lives of people in public life are largely irrelevant to readers and they should be allowed to 'stand or fall by what they achieve or fail to achieve'. Snow prefaced his remarks by recounting the frustrating time he had with *The Mail on Sunday* in 2007 over a five-page article about his private life, including allegations which the paper later admitted were false when it published an apology. He said he had not intended to bring the incident up but it 'burned a hole in my soul'.

The hearings conclude

The hearings ended on 24 July. David Sherborne, counsel for 50 victims, told the inquiry that the arguments put forward by media lawyers suggesting statutory regulation would lead to interference by politicians and have a 'chilling effect' on investigatory journalism were 'specious'. He went on: 'We say there should be an entirely new regime, a clean break not just in name but in substance from everything that has come before and failed.' He added: 'The public wants more objective standards and the starting point for that is an independent statute-backed regulator, which is created for the public and is not run by a serving editor.' Alan Rusbridger, *Guardian* Editor, was also invited to say some final words. He said many of the abuses uncovered by the inquiry would not have happened if Rupert Murdoch's News International had been prevented from holding such a dominant position in British media. Warning that there was likely to be more consolidation, rather than less, he urged Lord Justice Leveson to consider 'the significant dangers to democracy' of media power being concentrated in too few hands. He added that over his newspaper's three-and-a-half-year investigation into hacking, it had encountered examples of people who lived, and in some cases still live, in fear of one particular newspaper company. *The Guardian* had never believed there would ever be a public inquiry, which put the practices of all newspapers under the spotlight. 'The Murdoch influence, power, money, dominance and reputation was such that it seemed to confer a form of immunity from scrutiny.' It was the courage of a small number of phone-hacking victims such as Sienna Miller, one of the first to take civil action, that helped 'prise open the evidence'.

The inquiry heard from 135 organisations and 474 people. They included 202 media people, 48 police officers, 41 lawyers, 38 politicians or their aides, 36 academics, 21 regulators or watchdogs, and 14 charities or pressure groups. Who had the worst memory? According to a BBC search – for variations on the words 'I don't know' or 'I can't recall' – Cameron came top with 49 times, followed by James Murdoch 41, Rebekah Brooks 35, Rupert Murdoch 30, Andy Coulson 28, Jeremy Hunt 23 and Tony Blair 19.

The first new criminal hacking charges

As the hearings closed, the criminal prosecutions picture became clearer. On 24 July the first eight criminal hacking charges were laid. Andy Coulson, the Prime Minister's former communications director, and Rebekah Brooks, Rupert Murdoch's closest confidant, were among eight former senior *News of the World* employees charged with conspiring to hack the phones of more than 600 people, including the murdered schoolgirl Milly Dowler, between October 2000 and August 2006. Both Brooks and Coulson had edited the paper during that period. The eight people were charged with 19 counts of conspiring to hack the phones of, among others, Labour Cabinet ministers, a host of celebrities, and ordinary people. Other defendants were: Stuart Kuttner, the paper's retired managing editor; James Weatherup, former news editor; Greg Miskiw, former assistant news editor; Ian Edmondson, another former assistant news editor; Neville Thurlbeck, former chief reporter; and Glenn Mulcaire, employed private detective. All eight faced two charges, Thurlbeck and Weatherup faced seven, Miskiw nine, and Edmondson 11.[52] In a later hearing, a further six former NoW employees were added to the charge sheet. All 14 were told on 26 September 2012, that their trials would start on 9 September 2013.[53]

A silly summer story

A silly summer story was prompted by Chris Blackhurst, Editor of *The Independent*, who claimed Leveson was 'loading a gun' against the industry. He claimed a letter, issued by Leveson warning national and regional editors of potential criticisms in his report, amounted to 'a demolition of the industry'. He went on the BBC's *The Media Show* on 29 August describing his 'shock and anger' at the 'one-sided letter' that was 'a point-by-point demolition' of the industry. The letter was issued under rule 13 of the 2006 Inquiry Rules, which require inquiries to send any potential criticisms they are intending to make of people, in order to give them a right of reply. By their very nature, such letters are one-sided as Blackhurst should have known, as should Steve Hewlett presenting *The Media Show*. It was a non-story.[54] Blackhurst was an early critic of the inquiry, claiming 'the press could deliver a credible package of reforms without a public inquiry'.[55]

A serious summer story

Three years after James Murdoch's MacTaggart lecture in 2009 (see p 36), his older sister Elisabeth was invited to give the prestigious address on 23 August 2012. What a contrast. Where the first was full of self-serving bombast, bravado and bluster, the second was thoughtful, intelligent and discerning. Whereas her brother had engaged in a long and sustained attack on public broadcasting, his sister chose to praise the BBC. James had concluded his address with the arrogant assertion that 'the only reliable, durable and perpetual guarantor of independence is profit'; Elisabeth punctured that statement with the observation that 'profit without purpose is a recipe for disaster'. She said that people needed to 'reject the idea that money is the only effective measure of all things or that the free market is the only sorting mechanism'. Instead, she said that 'the absence of purpose' could be 'one of the most dangerous own goals for capitalism and freedom'.

After leaving college, Elisabeth began working in her father's business, first in Australia, then California, before moving to London. She left BSkyB in 2001 to set up her own television production company, Shine, which made popular programmes such as MasterChef. She later sold it to her father's company for £415 million in 2011, but continued to run it until September 2012. Speaking in public for the first time about the hacking scandal, she said News Corp had to ask 'significant and difficult questions about how some behaviour fell so far short of its values' in the wake of what happened. The organisation needed to 'discuss, affirm and institutionalise a rigorous set of values based on an explicit statement of purpose' – in contrast to News Corp's traditional mode of governance based on executives second-guessing what Rupert would do. She went out of her way to praise the BBC, which frequently airs Shine programmes, in marked contrast to her father and brother. 'Let me put it on the record that I am a current supporter of the BBC's universal licence fee,' she said. There was also praise for the outgoing BBC Director General, Mark Thompson, for working collaboratively across the television industry. According to a long article in *The New Yorker* on 10 December 2012, her father refused to speak to her for nine weeks after the lecture for attacking her brother.[56]

The politics below Leveson

Behind the scenes two separate groupings were energetically seeking to widen public support for their cause. On the pro-regulation front, Hacked Off emerged after the Milly Dowler hacking revelations, intent on pushing for a public inquiry into the scandal. One of its founders, Brian Cathcart, was formerly a journalist (Reuters, the *Independent* papers and the *New Statesman*) before becoming Professor of Journalism at Kingston University. He is a prolific writer – punching out regular well-informed blogs on the Hacked Off website, as well as commentary pieces for *The Guardian* – and has a waspish pen. The pressure group quickly won the support of victims and celebrities, foremost of whom was Hugh Grant. It covered every day of the Leveson hearings, commented on them, and contributed evidence to them. It is very media savvy and staged very effective fringe meetings at the three major political party conferences in the autumn of 2012. Initially housed by the Media Standards Trust, it became an independent non-profit company based at Victoria Street, London, in the summer of 2012.

Hugh Grant became a donor and a board director of the organisation, which has a distinguished board including two leading media lawyers, two media academics and the director of Full Fact, a pressure group pursuing inaccuracies in the media. Grant, who has been a prominent critic of privacy intrusions, has been a particular target for the venom of the *Daily Mail*. Hacked Off and Cathcart have proved effective counter-punchers, exposing the *Mail*'s many inaccuracies and hypocrisies in newspaper columns and on its website.

The Media Standards Trust, set up in 2006 to help raise the standards of British journalism, quickly got to work under its director Martin Moore, documenting the abysmal failings of the Press Complaints Commission. This first report, *A more accountable press*, was followed by a second in 2010, on how it could be improved, *Can independent self- regulation keep standards high and preserve press freedom?*. It has a website providing more information on the background of journalists; and, in conjunction with Tim Berners-Lee and the Web Science Trust, launched the Transparency Initiative to make searching online news easier and more intelligible.

The spearhead of anti-statutory reform

On the other side have been two active Tory peers, Lord (Guy) Black and Lord (David) Hunt, drafting what they purported to be a tough independent non-statutory press regulation system in place of the PCC. Lord Hunt, a lawyer, former Cabinet minister in the Thatcher and Major governments, was appointed chairman of the PCC in October 2011 by Lord Black, executive director at the Telegraph Media Group. Hunt's remit was to oversee its phasing out. Lord Black, who was chair of the PCC's finance board, by far its most powerful body, began drawing up an alternative to the PCC with the assistance of Hunt. At first glance their proposal looked attractive. Newspapers would be bound into the system by commercial contracts. There would be an investigatory arm – which the PCC never had – to undertake inquiries into systematic breaches of the new body's code of standards. There was commitment to impose sanctions for breaches of the code, with fines of up to £1 million or 1 per cent of total turnover. And there was readiness to explore an arbitration arm, which would provide a faster and cheaper way of resolving complaints, although ironically this would need a statute to make it a really effective alternative to libel actions in the courts.

But this first version, which Cameron suggested at the Leveson hearing had 'good ideas', was clinically dissected: first by Robert Jay in a 9 July hearing with Lord Black, followed by an even more comprehensive analysis by Martin Moore, in a 20-page report from the Media Standards Trust. He identified '10 serious failings'. It was not 'a new system entirely'; not independent; it maintained the dominance of the key vested interests; it remained mediation rather than regulation; the incentives to join would damage journalistic freedom; news organisations would be able to bail themselves out of the contracts; it was unwieldy, bureaucratic and under-costed; third parties would find it as hard, if not harder, to complain; and it had a five-year sell-by date.[57]

One of the ways the Black/Hunt plan would damage journalistic freedom was in its suggestion that press cards should be restricted to journalists working on newspapers subscribing to the 'regulatory' body. A second proposal involved restricting PA news feeds to signed-up newspapers. Moore noted: 'Together it is hard to see how they can be distinguished from a licensing system run by the big news organisations.'

The entire structure of the new system would be in the hands of the industry, just like the PCC. The editors' code would remain the prerogative of 12 serving editors; the complaints adjudication body would have five serving editors, with seven lay members. The powerful PressBof (the Press Standards Board of Finance) would be renamed the Industry Funding Board but maintain almost all its old powers. It would be entirely composed of industry figures. Its powers would include: deciding who is in or out of the system; appointing two out of the four members of the appointing panel; appointing the three press members to the Board of the proposed regulator; firing the chair or the three press members; extending the terms of the chair; defining and approving amendments to the regulations; determining the sanctions. These last powers would raise other problems: high initial hurdles; a lengthy process involving multiple representations and objections; no ladder of tariffs for fines below the upper limit. As for third party complaints (such as would be needed to stop the systematic way the tabloids were distorting the coverage of asylum as set out in Chapter Five), Lord Justice Leveson noted the hurdles: 'There has to be a significant breach of the code, not just a breach. There has to be a substantial public interest – not merely a public interest – and even then, that's in the discretion of the head of complaints.'

Both peers, egged on by the right-wing press, became hardened against any statutory element. Both believed their system could be put into operation early in 2013, no matter what Leveson proposed. Both believed it was important to safeguard press regulation from parliamentary intervention, yet both were active Conservative peers.

Hunt voted in 102 out of the 112 divisions in the year ending 1 December 2012; Black in 92 out of 112. Both had long backgrounds in politics. Hunt was first elected to the Commons in 1976. Black joined the Conservative Research Department in 1986; in 1989 became a special adviser to John Wakeham, the Conservative Energy Secretary; and then in 2003 became Director of Communications for the Conservative Party and Press Secretary to the party leader Michael Howard, then leader of the opposition.

With their first proposal panned by the Leveson inquiry, they went back to the drawing board to produce a more independent model.

Covert politics become overt

Stories began running in September 2012 that Cameron had decided to give newspapers 'another chance to improve self-regulation', even if Leveson concluded there had to be an element of statutory law. Downing Street dismissed the story as 'speculative'. But on Sunday, 7 October, *The Observer* front page splashed on an open letter from 50 victims of hacking expressing fury over the suggestion that the Coalition would reject statutory-backed regulation. Organised by Hacked Off and deliberately sent on the eve of the annual Conservative Party conference to send the issue to the top of the political agenda, the letter spoke of 'a betrayal of us and your precious commitment'. In establishing the inquiry, Cameron had pledged that the test for the future system of press regulation was not whether it suited politicians or the press but instead 'the people who have been caught up and absolutely thrown to the wolves by the process'. The letter was signed, among others, by Jude Law, Hugh Grant and Charlotte Church.[58] Asked on the BBC's *Andrew Marr Show* on the morning of Sunday, 7 October, whether he would stick to his reported promise to implement Leveson's proposals provided they were not 'bonkers', he replied 'Absolutely'.[59] By early October, the megaphone of the major big right-wing media groups – Murdoch's News International, Telegraph Media Group, and the *Mail* group – were blaring at full force of the dangers of a state-regulated press. As Brian Cathcart accurately noted in a comment piece: 'Nobody wants that, least of all Leveson, who insisted on the point at almost every public inquiry session. You won't be told this in most papers ... we don't know what he will say, but it looks likely that he will give a new regulator teeth by underpinning it with a statute.'[60]

A new lobby group

In late October a Free Speech Network to counter Hacked Off was launched to act as an umbrella group for all who 'share concern over protecting freedom of expression against any attempts to introduce a statutory backstop to press regulation'. It produced a two-page summary of the Black/Hunt latest plan on its bare website and another two pages setting out 20 reasons why a statute would be wrong. There was no attempt to take in the very many different forms of statute. The launch, on 21 October, coincided with publication of a pamphlet from Tim Luckhurst, a professor of journalism at Kent University, entitled *Responsibility without power*. It was a call to arms with the following declaration: 'An officially regulated press is the glib, easy, dangerous solution. It would spell the slow painful death of a raucous, audacious and impertinent press able to speak truth to power on behalf of its readers and entertaining enough to secure their loyalty. We would all be losers.'[61]

An earlier case of police immunity

Just two weeks before Leveson reported, there was a dramatic reminder of the dangers of the of politicians and police getting too close with the national press on 12 September 2012 with the publication of the report of the third inquiry into the worst disaster in British sporting history. Some 23 years after 96 Liverpool football fans died crushed against barriers in Sheffield's Hillsborough Stadium in 1989, the truth finally emerged. Two earlier inquiries by respected senior judges had concluded that the main cause was incompetent stewarding by the police. This third, by an independent panel chaired by the Bishop of Liverpool, found that the police were guilty of something more serious than just gross mismanagement of crowd control. They had deliberately and successfully shifted the blame from senior officers onto the victims.

This was achieved by multiple tactics: all reports by police officers at the ground were systematically scrutinised and 164 amended, 116 of them 'to remove or alter comments unfavourable' to the police operation, including its lack of leadership at the top and poor communications. Redacted statements, private press briefings and blatantly false stories about drunken ticketless fans forcing their way into the grounds were found by the panel to be groundless. So were suggestions of fans urinating on the police, picking the pockets of dead victims and attacking officers trying to help the injured, all of which were emblazoned on a notorious front page of *The Sun* under the banner headline 'The truth'. The depth to which the police descended to escape blame was breathtaking: systematic blood samples of all the victims, one as young as 10, to scrabble evidence that alcohol had fuelled the disaster. When that failed, they combed criminal records in a bid to blacken their reputations.

The panel examined 450,000 documents gathered from 80 organisations along with many hours of videos taken at the scene and concluded there had been a concerted campaign by senior officers to shift the blame. There was an unreserved apology from the police, a much belated one from the former Editor of *The Sun*, Kelvin MacKenzie, and a moving one by the Prime Minister on behalf of the country.

Jack Straw was the Labour Home Secretary who set up the second judicial inquiry into the disaster when Labour came into power in 1997. He expressed his regrets on the BBC Radio 4 *Today* programme that it had not uncovered the police cover-up but went on to note that the government of the day (Margaret Thatcher's) had been heavily reliant on the police in dealing with angry public and industrial disputes and that had helped create "a culture of immunity" within the police.[62] This provoked denials from her former ministers, but support in several newspapers.

One police officer told the *Financial Times*: 'Margaret Thatcher said "jump" and senior officers responded "How high?".' The paper went on to note: 'Thus one policeman recalls the famously close relationship between the Iron Lady and the UK's top cops during the fraught days of the miners' strike, the poll tax riots, and the Wapping (print) trade union dispute.' It went on to add that the party's relationship with the police had radically changed since then, with the current government's moves to reform police pay, make a 20 per cent cut to the police budget, and introduce directly elected police commissioners.[63] Philip Johnston in a full-page feature in *The Daily Telegraph* noted the pride with which the police were viewed in Britain, but went on: 'Perhaps that was always a naive caricature, but it was a view so deeply ingrained in our national psyche that we were unwilling to give credence to powerful evidence that suggested otherwise. However it was not only the police who let down the Hillsborough families: the very institutions that most of us trust to get to the bottom of things – the courts, the media and parliament – were all culpable.'[64] *The Economist* praised the panel's careful and fact-filled report and suggested 'the worst sporting disaster in British history may also be the worst police cover-up of all time'.[65]

There was a familiar list of earlier miscarriages of justice involving the police in many editorials, and calls for the reform of the Independent Police Complaints Commission and coroners' courts. The most interesting proposal to emerge was a call by Michael Mansfield QC, the barrister representing the families of the victims, for 'a commission of truth' that could hold state institutions to account. He suggested that although the panel's findings were proof that the state could not be trusted to investigate itself, its conclusions also showed how a historical pattern of 'institutional denial followed by institutional deceit' could be finally challenged.[66]

The debate gets dirtier

As the publication date for the Leveson report got pushed back, the debate got dirtier. In a move on 16 November which perfectly illustrated the criticisms set out by Jon Snow and Tony Blair of the *Mail*'s 'mendacious' attacks on people in public life, the paper chose to make an extreme attack on one of Leveson's six advisers, Sir David Bell. Even by the *Mail*'s deplorable standards, the 11 pages of skewed arguments and fact, all focused on one person, hit a new low. Its previous attacks had generated a new verb, 'to monster', an ugly word but it describes an ugly action. Here was a serious journalist, who had worked his way up the *Financial Times* rungs from the newsroom to managing editor, then chief executive and finally chairman in 1996. He has been a chair or trustee of a huge list of voluntary bodies involving dance, music, leadership, the homeless and journalism. In 2006 he helped to launch the Media Standards Trust, with the aim of raising standards of British journalism, which had reached a new low. He was also an early supporter of the Bureau of Investigative Journalism, which was launched in 2010 at a time when many papers had cut back on investigations because of their cost. The Bureau had received a number of awards, before making serious mistakes in the BBC *Newsnight* programme that falsely accused Lord McAlpine of child abuse. This latter event was manna from heaven for the *Mail's* malicious rant.

In its Editorial attempting to justify its 11 pages of venom, the Mail asserted its 'investigation paints a picture of how a small, intertwined nexus of Left-of-centre individuals – some with links to Ofcom, the media regulator, and virtually all with links to Bell – have sought to exert huge influence on the inquiry'.[67] Roy Greenslade opened his analysis of the 11-page diatribe, with an irreverent voice: 'I have been worried about *The Daily Mail's* editor, Paul Dacre, for some time. After seeing today's issue of his paper, I really think it's time for men in white coats to visit its Kensington offices as soon as possible.' He went on to show the leaps of logic and phoney revelations used by the *Mail* to turn a do-gooder into a 'do-badder'. Greenslade concluded: 'For a national paper to devote the best part of a dozen pages to an investigation so obviously based on prejudice against Leveson inquiry is surely counter-productive. It is very likely to reinforce the view of politicians that *The Mail's* brand of journalism is too often born of bias. And that that bias is located in the person of the editor.... The likeliest effect will be to convince MPs that statutory press regulation is a good thing.'[68]

The prediction gained some credence when David Aaronovitch, the *Times* columnist, tweeted: 'I was opposed to statutory press regulation until the *Mail* hatchet job on Leveson.'

Two days later *The Sunday Times* joined in the monstering with a large unfavourable profile of Sir David: 'Part of an unelected elite, he has links to victims of phone hacking and to journalists behind the BBC debacle and yet, as an adviser to Leveson, is about to sit in judgment on press freedom.' It too was concerned that the Leveson report would be 'unfairly skewed towards the views of an unelected, centre-left elite, of which he is seen as a leading light'.[69]

Distorted poll reporting

In mid-November 2012 a YouGov poll for Hacked Off found 77 per cent of the public no longer thought newspapers should control the complaints system. Only *The Independent* and *The Guardian* reported that fact. Martin Hickman on the Campaign for Press and Broadcasting Freedom (CPBF) website pointed to other distortions. It followed Hacked Off's complaints that the industry was selectively reporting polls, such as Hacked Off's, to give the impression that it enjoyed public support.[70] *The Sun* on 15 November, under a headline 'State-run watchdog "will gag free press"', reported that 75 per cent said there was a risk that politicians would use a statutory system to silence papers. The paper neglected to mention less helpful data from the same poll, notably that 63 per cent did not trust newspapers or journalists to set up a fair system of regulation.

The Times reported on 20 June that 61 per cent of respondents in a Populus poll thought 'the Leveson inquiry had lost its way as a procession of politicians, journalists and celebrities have simply tried to defend themselves against one another's allegations'. It ignored a second question, which showed 59 per cent supported that the inquiry 'will lead to more effective regulation of the press offering better protection to members of the public against unwarranted intrusion in their private lives'. *The Daily Telegraph* deleted a last line from the conclusion of a letter it published from Christopher Jefferies, one of the victims of media frenzy, which stated that the reform of press regulation would require statutory underpinning. The last line that was deleted read: 'The evidence of opinion polls show that more than 75 per cent of the country wants this too.'

The last poll to be released before the publication of the report, again carried out by YouGov but this time for the Media Standards Trust, showed that 79 per cent were in favour of 'an independent press regulator, established by law, which deals with complaints and decides what sanctions should be'. Only nine per cent believed that 'newspapers should establish their own body to do this'. A third finding was that 86 per cent believed there was a risk, if the press continued to regulate themselves, that there would be a return to unethical and illegal practices. Interestingly, for all the distorted reporting of Leveson, there were large majorities in favour of the last question from readers of all newspapers: *Sun* readers, 79 per cent; *Mail*, 91 per cent; *Times*, 91 per cent; *Telegraph*, 93 per cent; *Guardian*, 99 per cent.

Bubble and trouble in the Commons

In the final days before publication of the report on Thursday, 29 November 2012, there was much political jockeying, particularly within the Conservative Party. On 21 November, *The Times* reported that some 70 Tory MPs were ready to publicly support a new press regulator being enshrined in law. About 40 of them had signed a letter to *The Guardian* earlier in the month saying the inquiry presented a 'once-in-a-generation' opportunity to put things right'.[71] *The Times* suggested that the number was large enough to defeat Cameron in the Commons, if he decided to support giving newspapers another chance of self-regulation, given the support from Labour and Lib Dem MPs for ending this system. But by 28 November, a 76-strong group of MPs and peers – the vast majority Conservative – urged Cameron to resist legislation. Their letter declared: 'As parliamentarians, we believe in free speech and are opposed to the imposition of any form of statutory control even if it is dressed up as underpinning. It is redress that is vital, not broader regulation.'[72] But by five days later the pro-Leveson group were backing down and a threat of a revolt was lessening.[73]

The report is born – but the press want to mark their own homework

The four-volume 2,000-page report was launched at a crowded London press conference on 29 November 2012. Leveson noted that this was the seventh time in 70 years that a new report commissioned by a government dealing with concerns about the press had been produced. He was all too well aware of the fact that the previous six (or seven if you count the second Calcutt report) had had little effect. He had mentioned throughout the hearings that he did not want this one to lay on a Whitehall shelf accumulating dust. He rightly asserted that his inquiry had been the most concentrated of the seven. It had taken only 16 months and over almost nine months of hearings there had been 337 witnesses giving evidence and 300 others read into the record.

Leveson emphasised his recognition of the importance of the press as 'guardian of the interests of the public, as a critical witness to events, and as a standard bearer for those who have no one else to speak up for them'. He went on: 'Nothing in the evidence I have heard or read has changed that view.' But this power and influence carried with it responsibilities. Unfortunately, these responsibilities on too many occasions, as the inquiry had documented, had been ignored. This had damaged the public interest, caused real hardship and, on occasion, wreaked havoc in the lives of innocent people.

> What the press do and say is no ordinary exercise of free speech. It operates very differently from blogs on the internet and other social media such as Twitter. Its impact is uniquely powerful. A free press in a democracy holds power to account. But, with a few honourable exceptions, the UK press had not performed that vital role in the case of its own power. I know of no organised profession, industry or trade in which the serious failings of the few are overlooked or ignored because of the good of the many. Were it so in any other case, the press would be the very first to expose such practices.

Leveson reported that three days earlier when his massive report was already being printed, he had received two submissions from the press telling him that the industry was now prepared to sign self-regulation contracts. The first (from the *Financial Times*, *The Independent* and *The Guardian*) recognised that this procedure could be improved. The second (from the other seven national titles) believed the model based on the Black/Hunt plan had already answered the criticisms expressed at the inquiry. He acknowledged that the model was an improvement on the PCC, but it did not come close to delivering, in the words of the submission, regulation that was 'genuinely free and independent both of the industry it regulates and of political control'. Leveson continued 'Any model with editors on the main board is simply not independent of the industry to anything approaching the degree required to warrant public confidence. It is still the industry marking its own homework. Nor is the model stable or robust for the longer term future.'

In the report he went further, noting that under the Black/Hunt proposals: the new finance body would have even more power than the PCC's PressBof, including overseeing the standards code; the body adjudicating complaints would include serving editors; and there was no indication that the initial standards would continue beyond the first five years, thus failing to provide sufficient long-term stability and durability. The report leaves it to the press to organise their own body, but sets down strict criteria to ensure it is independent of both the industry and Parliament. The appointments panel should have no more than one editor and a clear majority of independent members; the new board should have no serving editor, although former editors, media academics or senior journalists could be members as long as the majority had no media background; and the standards code committee would no longer be confined to serving editors but include a mixture of independents and editors. All member newspapers should have their own complaints system, with no referral to the new organisation until the newspaper's system had tried to resolve the issue.

The remit of the new board would be much wider than the PCC's. As well as complaints it would have an important regulatory role, investigating serious breaches of the standards code and failures to comply with the board's rulings. It could impose fines of up to one per cent of turnover, or £1 million. There should also be an arbitration arm, providing a quicker, more accessible and cheaper way of resolving libel or other disputes. This would make it easier for complaints to be dealt with but also provide a financial incentive for newspapers to sign up. As well as this carrot, there was a stick: no newspaper in the system would be liable for exemplary damages, but those not signed up would be liable for such damages and would not receive their own legal costs even when they won in the courts. To ensure that these provisions would be recognised by the courts, the board would need a statutory base. In anticipation of political and media objections, the report notes the advantages of the statute. First it would enshrine for the first time a legal duty on governments to protect the freedom of the press – a UK version of America's First Amendment, which has been so important in the US. Second, it would provide an independent assessment of the new board's effectiveness and independence every two years or so. Controversially, Leveson proposed that this should be done by Ofcom, the regulator of broadcasting. Third, it would integrate the arbitration scheme into the legal system.

Findings

In its findings the report avoided naming individuals involved in hacking so as to avoid prejudicing forthcoming criminal prosecutions, but it dismissed the idea that it only involved one or two people: 'the evidence drives me to conclude that this was far more than a covert secret activity, known to nobody save one or two practitioners of the "dark arts"'. This was a further torpedo in the already discredited News International defence. Other findings included the following.

- Newspapers had recklessly pursued stories 'almost irrespective of the harm the stories may cause and the rights of those who would be affected'.
- Families of actors and footballers had a right to privacy. Leveson found 'ample evidence' that parts of the press had decided that actors, footballers, writers and pop stars were 'fair game, public property with little if any entitlement to any sort of private life or respect for dignity'.
- There had been a failure of compliance and governance at the *News of the World*. The paper's 'casual attitude to privacy and the lip service it paid to consent demonstrated a far more general loss of direction'.

- Complaints were not taken seriously. There was 'a cultural tendency within parts of the press vigorously to resist or dismiss complaints almost as a matter of course'. Even when an apology was agreed, some papers resorted to 'high-volume , extremely personal attacks on those who challenge them'.

- On Jeremy Hunt's handling of the BSkyB bid: despite the huge imbalance in the communication of Hunt's office with Murdoch's office compared to the opposition media groups, Leveson concluded 'there is no credible evidence of actual bias' in the handling of the bid.

- On police relations with the press: the perceptions that senior Met officers were 'too close' to News International were 'entirely understandable'. The report lists a long list of 'poor decisions, poorly executed': the failure to review the original phone-hacking investigation papers after the 2006 trial that involved only two *News of the World* employees being prosecuted; 'the incredibly swift dismissal of allegations in *The Guardian* article of 9 July 2009', which suggested there could be 3,000 victims of phone hacking; the failure to warn the victims of hacking, including the Deputy Prime Minister, that their phones were being hacked; the dismissal of a *New York Times* investigation into the scandal in 2010; and the friendship between John Yates, Assistant Metropolitan Commissioner, and Neil Wallis, Deputy Editor of the *News of the World*. Given this friendship, Leveson declared that Yates would have been better advised to arrange for a different officer to decide whether there were grounds for reopening the investigation with the material seized from the private detective Glenn Mulcaire in the original hacking operation in 2006. 'Even more so when he (Yates) decided within hours and even before the case papers were recovered and could be properly reviewed, that there were no grounds for reviewing the decision ... furthermore, publicly to announce that conclusion, on camera, on the same day meant no turning back. A defensive mindset was then established which affected all that followed.' Three years later Yates dismissed *The Guardian's* 2009 investigation, suggesting it contained nothing new, a verdict he later described as 'pretty crap'. He resigned in 2011 after his friendship with Wallis emerged, causing widespread criticism.

- Other officers also came in for criticism. Andy Hayman, who was in overall charge of the hacking investigation during his time as Assistant Commissioner, went to dinner with the Editor and Deputy Editor of the *News of the World* the day before Scotland Yard's investigation into the tabloid formally began. His decision to accept this hospitality was described in the report as 'extremely unwise'. Despite these failings the report concludes there was no evidence to show that the decisions to limit the hacking investigation were due to influence or corruption. Nevertheless it called for mandatory records to be kept of meetings between chief police officers and the media, and for those records to be available publicly for transparency and audit purposes.

- On relations between the press and senior politicians: Leveson could find no evidence of explicit deals by Rupert Murdoch with prime ministers in return for support from his papers, but concluded that politicians competed for his support, knowing that taking him on would lead to a backlash from his papers. He explained:'Sometimes the very greatest power is exercised without having to ask, because to ask would be to state the blindingly obvious and thereby diminish the very power which is being displayed. Just as Mr Murdoch's editors know the basic ground rules so did the politicians. The language of trades and deals is far too crude in this context.' He concluded that 'politicians' interests ... would find themselves highly aligned with Mr Murdoch's', even if the newspaper owner never asked for a single favour.

- On James Murdoch: the report expressed 'concerns' with claims by James Murdoch that he was unaware that phone hacking was 'rife' at *News of the World*. Leveson found it 'surprising' that Murdoch was unaware that the tabloid's own barrister had warned that there was 'a culture of illegal information access' at the paper. His concern related to an email sent by the *News of the World* editor about phone hacking being 'rife', which Murdoch said he had not read in full. Tom Crone, former NoW lawyer, said he subsequently provided Murdoch with 'direct and hard evidence' about the extent of the hacking, Murdoch denied the claim. Leveson writes: 'I conclude that Mr Crone's version of events as to what occurred on June 10, 2008 should be preferred to that of James Murdoch.'

This dispute will be examined more fully if the proposed second stage of the inquiry, which was due to begin after all criminal trials and police investigations end, goes ahead. Leveson had signalled during the inquiry that that may not be necessary, but David Cameron in his Commons statement said he remained committed to a second stage. Police estimates suggest there could still be trials proceeding as late as 2015.

Summing up the report

The report is a treasure trove for researchers, policy-makers, media analysts, political anoraks and social policy academics and students. True, some of it is a cut-and-paste job from Wikipedia and other sources, the first source leading to an embarrassing gaff on *The Independent*'s three founders, one of whom had been deleted from the site by a prankster, and an unknown name, Brett Straub, inserted. But the Leveson website is superb, with the recordings of all hearings well indexed to provide easy access, as are the full four volumes of the report. Take a rucksack if you intend to buy the report: it weighs 10 kilos, costs £250, and is only sold as a package of all four volumes.

The judge produced the right structure but the report was not without its own shortcomings: just a single page on 'the relevance of the internet' despite its existing power and growing dominance – dismissed as not relevant, first because it does not claim to operate by any particular ethics, and second because of the difference in impact of a private photo or personal news item posted online compared with being blazoned on the front page of *The Sun*, which 'multiplies and magnifies the intrusion'. It was wrong to suggest Ofcom as the monitor of the new press board's effectiveness and to allow it to be a backstop regulator for newspapers refusing to join the new board, given that the broadcasting regulator's head is a political appointee. It should have done more to develop a robust legal public interest defence for serious investigatory journalism; there needed to be greater emphasis on the importance of improving plurality; it was pretty feeble on the failures of the police investigations of hacking; even more feeble on the huge bias of Jeremy Hunt's office in the access given to James Murdoch's office (158 emails, 191 phone calls,

799 texts) compared to the miniscule correspondence with the media opponents in the BSkyB bid. And it was not even an easy read, with cumbersome sub-clauses and caveats sprayed everywhere, leading to lumpy sentences of torturous length. To apply one of the many unusual words of the inquiry's counsel Robert Jay, a little more pellucid style would have been welcome.

The media's immediate response

Speaking in the Commons on the day the report was released, David Cameron accepted the main thrust of Leveson but rejected its cornerstone: the need for the new body to have statutory backing. The next day he was the hero of Fleet Street. The *Daily Mail* headline declared: 'Cameron's stand for freedom – defiant PM says he won't back key proposal'. The *Daily Telegraph* headline was equally upbeat: 'Unexpected decision makes PM a leader in defence of liberty'. He won plaudits in *The Times* Editorial (for showing courage and principle) and in the *Financial Times* (Cameron deserves commendation). *The Guardian* suggested in its Editorial that the industry should treat the report 'with respect and a little humility' because 'the fact that the industry is now threatened with statutory controls is no one else's fault'. *The Sun's* Editorial was the absolute opposite, wrongly declaring that Leveson's proposals would allow 'state officials to walk into papers like *The Sun* and censor stories'.

Cameron broke two pledges with his response. He had pledged, at different times, that he would support the report so long as it had the support of victims, and, later, so long as there was nothing 'bonkers' in it. His purported reason for opposing statutory backing was that it would cross 'the Rubicon of writing elements of press regulation into law'. As one Lib Dem MP noted, he had his waterways wrong, 'not a Rubicon, barely a brook'. But he also knew that his opposition would win plaudits in the media and with his own right-wing back-benchers. Far from being brave and principled, he followed his predecessors' readiness to meekly appease the bullying media barons and ignore the need for more protection for the weak and vulnerable.

The Sun is not alone in not understanding the difference between a state body and a public body. James Murdoch in his infamous

MacTaggart lecture in 2009 demonstrated he had not learned the difference between a state broadcaster (owned and run by governments) and a public broadcaster like the BBC (independent of the government and financed by a public licence fee). It is absurd to describe the Leveson proposals as state control. All the legislation ensures is that the body which the press sets up to police itself has the powers to pursue its various objectives. It is not state control, but even state sanctions in some democracies – like Finland and Denmark – do not lead to totalitarian control found in communist states. Finland passed a law in 2003, which provides people with a statutory right of reply and news groups with a duty to correct – yet in eight out of the last 10 years the country has come top in the World Press Freedom index. Denmark has something similar.

Moreover, the idea that UK governments are eager to rein in the media is a myth. History documents not six but seven reports in the last 63 years demonstrating their reluctance: three Royal Commissions (1949, 1962, 1977), Younger (1969), Robertson (1983), along with two from Calcutt (1990 and 1993), all producing proposals which successive governments declined to pick up. Stephen Dorrell, Media Minister in 1993, explained to Leveson why the Conservative government declined to take up Calcutt's 'last chance saloon': the depth of media opposition. True the media is in a weaker position now than then. But having had seven chances to reform itself, it does not deserve an eighth. Leveson was right to reject the media's own amended proposals. As Harriet Harman, Labour's Shadow Media Secretary, noted in a Commons debate four days after publication: 'The definition of insanity is doing the same thing over and over again and expecting a different outcome.' As an Editorial in *The Observer* noted, Leveson 'is proposing that the privately owned organisations that shape our access to public information accept they constitute and are part of the public square – for all that they are privately owned. The way they report, the methods they use to acquire information, and how they subsequently use it can be as damaging as any exercise of state power. "Facts" can be printed that are not true and there is little or no comeback. At the limit, as we witnessed, a newspaper group was able to abuse the public realm so much that in effect it became a state within a state – cowing politicians, abusing press freedoms, invading private space and allegedly paying backhanders to the police – while being reckless with the accuracy of the information it put into public domain. To want to put an end to this, or at the very least make it very hard for it to happen again, is to assert the public interest in genuine press freedom.'[74]

Seeking a consensus on reform

For all the disappointment over Cameron's cave-in on statutory backing, the prospect of achieving most of Leveson's package initially looked promising. Cameron summonsed national editors to a meeting at Number 10 on 4 December to tell them that, with the exception of statutory backing, use of Ofcom and some changes to data protection law, they must implement the Leveson recommendations in their entirety, otherwise the government would introduce a new press law. The Prime Minister gave them two days to demonstrate they were making progress towards an agreed regulatory change.[75] Less than 24 hours after that injunction, the editors agreed at a breakfast meeting in the Delaunay Restaurant on the Aldwych to sign up to 40 of Leveson's 47 recommendations on the media. Lord Hunt was told that he must work to the Leveson plan, agreed by the editors, rather than the Black/Hunt proposal. He would no longer be able to appoint the chair of the appointments panel that will choose the chair and board of the new regulator. It was even agreed that there should be a whistleblowers' hotline for journalists who believed they were being asked to breach the industry's code of conduct. And in a concession to a demand by the National Union of Journalists, it was also agreed that newspapers should consider providing a 'conscience clause' in their contracts with employees, protecting them from disciplinary action if they refused to break the code. As Dan Sabbagh noted in *The Guardian*, 'The speed at which a settlement has been reached risks leaving Nick Clegg, Ed Miliband and the press reform campaign trailing.'[76] In fact it should not have come as a complete surprise. A five-page memo distributed to national newspaper editors before the breakfast meeting indicated there was a willingness to accept almost all of Leveson's proposals.[77]

Caveats

Inevitably some important caveats emerged. They tell their own story about Fleet Street values and ethics. In a public hearing before the Select Committee on the Media on 11 December, Alan Rusbridger identified five proposals that some editors were nervous about. Two important provisions, which would curb outrageously distorted coverage of stories such as asylum (see Chapter Five), would allow third party complaints. (Remember the *Express* journalists who had their complaint about the paper's distorted coverage of asylum turned down by the PCC because they were third parties, not victims.) A second much needed reform would allow the new regulator to intervene in cases of discriminatory reporting in line with 'the spirit of equalities legislation' – other areas badly covered by the tabloids include mental health, poverty, drug addiction and homelessness. Some tabloid editors were clearly worried by these two reforms but had an easy solution to their worries: improve the accuracy of their reporting. A third issue, which worried Paul Dacre, Editor of *The Daily Mail*, was the new Trust board having the final say on the code of conduct. Dacre was chairman of the PCC's editors' committee. His predecessor, Les Hinton, turned down the Information Commissioner's request to make it clear in the code that obtaining information about a person's private life by bribery, impersonation or subterfuge is illegal. Leveson was right to take the final say away from the editors. Other editors wanted to know what consequences would flow if they sought pre-publication advice on a story, but did not heed it. And there were even some editors wanting to restrict the publication of the new board's rulings to online, rather than in the paper.[78]

A Middle Ages solution: Royal Charters

In another part of the forest there were interesting developments in the Cabinet Office, where Oliver Letwin, Cameron's chief adviser on the issue, was finalising a plan to use the ancient power of a Royal Charter to create a new press regulator. Supporters of the plan said it would allow all the principles of independent regulation set out by

Leveson to be implemented, while stopping short of new legislation, which Cameron and most newspaper editors were seeking to avoid. The BBC was set up under a similar scheme.[79] But a week after this story broke, an even more interesting development had occurred. At a meeting with Labour and Lib Dem senior MPs, Letwin for the first time accepted there would need to be legislation even using the Royal Charter procedure in order to prevent the plan being overturned by the executive. People present said he had also accepted that legislation might be needed to embed the new arbitration scheme into the legal system.[80]

Prospects turn sour

But then on 14 December depressing news broke that five UK newspaper- and magazine-publishing bodies had written a joint letter to the Media Secretary, Maria Miller, reminding her that publishers, rather than editors, were responsible for funding the regulator. Moreover, it was the publishers, not the editors, who would be 'the signatories to the contracts that will under-pin it'. The publishers went on to explain that work was under way – coordinated by a working group of industry lawyers, editors and senior executives reporting to Lord Hunt – on a draft contract and regulations that would be Leveson-compliant.[81] Worse still, the news coincided with reports that James Harding, Editor of *The Times*, had resigned after Rupert Murdoch had made it clear he wanted him to go. Harding had been a good chair of the meetings of editors and a key link relaying their needs to ministers.[82]

There were three depressing aspects to these two news items. First, Leveson had made it clear that he believed the media's plan to bind newspapers by contract was complicated, unstable and contained 'a degree of built-in failure' by its time limits. Whatever revisions Lord Black was going to make to his idea, they were extremely unlikely to meet Leveson's strict criteria. Second, Lord Hunt had ignored the editors' injunction to follow Leveson and had been happily engaged in setting up a new shadow board he was calling 'the Press Trust' – ignoring the fact that the editors were drawing up their own plans for a new press regulator.[83] Third, as Dan Sabbagh noted in *The Guardian*:

> The loss of James Harding from *The Times* seems to have mortally wounded the editors' initiative, which began so well at Delaunay. Now a faceless collection of trade bodies seems to be in the driving seat with manoeuvre-in-chief Lord Black cemented in their ranks. Where the editors signed up to 40 out of 47 Leveson recommendations, with a handful of tweaks, the alphabet crew (the publishers) have only signed up to the 'five Leveson principles' as outlined by David Cameron.[84]

Has the last-chance saloon got yet another extension?

At the close of 2012 it was impossible to predict what would emerge. It was unclear how many of the five important Leveson changes causing some editors anxieties – listed above under 'Caveats' – would be watered down. More fundamentally, it was unclear whether the national editors' expressed wish – and the Prime Minister's injunction – to stick with Leveson's outline was being ambushed by the intervention of the publishers with their desire to stick with the Black/Hunt formula of contracts. All was still up for negotiation. Some sources suggested the contracts could be an add-on to Leveson, not a substitute. The national editors were divided on different issues; a separate group of 100-plus regional editors were exploring whether they could have their own system. They didn't like the arbitration arm: first, because of its cost; second, because they rarely if ever face libel suits; and third, because they fear ambulance-chasing lawyers might encourage their readers to seek damages. The Conservative Party was divided, with a minority in favour of legislation. Various draft Bills to produce a statutory back-up for the new press board – versions from Labour, a private Lib Dem peer, Hacked Off and a draft but unpublished Government Bill – were circulating at joint party talks. Labour, led by Ed Miliband, whose leading charge against Murdoch in July 2011 was one of his defining moments, was united behind having a statutory back-up. The Lib Dems would go along, but with not the same fervour. In theory, Labour and Lib Dem MPs, along with supportive Tory MPs, would have a majority in the Commons for a statutory-backed press regulator. As the issue involved free speech, it would need a free vote. In practice, the idea of the Lib Dems joining with Labour to defeat Cameron on such a high-profile issue seemed extremely unlikely. There was even a report in *The Times* in mid-January that the national press publishers were poised to launch a regulator without waiting for the politicians.[85] In short, the future of press regulation in England and Wales in early 2013 remained, to use a Churchillian phrase, 'a riddle, wrapped in a mystery, inside an enigma'.

Notes

[1] Rob Evans (2012) 'Spotlight on an industry that often lurks in the shadows', *The Guardian*, 24 May.

[2] *Tabloid Girl* by Sharon Marshall, quoted in *The Observer*, 5 September 2010.

[3] BBC and national press websites 24 February 2010.

[4] BBC and main national press websites covering the Commons debate, 10 September 2010.

[5] Alex Spillius (2011) 'Phone hacking: Rupert Murdoch claims "minor mistakes" have been made', *The Daily Telegraph*, 15 July.

[6] BBC Radio 4, *The Media Show*, 27 July 2011.

[7] 'Thought for the day' on BBC Radio 4 Today programme, 14 July 2011.

[8] David Leppard (2011) 'Met boss took £12,000 freebie', *The Sunday Times*, 17 July.

[9] Vikram Dodd (2011) 'We quit, now others should resign at News International', *The Guardian*, 20 July.

[10] Fiona Hamilton and Richard Ford (2011) 'Met plunged into crisis as scandal engulfs 3 more officers', *The Times*, 19 July.

[11] Patrick Wintour (2011) 'Phone hacking: Theresa May announces more inquiries', *The Guardian*, 18 July.

[12] Richard Ford (2011) 'News International deliberately thwarted inquiry', *The Times*, 21 July.

[13] Ed Pilkington (2011) 'US authorities prepare to issue subpoenas as net widens', *The Guardian*, 23 July.

[14] *The Times* (2011) Editorial, 'Power relations', 23 July.

[15] Andrew Porter (2011) 'Cameron finally says hiring Coulson was a mistake', *The Daily Telegraph*, 21 July.

[16] Esther Adderley (2011) 'Lives casually ruined', *The Guardian*, 26 November.

[17] Ben Webster (2011) 'Actor reveals more of himself than the tabloids', *The Times*, 22 November.

[18] David Leigh (2011) 'Anatomy of a cover up – what new hacking documents reveal', *The Guardian*, 3 August.

[19] David Leigh (2012) 'Police files expose NoW interference', *The Guardian*, 20 January.

[20] Dan Sabbagh (2012) 'Lies, evasions, cover-ups – how Murdoch firm hid hacking trail', *The Guardian*, 20 January.

[21] Daniel Brown (2012) 'Celebrities and politicians settle claims claims over hacking', *The Times*, 20 January.

[22] Ben Webster (2012) 'Emails were deleted says hacking case judge', *The Times* , 20 January.

[23] Peter Preston (2012) 'Hack behind the payoffs and you find a pack of lies', *The Observer*, 22 January.

[24] Lisa O'Carroll (2012) '21 payouts, 50 new claims', *The Guardian*, 9 February.

[25] Trevor Kavanagh (2012) 'Witch-hunt has put us behind ex-Soviet states on press freedom', *The Sun*, 13 February.

[26] Brian Cathcart (2012) 'News International needs to decontaminate *The Sun* brand', *The Guardian*, 16 February.

[27] Dan Sabbagh (2012) 'Murdoch's News Corporation hit by feud over *Sun* arrests', *The Guardian*, 14 February.

[28] Dan Sabbagh (2012) 'Power, corruption, and lies', *The Guardian*, 28 February.

[29] David Leigh (2012) 'Yard's investigation shows "culture of illegal payments"', *The Sun*, 28 February.

[30] Ibid.

[31] Mark Hughes (2012) '*Sun* paid police thousands for stories', *The Daily Telegraph*, 28 February.

[32] Ben Webster (2012) 'James Murdoch resigns as NI chief', *The Times*, 1 March.

[33] Michael Wolff (2012) 'Heir to the empire slips into shadows', *The Guardian*, 1 March.

[34] Ben Fenton (2012) 'Timing of Murdoch exit will not spare the scrutiny', *The Financial Times*, 1 March.

[35] Gordon Rayner (2012) 'One day they were off racing, the next they were under arrest', *The Daily Telegraph*, 14 March.

[36] James Cusick (2012) 'Met Press Chief reveals "incestuous" Murdoch ties', *The Independent*, 14 March.

[37] Harold Evans (2012) 'Myths, memory and Murdoch's imagination', *The Guardian*, 26 April.

[38] Lisa O'Carroll (2012) 'Rupert Murdoch: I have never asked a prime minister for anything', *The Guardian*, 25 April.

[39] Nick Davies (2012) 'He wriggled. He railed. But finally Murdoch met his match', *The Guardian*, 26 April.

[40] Tim de Lisle (2012) 'Rupert Murdoch's evidence was like one of his tabloids', *The Guardian*, 26 April.

[41] David Leigh (2012) 'Milly's phone: the truth may never be known', *The Guardian*, 10 May.

[42] Ben Webster (2012) 'Cameron did not question me about hacking, says Coulson', *The Times*, 11 May.

[43] Christopher Hope (2012) 'Analysis: Decision to charge Rebekah Brooks means hacking will hang over Government until election', *The Daily Telegraph*, 15 May.

[44] Ben Webster (2012) 'Piers Morgan gave me a lesson on phone hacking, Paxman tells', *The Times*, 24 May.

[45] *The Times* (2012) Editorial, 'Hunt for the truth', 25 April.

[46] *Daily Mail* (2012) Editorial 'Mr Hunt, BSkyB, and a grim day for integrity', 25 April.

[47] Vernon Bognador (2012) 'No matter what he says to Leveson, Hunt must go', *The Guardian*, 30 May.

[48] Andrew Rawnsley (2012) 'The prime minister has put his judgment and integrity on trial', *The Observer*, 27 May.

[49] Stephen Glover (2012) 'Kid gloves and the damning questions Mr Blair wasn't asked', *Daily Mail*, 30 May.

[50] Quentin Letts (2012) 'Like a spaniel begging for scraps, Jay's beardlet moved from side to side', *The Daily Mail*, 15 June.

[51] Lisa O'Carroll (2012) 'Leveson defends inquiry against "hidden agenda" claims', *The Guardian*, 25 June.

[52] Dan Sabbagh (2012) 'Eight face hacking charges', *The Guardian*, 25 July.

[53] Lisa O'Carroll (2012) 'Brooks and Coulson face one year wait', *The Guardian,* 27 September.

[54] Lisa O'Carroll (2012) 'Leveson loading a gun against papers', *The Guardian*, 29 August.

[55] Josh Halliday (2012) 'Leveson "deeply flawed", claims *Independent* Editor', *The Guardian*, 27 August.

[56] Ken Auletta (2012) 'The Heiress: the rise of Elisabeth Murdoch', *The New Yorker*, 10 December.

[57] Martin Moore (2012) *The Lord Black plan for reform of press self-regulation: A short critique*, Media Standards Trust, November.

[58] Jamie Doward (2012) 'Phone hacking victims turn on Cameron over "betrayal"', *The Observer*, 7 October.

[59] Helene Mulholland (2012) 'Cameron insists he will not pre-judge Leveson proposals', *The Guardian*, 8 October.

[60] Brian Cathcart (2012) 'The Leveson inquiry backlash is already under way', *The Guardian*, 29 October.

[61] Tim Luckhurst (2012) *Responsibility without power*, extracts on the *Press Gazette: journalism today* website (www.pressgazette.co.uk/), 26 October.

[62] BBC website (2012) 'Hillsborough: Straw blames Thatcher for police "immunity"', 13 September.

[63] Helen Warrell (2012) 'Hillsborough compounds police siege mentality', *Financial Times*, 15 September.

[64] Philip Johnston (2012) 'Could a cover-up like this happen now?', *The Daily Telegraph*, 14 September.

[65] *The Economist* (2012) 'Truth, but not yet justice', 15 September.

[66] Paul Gallagher (2012) 'Hillsborough: lawyer calls for permanent "truth commission" to prevent cover-ups', *The Observer*, 16 September.

[67] *Daily Mail* (2012) Editorial, 'Leveson: Disturbing questions over his key adviser', 16 November 2012.

[68] Roy Greenslade (2012) 'Laughable *Daily Mail* investigation smears Leveson inquiry assessor', *Guardian* blog, 16 November.

[69] *The Sunday Times* (2012) 'Profile: Sir David Bell: Weaving a gag from Mr Network's web', 18 November.

[70] Martin Hickman (2012) 'Newspapers accused of keeping readers in the dark on press regulation', CPBF website, 17 November.

[71] Roland Watson (2012) 'Backbenchers threaten to rebel if Prime Minister defies Leveson', *The Times*, 21 November.

[72] Roland Watson (2012) 'MPs' letter sets scene for "almighty row" over Leveson', *The Times*, 28 November.

[73] Roland Watson (2012) 'Tory MPs back down over press law as battle rages on', *The Times*, 3 December.

[74] *The Observer* (2012) Editorial, 'Newspapers must respond in a reasoned manner to Leveson's proposals', 2 December.

[75] Dan Sabbagh (2012) 'You've got two days to comply with Leveson report, PM tells Fleet Street', *The Guardian*, 5 December.

[76] Dan Sabbagh (2012) 'Editors agree to most of Leveson's recommendations', *The Guardian*, 6 December.

[77] Roy Greenslade (2012) 'Editors' memo suggests willingness to accept almost all of Leveson's proposals', *The Guardian*, 5 December.

[78] Dan Sabbagh (2012) 'Leveson report: editors seeking advice on third party complaints', *The Guardian*, 11 December.

[79] Michael Savage (2012) 'Royal Charter could implement press proposals without new law', *The Times*, 6 December.

[80] Patrick Wintour (2012) 'Leveson report: parties discuss plan to safeguard Royal Charter on the press', *The Guardian*, 19 December.

[81] Roy Greenslade (2012) 'Publishers remind minister that they, not editors, will do Leveson deal', *The Guardian,* 14 December.

[82] Ben Webster (2012) 'Harding to stand down as Editor of *The Times*', *The Times*, 13 December.

[83] Lisa O'Carroll (2012) 'Press regulation: Hunt to announce "transition board" members', *The Guardian*, 11 December.

[84] Dan Sabbagh (2012) 'Press regulation: the post-Leveson deal to satisfy Nick Clegg', *The Guardian*, 17 December.

[85] Ben Webster (2013) 'Press poised to launch regulator without waiting for politicians', *The Times*, 15 January.

Afterword

How did it go so wrong?

Why did British journalism descend to such depths? First, because of the power which the Murdoch group was allowed to accumulate and the fear that this generated within governments and oppositions. Alan Rusbridger, in a BBC Radio 4 programme on 2 August 2011, described how the Murdoch empire's power led it effectively to assume immunity from press, police, Parliament and regulator scrutiny.[1] This immunity was based on a group stretching from posh papers down to tabloids, with underhand criminals behind them. It was fear of the use of criminals and their ability to get information on private lives that increased the group's power. Onora O'Neill, on the same programme, confirmed this analysis, saying she had been struck by how many politicians had quite openly confessed that they were afraid and had pulled their punches, did not ask about or look at certain things, because they were fearful of the consequences.[2] But it was not just Commons Select Committee members expressing hesitations about rigorously examining Murdoch executives for fear of retaliation. Tony Blair, when Prime Minister, demonstrated his trepidation about taking on tabloids. As noted in Chapter One, Blair was widely criticised for picking on *The Independent*, the smallest and weakest paper, for special criticism in his speech on the 'feral media'. Both Adam Boulton in *Memories of the Blair administration*[3] and Alastair Campbell in his 2008 Cudlipp lecture[4] suggested he would have preferred to have targeted the *Mail* but feared for what the paper would do to him and his family.

A second reason for the decline in journalism was set out in Chapter Ten, drawn from Roy Greenslade's inaugural lecture as Professor of Journalism at City University, London, in 2004. To re-quote: 'Popular newspapers have forgotten what journalism is about. They have become organs of entertainment. Even that old halfway house – infotainment – is no longer an appropriate description of what they purvey in their meretricious diet of glitz, tits and naughty bits. Celebrity is no longer an aspect of the popular press agenda: it is now its raison d'être.'

He went on to argue that celebrity had replaced religion as the opium of the people. A celebrity culture, which had been created by the media, had ended up hoisting the media by its own petard. Tabloids' survival had become dependent on satisfying the appetite they had stimulated so successfully among their audiences. They are now forced to go on producing and reproducing the famous. 'They have become the drug pushers and the drug addicts.'

I could add that new technology bears some of the blame. It is so much easier today than it used to be to tap into phones. Faced with record falls in advertisers and circulation, the tabloid market had become even more competitive. The temptation to hack had become more irresistible. One of the uplifting aspects of the scandal was the unanimity of public revulsion over the hacking of Milly Dowler's phone. As Madeleine Bunting put it in *The Guardian*, 'it was a rare moment of clear moral consensus in public life – we'd forgotten such things were possible'.[5]

Murdoch people speak out

James Harding, the Editor of *The Times*, in a brave column in his paper on the eve of the Leveson report, provided another insight: 'The *News of the World* was an example of a newsroom not only whose methods were wrong, but which had also lost its moral bearings. The failure of News International to get to grips with what had happened at one of its newspapers suggested that the company had succumbed to that most dangerous delusion of the powerful, namely that it could play by its own set of rules.'[6] It was by no means the first criticism he had levelled at his own publisher, but insiders pointed to that paragraph two weeks later when they heard he had resigned at the request of Rupert Murdoch. Elisabeth Murdoch, his daughter, survived her criticism of her father's company, News Corp, in her 2012 MacTaggart lecture where she said it needed to ask 'significant and difficult questions about how some behaviour fell so far short of its values' in the wake of what had happened. As reported in Chapter Eleven, contrary to her brother James' statement three years earlier at the same event – 'the only reliable, durable and perpetual guarantor of independence is profit' – she asserted: 'profit without purpose is a recipe for disaster'. She said the lesson to be drawn from the scandal was the need for the company to 'discuss, affirm, and institutionalise a rigorous set of values based on an explicit statement of purpose'. She added an 'absence of purpose' could be 'one of the most dangerous own goals for capitalism and for freedom'.[7] A former *News of the World* Editor, who cannot be named for legal reasons, illustrated just how far the paper's moral values had fallen with his well-known admission: 'This is what we do. We go out and destroy other people's lives.'

Three other voices

Max Clifford, a consummate provider of stories for Fleet Street, was asked by Leveson about his perception of the tabloids: 'Are they savage? Absolutely right. Of course some of the most successful papers are the most savage because an awful lot of people would much rather read nasty things about other people than nice things.'

Philip Stephens, the *Financial Times* chief political commentator, summed up the report's findings in a powerful piece which widened the indictment to three other tabloids:

> The narrative reads like a journey through the sewers ... the really damning indictment lies in the exposure of a culture of casual contempt for decency, fairness and privacy in newspapers representing a sizeable chunk of what used to be called Fleet Street. Traducing the innocent; routine disregard for truth; and riding roughshod over individual rights – all were deemed acceptable in the cause of 'a good story'. It should be obvious to everyone but a handful of cynical proprietors and editors that the media cannot, in Lord Justice Leveson's phrase, forever be allowed to 'wreak havoc with the lives of ordinary people'. The behaviour of newspapers such as the now defunct *News of the World*, *The Sun*, *The Express*, and the *Daily Mail* has put freedom of the press in direct conflict with the rights and liberties

> of ordinary citizens. The role of newspapers is to speak
> truth to power, not to trample over the powerless.[8]

Summing up his views on the culture, practices and ethics of the press and how they had deteriorated, Leveson pointed to a long list of root causes: a competitive market, growth of mass media, declining circulation, reduction in journalist headcount, reduced budgets, a casualisation of the workforce, a lack of support for whistleblowers, and a sometimes bullying culture. All these combined to give the pursuit of a story a higher priority over all other ethical considerations. He noted that Sharon Marshall, author of *Tabloid girl*, had told the inquiry there were no ethical conversations in tabloid journalism. Richard Desmond, proprietor of the *Star* and *Express* had added: 'We do not talk about ethics or morals because it is a very fine line, and everybody's ethics are different.' He concluded: 'to be blunt, a fairly basic understanding of human nature suggests that the problems identified are unlikely to be eliminated by self-control.' But this was not unsolvable: it demanded 'a more robust system of independent press regulation which is capable of addressing the problem head on'. Do not forget what a fourth voice said 20 years ago. Rupert Murdoch downplayed his power before the Commons committee on the media and the Leveson hearings, but remember what he told his biographer, William Shawcross, as mentioned in the Preface: 'That's the fun of it, isn't it? Having a little smidgen of power.'

The dangers of delay

Reformers were rightly worried that the momentum for reform could drop if the government delayed too long in implementing the report. The current government does not like regulation. One of its first initiatives was the abolition of one of the best regulators, the Audit Commission, whose main focus was on value for money and improving services. Not even the fact that it was created by the Thatcher government saved it from the axe. But the Labour opposition and the campaigners for press reform are not going to let Cameron use this ploy. He is notorious for his policy U-turns (over 40, counting his refusal to fully back Leveson) but he did set up the inquiry and his words in doing so are on the record: 'This is a wake-up call. It is on my watch that the music has stopped and I am saying loud and clear that things have got to change.' Even better, unlike the seven previous reports on reforming the press, the issue is not going to disappear with its publication. Three separate police investigations involving 170 officers were still at work on publication day. This did restrain the judge in so far as ensuring his report did not prejudice any future trials, but it does mean for the next two years even murkier stories of what the tabloids have committed will be making regular appearances. Both criminal and civil court actions are due to continue for the next two years. Indeed, the first major trials involving 14 defendants do not start until September 2013. These will include senior people: Rebekah Brooks and Andy Coulson, both former Editors of the NoW, a former managing editor, news editor, two assistant news editors, and chief reporter. By the end of 2012, the police had arrested over 90 people suspected of being involved in one or more of four offences: hacking phones; hacking computers; corrupt payments to public officials; or perverting the course of justice through destroying evidence.

By that time, the police had contacted 2,500 potential victims of phone hacking. These will extend the already long queue pursuing News International for civil damages. And for the first time since the NoW hacking scandal began, the first formal move for damages against a media company outside Rupert Murdoch's News International was filed in the High Court in late October 2012, against the *Daily Mirror*, *Sunday Mirror* and *The People*, all part of Mirror Group Newspapers (MGN). Mark Lewis, the lawyer who acted for a significant number of claimants against Murdoch's company, filed the new claims on behalf of Sven-Goran Eriksson, the former England football coach; Abbie Gibson, a former nanny for David and Victoria Beckham; Garry Flitcroft, former football captain of Blackburn Rovers; and the Coronation Street actor Shobna Gulati. The claim filed by Eriksson against the *Daily Mirror* covers the period when Piers Morgan was Editor. MGN faced accusations of hacking during the Leveson hearings, but has always said: 'All our journalists work within the criminal law and the PCC code of conduct and we have seen no evidence to suggest otherwise.' Morgan edited the paper between 1995 and 2004. He now hosts a major chat show for CNN in the United States. He gave evidence to Leveson in December 2011 when he repeatedly denied any knowledge of illegal news gathering. Given the well-known names associated with this batch of claims, there is bound to be widespread coverage.[9] Finally, there could still be litigation in the US by unhappy shareholders upset by the cost of the scandal or even by US federal agencies if the UK criminal trials end in convictions. This could make Murdoch's headquarters in New York, News Corp, liable under the Foreign Corrupt Practices Act – passed to make American-based companies accountable in the US for their overseas activity.

But it is not just a new regulator of media conduct that is needed. We need stricter controls over media ownership. As noted in Chapter One, Britain's media ownership laws are far more lax than those of many developed states. What Murdoch almost obtained in the UK would never have been allowed in his country of birth, Australia, nor in his country of choice, the US. In July 2011 all three main parties were agreed on stricter controls of ownership. Ed Miliband, the Labour leader, stated that Murdoch's bid to own both Sky News and his newspapers was 'democratically unhealthy ... because that amount of power in one person's hands has clearly led to abuse of power within his organisation.'[10] David Cameron, the Conservative Prime Minister, told the Commons: 'Never again should we let a media group get too powerful.'[11] Vince Cable, the Lib Dem Secretary of State for Business, appearing on the BBC's *Andrew Marr Show* on Sunday, 24 July 2011, declared that no other media company should ever have the same influence in the UK as Rupert Murdoch's News Corp. But there are already signs that Murdoch's cheerleaders within the Conservative Party would be able to rally opposition to any new laws curbing ownership. As the 2015 election grows closer, so the resolve to do something about it will wain.

To go back to the original five questions

This book set out to answer the five questions listed in the opening paragraph of the Preface. First, how big a role do the media play in formulating social policy? In some areas, it is a major one, as described in Chapters Three, Four and Five, on law and order, drugs reform and asylum. It is also present in the fields of poverty, education, and health and social care, as Chapters Six, Seven and Eight document. Second, has the role of the media changed over time? Yes, and dramatically. Read Chapter Two on how specialist reporters grew with the growth of the welfare state. In my 38 years on *The Guardian* I saw its specialist staff grow from three in 1969 to over 30 in 2006, counting the two weekly specialist sections – *Education* and *Society* – and the website. Third, to what extent do the media change public opinion? Academics are wary of making such claims given the multiplicity of factors which contribute to such positions, and are understandably chary of being dismissed by their colleagues for making simplistic interpretations. The well-argued Glasgow Caledonian University study on the reporting of poverty discussed in Chapter Six is one step on from this tradition: 'although public attitudes cannot be attributed to the influence of mass media, it is important to acknowledge the media's pivotal role in responding to and reinforcing public ideas about poverty'.

Professor Mike Hough, former Deputy Director of Research at the Home Office, was more robust in his study drawn from the huge British Crime Survey (BCS). As reported in Chapter Three, it showed that two thirds of the population wrongly believed that crime was still going up and blamed the government; one third rightly believed it was going down, but gave no credit to the government. Hough noted that there were various academic and political arguments about the cause of these findings, but he came down on 'the simplest explanation for this trend is that people think crime is rising because they are told by the media that it is'. There is an even more compelling example than this: the media campaign against the MMR vaccine set out in Chapter Eight. In the wake of the massively over-hyped anti-vaccine campaign, with its gross distortions of the risks, there was a dramatic and damaging reduction in the proportion of parents taking their children to be vaccinated. The Department of Health and most other health observers are in no doubt what caused this dangerous slump: the anti-MMR media campaign. It did not just change attitudes, it changed behaviour.

Fourth, to what extent do ministers believe that tabloids influence public opinion and adjust their decisions accordingly? A great deal in certain policy areas. Read the leaked Blair memos in Chapter One calling on his aides for 'tough on crime' soundbites, or Lance Price on 'feeding the hungry beast' with tough headlines. Read Chapter Three to see the degree to which both major parties indulged in the penal populism that tabloid papers promulgate. Read Chapter Seven to learn how a crucial reform of vocational education was abandoned by Tony Blair in the belief that it would not be popular with *Mail* (or *Telegraph*) readers. But also read Chapter Four on how ministers misread the reaction of the media to reform of the current drug laws. And fifth, why was there a three-way breakdown of trust between media, government and the public? This is set out in Chapter One.

Lessons to be learned

Readers will have their own list of lessons to be learned, but here are five I would suggest:

- Where there is a policy vacuum, as there was with asylum, the media's influence can become disproportionate.
- Conversely, where there is an unequivocal pledge with clear targets, which is what emerged from Tony Blair's promise to end child poverty within 20 years, then the media can apply pressure on ministers to meet their commitment as each milestone comes up. Crucially, this was in a category where the numbers were collected every year and published. Where, alas, this does not happen, such as in neighbourhood renewal, even the boldest pledge, as set out in Chapter Nine – 'within 10 to 20 years no one should be seriously disadvantaged by where they live' – achieved no traction. The promise was too vague, lacked clear criteria and was not subject to annual measurement and monitoring. Hence it received no media coverage.
- Where things are going wrong in a public service – such as the genuine run of bad news reports on the health service in the second half of 1999 – the media can both accelerate decisions and help make them more generous. A government which came into office

declaring its priorities were 'education, education, education' ended up giving the NHS much more funding than the education service.

- Ministers should be more ready to take on the tabloids, and also recognise, as the drug reform case in Chapter Four illustrates, that they are not always as predictable as sometimes believed. Even more important for a government purporting to pursue evidence-based policy-making is to do just that.
- For all the bravado of the trade, the media are still too ready to meekly follow the agendas of governments – as set out in the housing case study in Chapter Nine – rather than challenge them.

Doubters of the policy chapters above should read Leveson

Finally, readers who are not totally persuaded by the arguments in this book should turn to volume two, page 592, of the Leveson report and read the following 145 pages documenting the many sins and crimes of the reptiles: inaccuracies, intrusions, distortions, harassment, breaches of privacy, unlawful acquisition of information, illegal payments to public officials. The damning evidence is drawn not just from the victims who gave evidence but also research studies, submissions from interest groups (representing immigrants, asylum seekers, disabled people, the mentally ill, prisoners and drug treatment specialists) along with former tabloid reporters who appeared before the inquiry. The latter openly admitted they made up reports to fit the narrative of the particular papers, frequently with anti-asylum, anti-Muslim and anti-welfare claimant slants, as well as writing totally fictitious stories about celebrities. Far from speaking truth to power, they admitted to telling untruths to tabloid readers because they were in too weak a position to challenge the editorial ethos. Hence the importance of Leveson's package of whistleblowers' hotlines and conscience clauses in journalists' contracts, as well as a robust new press regulator.

Notes

[1] *Beyond Hackgate: Who do we trust now?*, BBC Radio 4, 2 August 2011.
[2] Ibid.

[3] Adam Boulton (2008) *Memoirs of the Blair administration: Tony's ten years*, New York: Simon Schuster, p 180.

[4] Alastair Campbell (2008) *The Cudlipp lecture* (www.independent.co.uk/news/media/alastair-campbell-the-cudlipp-lecture-775278.html).

[5] Madeleine Bunting (2011) 'Our crisis is not about trust', *The Guardian*, 25 July

[6] James Harding (2012) 'Don't force the press into politicians' arms', *The Times*, 27 November.

[7] Dan Sabbagh (2012) 'Elisabeth Murdoch turns on her father and brother in MacTaggart lecture', *The Guardian*, 23 August.

[8] Philip Stephens (2012) 'An opening gambit for a grand bargain with the press', *The Financial Times*, 30 November.

[9] Josh Halliday (2012) 'Daily Mirror publisher faces being sued over alleged phone hacking', *The Guardian*, 23 October.

[10] Dan Sabbagh (2011) 'Three weeks that made a revolution', *The Guardian*, 23 July.

[11] Ibid.

Index